BERNARD ON RUTH.

RUTH'S RECOMPENCE:

OR,

A COMMENTARY UPON THE BOOK OF RUTH

DELIVERED IN SEVERAL SERMONS;

THE BRIEF SUM WHEREOF IS NOW PUBLISHED FOR THE BENEFIT OF THE CHURCH OF GOD.

BY

RICHARD BERNARD,

PREACHER OF GOD'S WORD AT BATCOMBE IN SOMERSETSHIRE.

WIPF & STOCK · Eugene, Oregon

Wipf and Stock Publishers
199 W 8th Ave, Suite 3
Eugene, OR 97401

The Last Discourse and Prayer of Our Lord
A Study of St. John XIV-XVII
By Swete, Henry Barclay
Softcover ISBN-13: 979-8-3852-1465-5
Hardcover ISBN-13: 979-8-3852-1466-2
eBook ISBN-13: 979-8-3852-1467-9
Publication date 1/25/2024
Previously published by Macmillan and Co., Limited, 1914

This edition is a scanned facsimile of the original edition published in 1914.

RICHARD BERNARD.

THOSE who have anything to do in the shape of researches among the old Literature of England, are somewhat puzzled about the identity of a very frequently recurring name, to wit, RICHARD BERNARD. Only other two Richards—the authors of 'The Saint's Everlasting Rest' and of 'The Bruised Reed,' Richard Baxter and Richard Sibbes—turn up in so many title-pages. But there is this difference with Richard Bernard from the other two, and indeed from all the numerous Richards we know,* that it is found in the most opposite kind of title-pages, the one as unlikely to represent the other as if Richard Baxter or Richard Sibbes appeared here to a 'Book of Jests' and there to a 'Sermon.' You find Richard Bernard now as the quaint and racy translator of Terence, and now as author of the oddest of odd treatises on 'Witchcraft;' again fronting a little volume that Sir Philip Sidney might have written on the 'Bible Battles,' and anon you have it to some rich, 'savoury,' quickening, practical book, exalting Christ. But as you are perplexed over these, you have still again the name of Richard Bernard at these two widely sundered poles, on a curious tractate demanding respect to conscience, and with biting sarcasm exposing the High Church claims of the Prelates, and the like;† and, on the other hand, you have it to at least two volumes angrily denouncing all

---

* It may be remarked in a footnote, since the thing comes up, that the name 'Richard' is singularly frequent among our old Divines and Worthies. We offer our note of some of them as a contribution to the Literature of 'Names' now being so largely augmented. Of the Puritans and 'Ejected' *proper* there were Richard Adams, Richard Blackerby, Richard Alleine, Richard Capel, Richard Clifton, Richard Astley, Richard Crackenthorp, Richard Avery, Richard Denton, Richard Batchelor, Richard Crick, Richard Batten, Richard Gawton, Richard Babbington, Richard Greenham, Richard Culmer, Richard Davis, Richard Bickle, Richard Binmore, Richard Mather, Richard Proud, Richard Chantyre, Richard Blinman, Richard Clayton, Richard Buress, Richard Byfield (Shakespeare's minister), Richard Rothwell, Richard Rogers, Richard Stocke, Richard Sedgwick, Richard Taverner, Richard Vines, Richard Cook, Richard Cooper, Richard Coore, Richard Wavel, Richard Whitehurst, Ritchard Whiteway, Richard Wooley, Richard Worts, Richard Wyne, Richard Martyn, Richard Herring, Richard Kennet, Richard Mayo, Richard More, Richard Morton, Richard Serjeant, Richard Smith, Richard Southwell, Richard Steel, Richard Stretton, Richard Swift, Richard Swynfen, Richard Symmonds, Richard Eeds, Richard Thorpe, Richard Thorp, Richard Dowley, Richard Dyer, Richard Fairclough, Richard Farrant, Richard Fincher, Richard Flavel, Richard Fowler, Richard Gilpin, Richard Holbrook, Richard Hawes, Richard Heath, Richard Hopkins, Richard Taylor, Richard Turner, Richard Dowler, Richard Down, Richard Drayton, Richard Frankland, Richard Garret, Richard Vin, Richard Goodwin, Richard Gyles, Richard Hilton, Richard Hincks, Richard Hook, Richard Jennings, Richard Kentish, Richard Lawrence, Richard Maudesley, Richard Moor, Richard Northam, Richard Parr, Richard Penwarden, Richard Perrot, Richard Rand, Richard Resbury, Richard Roberts, Richard Saddler, Richard Saunders, and, finally, there is RICHARD HOOKER. It were easy to extend the roll. What is the explanation of this former plenty, as compared with the modern scarceness of Richards?

† 'Twelve arguments proving that the Ceremonies imposed upon the Ministers of the Church of England, by the Prelates, are unlawful; and, therefore, that the Ministers of the Gospel, for the bare and sole omission of them, for conscience' sake, are most unjustly charged with disloyalty to his majesty.'

'Separation,' and treating the Nonconformists as if they were the 'offscouring of the earth,' and thereby fetching down upon himself the mailed hand of John Robinson of the '*Mayflower*' Pilgrim Fathers, and the no less powerful Henry Ainsworth, not to speak of the termagan ribaldry of John Smyth.

You read the present reprint of an exposition of 'Ruth;' and as you feel refreshed as with the blowing of bean-blossom-scented breezes in your evening walk, you fancy its author as a 'gentle spirit,' living apart from the crowd in cloistered piety, the *pastor* of some small rural flock, bringing the odours of kine and grass into some antique village church ; but as you open the 'Threefold Treatise on the Sabbath,' there looks out upon you the leonine and craggy face—recalling 'rare Ben's'—of a man of gigantic mould, self-evidently one to snuff the 'smell of battle' afar off, and to revel in mighty Controversy, Papist or Brownist.   Yet again there is put into your hand the 'Thesaurus Biblicus,' second only in laboriousness to the 'Concordance' of Alexander Cruden, telling of immense midnight labour over the words of The Bible ; and as you put it gratefully down, you have to turn next to still another pastoral volume, 'The Faithful Shepherd,'—meet to lie on the same shelf with the *Gildas Salvianus* itself ; or mayhap you are held as with *the* 'glittering eye' by that book so far ahead of its age, his 'Ready way to Good Works;' or not less so with 'The Isle of Man, or Proceedings in Manshire,' which, if it be not the prototype of Bunyan's immortal Allegory, is full of wit, wisdom, penetration, and ineffable touches, as of the tints in sea-shells, or in the cups of flowers.

And so we might go on through very many more books, some larger, some lesser, some stormy, some peaceful, some practical, even finely spiritual, and some, alas ! 'set on fire of hell' with the wildest fanatic fire of passion.   And yet it is certain the RICHARD BERNARD is one—a many-sided, opulent, remarkable man, of whom it were surely desirable to know more.   'The more's the pity' that, except what his own books supply, there are few memorials left us.   These we proceed to gather up ; and perchance, in this case and the others, our Memoir may incite to inquiry and interest, those to whom more leisure is given than to ourselves.

RICHARD BERNARD was born in the year 1567, as his age at death informs us, which age is inscribed on the striking portrait already alluded to.   But neither the birth-date exactly nor his birth-place appears to be known.   He is not among the 'Worthies' of any of the Shires in Fuller's all-embracing and never-to-be-made-old 'History,' though placed by him among the 'learned writers' of his College.   Curiously enough there is no Bernard in all his roll.   A Richard Bernard appears in the Registers of Christ's College, Cambridge, as proceeding B.A. 1567–68.   He is *supposed*, but improbably, to have been the father of our Richard.   Though Fuller and all other authorities thus fail us in regard to the birth-place, an incidental expression in one of his Latin 'Epistles Dedicatory' designates Nottinghamshire as his 'native soil,' as we shall see in the sequel.

Our Richard Bernard was, like the other named, of Christ's, Cambridge.   Though his matriculation is not now to be found, he probably proceeded B.A. 1594–5 (but at that period the University Registers are defective), and certainly passed M.A. in 1598.   This is all that our excellent friend Mr Cooper of Cambridge has been able to send us from the Cambridge *archives*.

We learn from other sources that when a mere youth, he fell under the notice of two ladies, daughters of Sir Christopher Wray, Lord Chief-Justice of England, pre-eminent even in those days for Christian large-heartedness and 'labours of love.'   One of them was the wife successively of Godfrey Foljambe, Esq. ; Sir William Bowes of Walton, near Chesterfield ; and of John, the good Lord Darcy of Aston.   The other married Sir George Saint Paul (spelled 'Saintpoll') of Lincolnshire ; and afterwards, the Earl of Warwick: as Countess of Warwick appearing in very many old 'Epistles Dedicatory.' It was these truly noble sisters who sent Master Richard to Cambridge, and he is never weary of acknowledging their kindness to him. Thus it will be observed that in the 'Epistle Dedicatory' to his 'Ruth' to the Countess of Warwick, he speaks very gratefully of all that she had done for him. Earlier in his 'Dedication' of his first book, 'Terence,' he describes these two sisters as those 'to whom, next to God and nature, he owed all that he had;' and in the same of his 'Christian Advertisements and Counsels of Peace,' addressing 'Sir George Saintpoll and his virtuous Ladie,' he makes the same acknowledgment. It is pleasing to find that the friends of his youth remained stedfastly his friends in his old age.

Richard Bernard was living at Epworth, in Lincolnshire, in 1598, whence he dated his translation of 'Terence.' Thus one noticeable man preceded SAMUEL WESLEY in this now famous 'parish,' where was born JOHN WESLEY, and later Alexander Kilham,—names venerable beyond the pale of Methodism.

One is vexed on turning expectantly to Archdeacon Stonehouse's 'History of the Isle of Axholm,' within whose boundaries Epworth lies, to find no notice whatever of our Worthy, albeit the Smiths, Browns, Robinsons, and Joneses, are superfluously chronicled.

From Epworth he was 'presented to the living,' which is a vicarage, of Worksop, in Nottinghamshire. The presentation was by a Richard Whalley,—whether of the regicide's family we know not,—and he received institution on the 19th of June 1601.*

Of his Worksop 'ministry' it is said, 'he experienced great encouragement in his ministry, and was exceedingly beloved by his people. As a preacher he was much followed, and his labours were rendered a blessing to many.' †

He sent out several of his books from Worksop, as the dates 1605 and onward shew. One of the most memorable biographically is the following :—

'Christian Advertisements and Counsels of Peace. Also disuasions from the Separatists schisme, commonly called Brownisme, which is set apart from such truths as they take from vs and other Reformed Churches, and is nakedly discoured, that so the falsitie thereof may better be discerned, and so iustly condemned and wisely avoided. Published for the benefit of the humble and godlie louer of the truthe. By Richard Bernard, Preacher of God's Word. Reade (my friend) considerately ; expound charitably ; and judge I pray thee, without partialitie : doe as thou wouldest bee done vnto. At London, Imprinted by Felix Kyngston. 1608' (18mo.)

This quaint title-page recalls one of those epoch-making events in the History of England and of the World, which, in their apparent outward insignificance originally, contrast astoundingly with the greatness, even magnificence, of their after-development. Joseph Hunter has told, with much loving detail, the story of the 'Church' of Scrooby, from whence went forth the Pilgrim-Fathers, the Founders of New England, and in *it* of the mighty Republic of the United States of America (which may God deliver from its present agony !). Thither,‡ and to the many memorial-volumes furnished by America itself—for Scrooby is to Americans what Runymede is to Englishmen and Bannockburn to the Scot—the reader is referred. Suffice it here that Richard Bernard by his *locale* and opinions and feelings, was brought into union and communion with the 'Separatists,' and treacherously and falsely as they alleged, but conscientiously as he himself affirmed and we are bound to believe, withdrew from them. Thereafter commenced *his* invec-

---

* Collections concerning the Church or Congregation of Protestant Separatists, formed at Scrooby, in Nottinghamshire, in the time of King James I., the founders of New Plymouth, the parent colony of New England. By the Rev. Joseph Hunter, London. One vol. 8vo, 1854, p. 37.

† Brook, Lives of the Puritans, ii. p. 460.

‡ See title-page, *supra*.

315

tives and *their* replies, through many a passionate, criminatory and recriminatory, volume and tractate.

It were pity to stir the long cooled embers of this ancient Controversy. Churchman and Nonconformist alike have admitted that while on each side there can be no question of sincerity and loyalty to what they believed to be The Truth, nevertheless the good men were morbidly jealous, mutually exaggerated difficulties and differences, and sadly lacked that charity 'which thinketh no evil' in construing others' motives and doings. Bernard we may allow, briefly, to speak for himself: —In his 'Christian Advertisements,' he says with reference to the 'Separation :'—'It grieveth me much to see this breach made amongst us; loss it is to the Church, gain to the enemy, and then what true good to themselves? Many laugh at it, some account it a matter scarce worthy thinking upon, and so few or none lament it. To me hath it been just cause of sorrow, and therefore could I not lightly pass it by; but in love to such as yet abide with us, and in desire to do my best to recover again mine own whom God once gave me, I have published these things.' Again :— 'Confidence in our cause (that here is a true Church of God, from which we may not make separation) hath made me adventurous : and the spiritual injury which some of late have done to me, more than to many, hath called me hereunto. They have taken away part of the seal of my ministry.'*

Once more, here are certain personal admissions :—'Such as have had a little taste of the way, and affection to the same, *misled by imagined truths, and by the honesty of the men for their lives, and some former familiarity had with them in an even way* (which indeed are the ordinary baits by which many are catched); yet at length perceiving the falsehood thereof, which is called Brownism, they have upon good considerations deliberated, and on deliberation and searching found out the errors thereof, and so left them. These, they condemn as apostates and what not.'†

Further, in his 'Plaine Evidences The Chvrch of England is Apostolicall, the Separation Schismaticall. Directed against Mr Ainsworth the Separatist and Mr Smith the Se-Baptist : Both of them severally opposing the Book called the Separatist's Schisme. By Richard Bernard, Preacher of the Word of God at Worksop. For truth and peace to any indifferent iudgment. Printed by T. Snodham for Edward Weaver and William Welby, and are to be sould at their shops in Paules Churchyard' (1610. 4to.), he thus notices Ainsworth's sarcastic and contemptuous retort : 'He calls that light which I knew of their way ; but I *now* judge it darkness, *through knowledge of the truth now, whereof I was ignorant then.* I see now by the light, their darkness, our truth, their errors, and yet bewail personal corruptions.'‡

We have in these,—a few out of many similar personal passages,—the real state of the case as between Bernard and his former friends and associates, the despised 'Separatists.' Equally with them he was a Puritan in 'doctrine' and in life, and a Nonconformist in well-nigh everything they objected to, 'carrying,' in the words of another, 'to an extreme length the Puritan scruples, going to the very verge of separation, and joining himself even to those of his Puritan brethren who thought themselves qualified to go through the work of exorcism.'§ Not only so, but he was 'silenced' by the Archbishop. Was it unnatural or unreasonable that his fellow-labourers expected that he would 'break' from The Church? But, as Mr Ashton remarks, 'he was a zealous and devoted minister of the Gospel, and a distinguished Puritan, but deficient in the moral courage requisite to constitute him a Reformer. He vacillated between the Church and the Separation, often avowing his determination to leave the Establishment ;

---

* and † The 'Epistles' to the Reader, &c., and p. 51. | ‡ Page 2.   § Hunter, as before, p. 37.

and on one occasion actually resigned the living of Worksop, but afterwards repented, subscribed again, was restored to his preferment, and continued a Churchman till his death.' *

We get a glimpse of him during this vacillating period, through the lurid pages of John Smyth. Referring to a particular place in his book, this undoubtedly over-vehement writer, but loyal man to conscience, says :—' By this place Mr Bernard intended to sin against conscience, for he did acknowledge this truth we now profess, divers times, and was upon the point of separation with some of his people with him ; yet loving the world and preferment, as Naaman is thought to do, he chose rather to stay still in the vicarage against his conscience, than to lose it and to follow Christ with a good conscience. Do you not remember, Mr Bernard, *what you said to me and Mr Robert Southworth,* coming together from W[orksop], that, speaking of the danger of walking in this truth of Christ we now profess, you said you could easily die upon the tree for the truth, *but you could not, without great horror, think of being burned as the martyrs were in Queen Mary's days ;* and that all the journey you were casting how to despatch your estate, and get away with safety ?' † On the whole, without imputing sin against conscience so harshly and recklessly as John Smyth, and even John Robinson and Henry Ainsworth did, it must be conceded that Bernard sought, according to Robinson, 'rather to oppress the person of his adversary with false and proud reproaches, than to convince (= convict, refute) his tenets by sound arguments.'‡ Sadly true, as might be abundantly illustrated ; nevertheless, —so strange a thing is conscience with an infirm will,—we unhesitatingly accept Bernard's own final declaration :—' If I were not persuaded in my soul that here is the true Church of God, I profess unfeignedly (by God's help), that I would renounce my standing, whatever wicked and uncharitable hearts censure to the contrary.'§ Pity that the excellent man could not accredit others with equal honesty and ' liberty !'

RICHARD BERNARD remained at Worksop until about 1613, in which year he was called upon to transfer his services to that place which is most of all associated with him, viz. Batcombe in Somersetshire. Thither he was summoned by the devout, and indeed well-nigh angelic, Dr Bis or Bisse. This venerable man had been himself pastor from the dawn of the Reformation, and had purchased the advowson of his ' living,' to present once only, for £200. To his honour be it told, that though he had a son in the church, he stedfastly resolved to bestow it ' as the Lord should direct him.' On ' presenting ' Bernard to it, he thus, like another Patriarch, spoke : ' I do this day lay aside nature, respect of profit, flesh and blood, in thus bestowing as I do my living, only in hope of profiting and edifying my people's souls,' after which he did not live above three weeks. This, his last act, he called his ' packing-penny ' between God and himself. ‖

We have an interesting retrospective reference to the Worksop ' ministry ' in the ' Epistle

---

* Works of John Robinson, vol. ii. p. vi. We have these and other similar *data* in another passage from Smyth: —' Master Bernard,' he says, ' I have sufficient reason that has moved me to break silence in respect of you, and by this letter to attempt a further trial of your pretended zeal for the truth and faith of Christ. I have long time observed the applause yielded you by the multitude. Likewise I have taken notice of your forwardness in leading to a Reformation by public proclamations in several pulpits, as if you had meant, contrary to the king's mind, to have carried all the people of the country after you against the ceremonies and subscription. Afterwards, having lost your Vicarage of Worksop for refusing subscription or conformity, I have observed how you revolted back, and upon subscription made to the Prelate of York, have re-entered upon your Vicarage. Again, I have noted your vehement desire to the patronage of Sowerby, and your extreme indignation when you were defeated of it ; further, your earnest desire to have been Vicar of Gainsborough, and all this after your subscription ; besides, I have carefully weighed with myself your steadiness to embrace the truth we profess.' (P. 5.)

† Quoted by Hunter, as before, p. 117.

‡ ' The People's Plea for the Exercise of Prophecy: against Mr John Yates his Monopoly. By John Robinson. 1618. 12mo, p. vi. § ' Plaine Evidences,' p. 4.

‖ Brook, as before, ii. p. 460.

Perhaps by ' packing penny' good Dr Bisse accommodated the old Charon fee to Christian use. It reminds us of the saying of an old Scotchman upon his death bed. Visited by his minister, and questioned as to his state, his reply was, ' I'm just packing, sir, just packing,' *i.e.* making ready.

It is of Dr Bis or Bisse that Fuller records the punning epitaph,—

' *Bis* fuit hic natus, puer et *Bis, Bis* juvenisque,
  Bis vir, *Bis*que senex, *Bis* doctor, *Bis*que sacer.'

Worthies, as before, iii. p. 107.

Dedicatory' to 'The Faithfull Shepherd : Wholly in a manner transposed and made anew, and very much inlarged, both with precepts and examples, to further young Divines in the studie of Divinitie. With the Shepherd's Practise in the end. By Richard Bernard, Minister and Preacher of God's Word at Batcombe in Somerset. London : Printed for Thomas Pavier, 1621 (12mo).'* Addressing the Archbishop of York, he says,—

'I call to mind mine own happiness in particular, above many, when I lived in those parts : I enjoy God's blessing (praised be his name) where I am, and it was *digitus Dei* that reached it out unto me, *agnoscunt omnes, qui nôrunt :* but yet my then present means, in the presence of my many honourable and other good friends, and your grace's so large provision for me for the time to come, should have contented me. *My removing was loss,* especially in the want of so gracious a diocesan.'†

Again, in the Latin 'Epistle Dedicatory,' already mentioned, he makes like reference to the providential character of his call from Worksop to Batcombe. As stated before, too, he herein informs us that Nottinghamshire, in which Worksop is, was his native county. The passage has been overlooked, and as it is of interest, may here be given. Addressing the Bishop of Bath and Wells (Arthur Lake, if we err not,—whose folio of 'Sermons' is full of riches), and gratefully acknowledging past goodness, he proceeds :—

'Nam, dum in Academia Cantabrigiensi, bonis literis operam darem, paupertatem meam ille sublevavit ; ex quo autem, relicta Academia, in publicum prodirem, humanissime semper habitum consilio, atque auxilio juvit, et cohonestavit ; pro sua demum singulari in me benevolentia, *ex natali solo* evocatum, haud vanâ spe detinuit : donec, numinis divini suasu, vir ille venerabilis, Phil. Bissus, sacræ Theologiæ Doctor (et pastor vigilantissimus, quem hic etiam non possum non honoris gratia nominare, Beneficii sui cujus advocationem esset nactus successorem me diceret, scriberetque), tamen ne rem meam pluris quam Ecclesiam Dei,' &c.‡

The former Patron and Bishop-Friend who is so affectionately remembered in this Epistle and elsewhere, was the Bishop of Winchester, his Diocesan while at Worksop, who was a fellow-student at Cambridge and brother to one of his lady-friends, as he tells us in his 'Epistle Dedicatory' to the 'Ready Way to Good Works.' Addressing Sir John Wray and his Lady, he thus recalls and combines the family goodness to him :—

'Who ever tasted more deeply than myself, of the charitable liberality and singular bounty of that right honourable lady, the Lady Frances, Countess of Warwick, Dowager, lately deceased, who first sent me unto, and planted me in, the University ? How bountiful, likewise, was the hand of that noble lady, Isabell, the Lady Darcy, to many, and to me in particular, while my abode was in those parts, with my loving parishioners of Worksop. I cannot but commemorate so transcendent goodness of those your right honourable aunts to you, so noble-minded friends towards me, imitating therein your worthy father and your blessed mother, sister to that my honourable good lord, the right reverend father in God, James, the Lord Bishop of Winchester, who when he was Lord Bishop of Bath and Wells, sent for me into these parts, whereunto I dwell, not by solicitation of friends, but only out of his former remembrance of me in Cambridge, where he was then to me a liberal and memorable benefactor.'

Set down in the county of JOHN HOOPER, Bishop and 'Martyr,' if RICHARD BERNARD shewed not his 'striving unto blood' for the truth, he certainly sought to preach the same 'everlasting Gospel ;' while in his love of 'wise saws and modern instances,' he ranged himself with another Somerset son, Thomas Coryat,—in whose extraordinary farrago-volume there is more of wit and sparkle than in a score of more reputed books.

All accounts go to shew that, not in name only (and it is his favourite name, as his title-pages

---

* It is worth while to note that, among others, 'The F. S.' is dedicated to 'Thomas Adams,' as one of B.'s friends.
† Epistle Dedicatory.
‡ Ep. Ded. to 'A Key of Knowledge, for the Opening of the Secret Mysteries of St Iohn's Mystical Revelation. By

Richard Barnard, preacher of God's Word at Batcombe in Somerset. The contents ar (*sic*) in the next page before the booke. At London, imprinted by Felix Kyngston, 1617.' 4to (Engraved emblematic title).

evidence), but as a blessed reality, the 'Minister' of Batcombe was a 'Preacher of God's Word ;' faithfully, earnestly, anxiously, in season and out of season, watching for souls. In spite of his unworthy accusations and 'flouting' of the 'Separatists,' he still 'held fast' to his objections to the 'Ceremonies,' never using them, never compromising. He was 'indulged' by the good Bishop. The position he took was very much that of THOMAS CARTWRIGHT, who, it must be remembered, equally with him, wrote against the 'Brownists,' and also against 'Separation' from the Church. Indeed, with all the Puritans the idea of 'Separation' was a terror as well as a sorrow. The wisest and holiest were 'driven' out with bleeding hearts. Hence the reiteration of sentiments such as these, which we cull from Bernard's 'Seven Golden Candlesticks :'* 'Be no fantastical Anabaptist; the true Spirit informeth the mind out of the Word. . . . Be no schismatical Brownist.'† Again, 'Heresy razeth the foundation; schism cuts off communion.'‡ Therefore, 'be not a Laodicean Conformitant, nor yet a preposterous Reformitant.' § Once more : 'Bear with lighter faults for a time till fit occasion be offered to have them mended,' and 'likelihoods of evil, make them not apparent evil, by ill interpretations, when neither the State intendeth it nor so maintains it.' ‖ Finally, 'Wholly condemn not that ministry which a godly man may make for good.'¶ It is easy to see how, conscious of his own integrity, though forgetful to admit like integrity in his opponents, our Worthy reconciled himself to adhesion to the Church, hoping against hope to 'reform' from within, not from without. All very well ; if only those who saw no other course than to 'come out and be *separate*' had been spared reviling and scorn, slander and injury. It is a satisfaction to know that his 'controversies' occupied but a small space in the 'Life' of Richard Bernard, that for the days and pages devoted to them there were long years and many volumes, given with a beautiful consecration to the SERVICE of The Master ; for the Pastor of Batcombe was the antitype of his own 'Faithful Shepherd.' He died in March 1641. It must have been very near to the close of the month ; for his 'Epistle Dedicatory' to his 'Threefold Treatise on the Sabbath' bears date 'London, March 20th 1641.' Fitting close to a noble 'Life,' a Book on 'The Sabbath ;' and then away to enjoy the 'Everlasting Rest.' As he had Robert Balsom, one of the saintliest of the early Puritans, for 'assistant' at Batcombe, and afterwards good Edward Bennet, so his successor was the great and good Richard Alleine, who was one of the 'Ejected' in 1662. Conant has left an excellent summary of his character and labours. We may read it :—

'I had for sundry years past,' he says, 'some intimate acquaintance with him, during which time, as, by the testimony of many godly and learned persons long before, he hath constantly been very laborious in the public exercise of his ministry ; the fruit whereof was sealed by the conversion of many souls to God. His labours in the ministry were bestowed not only in his own congregation, but in several of the adjacent market towns, where weekly lectures were for many years continued, by the free and voluntary assistance of pious, godly, and orthodox divines, until they were, by the last bishop of that diocese, to the great prejudice of many souls, imperiously suppressed. In his ministerial work he was a leader and pattern to many, exemplifying in his sermons that method of preaching which many years since, in his "Faithful Shepherd," he prescribed, or at least proposed, in writing. Divers painful and profitable labourers in the Lord's vineyard had their first initiation and direction from and under him, to whom also many others had recourse, and from whom they borrowed no small light and encouragement. His people, by his constant pains in catechising (wherein he had an excellent facility), as well as his preaching, were more than ordinary proficients in the knowledge of the things of God : and the youth of his congregation were very ready in giving a clear account of their faith, whereof he would often speak with much rejoicing. That the knowledge of his people was not merely speculative, appeared by the many liberal contributions which, for pious and charitable uses, were made by them ; wherein, I suppose, they were not inferior to any congregation in the

---

* 'The Seaven Golden Candlestickes, England's Honour. The Great Mysterie of God's Mercie yet to Come. With Peace to the pure in heart, aduising to Vnitie among our sclues. By Richard Bernard, Minister at Batcombe in | Somersetshire. London, Printed for Iohn Budge, dwelling in Paul's Church-yard, at the signe of the Green Dragon, 1621. 12mo. † *Ibid.* p. 2. ‡ *Ibid.* p. 3. § *Ibid.* p. 4. ‖ *Ibid.* p. 5. ¶ *Ibid.* p. 6.

whole county wherein he lived.' . . . . . . 'His preaching and catechising were accompanied with zeal, frequency, and fervency in prayer, wherein he was very ready and powerful, and whereby all his other labours became the more successful. With all these, his ordinary and more private conversation held a good correspondence; he being bold, expert, and candid in admonishing or reproving, as occasion presented; tender also and cordial in comforting the afflicted or wounded spirit; and, in a word, he shewed much integrity in all his actions. He was, in his private studies, according to that strong constitution wherewith God had blessed him, indefatigable; the benefit whereof the church of God enjoyeth, in those many tractates written and printed by him, as most men versed in theological studies will give testimony."*

We have already, in the course of our Memoir, mentioned the leading writings of Richard Bernard, and also indicated their general character. We place below the title-pages of his rarer books and tractates not already given, or to be given,† and would only more specifically notice three of them, because of the opinions they advocate, and one of the three, from the reflected honour cast upon it, as having been regarded as the prototype of John Bunyan's 'Pilgrim's Progress.'

First of all, let it be noted, to the honour of the 'minister' of Batcombe, that on three questions that have subsequently received large and enlarging attention he spoke out faithfully, passionately and compassionately, when all others were in a manner silent. The 'Epistle Dedicatory' of his 'Isle of Man' makes a most arousing and generous appeal in behalf of 'poor prisoners.' Sure we are JOHN HOWARD had thanked RICHARD BERNARD for his burning and thrilling words. We can only select a few out of many similar ones. 'The state of poor prisoners,' he says, 'is well known, and how their souls' safety is neglected; and yet our Saviour gave such a testimony to a penitent thief, as he never gave to any mortal man else; for he told him that he should be that day with him in Paradise.' Again, 'How blessed a work would it be to have maintenance raised for a learned, godly, and grave divine, that might attend to instruct them daily? Twelve pence a quarter of one parish with another in our county, would encourage some compassionate holy man thereunto. And what is this? Not a mite out of every man's purse to save souls.' There then follow admirable suggestions as to work to be imposed and other arrangements; and having, by name, brought up the different magistrates of the county, he breaks out, 'Oh let me be bold earnestly to beseech you, and in all humility to crave your merciful and tender bowels of compassion towards them.' Again, a most urgent appeal to judges, sheriffs, and all magistrates, and finally these affecting words: 'The work surely would bless you all. Alas! the prison now is a very picture of hell, and (more is the pity) as the case now stands, is no less than a preparative thereto, for want of daily instruction.' . . . . . 'The Father of our Lord Jesus Christ persuade your well-disposed hearts *to such an unbegun work*, among so many deeds very famous in this renowned nation.' Surely in the History of Philanthropy in relation to the 'prison-house,' this pioneer to a blessed Reform deserves no stinted honour.

---

* From the 'Epistle' to 'The Reader' prefixed to Bernard's posthumous work, 'Thesaurus Biblicus,' folio, 1644, pp. 2, 3.

† The Fabvlous Fovndation of The Popedome: or a Familiar Conference between two friends to the truth, Philalethes and Orthologvs, shewing that it cannot be proved, That Peter was ever at Rome. Whervnto is added a Chronographicall Description of Paul's peregrinations, with Peter's travells, and the reasons why he could not be at Rome, that so the truth in one view may more fully and easily be seene of every one. At Oxford, Printed by John Lichfield and James Short, for William Spier, An. Dom. 1619. 4to. *.* Dedicated to Dr Thomas Goodwin, Prideaux, and Benefield.

‡ Looke beyond Luther: or an Answere to that Question so often and so insultingly proposed by our Adversaries, asking vs: Where this our Religion was before Luther's time? Whereto are added Sovnd Props to Beare vp honest-hearted Protestants, that they fall not from their sauing-faith. By Richard Bernard of Batcombe in Somerset. London, Imprinted by Felix Kyngston, and are to be sold by Edmund Weaver, at his shop at the great North doore of Pauls. 1623. 4to. *.* The original Manuscript of this, with curious memoranda, is in my Library.

The Bible-Battells or The Sacred Art Military. For the rightly wageing of warre according to Holy Writ. Compiled for the vse of all such valiant Worthies and vertuously Valerous Souldiers, as vpon all iust occasions be ready to affront the Enemies of God, our King, and Country. By Ric. Bernard, Rector of Batcombe, Somersetshire. Printed for Edward Blackmore, and are to be sold by Iames Boler at the signe of the Flowre de Luce in Paule's Church-yard. 1629. 18mo.

Further: The second portion of the 'Seven Golden Candlesticks,' which is entitled 'The Great Mysterie of God's Mercie yet to Come,' is one earnest pleading in behalf of the Jews. This too, when to be a Jew was to be the butt of all scorn and insult. Very wistful and very eloquent, with the fine eloquence of emotion, is his setting forth of the claims of the 'children of Abraham.'

The third thing, wherein RICHARD BERNARD proved himself to be far in advance of his age, is found in one of his very best books, to wit the following : 'The Ready Way to Good Works, or a Treatise of Charitie, wherein, besides many other things, is shewed how we may be always ready and prepared, both in affection and action, to give cheerfully to the poor, and to pious uses, never heretofore published. By Richard Bernard, Rector of the parish of Batcombe in Somersetshire. London : Printed by Felyx Kyngston, and are to be sold by Edward Blackmore, at the signe of the Angell in Paul's Church-yard. 1635.' (12mo). The whole argumentation on this vital subject is to be found in this little-known volume. Its watchword is precisely that of our 'Systematic Benevolence Society,' and the like. Here is one sentence ; ' *Laying aside weekly every Lord's Day ;* for the performance of which duty I did principally set my hand to this work.' We would commend the sections ' *When* to lay aside,' ' *How* to lay aside,' ' *Certain objections,*' ' *Quantity,*' to our readers. And we may be permitted very respectfully to suggest that our Societies, such as that just named, would go far toward the end they aim at, by a cheap reprint (worthily edited and annotated from similar early books, of which there are several) of this treatise. All praise to RICHARD BERNARD for the wisdom, the unction, the logical force, the pungent reproof, the awakening calls, the munificent consecration, of his masterly little book.

We pass now to his 'Isle of Man—Proceedings in Manshire.'* It were inexcusable not to furnish a specimen of this most original and picturesque, vivid and memorable treatise. In proceeding to submit this, however, we must testify that a careful perusal of the volume, in common with all the alleged sources of the 'Pilgrim's Progress,' leaves John Bunyan's own averment, intact,

'Manner, and matter too, was all MINE OWN.'

The chief characteristics, merits and defects, of the book, are represented in what now follows. Marshalling the subjects of the 'Proceedings in Manshire,' he thus goes on :—

' Sin is the Thief and Robber ; he stealeth our graces, spoileth us of every blessing, utterly undoeth us, and maketh miserable both body and soul. He is a murderer: spares no person, sex, or age ; a strong thief: no human power can bind him; a subtle thief: he beguiled Adam, David, yea, even Paul. The only watchmen to spy him out is Godly-Jealousy. His resort is in Soul's Town, lodging in the heart. Sin is to be sought in the by-lanes, and in Sense, Thought, Word, and Deed Streets. The hue and cry is after fellows called Outside, who nod or sleep at Church, and, if awake, have their mind wandering : Sir Worldly Wise, a self-conceited earthworm ; Sir Lukewarm, a Jack-on-both-sides ; Sir Plausible Civil, Master Machiavel, a licentious fellow named Libertine ; a snappish fellow, one Scrupulosity ; and one Babbling Babylonian ; these conceal the villain Sin. To escape, he pretends to be an honest man ; calls vices by virtuous names ; his relations, Ignorance, Error, Opinion, Idolatry, Subtilty, Custom, Forefathers, Sir Power, Sir Sampler, Sir Must-do, Sir Silly, Vain Hope, Presumption, Wilful, and Saintlike, all shelter and hide him. The Justice, Lord Jesus, issues his warrant—God's Word—to the Constable, Mr Illuminated Understanding, dwelling in Regeneration, aided by his wife Grace ; his sons Will and Obedience, and his daughters, Faith, Hope, and Charity ; with his men, Humility and Self-denial, and his maids, Temper-

---

* This appears to have been not only his most popular book, but one of the most popular of the age. We have seen a 12th and 13th edition within a brief period of publication. The last modern edition is this: ' Sin Apprehended, Tried and Condemned ;' being the (*sic*) reprint of a book entitled, 'The Isle of Man.' By D. F. Jarman, B. A. (Nisbet, 1851.) This editor has the impertinence to abridge and change as it suits him ; utter rubbish: Jarman not Bernard.

ance and Patience. Having got his warrant, he calls to aid his next neighbour, Godly Sorrow, with his seven sons, Care, Clearing, Indignation, Fear, Vehement Desire, Zeal, and Revenge: these are capable of apprehending the sturdiest thief. He goes to the common inn, an harlot's house called Mistress Heart, a receptacle for all villains and thieves, no dishonest person being denied house-room. Mistress Heart married her own father, an Old-man, keeping rest night and day, to prevent any godly motion from lodging there. The house has five doors, Hearing, Seeing, Tasting, Smelling, and Feeling. Eleven maids, impudent harlots, wait upon the guests, Love, Hatred, Desire, Detestation, Vain-hope, Despair, Fear, Audacity, Joy, Sorrow, and Anger, and a man-servant Will. The Dishes are the lusts of the flesh, served in the platter of pleasure; the lust of the eyes, in the plate of profit; and the pride of life. The drink is the pleasures of sin; their bedroom is natural corruption. "In this room lieth Mistress Heart, all her maids, her man, and all her guests together, like wild Irish." The bed is Impenitency, and the coverings Carnal Security; when the Constable enters, He attacks them all with "apprehensions of God's wrath," and carries them before the Judge, who examines the prisoners, and imprisons them until the assizes, in the custody of the jailor New Man. "If any prisoner breaks out, the sheriff—Religion—must bear the blame; saying, This is your religion, is it?" The keepers and fetters, as vows, fasting, prayer, &c., are described with the prison.'

The second part is the trial of the prisoner, and judgment without appeal:

'The commission is Conscience; the circuit, the Soul; the council for the king are Divine Reason and Quick-sightedness; the clerk, Memory; the witness, Godly Sorrow; the grand Jury, Holy Men, the inspired authors; the traverse jury, Faith, Love of God, Fear of God, Charity, Sincerity, Unity, Patience, Innocency, Chastity, Equity, Verity, and Contentation; all these are challenges by the prisoners, who would be tried by Nature, Doubting, Careless, &c., all freeholders of great means. This the Judge overrules; Old-man is put on his trial first, and David, Job, Isaiah, and Paul, are witnesses against him. He pleads, "There is no such thing as Original Corruption; Pelagius, a learned man, and all those now that are called Anabaptists, have hitherto, and yet do maintain that sin cometh by imitation, and not by inbred pravity. Good my lord, cast not away so old a man, for I am at this day 5569 years old." He is found guilty, and his sentence is: "Thou shalt be carried back to the place of execution, and there be cast off, with all thy deeds, and all thy members daily mortified and crucified, with all thy lusts, of every one that hath truly put on Christ." Mistress Heart is then tried; Moses (Gen. viii. 21), Jeremiah (xvii. 9), Ezekiel Matthew (xv. 9), and others, give evidence, and she is convicted, and sentenced to perpetual imprisonment under the jailor, New Man. All the rest of the prisoners are tried.'

This may suffice. It will be seen that there is much ingenuity, clever adaptation of Scripture names, and admirable 'keeping' throughout. No doubt the Impersonations are but as the 'dry bones' compared with Bunyan's 'living army' of Spirit-quickened, breathing, real flesh-and-blood actors, whom we mourn or rejoice with, smile, approve, disapprove, acquit, condemn. Still there is the same 'faculty,' if it be without the indefinable stamp of genius. The allusion to the Anabaptists is unworthy of Bernard. The 'Separatists,' or Nonconformists, who were so slandered, held and avowed the very doctrine he himself taught; none more articulately proclaimed alike the 'pravity' and depravity of man. It is painful to find these plague-spots in such a fine, quaint, rich, old book; and the only palliation (a poor one enough certainly) is that in the rebound from 'The Church' there were fragments of the 'Separation' who lifted up not only the anchors but went adrift and struck on the reefs of Error. But it was an unworthy trick to confound the 'Separatists' of Scrooby, and men like John Robinson and Henry Ainsworth, with such wanderers from 'the Truth.'*

The work now reprinted is perhaps as perfect an example of all Bernard's merits as any that could be selected. It is expository, doctrinal, practical, 'savoury,' and full of living appli-

* The literature of the Controversy is extensive. Besides the masterly 'Replies' of John Robinson, contained in his Works edited by Ashton, 3 vols. 12mo (vol. ii.), those wishing to get at the stand-point of 'the Separatists' would do well to study the following:—
1. Certayne Letters translated into English, being first written in Latine. Two by the reuerend and learned Mr Francis Iunius, Divinitie Reader at Leyden, in Holland. The other by the exiled English Church, abiding for the present at Amsterdam, in Holland. Together with the Confession of Faith prefixed, whereupon the said letters were first written. Isaiah liii. 1. Printed in the yeare 1602. 4to. Signed by F. Johnson, Ainsworth, &c.

cations to everyday experience and life. It abounds with apophthegms and compressed thoughts that cleave to the memory. It has hitherto been excessively rare and costly.

ALEXANDER B. GROSART.

KINROSS.

---

2. Counterpoyson: Considerations touching the points in difference between the godly ministers and people of the Church of England, and the seduced brethren of the Separation. Arguments that the best assemblies of the present Church of England are true visible Churches. That the Preachers in the best assemblies of England are true Ministers of Christ. Mr Bernard's book intituled the Separatists Schisme. Mr Crashawe's Questions, propounded in his Sermon preached at the Crosse. Examined and answered by H. A. [i. e. Henry Ainsworth], Ao. Di. 1608. 4to. *⁎* Name in full to 'Epistle to the Reader.'

3. A Defence of the Holy Scriptures, Worship, and Mysterie, used in the Christian Churches, separated from Anti-Christ, against the challenge, cavils, and contradictions of M. Smyth, in his book intituled, The differences of the Churches of the Separation! Hereunto are annexed a few observations upon some of M. Smythe's Censures, in his answer made to M. Bernard. By H. A. [i. e. Henry Ainsworth] of the English exiled Church in Amsterdam. Imprinted at Amsterdam, by Giles Thorp, in the yere 1609. 4to.

4. The Saint's Apologie, or A Vindication of the Churches, (which endeavour after a pure communion), from the odious names of Brownists and Separatists, in a letter sent to an eminent Divine of the Assembly, shewing that they separate not from true Churches, but keep themselves free from other men's sins. In repositing from the corruptions only which such Churches maintain in their externall communion, and from that yoke of bondage, which they subject themselves unto, under Prelates and humane Devices. London: Printed with order, by A. C. Anno MDC.XLIV. 4to. To the reader Signed 'Thos. S.'

☞ In the Bodleian Catalogue, and in that of Trinity College, Dublin, the following anonymous tractate is ascribed to our Bernard :—' A short View of the Prelaticall Church of England: Wherein is set forth the horrible abuses in Discipline and Government, layd open in tenne Sections, by way of Quære and Petition, the severall heads whereof are set downe in the next Page. Whereunto is added a short draught of Church-government. Printed in the yeare MDCXLI.' 4to. It is simply impossible that Richard Bernard could have written this very able but unmeasured assault upon the Church of England. Let one brief extract suffice: 'The Church of England now so called, is the Church of our Prelates, and may be rightly termed the Prelatical or Hierarchical Church of England, received from Rome, the seat of anti-Christ, and set up here after the Protestants fell off from that Papal Church for its, framed of Prelates and also of prelatical Clergy, and only ruled by them. Quære, Whether any such Church was ever in the Apostles' days, or any time shortly after within 2 or 300 years? Whether any such Church be among any of the Reformed Churches; or anywhere else, but under the Pope, the Beast,' &c. ?

There was a second edition of this tractate published the same year (1641), 'Newly corrected with additions.' The 'additions' consist chiefly of an address (one page), to 'the Honourable and High Court of Parliament.' This is a bona fide new edition; type different, and consists of forty-three pages, whereas the other has thirty-nine pages only. There was a third edition published in 1661, along with Vav. Powell's well-known 'Anatomy of the Prayer-Book' and other things. Probably the mistaken ascription of the authorship originated in this reprint, of which the title is as follows : 'A Short View of the Prelatical Church of England. Laid open in Ten Sections, by way of Quere and Petition to the High and Honourable Court of Parliament, the several Heads whereof are set down in the next two pages. Written a little before the fall of that Hierarchie, about the year 1641, by Iohn Barnard, sometimes Minister of Batcomb in Somersetshire: Whereunto is added, The Anatomy of the Common-Prayer. Printed in the year 1661.' 4to. It will be observed that name and surname are blundered, the former in all likelihood, because in his 'Bible Abstract and Epitome' (folio, 1642), usually bound up with the 'Thesaurus' his name is stupidly given, 'Pro Richardo Barnardo' Copies of the three editions are in Trinity College, Dublin: that of 1661 is P. kk. 59.

ADDENDA ET CORRIGENDA.

WE embrace the present opportunity of correcting and supplementing one or two statements in our former Memoirs :—

1. Airay, p. xi, for 6th read 10th October, as the date of his death by our reckoning. Cf. p. xii.
2. King, p. ix, line 17 from top : It appears that this was the unrenowned father of *the* Ralph Cudworth, not the metaphysician himself, and that this was not *the* John Norton of New England, but one obscure.

> *Ibid.* p. xi, foot-note ‡. I gladly transfer from " Notes and Queries " the following communication from an accomplished correspondent :—

> " *Bishop King and Dr John Rainolds.*—Mr Grosart has just edited* for Mr Nichol's *Series of Commentaries*, the Lectures of Dr King on Jonah, and of Rainolds on Obadiah and Haggai. Biographical notices are prefixed to each. In the first, reference is made to the fiction which was circulated, affirming that Dr King had professed himself a Roman Catholic. Allow me to add a reference to those which Mr Grosart has given. Some account of the matter may be found in " The New Art of Lying, covered by Iesuits under the Vaile of Equivocation ; discovered and disproved by Henry Mason, Parson of St Andrew's Vndershaft, London," 12mo, 1634, p. 206.

> " The same book also contains an interesting anecdote concerning Dr Rainolds (pp. 199–206). It appears that a stupid report was set afloat about Dr Rainolds ; and to prepare against anything worse, his friends drew up for him a Confession of Faith, which he was too weak to write himself, but which he signed, and which was witnessed by nine persons, May 20. 1607. You may not wish to have the document, but here are the names : Henrie Airay, vice-chancellor ; Henry Wilkinson, Edward Bilston, Richard Taylor, Henrie Hindle, Daniel Fairclough, Henrie Mason, Alexander Hord, and Iohn Dewhurst."

> Mr Mason adds that he was in possession of the original, from which he makes " a faithful transcript." Of this Henry Mason I have no further information, except what Wood says in Athen. Oxon. II. 56, ed. 1691. B. H. C. (January 28. 1865, 3d S. VII.). It were easy to supplement concerning this Worthy, Henry Mason, than whom there are few of our old writers more racy and quickening. It may suffice to add that he was chaplain to Bishop King, that he died in 1647, and to refer to Dr Bliss's A. O. III. 219, 220, and Fasti, *sub nomine.*

> A. B. G.

---

* A mistake : I am only responsible for the Memoirs. The Rev. Thomas Smith, M.A., Edinburgh, is the alone Editor of this Series, as he is the ' General Editor' of the Series of Puritan Divines, in which only Sibbes, thus far, has been edited by me.—G.

THE LADY FRANCIS,

COUNTESS OF WARWICK, DOWAGER,

The increase of all saving graces, and the fruition of that eternal bliss with the saints in glory, is heartily wished.

RIGHT Honourable Lady,—Though a woman was the mother of all man's misery, yet of a woman came salvation, to bring us out of that estate unto grace and glory; and for women's comfort, God of his mercy hath been pleased to make their sex renowned in many examples. To some he hath given supernatural knowledge, by enduing them with the spirit of prophecy, as Miriam, Deborah, Huldah, and Anna. Upon other some he hath bestowed singular wisdom, as upon the woman of Tekoah, and the wise woman of Abel in Bethmaacah. Rare was the faith of many, as the faith of Sarah, of Rahab, of the widow of Sarepta, and of the Canaanitish woman; who have put on better resolutions, and greater courage for the church in the time of peril, than some men have done. Did not Deborah encourage Barak to the wars, adventuring herself with him, when otherwise he without her was afraid to go? Did not Jael, the wife of Heber, kill the great captain and general Sisera? And who more resolved to jeopard her life for God's people then beautiful Esther, with her *If I perish, I perish ?*

Have there not been of them famous in many other things? For attention to the word, as the virgin Mary and Lydia; for going far for knowledge, as the queen of Sheba, to hear the wisdom of Solomon; for works of charity, as Dorcas; for works of piety, helping forward the building of the tabernacle, as were many women, Exod. xxxv. 21, 22, 29; for fervency in prayer, as Hannah; for daily devotion in fasting and prayer, as Anna; for entertainment of God's messengers, as the Shunamite, as Lydia, and one Mary, Rom. xvi. 6; for the fear of God, as the midwives of Egypt; for courtesy to a mere stranger, as Rebekah; for humility and patience, as old Naomi. Who can outstrip Ruth in love? Are there not recorded not mean ones only, but also honourable personages for religion and grace? as we may read in the

Acts xvii. 4, 12. Will a Dionysius become a believer in an university from among the Athenians? You shall find a Damaris to second him.

In what have men been renowned, wherein some women (according, yea, and beyond the nature of their sex) have not been remarkable? In wisdom, faith, charity, love of the word, love of God's messengers, fervent affection, and desire of heavenly things? If men have suffered imprisonment, cruel persecution, and bands for Christ, were women behind? No, verily, Acts viii. 3, and ix. 2.

Nay, have they not in somewhat excelled men sometimes? Who entertained Christ so much and so often as Martha and Mary? Who are noted to contribute to Christ's necessities but women? Luke viii. 3. Who (saving John the apostle) followed Christ to his cross, lamenting and weeping, but women? Who of all the ordinary followers of Christ observed where Christ was buried but women? Luke xxiv. 24. Who first went to his sepulchre with sweet spices to anoint Christ's body but women? Mark xvi. 1, 2. We may read of a congregation of women, to whom St Paul preached, being gathered together to the accustomed place of prayer, Acts xvi. 13, as more forward as it may seem at that time than men.

It would be tedious to repeat by name all the notable women in the holy Scriptures, and their excellent graces; yet can I not let pass Priscilla her knowledge, with her husband Aquila in the ministry of the gospel, able to teach an eloquent Apollos; nor Lois and Eunice, trainers up of the famous evangelist Timothy in the holy Scriptures; nor Persis, Philip. iv. 3, which laboured much in the Lord, as many other women did. Not to stand upon more instances, one thing for their more worthy praises is to be observed, and not to be forgotten; I have read of men well-esteemed of to have been apostates, as Demas, Alexander, Phyletus, and others, but of never a woman by name, once reckoned among the saints in all the New Testament. This is singular glory.

But the Lord hath not thought it enough to honour women thus, by endowing them with excellent gifts, and by their praiseworthy works, but also he hath graced them otherwise. To whom did Christ first manifest himself after his resurrection, but unto women? Of what act did ever Christ so speak, to make it perpetually famous, as that of the woman, Mat. xxvi. 7, 17, that poured upon him an alabaster box of ointment, promising that wheresoever the gospel should be preached in the whole world, there should her work be remembered? Hath not also the Lord directed his penmen, and by name his beloved apostle, to write an epistle unto an 'elect lady'? And are there not whole books of Scripture dedicated to their names, as this of Ruth, and the other of Esther, for an eternal remembrance of them?

I hope, Right Honourable Lady, therefore, that I may be bold to present your Honour with this my *Commentary upon Ruth*, which you may challenge of right before all others, for your bountiful and liberal contribution towards my maintenance in the univer-

sity of Cambridge, by the which I am now that I am; and for which, as also for your Honour's ever-continuing favours to me and mine, I remain ever-lastingly a debtor.

Accept, therefore, I humbly beseech your Honour, this my best testimony of all dutiful services, and of the acknowledgment of my most thankful remembrance of the same. And my hearty and daily prayer is, that the Lord would bless your Honour, that as both you have intended and also begun good works, so you may go on with increase therein to the end; it being the greatest honour before God and men, to be great and rich in good works, for which you shall have, for the present, many people's prayers; for the time to come, of mindful posterities, also great praises; and withal in heaven (which is the best of all) reward with God, who ever preserve your Honour in all happy peace and prosperity!

Your Honour's ever bounden to be commanded,

RICHARD BERNARD.

BATCOMBE, March 22.

RUTH'S RECOMPENCE:

OR,

A COMMENTARY UPON THE BOOK OF RUTH.

———o———

*T*HE *book of Ruth*. This is the title of this part of Scripture; and hereby is shewed of whom it chiefly entreateth: even of Ruth, the virtuous and godly young woman and widow, a heathen and idolater by her country and birth, but by the Lord's call a gracious saint at length, a mother in Israel, and one of whom Christ came. The titles of the books of holy writ, shew either the principal matter thereof, as *Genesis, Exodus, Leviticus, Numbers, Psalms, Proverbs,* and many other; or who were the penmen, as the books of *Samuel, Ezra;* or what person chiefly is there spoken of, as *Job, Esther, Nehemiah,* and *Ruth* here; who, though but a woman, and of that weak sex, yet being truly religious, see how the Lord doth her honour to all posterities: a singular encouragement unto virtue and godliness.

Who penned this, is not certain; but certain it is by the genealogy, chap. iv. 18, 22, that the scribe lived in David's time, and therefore is it held to be Samuel's by some. But it is not necessary ever to know the penners of every book of Scripture, especially of historical and dogmatical, whose truth and authority depend not upon the writer or speaker, as prophetical books do, but upon the verity of the things spoken and written. The scribe's name is concealed; the Lord's pleasure was not to have it mentioned, and therefore after hidden things we will not make further inquiry, especially in a matter of no more moment.

The book is divided into four chapters, being, as it were, the parts of the book: the first sheweth Ruth's journeying to Judah, with the occasions thereto, and causes thereof; the second, her entertainment and her carriage and pains there; the third, her contract with Boaz, a nobleman of Bethlehem, and how it was procured; and the fourth, her solemn marriage, with the joyful issue thereof.

CHAPTER I.

*T*HIS chapter telleth us how Ruth came to Bethlehem, who, being married to a man's son of Judah, in her own country, for the grace of religion in her heart, and the love she bare to her mother-in-law, after the death of her husband and father-in-law, forsook her people, country, and idolatry, and went into the land of Judah, to dwell with God's people, and came thither with her mother-in-law, in the beginning of barley harvest.

Ver. 1. *And it came to pass in the days when the judges ruled, that there was a famine in the land; and a certain man of Bethlehem-Judah went to sojourn in the country of Moab, he, and his wife, and his two sons.*

This verse is an entrance into the story, and is the description of a journey; and therein note, when, upon what occasion, from whence, whither, and who took it in hand, and with what company he finished it.

And it came to pass. To wit, by the hand and providence of God. Thus he beginneth this history, to note a special hand of God in all this business, beyond man's purpose and thought, in bringing a famine, and in Elimelech's going into Moab, to take a wife for his son, even this Ruth, to make her a mother in Israel. And therefore are we diligently to mark the providence of God in reading this story.

In the days when the judges ruled. This telleth us when this happened. In historical narrations, the time with other circumstances are set down for more credit to the story, Judges i. 1, 2 Sam. i. 1, 1 Kings i. 1. As in human stories this is observed, so here in divine. Thus God in mercy descendeth to us, for the better confirmation of our weak faith, for which he is to be praised. We may note out of these words,

I. That the Israelites were ever under government, under Moses, Joshua, the judges, and then kings. This was needful to prevent disorder and confusion of state, when men are not under rule and government; for then will every one do what he listeth, Judges xviii. xx., which condemneth anarchy and all loose liberty, destruction to church and commonwealth.

II. That their government was first by judges, that they might see the Lord's extraordinary hand in this governing of them,* 1 Sam. viii. 6, 7, and that they might not be as other nations, 1 Sam. viii. 5, nor in bondage, 1 Sam. viii. 9, 18. These judges were raised up for the most part extraordinarily, to shew more fully the Lord's care of his people. They were worthy and excellent men; not all of the same tribe and family, but sometimes of one, then of another; they ruled not by tyranny, or the advice of man, but by the counsel and guidance of God; they loaded not the people with heavy burdens to maintain great state. In their days they sought the welfare of the people, the glory of God; not their own wills and pleasures, to rule after their own lusts. They would not reign themselves, but the Lord, as Gideon said, Judges viii. 23, should reign over the people. Thus happily did the Lord provide for his people, till they did shake off his yoke, and brought themselves into bondage. For so it falleth out, if men like not of God's choice, he leaveth them to their own, of which they shall be sure to repent.

III. That such as be set over a people are to rule them, but yet in judgment; for the Hebrew word translated *ruled*, is *judged*, and rulers were to judge, 1 Sam. vii. 15. And this must they do, even labour wisely to rule and govern in judgment. They are to rule, to maintain their authority, which else will lie through contempt in the dust; and they must do it in judgment, that equity may be upheld, and nothing be done rashly, partially, and to the hurt of innocency.

That there was a famine. This might happen many ways: by the incursion of foreign enemies, by civil wars among themselves, or by restraint of seasonable showers from heaven. Howsoever it came, sin was the cause thereof; for we may read in the time of these judges, howsoever they themselves did valiantly and right worthily in Israel, yet the people would run into many mischiefs, so as we by searching may find these evils among them: a toleration of idolaters and public monuments of idolatry, Judges i. 21, 27, 29, 30, and iii. 5 and ii. 2, contrary to God's express commandment by the hand of Moses. They fell themselves unto idolatry, chap. ii. 11, 12, 13, 17, and viii. 27; for but

* Josephus in Antiq. lib. iv. cap. 8.—*De Aristocratia.*

tolerate it in others first, then we like it at length in ourselves, as many examples witness. They would defend it, and that with bloodshed, chap. vi. 30, for idolaters are of a murderous disposition, as their god-devil is whom they worship, as Manasseh, Joash, Jehoram, and other kings do manifestly declare, and as we have experimentally found at the hands of papists. See here a toleration first, then an approbation, then an open defence of an idolatrous worship; and when this is once on foot, what darkness doth not over-spread! They did what themselves listed, chap. xvii. 6, and xviii. 1, and xxi. 25. They fell to adultery and filthy Sodomitry, chap. xix. Thus they forgot the Lord's mercies, and therefore he severely punished them, as the story of the Judges shew, in giving them into the hands of their enemies, grievously to oppress them, and here by famine to plague them. From whence we may observe,

I. That sins, especially these aforenamed, deserve the judgments of God, Deut. xxviii., 1 Kings viii. 35, 36, 37, because sins provoke and incense the wrath-ful indignation of the Lord against men, as appeareth by his terrible threatenings, Ps. xi. 6, Rom. ii., and his inflicted punishments upon evil-doers, of which there want not examples in the Scripture: as the old world, Sodom, Israelites, in wilderness, in Canaan; and therefore to escape plagues, let us take heed of sin, Ezek. xviii. 31, Rev. xviii.

II. That famine and dearth is a punishment for sin, and that a great plague, Ezek. v. 16; Deut. xxviii. 23, 24; Lev. xxvi. 19, 20; Amos iv.; therefore to avoid it, either prevent sin, that it be not committed; or if we be overtaken, repent of sin, and that sincerely and speedily. And when this hand of God cometh upon us, let us search our ways, and let us humble ourselves, 2 Chron. vii. 14, that the Lord may heal our land, for it is a terrible judgment, 1 Sam. xxiv. 14, and without mercy, 2 Kings vi. 10, 29, Ezek. iv. 10. This famine men do know; yet there is another famine which few know, or if they know it, they fear it not, the 'famine of the word,' Amos viii. 11, which the Lord threateneth by that prophet, as a greater plague than the famine of bread and water, the food of the body; and yet, alas, who feareth it? who are touched with the terror of this plague?

III. We may hereby see how God made his word good upon them, and that he dallieth not with his people, in denouncing judgments against them; for Moses had told them, Deut. xxviii., that God would thus afflict them, if they would be rebellious against him: and here the story telleth us, that in the days of the judges this famine came upon them. This Ezekiel verifieth in chap. vi. 10; and the punishments inflicted, as the Lord denounced them, shew the truth hereof, that the Lord speaketh seriously. He doth not jest with sinners; he will certainly make good upon them what he threateneth, as may be seen upon Jezebel, Eli's sons, and upon his house, upon Jeroboam, Joa-chim, Zedekiah, and on Jerusalem. For the Lord is the God that hateth iniquity, and is just in his word, even the God of truth, as well in threats as in promises. And therefore let us fear the lion's roaring, and not be like him that blesseth himself, and dreadeth not the curse, Deut. xxix. 18, but presumeth of mercy, as if God were not also just to punish offenders. But such must know they deceive themselves, they harden their own hearts, they abuse God's mercy, which is to work fear, Ps. cxxx. 4, Jer. xxx. iii. 9, and obedience, Rom. xii. 1. They spoil God of his justice and truth in his threats, and incense the Lord's wrath to plague them in a high degree, as he threateneth in Deut. xxix. 19.

In the land. In the land of Canaan, the kingdom of Israel, where God had placed them, planted them, and promised to them his blessings plentifully. Yet see now, for their sins, in a land once flowing with milk and honey, Ezek. xx. 6, they find scarcity. Hence note,

I. That people deprive themselves, by their sins, of that which God had given, and they enjoyed, according to his promise. For sin will deprive angels of heaven, Adam of paradise, Cain of his honour, Reuben of his birthright, thousands of the land of Canaan, though they came out of Egypt; Jerusalem of her kings, her temple, peace and prosperity; men of their honours, as Jeroboam, Haman; of their liberty, as Manasseh; of health, as Uzziah; of their lives, as Korah with his company. Let us then blame ourselves for our miseries, and not the Lord, for punishing us as we deserve; and if we would hold the blessings which we do enjoy, beware of sin, which will rob us of all we have.

II. That a fruitful land is made barren for the sins of the inhabitants thereof, Ps. cvii., Lev. xxvi. 19, 20. And these sins in particular procure this plague: the abuse of God's mercies, Luke xv. 14; idolatry, 1 Kings xvii. 1, 2 Kings iv. 36; the murdering of innocents, 2 Sam. xxi. 1; and the oppression of the poor, Amos iv. 1, 6. Know, then, how to prevent hereby scarcity, and in the time of want turn from sin by repentance, and blame not the heavens or earth; murmur not against unseasonable weather, but be displeased with our sinful selves.

III. Judgment begins at the house of the Lord, 1 Peter iv., Ezek. ix. He will shew his hatred of sin upon the land of the living, for he cannot suffer evil in his people; if a Moses, an Aaron, a David, a Josiah sin, they shall feel the smart of it. Now therefore, if judgment begin at God's house, what shall become of God's enemies? If the church feel wrath, what may the adversaries expect?

A certain man of Bethlehem-Judah. Judah, the royal tribe. And this is added for distinction, because there was another Bethlehem in Zebulun, Joshua xix. 15. This Bethlehem was called Ephrata, Gen. xxxv. 18, six miles from Jerusalem, as some say. Here Jacob fed his sheep, Gen. xxxi.; here Rachel died, David was born, and Jesus Christ our Lord. It had

the name from plenty, and signifieth the *house of bread.* So as we see the noble tribe of Judah, and this honourable place of Bethlehem, felt this scourge of God. No place is exempt from the punishment where sin is suffered to reign; it bringeth famine upon Bethlehem-Judah, and on the land of Israel; it bringeth the sword and famine into Jerusalem. There is then no place to keep us free from feeling the punishment, if sin be not removed; chase out this, and call home again the Lord's blessings.

Went to sojourn. As a stranger, in another country, from his own home. We here see how God can remove by one means or another men out of their homes and harbour: David, through just fear of Absalom, out of Jerusalem; Manasseh, by force, out of his kingdom into prison; others, by unthriftiness, cast out themselves; some voluntarily leave their habitation and place of abode, and return not again; all which came about by the hand of God, who hath all things at his disposing, that no man may think himself securely settled, especially if he be a Shebnah, Isa. xxii. 15–17; the Lord will drive such out, Amos iv. 2, 3. Note again, how fear of corporal wants will make men leave their home, their native soil, their friends and kindred, to go into a strange country: so forcible is nature for preservation of bodily life, which man so much esteemeth and loveth. This should then make men care to keep the blessings providently and frugally, also to avoid the occasions and means of wasteful misspending, seeing fear of want will thus work. And if the love of corporal life be so forcible, how much more the love of eternal life, for which we should be willing to forsake all·! But, alas, the least worldly gain or carnal pleasure banisheth this love out of many men's hearts, who rather follow here Elimelech, to leave the people of God to go into Moab for the world, than Abraham, to forsake his country at the commandment of God.

In the country of Moab. This Moab was inhabited by those which came of Lot's eldest son, incestuously begotten, Gen. xix. 37. Of this was Balak king, who hired Balaam to curse Israel, Num. xxii. 6; who committed fornication with the daughters thereof, to the destruction of thousands. Over this land reigned Eglon, who smote Israel, and possessed some part of the land, and kept them in bondage eighteen years, Judges iii. 12–14. Some think that Elimelech journeyed to Moab in his days. Howsoever, by this we may learn that wicked idolaters may have sometimes plenty when the people of God are in want. Here Moab had plenty when Israel was under a famine. Of the prosperity of the wicked, read Ps. lxxiii. 4, and xvii. 14, and xxxvii. 15, Job xxi. 7, 13; and of the troubles of the godly, Heb. xi. 37. And this cometh to pass because the wicked are at home here; here their heaven and time of rejoicing. But the godly are not here at home; the Lord looketh for their coming to him, and therefore prepareth them by crosses; he loveth them, and therefore doth he correct them, that they might not be damned. Hence, then, it followeth that we are not to judge men's spiritual estates by outward prosperity or adversity, for the wicked have the greatest portion of the things of this life; see it in the parable of the rich man and Lazarus. Why do men then bless themselves for their wealth and honour, and despise their poor brethren, in a far better estate before God than they?

Quest. Whether did Elimelech well to go from Bethlehem into such an idolatrous country?

Ans. It may seem not, because he went of distrust rather than of present want, verse 21, and for that he left the place of God's true worship, and where the Lord promised his blessing, Canaan also being a type of the kingdom of heaven, to go among the wicked idolaters, whom the Lord by name also had forbidden to be received unto his people, Deut. xxiii. 3, Neh. xiii. 1. Further, hereby he could not but endanger his family to be defiled by idolatry, if the Lord had not been more merciful. And to conclude this, we see how the Lord's taking both him and his sons away may somewhat persuade that he did not well, seeing the Lord suffered him not to return home again. True it is that David went out of Judah unto idolaters for fear of Saul, but it was against his will, and with much sorrow of heart. Abraham he travelled into Egypt, but it was at God's bidding, and the Shunamite might by the prophet's warrant go into some place out of Israel to prevent the misery of famine, 2 Kings viii. 1, 2. But what is this to such as have no such warrant, but such moving causes as here?

He, and his wife, and his two sons. This is praiseworthy in him, for an honest man careth for his wife and children as well as for himself. Abraham took his wife with him into Egypt, Gen. xii. 18; Jacob, all his with him, Gen. xlii.; for the wife is as himself, Gen. ii., and so to be loved, Eph. v., and the children are bone of his bone. Reason and nature tied Elimelech to this, an example of a loving husband and of a natural parent to be imitated, and which condemneth those which run away from wife and children, and are worse than infidels, 1 Tim. v. 8, yea, than the brute beasts. This man led them, they followed him; so wives and children are to be companions with their husbands and parents in adversity. Sarah will follow Abraham, Rachel and Leah Jacob, from their country and father's house; and Mary, the mother of Jesus, will follow Joseph; for the husband is the head, and bond of law bindeth them thereto, which checketh the contrary, if husbands and parents do command to be followed and obeyed in things lawful. If Elimelech, as it may seem, did not well to go, it may be questioned whether these did well to follow him? He might do amiss, and not they, being under his government, so long as he led them not to do evil, and to commit idolatry, but for sustentation of life,

and in that country where they were not outwardly compelled to idolatry, but might serve God as they had learned at home. If any think otherwise, either of Elimelech's going or of his company, I contend not.

Ver. 2. *And the name of the man was Elimelech, and the name of his wife Naomi, and the name of his two sons Mahlon and Chilion, Ephrathites of Bethlehem-Judah: and they came into the country of Moab, and continued there.*

The historiographer goeth on with the former narration of the journeying, first expressing by name the man, the wife, and the sons, shewing plainly who they were; then the finishing of their journey; and thirdly, their abode there. Into these three things this verse divideth itself, the declaration of their persons, what they were called, both in respect of their names and place whence they came, the perfecting of their journey, and their stay there.

And the name of the man was Elimelech. By naming the parties, and not speaking in general, as before, the Holy Ghost would have notice taken of them, the better either to see their graces or to discern their wants, and so to have a more certain knowledge what to follow or what to take heed of; for the knowledge of persons maketh the things which they do either more or less apparent to us. Elimelech signifieth *the Lord my King*, a man well descended. He was of the chiefest tribe, to wit, of Judah, a nigh kinsman unto Boaz the lord of Bethlehem, and one of note, as appeareth by the article in the Hebrew, and in the Greek Septuagint also, as likewise by the notice taken of Naomi his wife at her return, ver. 19; yea, he went out of Judah without want, as may be noted from verse 21, and as learned men from thence do collect. And if so, his going away was more of fear to want than present necessity, which sheweth his great weakness, worthy reproof. See here a man well born, of good means, of good note, and carrying a name of trust in God, yet slipped through distrust of God's providence, and too much relying upon his own devised course, which yet failed him in the end. Great birth, good means, high name and fame, save not from falling either into sin or outward misery, if a better blessing than all these be not given men from God, and therefore not to rest upon them.

And the name of his wife Naomi. Whose daughter this was the Scripture recordeth not; her name signifieth *my pleasantness* or *sweetness*, as wives should be such to their husbands, and so husbands should account them. She was fair, a wise woman, of great note in the city, and a very godly and meek-spirited woman, full of true love, patient in want, thankful and humble, all which, to be true, her words and deeds in this history do plainly shew. So she was fair inward and outward, an example and looking-glass for women, the gallant dames which would be Naomis for outward beauty and bravery, but are foul Marahs for want of grace and true goodness. Naomi is named before her children, both in the former, as a wife to Elimelech, and here as a mother to them ; and this reckoning of her name in this order declareth her dignity and place before them. She, as a wife, is to have place next Elimelech the husband, who is to prefer wife before children, for she is himself, and as a mother to go before them that be her children, who are to honour their parents.

And the name of his two sons. Why not *her* sons, for she was not their mother-in-law, but they were sons born of her body ? verse 11. But they are called his for the more honour, for the father chiefly giveth honour to the child.

Mahlon and Chilion. The former signifieth *infirmity*, the latter *finished*. Why so called is not shewed, but they answer the event of things : the first, his father's infirmity in going from among God's people to live with idolaters for preservation of his outward estate ; and the other, his father's death, being taken away in Moab, verse 3. He was *Mahlon* in his leaving of Bethlehem, and *Chilion* in abiding in Moab. And here note in all these names how significant they be, which the Hebrews did ever observe in naming their children, yea, the Lord himself in giving a name to any one, as in calling Abram *Abraham*, Sarai *Sarah*, which is of us to be imitated, thereby expressing our faith and grace towards God, and admonishing them of some duty. True it is that good names have no virtue in them to make men better, nor names without signification to make any worse ; yet for reverence to our holy profession, and that blessed sacrament of baptism, at which time names be given, and in imitation of the godly in Scripture, yea, of God himself, who called his first son of men *Adam*, and his blessed holy one *Jesus*, by the message of an angel, let us give our children good names, significant and comely, not absurd, ridiculous, and impious, as some have done, out of the spirit of profaneness.

Ephrathites of Bethlehem-Judah. So termed, because Bethlehem was called Ephrata, Gen. xxxv. 19, or for that the country where Bethlehem stood was so called, as may appear in Micah v. 2; and Judah is added, not only for a distinction of this Bethlehem, from the other in Zebulun, but for to make a difference of the Ephrathites here from other in the tribe of Ephraim ; for Jeroboam is called an Ephrathite, 1 Kings xi. 26. By which we see how careful the Holy Ghost is to make clear the history, and to free it from ambiguity of speech, that the truth might better appear, and not be mistaken. The penmen of this and other divine histories are faithful historians ; and such should others be, and not full of fables, falsehood, and deceit, written through fear, or favour, or ill-will.

And they came into the country of Moab. So they finished their journey. Howsoever the man might do amiss in leaving Israel for Moab, the land of the living

331

for a dead nation, yet it pleased the Lord to speed his journey, to bring to pass what he had intended for the conversion of Ruth, to make her a mother in Israel. Whence we see, that God, intending good to some, in his secret counsel, may prosper that which others undertake with no good warrant. Thus shall Nebuchadnezzar prosper against Jerusalem ; Jacob's sons act in selling Joseph their brother ; yea, the enemies of Christ to put him to death, as God had determined, Acts iv. ; for the Lord can work good out of evil, and can use ill instruments to good purposes. And therefore simply for the good issue which God maketh, we are not to approve of either the matter in hand, or the minds of men which God useth therein, as is apparent in the former examples ; for God's will and work was one thing, but theirs another ; he is to be praised, but they are to be reproved. The word *country* may be also translated the *field*, as in the original it is often used, שדה, Gen. ii. 5, Num. xx. 17, Prov. xxiv. 3 ; Septuagint, εἰς ἀγρὸν ; and hence some conjecture that Elimelech went not into the cities of the Moabites, but dwelt in tents, as did Abraham, Isaac, and Jacob, and not in the cities of the Canaanites. If men live where idolaters be, it is good to avoid the occasion of infection as much as may be ; for much conversing breedeth familiarity ; this, love of their persons, and so a liking of their ways, with neglect of true religion at the first, but it falleth into contempt at last. It is rare to be a righteous-hearted Lot in Sodom ; he was but one, and one alone. Israelites became idolaters in Egypt. This is it which made the Lord forbid communion and marriages to them with the Canaanites, lest they should learn their ways. Let us therefore take heed of conversing with the wicked, and with idolatrous people. It is good that idle travellers should consider well hereof.

And continued there. So then they had no repulse, but were allowed to dwell there, and that for a long time, as the words in ver. 4 do shew; yet these Moabites were formerly hard-hearted enough, Deut. xxiii. 3. But by this we see that none are so churlish and unkind at one time to some, but God can incline their hearts at another time to other some. The history of heathen emperors manifesteth the truth of this towards Christians, and the story of the Israelites coming forth of Egypt ; for men's hearts, yea, the hearts of kings, are in the Lord's hands, to turn them towards whom he pleaseth, as Nehemiah knew well, which made him to pray, Neh. i.; and Jacob also, when he feared the coming of Esau. When we have to do with ill and dogged-natured men, let us go to God, who can turn Esau's bloody heart, in his coming forth, into a kind welcoming of his brother at their meeting ; he can incline Ahasuerus's heart towards Esther, to make him hold out to her the golden sceptre. Consider the promise, Jer. xv. 11, and xlii. 12, and let us seek to please God, and he will work us favour in the eyes of men, Prov. xvi. 7 and Job v. 23 ; let this be our comfort. It may further seem, by the course of this story, that these Bethlehemites were not only suffered to dwell among the Moabites, but also that they were kindly used, in that they would be content to marry with them, which is a commendation to them, that would thus welcome such as came among them for succour. It is a matter praiseworthy to be harboursome to strangers. For this were the barbarians commended, Acts xxviii. 2, 7, 10, who received the apostle and the rest into their houses, made them fires because of the cold and rain in winter, courteously lodged them, and when they departed, being such as had suffered shipwreck, and were thereby in want, those barbarians helped them with necessaries. This was humanity and mercy ; for this Abraham, and Lot, and Job are commended ; and this goodness we must learn to practise, for so are we exhorted, Heb. xiii. 2 ; and these former examples lead us to it. This duty is to be done, not only to our kindred, to our friends, to our known countrymen, but to strangers, Heb. xiii. 2 ; yea, and to our enemies in their need, 2 Kings vi. 23, Rom. xii. 20.

Ver. 3. *And Elimelech, Naomi's husband, died; and she was left, and her two sons.*

This telleth us of the heavy cross which befell Naomi, which was in the death of her husband, and that, as it may seem, very shortly after they were come into Moab, before the sons did marry ; so she was left a widow with two fatherless children, to take care for them in a strange country. This verse is a narration of an event, what it was, and upon whom it fell to the great heaviness of Naomi. The event was death, and here is shewed whom it took, and whom it left.

And Elimelech died. His age is not reckoned. He could not be very old, if we may guess his years by his sons marrying so young women after his death ; yet he dieth, yea, and there also, whither he went for food to preserve life. He went first from Israel, the land of the living, and led them thence, and so he now goeth out of the world before them ; from whence note,

I. That death is the end of all, and it spareth none, Josh. xxiii. 14, Job xxi. 33, Eccles. vii. 2, and vi. 6, 1 Cor. xv. 51, Heb. ix. 27 ; 'for all have sinned,' Rom. v. ; and 'death is the reward of sin,' Rom. vi. ; and therefore let all prepare to die.

II. That a full supply of bodily wants cannot prevent death. The man must die in Moab, where was food enough ; the rich glutton must die also, and the rich man with his barn full, for the sentence of death is irrevocable, and man's life dependeth not upon the outward means of life, for then the rich and mighty would never die.

Let not men in their abundance think to escape death ; let them therefore not set their hearts on their wealth, for they must leave it. It is folly to trust in riches, for they cannot deliver from death, either ordinary or extraordinary, lingering or sudden, natural or violent, as examples and experience itself teacheth.

III. That where men think to preserve life, there they may lose it, as Elimelech doth here, fleeing from the famine in Israel, yet died where plenty was, in Moab ; for no place is free from death, and when the time appointed is come, man cannot pass it, Job xiv. 5. We cannot think therefore ourselves safe anywhere from death ; nay, many times where we may think ourselves secure, there death may take us away.

Naomi's husband. It is not said *her* husband, which might well have been spoken by way of relation to her, without her name, because she was named before, and no other woman. But this woman was a very virtuous woman, and this was a great cross to her, and therefore, both to express her excellency, and her begun misery, it is said, 'Naomi's husband died,' the husband of so rare a wife died. Note hence,

I. That it is a grace for some to be called the husbands of some women ; their name is a grace to them, if they be virtuous ; for such a one is ' a crown to her husband,' Prov. xii. 4. Now a crown is high glory to a man, and ' her husband is known in the gates,' Prov. xxxi. 23. Such wives are to be made much of, as rare birds ; for too many may sit down with shame and blush to be named the husbands of some wives. Foolish, though fair ; fair, but perhaps filthy ; rich but withal retchless ; wives, but without government ; husbands, named the head, but they must be masters ; sometime painful, but peacock-like proud ; often more mad, or sullen sad, than merry ; if merry, it keeps not in with modesty ; if she speak, it is loud, often heard farther than seen, and yet oftener seen by a quiet husband than well liked of. In a word, a wicked foolish woman is ' shame to his person, and rottenness to his bones,' Prov. xii. 4.

II. That grace in one prevents not death in another. Naomi's husband must die, so Abraham's wife also ; Jacob must bid his Rachel adieu, and Ezekiel the desire of eyes, Ezek. xxiv. 16 ; for no man's grace can free himself, much less another, from death, Ps. xlix. 7, 9, and married persons are not appointed the same length of days. No ; we come not together, and we go not together. Let none hope for life by the grace of another ; let the nearest and dearest look to part by death. Ruth loved Naomi most dearly, and saith that nothing should separate them but only death, ver. 17, because she knew that that must needs be yielded unto.

III. That it is a great cross for a woman to lose a good husband. This is implied, as I said, in naming her by name ; for in him the wife loseth her head, her guide, her stay, and comfort, if he be a virtuous man, and a good husband. I need not entreat good and loving wives to mourn for such ; sure enough they have cause, and wives cannot but mourn, except they conceit a new comfort very quickly, as some do, for fear the old grief should lie too long at the heart for him that is dead, and cannot be recalled. So with them, the living is better to be liked of than the dead, for they know their husbands would, perhaps, have so dealt with them.

And she was left, and her two sons. Death seized only upon Elimelech, and left Naomi and also her sons, that she might not be utterly comfortless in a strange country. From this may we note these two things:

I. That albeit death is due to all (inasmuch as all have sinned), yet it seizeth not upon all at once; but one dieth now, and another hereafter, as we see in all ages, which cometh not to pass for any good in one more than in another. But God will have mankind upon earth till the last day; he forbeareth some, and reprieveth them for their amendment; for the lengthening of life is for our further repentance, if we be the Lord's, or for the greater condemnation of such as shall perish. For this mercy God is to be praised, for we deserve death; and it might seize upon every one at once, and take us away, because we are born in sin, brought up therein, and none so free ever, but in his highest pitch of well-doing he may be tainted of sin, 1 John i.

II. That the Lord, in afflicting his children, sweeteneth the same with some comforts. He wholly leaveth not them without some taste of his mercy and goodness, as we may see in his dealing with Naomi. He took away her husband, and left two sons, and after took them away, but gave her an excellent daughter-in-law. Elisha had an earthly power coming against him, 2 Kings vi. 10, but he then saw a great help from heaven. It was a bitter affliction for Joseph to be sold of his brethren, but it was sweetened with Potiphar's favour; this at length imprisoned him unjustly, but the Lord gave him favour in the eyes of the keeper of the prison, to sugar this bitter pill with. And this the Lord doth in mercy, that his children might not be overwhelmed with grief, and swallowed up of sorrow; therefore by one means he casts them down, but by another sustaineth them. Let not therefore men, which fear God, be over sad when afflictions come; God will lay no more than they can bear; he layeth on them a burden, but he putteth under his hand. If we look upon the affliction, let us also consider what cause of comfort we have; mark when, for what, how long or short, what it is allayed with, that we be not wholly cast down.

Ver. 4. *And they took them wives of the women of Moab; the name of the one was Orpah, and the name of the other Ruth: and they dwelt there about ten years.*

This sheweth what course the sons took after their father's death; they returned not home. This cross brought them not to think of leaving that idolatrous country, but they settled themselves to marry there, so as this verse telleth us of two things: the first is

of a marriage, and herein who they were, the men, Elimelech's sons; the women, who are set out by their country, then by their names; the second is of their abode in Moab, and time how long.

Note (before I come to the words) that every cross bringeth not men home again; their father's death made them not resolve to go back unto God's people again. Lot was taken prisoner, yet would he still abide in Sodom after his deliverance. Jehoshaphat's danger with Ahab made him not wholly to forsake that house; but he must have more afflictions, and the prophet openly to rebuke him. And this cometh for want of weighing the true cause of afflictions, when they happen, or desire to please other, or the love of this world, or some such corruption of our heart. To bewail this our perverse nature not easily reformed; a great affliction must work on Manasseh, great distress the prodigal son, before they will come to themselves, and turn to the Lord; yea, some are worse for afflictions, as may be seen in Ahaz, 2 Chron. xxviii. 22, in Amon, chap. xxxiii. 23, in the antichristians, Rev. xvi. 11, and in the Jews, Jer. v. 3.

And they took them. This may seem an act of their own, as that of Lamech, Gen. iv. 19, and that of the sons of God, Gen. vi. 2, and not their mother's deed, as is said of Hagar, Gen. xxi. 21. If they did this with her consent, it was as godly children should do, to marry with consent of parents, for parents have authority in this case, 1 Cor. vii.; children owe this honour to them. Examples of the godly, as in Isaac, and Jacob, and Samson, move to it, and the contrary is found fault with, Gen. vi. 2, and in Esau; our laws require it, godly men and learned divines so teach out of the word. Let children therefore herein take advice of their parents, they shall thrive the better: if they do well, their parents will rejoice; if otherwise, then children may more boldly seek to parents for comfort, and expect help at their hands.

Wives. So women be called when they be married unto men, or betrothed. It is as if it had been said, They took young women for wives to live in God's ordinance, and not for wantons to live in uncleanness. Though they were not in Israel, yet they let not loose the unbridled lust of nature, but used marriage, the ordinance of God. So men are to take women as wives, to live together in God's holy ordinance, as the godly have ever made conscience to do, and not to live as brute beasts, to defile themselves, as Hamor did Dinah, and Zimri did Cozbi, in the sin of fornication. From this must we fly, as the apostle exhorteth, and from other degrees of uncleanness, as adultery, which God severely punished, 2 Sam. xxii. 10, Job xxxi. 9, 11; so incest, Gen. xix. 36, 1 Cor. v. 1, 2 Sam. xiii. 14, and other unnatural pollutions not to be named, Rom. i., which God giveth reprobate minds over unto.

Of the women of Moab. With these they were not to marry, Deut. vii. 3, and xxiii. 3 Ezra ix. 1, 2, Neh. xiii. 23, 25, 26. Young persons in their choice soon err, if they suffer lust to rule, and follow not the law of God, Gen. vi. 2. Herein wise Solomon was overtaken, Neh. xiii. 26, 1 Kings xi. 1. Therefore men are to bridle appetite and lust, and let the Lord rule them; religion and reason guide them herein. The children of God are not to marry with the daughters of men; it is condemned, Gen. vi. 2, the contrary commanded, Deut. vii. 3, 4. See there the reason and equity thereof. Ever such marriages are not made in the Lord as they ought, 1 Cor. vii. 36, and God hath punished such matches; see in Solomon, 1 Kings xi., and in Jehoshaphat, in marrying his son to Athaliah, 2 Chron. xxi. 6. If Rahab be a believer, Salmon may take her to wife, and so Boaz may marry Ruth; and if there were none other to match with in the world, Abraham may take one out of another country for Isaac, and Jacob may marry Laban's daughter; but there is no such want, but that the sons of Abraham may match with the daughters of Abraham now.

The name of the one was Orpah, and the name of the other Ruth. This was the wife of Mahlon, chap. iv. 10, the elder brother, and Orpah the wife of Chilion, the younger; whether sisters or no, or of what parents these came, is not mentioned. These heathen people refused not in those days to match with strangers. Jethro giveth his daughter to Moses, which must be for his virtue and not for his wealth, for he had none; he was brought up like a prince, but he humbled himself to keep sheep, and so obtained his wife. Men's manhood, virtues, and painfulness in those days got them wives. Caleb will marry his daughter for the man's virtue's sake, and valorous spirit; Saul will pretend as much towards David, but that was pretended in policy, not in truth; Laban the worldling will marry his daughters for the world, and sell them for gain; but a godly man preferreth grace before goods, and wisdom before the world; though where grace is, if goods may come with it, it is a blessing, and the better to be liked of, for help to uphold the burden of marriage.

And they dwelt there about ten years. Whether this time beginneth at their first coming, or after this marriage, is not certain, but it is ten years before Naomi hears of the Lord's visiting of Israel with plenty. It is a long time for a godly woman to be kept from God's people, and public service of his name. David lamented it much, Ps. cxx. 5, and desired the presence of God and his tabernacle, Ps. lxxxiv. 1, 4. In Moab was corporal plenty, but not spiritual; for the one the other was neglected. Such is our corruption, a common sin now; I wish it had not taken possession of the best. But besides this, we may further note, how a heavy calamity may long rest upon God's people; we may read of a famine three years and a half in Ahab's days, three years in David's time, 2 Sam. xxi. 1, 1 Kings xvii. 1, Luke iv. 25, and seven years at another time, 2 Kings i.,

and here also for a great many of years. And this cometh through men's obstinacy in sin, and for that such things are not reformed, as God commandeth, or for that some evils are not punished as they ought to be, as for innocent bloodshed, 1 Sam. xxi. 1, for open idolatry, and murdering of the saints, as in Ahab's days. We are in such continuing judgments, to look to our ways, and bewail our sins; also seeing thus God's hand against his people so long, we may learn patience in the years of scarcity, and bless God that never thus afflicted us in any of our remembrances; for such a famine would in these northen parts be most intolerable, far more unsufferable than in hot countries, where people could humble themselves with fasting many days together.

Ver. 5. *And Mahlon and Chilion died also both of them; and the woman was left of her two sons and of her husband.*

This verse sheweth a further grief which befell good Naomi, which was the death of both her sons; and so to be left a heavy soul in solitariness in a strange country, where she could have no spiritual comfort, and where now she had lost her chiefest corporal comfort.

And Mahlon and Chilion died also both of them. These enjoyed their young wives for some space, and had time to have returned home to the Lord's people, but they for bodily maintenance, and new friends gotten by their marriages, would not; the Lord therefore took them away in this strange land. Many things may be noted.

I. That the Lord gave them time to marry, and to enjoy their marriage for some space, though they made no better use of their father's death. Thus good and patient is God unto men, for their bettering, if it would be; for which praise him.

II. That when God hath proved men in patience, and they will not make right use thereof, then will he take them away, for he will not always strive in mercy. Here the abusers of God's goodness may learn to take heed.

III. That God can and will cut off sometimes young men in the flower of their youth. Thus he took away Nadab and Abihu, Hophni and Phinehas, Amnon and Absalom, two gallant young princes; so here these two, though some by violent death, and other by natural death. And this is sometime a punishment for sin, Ps. lv. 23, 1 Sam. ii. 31, but not ever; for God in mercy will take some from the evils of the world, as he did Josiah. Let none because of youth put far off the day of death. Death respecteth no age, no strength, no beauty: 'Remember thy Creator in the days of thy youth,' Eccles. xii. 1. Thy own sin may cut thee off in youth, as it did Absalom, and so the rest; or thy father's sin, as David's child was taken away, 2 Sam. xii. 14, and the ten tribes from Rehoboam, 1 Kings xi. 12, and xii. 6, and the sons of Saul.

And the woman was left of her two sons and her husband. This is added to aggravate the affliction of Naomi, and doth teach, that neither few nor light afflictions sometime befall the godly. Naomi lost her husband, then not one but both her sons, and left their widows without children, so as Naomi had none of his blood remaining in Moab. And as she was thus afflicted, so was David, who had proud and scornful brethren, a bloodily-minded father-in-law, a mocking Michal to his wife, lewd and unnatural children, besides many other great trials. What shall I speak of Job's trials, Jeremiah's troubles, and Paul's persecutions? Yet God thus suffers his to be tried, to make them know themselves, to shew them their graces and their imperfections, which in affliction they will manifest, to wean them from the world, to the love of a better life, to whip them from their sins, and to make our vile natures tame, to submit to his yoke. Let us look therefore for them, let us be contented and patient under them, and consider the troubles of others of old, and in the primitive church, and of later times. Let us not think our condition the worse before God, but rather the better, if instruction be with correction, for God loveth us then. It is a fault to murmur at him, it is an error to think our estate to be evil before God, because of sundry and great crosses, for many are the afflictions of the righteous; he saith not of the wicked, yet then righteous when they be afflicted; this is comfort against despair.

Note again that he saith, *the woman* was left. He saith not now, *Naomi,* as before and after, to express her dejected condition; for a widow, poor, alone, without friends, and in a strange country, is in an afflicted estate and contemptible. It is then not *Naomi,* but *the woman* in distress and misery. And lastly observe, that when death calleth, friends must part, and one leave another, husbands their wives, children their parents, and parents their children; as here, no band of love can keep them then together, death must be welcome, and unto dearest friends we must bid farewell.

Ver. 6. *Then she arose with her daughters-in-law, that she might return from the country of Moab: for she had heard in the country of Moab how that the Lord had visited his people in giving them bread.*

Here is at the length the return of Naomi, with whom, from whence, and the reason drawing her mind homeward.

Then she arose. She had long abode in Moab; now, after such crosses, she ariseth to go thence, unto the church and people of God. When the Lord thus afflicted her, when she saw herself destitute of her husband and children, and had none to go unto and to converse with but idolaters, the Moabites, then she arose to leave those coasts. Note how affliction shall follow affliction, to bring home such as be the Lord's: if one cross will not do it, another shall, as we see in

the prodigal son, and God's dealing with Manasseh; for the Lord is loath to lose his own; and therefore if one affliction happen, make good use thereof, else another shall follow, yea, and another after that, till we return home. Again, mark that it is then time to leave the place of our abode, when the godly are taken away, and none left but wicked to converse with. Thus, and for this cause, many left Israel in Jeroboam's days, 2 Chron. xi. 13, 16, for the godly should delight in the fellowship of the godly. David's delight was in the saints. It is also dangerous for the godly to frequent the company of the wicked, as a lamb to be among wolves. David will not dwell in the tents of the wicked, neither sit among them, Ps. xxvi., and it is a good man's property to avoid them, Ps. i. 1, and therefore let us flee the fellowship of idolaters, 1 John v., 2 Cor. vi., and the society of evil persons. For such as can live with delight among them are like them, are no true converts to God; and yet not a few which will be held religious can make themselves merry with vain persons, and condemn others for too stoical, too censorious, for that they cannot away with fleshly and carnal delights.

With her daughters-in-law. It appeareth that these two did voluntarily accompany her of their own minds, and not by Naomi's entreaty. This appeareth out of vers. 8 and 11. What moved them hereto but Naomi's virtues? So as we may see that the truly virtuous are of an attractive power, even as the loadstone, to draw others unto them, partly by instruction, partly by their godly conversation. Both which means we may think she used towards these while she abode in Moab; for the religious cannot but incite others unto piety. This is worthy imitation in Naomi; if practice shew our religion, it will win others, 1 Pet. iii. 1, without which even the most glorious profession in words hath no operation, no power to persuade. And here also was a mercy of God to this poor old woman, that she lost not all outward comfort; she had some to keep her company in her adversity. It is a good grace to be content to bear the poor company in a miserable estate: they be true friends which will sit down upon a dunghill with Job to mourn with him. Well, here were two daughters of Moab which would accompany Naomi, poor and afflicted Naomi. A reproof to counterfeit friends, of which now the world is full, never more.

That she might return from the country of Moab. This is the end why she arose, that is, left the particular place of her dwelling, not to go into some other place in Moab, as hoping of better success there, but quite to forsake the country. The kindness received there could not hold her, when she perceived the Lord to call her home, partly by afflictions in Moab, and partly by mercies now in Israel. Outward kindness of worldlings cannot keep the godly with them, when God calleth them away from them either by afflictions or by check of conscience, or by falling into sin by them, or by feeling the want of the godly and the use of God's public service, or else by seeing or hearing of God's favour to his people. When these or such like do call upon the godly to come away, they cannot by any wordly pleasure, profit, or familiar acquaintance, or kind entertainment, stay with such men; they be like Abraham's servant, Gen. xxiv., which could not be held with rest and good cheer to stay in Bethuel's house, nor David in Ziklag, when he had liberty to go into Judah, 2 Sam. ii. 2; for their spirits differ, so as they cannot truly affect one another; and the godly find crosses among the wicked to hunt them out from their society, and they cannot but fear, in a godly jealousy, to be made the worse by them, for that they know their own weakness. And therefore let us labour for this grace, to leave the society of the ungodly, lest we be ensnared by them; and if we be with them, let it be by warrant of our calling, or of necessity, and only so long as we have hope to do them good, and to win them; but if they be found obstinate, forsake them, Jer. li. 9.

For she had heard in the country of Moab. That is, while she did stay in that country, news was brought of plenty in Israel. As the famine did drive her from thence, so now food being there, and the crosses she found in Moab, moved her to return back again. As adversity maketh many to leave the church, so the prosperity thereof bringeth many unto it; some in truth and love, as Naomi here, others for the world, or for fear, Esther viii. 17. Let us then pray for the church's prosperity; yet not then are we to trust all that come within her lap. Note again how Naomi, in her greatest distress, heard of comfort to her country, to bring her home again. God is often the nearest in mercy to help, when in man's reason he seemeth to be furthest off. Thus was God with Jonah in the whale's belly, and with the three children in the furnace, with Daniel in the den, with David to help against most present danger, 1 Sam. xxiii. 26, 27. Peter, the very night before his intended death by Herod, must be delivered; and so the gunpowder plot here be discovered. And God thus suffereth his so long, and to come to so narrow a strait, before he set them free, and shew himself; to humble them, to beat them out of confidence in themselves, to shew his power and mercy the more, that they may see more fully his goodness to them, to make them thankful, obedient, and the more in utmost perils to rely upon him. We are not to despair in the greatest dangers, nor to think ourselves forgotten in great extremities, but then seek to God, trust in him, and doubt not of comfort. God will have Lazarus in the grave before Christ restore him to life, and Isaac bound upon the altar before he forbid Abraham to slay him. Till the ship be ready to sink, Christ will not awake, Mat. viii. 25, 26, for so the Lord is more seen in his power and mercy towards his.

How the Lord had visited his people in giving them

bread. By bread is meant all necessary food, but especially corn, of which bread is made. Here the Lord is made the giver thereof to the Israelites, called ' his people,' whom in mercy he visited, to bestow his blessings upon; for so is *visited* here taken, and in Gen. xxi. 1, Luke i. 68, Jer. xxix. 10. Note from hence these things :

I. That God seeth his people in adversity and want, and cometh in his due time to help them, Exod. iii. 7, 8, which is from his mere mercy, and the stability of his love and promise to his people; and therefore we may learn patience in affliction, and not be impatient, as if God had forgotten, nor murmur, lest the Lord punish us, Ps. xiii. 1, 1 Cor. x.

II. That God hath ever had more specially a people for his own, called ' his people.' Thus were certain called the sons of God, Gen. vi.; thus after were the Israelites his, Deut. vii. 6, and xxvi. 18; and such be now true Christians, 1 Pet. ii. 9, Rev. xviii. 4. These he chose not for any merit in them, but of his mere love, Deut. vii. 8, Eph. i. 4. This should make us to examine ourselves how we be God's people, whether according to creation, or after the work of regeneration; for these differ from the other greatly, in the graces of God's Spirit and holy conversation, Ezek. xi. 19, and xxxvi. 26, 27, Ps. xv.; in glorious titles, Deut. xxvi. 19, Exod. xix. 6, 1 Pet. ii. 9, Rev. i. 6; and in heavenly prerogatives, as in peace with God, Rom. v. 1; in free access, with a holy boldness to God in Christ, Heb. iv.; in having God ever with them, Mat. xviii. 20; in this blessing, that ' all things work together for the best to them,' Rom. viii.; and in being a ' communion of saints,' to whom is belonging ' the forgiveness of sins, the resurrection of the body, and life everlasting.' We are therefore to labour to be of this sort of God's people.

III. That corporal food and the necessaries of this life are God's gift, Lev. xxvi. 4, 5, Deut. xi. 14, 15, Hos. ii. 8, 9, Joel ii. 19. It is he that maketh the earth fruitful, he giveth rain, and withholds it, Hos. ii. 8, 9, Amos iv. 7, and man without him can do nothing, Ps. cxxvii. 2, Hag. i. 6, Deut. viii. 18. Praise him for these blessings, Joel ii. 26; in the want of them, acknowledge it from God, and go to him, pray to him, Mat. vi.; and this must be done in an humiliation of ourselves for the affliction, 2 Chron. vii. 14, Joel ii. 16, 17, 19. If we look for these blessings, we are to serve him, because they be his gift, and to such hath he promised them, Lev. xxvi. 3, Deut. xi. 13, 16. Let this reprove such as forget God, do not praise him, nor serve him for these blessings, and let it confute such as ascribe them to the heavens, or to the industry of man, never remembering the precept of Moses, Deut. viii. 18, and that saying in Job, xxxi. 26, 27.

Ver. 7. *Wherefore she went forth out of the place where she was, and her two daughters-in-law with her;*

and they went on their way to return unto the land of Judah.

In the former verse was Naomi her preparation for her journey; here is her setting forward, noting from whence, with whom, and whither.

Wherefore. That is, because she heard of plenty in her country: which giveth us this to understand, which before I noted, that the church's welfare procureth friends, and draweth her old acquaintance to her; for prosperity is of an attractive virtue, and men are affected with it. This will make Abimelech to seek to Isaac, Gen. xxvi. 26, and Job's friends gather unto him, Job xlii. 11. This should make us seek the church's prosperity, yea, and make men frugal to preserve their estates; for prosperity gets friends (though not a few counterfeit), and adversity maketh men to be forsaken; and yet many, which might live well, bring themselves, by prodigality and lewd courses, unto misery; unworthy they be of pity.

She departed out of the place where she was. In what particular place of Moab she was in, is not named, though here to be understood by the name *place.* There was food here, as well as in Judah, yet she would not stay, though she was an old woman, having poor and weak attendance, the journey somewhat long for her, her estate wasted, and therefore was she to return in a base estate, which other perhaps might cast in her teeth for leaving Judah, and going into that idolatrous Moab; but all these things did not withhold her from her godly purpose. And two reasons may be given for this: the love of her own country, and her piety, esteeming highly of the means of salvation. Whence may be noted,

I. That there is a love naturally in every one to their own country. See it in Jethro, Exod. xviii. 27, Num. x. 29, 30, and Barzillai, 2 Sam. xix. 27. Jacob would return into Canaan out of Mesopotamia, where he had gotten great riches. And this love unto their country made men to adventure their lives in defence thereof, 2 Sam. x. 12. Therefore such are unnatural, who will seek the destruction thereof.

II. That corporal means cannot keep the truly religious from the place where God is worshipped, if they may enjoy the means of life in a poor measure. Naomi would not stay in Moab, though she in Judah had nothing to maintain her, but her hands, and that Ruth must glean for bread, when they came thither. What a change Moses made we all do know; a crust of bread for the body is better, with the food of the soul, than all carnal abundance without it. And therefore if the choice of our dwelling be, either where bodily plenty is, without the word, or a poor estate for the body, and plentiful instructions for the soul's safety, let us choose this rather than the other. Seek, saith our Saviour, for the food which endureth unto eternal life, which perisheth not, John v.

And her two daughters-in-law with her. This their accompanying of her, argueth Naomi her singular
337

good carriage towards them while her sons lived; for if she had been proud, froward, and unkind, as some mothers-in-law have been, they would have despised her, and shaken her off; but we see, first, how good carriage procureth love; and, secondly, how true love sheweth itself in the adversity of a friend, Prov. xvii. 17, for these two forsake not poor and old Naomi in this her contemptible estate. Thus Jonathan shewed his love in David's trouble, and Job's friends, when they sat down by him; for true love is not tied to outward respects. Such love is false and hollow-hearted, the love of these times. We must imitate God in love, to love ever, and chiefly in adversity; for either love then or not at all. Be not as the shadow which sheweth itself only in sunshine; nor as the swallow which chatters, and sings over thy chimney in warm summer, but cannot be seen in winter. Friends only in appearance shape their love like to the devil, who only maketh a show of love to man, and is ever sinister in the intendment.

And they went on their way to return to Judah. It seemeth by this, that the two women came out to return with Naomi, who only is properly said to return, because she came out of Judah; and they had a purpose to go through with her to the end, and to leave their own native soil, their parents and friends, which was a great degree of love; but yet we may read that Orpah afterwards gave over. To begin well, and to make an onset to goodness, is easy to many; but to go on to the end, is of special grace. Cain began and made an onset to godliness, so did Joash king of Judah. Jehu did valiantly for a while. Judas seemed to be approved by his fellows, and to live without suspicion for a time. The same may be said of Ananias and Sapphira, of Simon Magus, of Demas, Hymeneus, Alexander, and Philetus, with many more; but their calling was not effectual. Called they were, but not elected; their hearts were full of hypocrisy, which will at length break out. Therefore let none think well of themselves for fair beginnings, because ' they that continue to the end shall (only) be saved.'

Ver. 8. *And Naomi said unto her two daughters-in-law, Go, return each to her mother's house: the Lord deal kindly with you, as you have dealt with the dead, and with me.*

Naomi seeth their kindness, and weighing aforehand all circumstances, beginneth to make trial of the fondness of their love, and to know upon what ground it standeth, as appeareth out of the verses 11–13. The words consist of an exhortation, and a petition to God for them, rendering a reason thereof.

And Naomi said unto her two daughters-in-law. To this place there is no mention of any speech of Naomi, but only what she did: First, in following her husband into Moab, ver. 1, 2, and then of her leaving that country to return into Judah, ver. 6, 7.

Hitherto her story is of her walking, and not of her words and talking; it seemeth her tongue did not hang loose, to be upon every touch tolling, as some women's be. And this her silence commendeth her virtue therein, and also giveth us to know, that she did not solicit her daughters to go with her, but that they voluntarily undertook the journey; for if she had requested them, their love had not so appeared, neither could she have tried them, by entreating them to return back.

Go and return. How far on the way they were come is not noted; but on the way they were before she spake thus to them; which she did not, as careless of their souls, or of any doubt, whether God would provide for them, who would forsake their country, and become proselytes; but two reasons may be alleged why she exhorteth them to return home again. First, was her love to them, for their kindnesses formerly to her and hers, as appeareth by her prayer, and therefore she might now seem to be loath to trouble them, though their company in the way might have been comfortable, except she had known certainly how to have recompensed their love. Taking this for one, we learn, that a true lover is loath to disadvantage a friend or friends for private respects to himself; for true love seeketh also the good of a friend beloved; and a sound-hearted friend will follow the apostle's advice, 1 Cor. x. 24, not seek his own, but his friend's welfare. But this, alas! is contrary to our times, when now men are all for themselves, which self-love is contrary to Christ's commandment to love our neighbour as ourselves; it is against the communion and fellowship of Christians, as 'members one of another;' it is contrary to the end of our labour in our callings, 2 Cor. xii. 14, Eph. iv. 28, which is, to do good to others; contrary to that care which God commandeth, for the preservation of other men's estate, Deut. xxii. 2, 4, Exod. xxiii. 4, 5; contrary to Abraham's practice, Gen. xxiii. 9, whose children we must be, and whose works we must do. This self-love is the original of all bribery, extortion, usury, deceit, fraud, oppression, and unjust dealings among men; this maketh men envious, that they cannot rejoice in other men's welfare; and this maketh men without compassion in another man's misery, if they themselves live at ease. This root of bitterness must be rooted out.

The second reason was her want of means to give them comfort in the world, to provide for them necessaries or convenient matches, as her words imply in verses 12, 13. She knew them to have friends and parents in Moab, but none in Judah, and therefore she was loath to make them worse, and to carry them to an unknown place, except she could better have provided for them with some certainty. True love will not make worse where it cannot make better. But here it may be demanded, whether Naomi did well to persuade them to return? I answer, if she had done it in carelessness of their souls, or in a coldness of religion, she had offended; but it was partly in her love to them for their outward estate, not knowing how to pleasure them, if they should take such pains to go with her, and leave their own country; and partly out of her wisdom, to try them whether indeed they fully resolved to go with her, let fall out what might fall out. And this was praiseworthy in her thus to try their soundness, for hereby she found one rotten at the core, and the other most sound. And thus should we also do in these deceitful days, try before we trust such as offer themselves to come among the godly, as also did our Saviour, Luke ix. 57, 58, lest when they hastily entertain religion they as suddenly fall back, to the reproach of the gospel and blemish of such as admitted them without trial.

If any ask why she persuaded them not to stay at home whilst they were there, but to let them go on the way, and then to will them to return back? I answer, it may be that she took their coming forth to be of courtesy to take leave of her, after she had gone somewhat on her journey, which kindness there was no reason to refuse; but perceiving that they would go on, she then fell to make trial of them, and to understand what might lead them thereto. And this was better done in the way than at home, to discern more fully of their resolution. In the trial of others, it is then best done, when the same may most appear; this is wisdom.

Each to her mother's house. Here is an argument to move them to return back, because they had natural parents alive, and she but a mother-in-law. She trieth them with this first, to see whether nature wrought more than grace. This she knew to be a strong pull-back, and that nature must first be subdued to follow soundly the course of godliness. We must forsake father and mother for the gospel, saith Christ, yea, and deny ourselves. If thus we can do, then are we to be admitted into the fellowship of the faithful. These words shew they were not natural sisters, because Naomi willeth each of them to go to her mother's house, as having either of them a mother. In that Naomi thus speaketh, we may further note,

I. That of either parent children are drawn with most affection to their mothers, because all children have most of their mothers, being conceived in them, long borne of them, and nursed by them; also, for that mothers are more tender-hearted towards them, and most familiar with them: therefore here is their mothers' house named, though afterwards Ruth's father, chap. ii. 11. And yet some children we see ready enough to despise their mothers, which is contrary to nature, contrary to the commandment, Exod. xx., Prov. i. 8. Yea, it is great ingratitude to requite so the great pains in conception, in bearing, in nursing, which a child can never recompense, and therefore a curse is pronounced against such children, Deut.

xxvii. 16, Prov. xx. 20; and of this the prophet Ezekiel complaineth, chap. xxii. 7.

II. That poor widows are to be maintained of their able parents when they be left alone, and cannot maintain themselves, Lev. xxii. 18, 1 Tim. v. 16. The law of nature, and, we see, the law of God leadeth thereto, and Naomi knew not whither else to send them. And whither should children go but unto their parents? If this be so, then let parents see to the well matching of their children, to prevent their poverty if it may be, and a second charge of them. Let children be then ruled of their parents in taking marriage upon them, seeing parents are to be troubled again with them if need require. Yea, and let husbands have care when they have received their wives' portions, so to husband the same that they may leave them to live after them, and not to be again chargeable to their friends.

The Lord deal kindly with you. Her prayer for them, which was her best recompence for their love, being now poor, and not otherwise able to requite them their kindness. Note hence,

I. That it is a duty to pray for those which do either us or ours good. So doth Naomi here; so Boaz for Ruth, chap. ii. 12; David for Abigail's good counsel, 1 Sam. xxv. 33; and Saul for David sparing his life, 1 Sam. xxiv. 19. And this duty lets us perform, as Christ in the form of prayer hath taught us, Mat. vi., and not pray only for ourselves, as worldlings do, nor to think a favour done is requited with *I thank you* only, and that prayer for a blessing upon them is not required, especially if they be superiors; and yet we see here the practice of superiors to inferiors.

II. That at parting friends are to pray one for another, as we may see the practice of it in Isaac, Gen. xxviii. 1, 3; Laban, Gen. xxxi. 55; Jacob, Gen. xliii. 14; and in Paul, Acts xx. 36. It is very Christian-like, an argument of love, and desire of their own welfare, which cannot be without God's protection. Put this, therefore, into practice. True it is that men now do it, but it is not with that reverence, nor expressed with that earnest desire, as is meet and befitting in such a case.

III. That the godly are persuaded that the Lord is a merciful rewarder of the duties of love which one doth towards another. This Naomi her prayer to God for them here teacheth, for the godly know that the Lord hath commanded such duties; and what he commandeth to be done, that will he reward in the doer. And hereof let us be well persuaded, this will make us do our duties cheerfully, though men requite not our pains, because God will. By this reason St Paul encourageth servants to their duties, and to do what they ought heartily, Col. iii. 24.

IV. That children should so well deserve of parents, yea, though but parents-in-law, as they may be moved heartily to pray for them, as Naomi doth in this place. A good carriage is a duty towards all, then much more to

parents; and the prayers of parents is a means to put a blessing upon their children. But some children are so far from doing their duties to their parents to procure a blessing, as they with Ham deserve a curse. Such a one was rebellious Absalom, bloody Cain; such a one was Reuben, Simeon, and Levi, whom the Lord punished.

V. That God will not only barely reward, but so deal with us as we deal with others. This Naomi begs for, this the Lord in mercy will do, Mat. vii. 2, for our encouragement to well-doing; he will reward us according to our works. This should stir us up to do our duties unto our brethren, knowing that as we do we shall be done unto.

As ye have dealt with the dead and with me. Here Naomi acknowledgeth their loving obedience and good carriage towards their husbands when they were alive, and now to her, they being dead; and this maketh her to pray thus for them.

Note here, first, that daughters of a bad race may prove good wives, and good children-in-law sometime, as these daughters of idolaters did, when God restraineth nature and giveth grace withal. For many times there are tractable and gentle natures, where religion is not grafted; these by good instruction and God's blessing may prove excellent wives. Children, therefore, are not ever to be censured according to their parents, though it is dangerous to graft in a bad stock, for an hundred to one but a Michal will make a David know that she is a Saul's daughter. But here women Christians are taught to shew themselves good wives and children, or else these daughters of the heathen will condemn them, whom Naomi commendeth for good wives. Now, to be a good wife, a woman must know her duty, and be very desirous to do it, which stands in love unfeigned, in fear to offend, in cheerful obedience, in meekness of spirit, and in sympathising with her husband in prosperity and adversity, Eph. v. 22, Col. iii. 18, 1 Peter iii. But where is the woman? where is this Sarah, this Rebekah? She will answer, perhaps, Where there is an Abraham and an Isaac, for a good husband will make a good wife; a good John a good Joan. The body will obey where the head knoweth how to rule well.

II. That good and truly loving wives love their husbands' parents for their husbands' sake, as these did Naomi. For the wife and husband are one, and should be of one heart, and the one love where the other liketh; and a good wife striveth to please and content her husband in shewing love to his friends. She will not be like such lewd wives, women not worthy to be wives, which hate their husbands' kindred, and browbeat them out of their houses.

Ver. 9. *The Lord grant you that you may find rest, each of you in the house of her husband. Then she kissed them: and they lift up their voice and wept.*

Naomi her continuing in prayer for them, as before

in general, now in particular, for a special blessing. This verse containeth a petition, an act of a valediction, and the passion which it wrought.

The Lord grant you that you may find rest, each of you in the house of her husband. She prayeth here for their second marriage, and that the same might be blessed of the Lord, the chief marriage-maker, so as it might procure them rest, and be a quiet, contented marriage to their comfort. Note hence,

I. That godly and wise friends pray not only in general, but in particular, as they know them to stand in need, for whom they do pray, as here Naomi for good husbands for her daughters-in-law; for we should take notice of our friends' wants, and so pray for them, and not rest in generals.

II. Godly mothers-in-law are hearty well-wishers to their children-in-law, whether they be such by a former husband departed, or by another husband living, or by the marriage of their children, as Naomi is here mother to these; for the love they bear to their husbands, and because godly women know themselves to be stepmothers, stepped in to be instead of natural mothers, and therefore do make conscience to supply their want; which if it be so, or ought to be so, it reproveth those stepdames which are unkind and cruel to their children-in-law, and cannot endure the sight of them.

III. That second marriages be lawful, 1 Tim. v. 11, 14. The reason is given by the apostle, 1 Cor. vii. 9, 36, which confuteth such heretics as in former times have denied this, contrary to the apostle's doctrine, and the example of Abraham, in marrying Keturah.

IV. That husbands are to be their wives' rest, chap. iii. 1; and they are so called, because of the desire of women to marry, and because they seek rest in their marriage, and for that loving wives take rest and contentment in their own husbands, who ought therefore to be rest unto them; which shall be if they do love them as they ought, Eph. v. 22, if they wisely govern them, 1 Peter iii. 7, if they provide and allow them what is meet, according to their ability, in all decency and honest contentment; if they keep their faith plight, and rejoice in them, and with them, they cannot but find rest. But unloving and fierce natures, Lamech-like husbands, a word and a blow, or terrible threats, miserable and niggardly Nabals, so prodigal and unthrifty, drunken or adulterous husbands, are so far from being poor women's rest, as they make them weary of their lives. But now if husbands must be their wives' rest, and that they look for it, then wives must care to make their husbands so to them, by willing obedience, by meekness of spirit, very acceptable to God, 1 Peter iii. 4, by seeking to please them, by speaking to them in a loving reverence, and to keep silence when words may offend, or not do good, as wise Abigail did, by a wise frugal course, and good housewifery, as the woman in the Proverbs, chap. xxxi.

Speak not foolishly, as Job's wife, to thy husband in his grief; nor mock him not, like a barren Michal; nor abuse him not, as Potiphar's wife would have done her husband; nor be impatient for not having thine own will, as Rachel was; but rest in his will, and thou shalt find him thy rest. Here is also an use for parents, to match so their daughters, as they may get husbands as rests for them; and this will be, when they marry their daughters betime to men of wisdom, fit for years, not unfit for birth and estate, well agreeing in qualities and good conditions, and in religion.

V. That it is God's blessing to be peaceably married, Prov. xviii. 22, and xix. 14. He is the marriage-maker, whosoever are the means; and he is the disposer and framer of their hearts one to another; therefore let God herein be sought unto, and let him receive praises and thanks for such a blessing, the greatest corporal comfort in this world.

Then she kissed them. This action we may find fourfold: carnal, as in fleshly lust; hypocritical, as was Joab's and Judas's kiss; holy, of which the apostle speaks, 1 Cor. xvi. 20; or civil, as here. This was used at the meeting of friends, Gen. xxix. 11, and xxxiii. 4; at their departing, Gen. xxxi. 55, 2 Sam. xix. 39, Acts xx. 37. This was used between men and men, Gen. xlv. 15, Exod. iv. 27, 2 Sam. xix. 39; between women and women, as here in this place; and between some men and some sort of women, as between husband and wife in meeting and departing, parents and children and nigh kinsfolk, Gen. xxix. 11, but not strangers, nor others not of kindred, to avoid the suspicion of wantonness. It was honestly used to testify love and unity, as Isaac did to Jacob, Gen. xxvii. 26; and therefore in the primitive church, before they received the sacrament, they thus saluted one another.*

And they lift up their voice and wept. Here was an answerable affection to the kindness of her action; her sign of love was not without love again to her: for it was not a few silent tears from the eyes, but a passion of the heart, breaking forth into wailing and weeping, so as their voice of mourning was heard, an argument of love and true affection towards her. This is rare love between mothers-in-law and daughters-in-law, in these days. But concerning weeping, it is used in Scripture,

I. To express sorrow, as at the parting of friends: Joseph, at his father's departing; Abraham, at Sarah's; Joash, at Elisha's, 2 Kings xiii. 14; and when friends must leave one another, though death separate them not, as when Jonathan and David parted, 1 Sam. xx. 41. And who can but weep, if true love be there, when friends must bid adieu one to another, and especially for ever, as we may see in Acts xx. 37?

II. For very joy, as Joseph's sight of his brethren, Gen. xlv. 14; and so Jacob at Joseph's coming to him, Gen. xlvi. 29; so did Jacob in meeting with Rachel, Gen. xxix. 11. Such true loving natures have

* Just. Apol. 2.   Beza on 2 Cor. xiii.

been in the godly in former times, but now men are lovers of themselves, without natural affection, 1 Tim. iii.

III. In pity and compassion, from a merciful heart, to behold the miseries of others, as Job did for the poor, chap. xxx. 25 ; Isaiah for the people, xxii. 4 ; so Jeremiah, chap. iv. 19, and ix. 1, and xiii. 17 ; Christ Jesus for the Jews, Luke xix. 41. This is a charitable and a holy weeping, when men can weep for the miseries of other, corporal but chiefly spiritual, as David did, because men kept not God's law, Ps. cxix.

IV. Sometimes some will weep in the apprehension of the kindness shewed to them, where none but utmost extremity is deserved, 1 Sam. xxiv. 16. Now, if David's forbearing of Saul wrought in Saul this passion, how should we be moved to consider of Christ's love to us, and our cruelty against him !

Ver. 10. *And they said unto her, Surely we will return with thee unto thy people.*

Before was noted their affection, here is set down their resolution, which was to accompany her, and also how far.

And they said unto her. All this while they heard her, they accompanied her, but no mention of any speech hitherto made unto her. But now necessity compelleth them to break silence ; which, though it be a special jewel in women, who are too tongue-ripe, yet sometime necessity enforceth them. If this might be the only key to make them speak, they then speaking were worthy attention, if withal they would speak in wisdom, and within compass, knowing when again to keep silence.

Surely we will return. That is, dissuade us not thus to leave thee, for we are resolved to go with thee in this thy return home. Where note, that an earnest affection suffereth not easily a separation from the party affected. For the truth of this, see it in any sort of love : as in carnal love, between Samson and Delilah, Judges xvi. ; in natural, between David and Absalom ; in friendly love, between Jonathan and David, and Mephibosheth to David also ; in Christian love, as in Paul to the Jews, Romans ix. 13, and in Moses to the Israelites ; and in divine love, as of God's to us, and of blessed martyrs towards God again. In all these, what provocations were there to break off, except it be in God's behalf towards us, who offereth no occasion to make us leave him ? Yet where affection is settled, there will hardly be a separation ; for true love liveth in the party beloved, and can no more forsake him than himself. It is also full of patience to put up wrongs, and taketh everything in the best part, and hopeth of better in the worst things. Let us hereby try our love, which is ever with peace and unity ; for where discord is, there is no love. Such then are hollow-hearted friends, which profess love, and yet upon every trifle break out into manifest signs of hatred.

With thee. As if they had said, Though thou beest

341

our mother-in-law, and art but one, and a poor woman, yet thy grace and virtue is such as we are content to forsake our country and carnal kindred for thee ; with thee will we therefore go. And indeed it is better to have the company of one sound Christian, than to enjoy the fellowship of a world of worldlings. Good Jonathan took more delight in one David, than in the society of all his father's house ; for the fellowship of the godly is comfortable and very joyous to the soul of such as be godly, but the company of worldlings vain and unfruitful to God-ward. The godly are worthy to be affected and loved ; they be the children of the Most High, and the world is not worthy of them, no, not when they be in the basest condition in the judgment of men, Heb. xi. 38. And the godly are such as with whom God is for ever, who go the way to eternal life, which whosoever looketh for must keep them company thither. And therefore let us join ourselves to them, sit down with them, delight in them, Ps. ci. 6, and xvi. 3, and cxix. 63, 79 ; and avoid others, Prov. xxiii. 1, Ps. xxvi. 4, 5, and ci. 3, 4, 7, 8.

Unto thy people. Thus they call the people of Israel, God's people and God's church, to shew that there is a right in every particular member to the church, as in the church to every member, and all to Christ, and Christ to them, 1 Cor. xii. 12. For the church is as a body, whereof Christ is the head, and every one one another's members. We may therefore claim a right in one another, to care for and watch over one another ; we may claim a right in all the church's rites and divine ordinances of God belonging thereto for our salvation ; and therefore should every member care for the preservation of the whole, and the whole for every member, and take their wrongs to heart. Lastly, note out of this verse, that both the women, in their passion, speak the same thing, but yet, upon more deliberation, one of them calleth back her word. By which we may see that in passionate affection more will be spoken than acted ; as we may here see in Orpah her promise, in Saul also, 1 Sam. xxiv. 16, 17, and xxvi. 21, and in David's heat of spirit, 1 Sam. xxv. 32. For passion causeth men to speak unadvisedly, and more than they would if they did consider thereof ; yea, in passion men are not themselves, neither can the hypocrisy of the heart be discerned, no, not of the parties themselves at the present instant of time, which maketh such to speak better than they either can or will do afterwards ; as appeareth here in Orpah, and in Saul. We are not to value words uttered in passion, nor to regard them, either to advantage ourselves or to harm the speaker, as many do, who catch men in their sudden speeches, sometime to gain by them, sometime to trouble them. This ought not to be ; charity would teach better things.

Ver. 11. *And Naomi said, Turn again, my daugh-*

ters; why will you go with me? Are there yet more sons in my womb, that they may be your husbands?

Naomi's reply unto their speech and second trial of them; wherein is an exhortation and a double interrogation: the first moving to a more serious examination of their resolution, and the second a reason of her continued exhortation.

And Naomi said. She maketh a second essay upon them, though she saw their passion and heard their resolution, for she knew that a sound trial is not made at once. We see Orpah withstood the first, and made as good a show as Ruth, both in her tears and talk, yet soon after she gave over. With these fair onsets Satan was well acquainted; and therefore both with Job and Christ, though he prevailed not at the first, yet hoped to overcome at the last. Constancy standeth not in one act, neither is therein to be discerned; and therefore let none think they have sufficient trial of any because they have made once an essay with them in any matter; neither let any man think that he hath done valiantly because he hath resisted a temptation once, and could not be overcome, for thou mayest be set upon again and again; and if after many thou beest overcome, thou hast lost thy glory in the rest.

Turn again, my daughters. Of the exhortation before in the 8th verse. Here Naomi kindly calleth them her daughters, which she might do both for her ancientness in years and also for that she was their mother by marriage. This is a term of love which here she doth express to shew that her exhortation came not for want of love, but even in love she did it, as before is noted, and as appeareth plainly in the last words of the ver. 13. And herein is a point of godly discretion, which is, that in giving counsel to or fro, it is good so to speak as may declare love and respect to the parties, as she doth here, Abigail to David, Jethro to Moses, yea, and Lot to the very abominable Sodomites; because the manifesting of love in advising, exhorting, admonishing, or reproving, doth make way in the heart of the party advised and reproved, and the contrary shuts up men's hearts and ears, as experience doth shew. And therefore in such cases let us shew love by using good and loving terms, by protesting our true affection, if so need require, by giving good reasons thereof that may fully shew it, and by being ready to do them good, offering them to do it if there shall be occasion of it. Note more, that it was a custom among the Jews for parents and children to speak most commonly one to another in the nearest and dearest terms of love, by the name of father, mother, son, daughter, and not by calling them only by their names, as parents do children now. See this in Gen. xxii. 7, and xxvii. 1, and xlviii. 19, and in many other places, which argued meekness of spirit, entire affection, and a loving natural kindness, worthy imitation.

Why will you go with me? This question is propounded to draw them to a consideration of some reasons within themselves why they should resolve to go with her; as if she had said, I love you as a mother her daughters, therefore I advise you to consider seriously of your resolution aforehand, and weigh with yourselves what may so lead you; for I can see no reason in worldly respects (for such only she urged both here and in the verses following) why you should go with me. And by this, as she taught them, so we may learn, that it is a point of wisdom to ask ourselves, why we will do this or that thing, before we undertake it or resolve upon it. And hereunto our Saviour advised, Luke xiv. 28, for that is well begun which is laid upon good grounds and sound reasons; it is a wise proceeding, it will prevent the after *Had I wist*, and future repentance. Let us therefore learn this wisdom, and not be foolishly rash in our attempts.

Are there yet any sons in my womb that they may be your husbands? Naomi now beginneth to bring in her reasons why she would have them to return, all drawn from the world, in which respect she giveth them no comfort to follow her; and it is as if she had said, If you will go with me for any worldly respect, alas, I cannot pleasure you, I am old, I have no sons to marry you again unto; and as for an outward estate, you see me very poor. In thus speaking plainly, and dissuading only by worldly reasons to try them, we may learn,

I. That the true honest-hearted, and such as fear God, in the kind offers of their friends, deal truly with them, and will not lead them into vain hopes. Thus Naomi dealeth; thus did our Saviour, Mat. viii. 20, for they would not deceive them. We must labour for this plain dealing, and not only look to ourselves, and what present benefit we may get to ourselves, as most do in these deceitful times, which is contrary to our Christianity, 1 Thes. iv. 6, to true love, 1 Cor. xiii., and to the comfort of our own consciences. Men now-a-days gladly make gain of all proffers of love, without any respect to their friends; because men are false-hearted and like such as David was troubled with, Ps. xli. 6.

II. That worldly respects are not the motives which should induce any to join themselves with God's people, for they want these things often. Of this our Saviour telleth the lawyer, Luke ix. 57. The godly here have their least share in the things of this life, because they have a better portion provided for them in the life to come. We are not, then, to become professors of religion with others for these worldly things. Naomi telleth thee this is not a good reason. Christ telleth thee he is poor, and such as follow him must take up their cross, must suffer affliction, saith Paul, 2 Tim. iii. 12, for to the godly it is given to suffer for him, Philip. i. 29. Beware of a Judas mind, to come for the bag; or a Demas-like disposition, to come before thou hast shaken off the love of the world: for if thou doest not, thou wilt sell Christ for the world, and bid the gospel adieu for goods.

Quest. Why is it said that she had no sons more for them to marry? Why should she thus speak to them? We must know that it was a law among the Jews, that a brother should raise up seed to a brother who left a wife and died childless, Deut. xxv. 5, Gen. xxxviii. 8, 11; to which law and practice her speech alludeth. And by this we may think it very likely, that these women were taught in the law of God, and made acquainted with the practice of God's people. This is very probable, because Naomi was so godly a matron, and it appeareth by Ruth's virtues; which being so, it commendeth the care of Naomi and her sons, for the souls of these young women, born of idolaters out of the church, to teach them the law of the true God. A good example for parents to follow, and for husbands; for fathers and mothers, see Prov. iv. 3, 4, Deut. vi. 7, Eph. vi. 4, Deut. xi. 19, Prov. xxxi. 1, 2, 2 Tim. i. 5 and iii. 15; and for husbands, read 1 Cor. xiv. 35. But, alas, many are so ignorant as they cannot teach them, and many so careless as they neglect them, many so wretched as they will not, and some so profane as they mock at it, and hold it no duty for them, but for the priest (as in scorn they call the minister of Christ) to perform.

Ver. 12. *Turn again, my daughters; go your way; for I am too old to have an husband. If I should say, I have hope, if I should have an husband also to-night, and should also bear sons.*

Naomi's third motion to have them to return, using still the same exhortation, with the like kind terms of love, and adding another reason to move them to return.

Turn again, my daughters; go your way. Naomi ceaseth not to urge them still, to try them to the utmost, not in want of zeal to gain them to God, but in a godly jealousy, fearing their constancy, if they should go on with her; of this before at large, and therefore here I omit the instructions.

For I am too old to have an husband. This reason is a preventing of an objection to her former reason; for they might say, Though, mother, you be not with child now, yet you may marry and have children. To this Naomi answereth, that she is too old to have an husband. From this we learn, that there is a time when women are too old to marry, by the opinion of godly Naomi. Now, if any ask when that is, I answer, as I suppose, when a woman is about sixty years of age; and therefore St Paul alloweth such a one for a widow, but not under, giving leave to others to marry; for under sixty women have had children, but none above, but Sarah's extraordinary blessing. And it is fit for women after sixty to follow the praise of blessed Anna, Luke i. 37. We read not in the Scripture of the marriage of such; and if they be poor among us, and do marry, we dislike it, and speak against it; if they allege the ends of marriage, they are easily answered. For the first is for procreation of children,

which in them is past; the other is to avoid fornication, which they should be far from, seeing the body is dead, the heart should not grow rank with filthy lust: the lecherous old person is hated of God. If they allege to marry for mutual comfort, I ask, with whom will she marry for such comfort? If with a young man, she may perhaps comfort herself in him, but not he himself with her; for young men marry old women's goods and lands, but not their persons; there is in nature no accord between them. Her wanton heart may seek her pleasure in matching with him, but he will take no contentment in her but for what she hath. If with an old man, where is comfort when two froward old persons meet together. Old age, all know, is hard to please, and therefore old persons can hardly afford kind comforts one to another. Lastly, marriage bringeth cares and troubles, 1 Cor. vii., saith St Paul. Now, it is time for old women to lay aside the cares of this world, and to give themselves to fasting and prayer, and to do good works, and to shew their care for the world to come; and therefore let such widows continue widows, and betake themselves to God and his divine worship, as best befitteth them.

If I should say, I have hope. To wit, to have children, and so might take an husband; implying thus much, that while a woman hath hope of children she may marry, for the first and chiefest end of marriage such a one is not deprived of; and therefore let child-bearing women use their liberty and marry, if they cannot abstain, 1 Cor. vii., 1 Tim. v. 28; yea, though they be poor, neither may any be offended thereat.

If I should have an husband also to-night. This circumstance of time is noted, that these women had gone nigh one day's journey with Naomi at the least. So they shewed herein great kindness to travel so far with her, or that it was far on the day before they came forth, if this was the first night; or else she speaketh thus, for that marriage was consummated at night. Here some may ask, Why needed Naomi thus to speak of her having an husband and bearing of children, seeing she knew that the next kinsman was to do the office for the dead? chap. iii. 1, 2. She might have said, Your husbands have kinsmen, which by our law are to marry you, if you will go with me, though I have no sons myself. Naomi knew this well enough, as it appeareth afterwards; but, first, she will not draw them to the Lord's people with such carnal reasons. Again, she knew not perhaps now whether such were dead or alive: if alive, yet they might be married, and so could not take them for wives; if unmarried, she yet knew not whether they would submit to the law in that case. For we see that what God commanded was not ever obeyed, and the story telleth us that one kinsman, chap. iv., refused her, and why not another? And therefore because she could not speak anything of certainty on which they might depend, she mentioneth no such thing; shewing this, that the wise will not make promises rashly for others, nor persuade to more than they well know, lest they be deceived, and so also deceive others relying upon their word. This reproveth all rash undertakers for others, though reason and religion should bind those for whom they so undertake to perform the same.

And should also bear sons. Naomi speaketh first of having a husband, and then of bearing children; for childbirth is to be the fruit of lawful marriage only. God first joined man and woman, and made them man and wife, and then said, Increase and multiply. Naomi was not of that mind to make herself a mother out of marriage, as many wantons and light-skirts do, making themselves whores and their children bastards, and all for satisfying the rage of present lust, though after they repent with grief and shame.

Ver. 13. Would ye tarry for them till they were grown? would ye stay for them from having husbands? nay, my daughters; for it grieveth me much for your sakes, that the hand of the Lord is gone out against me.

Naomi here dissuadeth them from staying for husbands from her, if it were granted that now she had born sons; and having thus spoken, she breaketh forth into a sorrowful complaint of her inability to do them good, for their sakes. The dissuasion is set out by a double interrogation, for more vehemency of speech, and by an answer made thereto. In the complaint she sheweth her grief, and that for whose sake chiefly, and how it came upon her.

Would ye tarry for them till they were grown? As if she had said, If I had now young sons, you could not marry them till they were of sufficient years, they must be grown up to marriage before they do marry; marriage is for them that are grown up for it, and are marriageable. God, when he made our first parents, made them of years fit for procreation of children before he married them. And this is to be observed for the due accomplishment of marriage, and for reverence to God's ordinance, which checketh those parents who, for other ends than the ends of marriage, do match their children together before they be marriageable. Here parents abuse marriage, for this is no conjunction for procreation of children, nor to avoid fornication. These parents take away their children's liberty, which is to marry, or not to marry, when they come to years of discretion. They are cruel and merciless parents, who bind their children in an inseparable knot and indissoluble bond, before they understand what they do. Such matches are commonly cursed of God, one forsaking another when they come to years, or hating one another, living in the gall of bitterness all their days; and so parents' expectation is frustrate, and children undone, with sorrow to friends on all sides: a just punishment of God, and reward of their sin.

Would ye stay for them from having husbands? As if she had said, You are young women, and there are men now fit husbands for you; it is not meet you should therefore stay so long for little children, and so be unfitly matched with them so young and you so old. It is not good for such as intend to marry to defer off too long. This is it which Naomi here teacheth her daughters; and this counsel is good if the parties cannot abstain, and that fit matches be offered. Let them yield to the good hand of God's providence, and not refuse an honest offer either of pride or of foolish fantasy, or of some nicety, or other light and idle womanish reason, against good reason and sound persuasion of godly and wise friends.

Nay, my daughters. This answer sheweth Naomi her meaning in the former interrogations, that she could not approve of their deferring off to marry, but that, being young, they should not refuse to marry again when God should send them fit husbands. A godly and wise mother-in-law like Naomi can not only be willing, but also will persuade her children-in-law should marry again; for they know this liberty is granted them of God, and in their own conscience they know it reasonable, and perhaps in others of necessity. She was not like those mothers-in-law which, after the death of their own children, cannot endure to hear of the second marriage of their children-in-law, whether sons or daughters.

For it grieveth me much. Here is the reason given why she willeth them to return and to take husbands again, even for the grief of her heart; for that, seeing them as poor widows as herself, and remembering her sons and how little she could do for them, she heavily sustained the grief, and therefore persuaded them to take husbands again, in whom they might have comfort. Note here how the most godly sometime do take their afflictions very heavily, as Naomi here, so Job, chap. iii., Jer. chap. xx. 9, 12, which cometh through weakness of faith, want of patience, want of humility, through also the strength of corruption and the aggravating of the affliction, ever looking upon it but not weighing the will of God, the necessity of the cross, and the good which might come thereby. Well, yet if the best may be much cast down, then let not such as be free, not under the cross, not knowing how they can bear it, censure others for their weakness under the burden, but rather take notice thereof, and be a staff of comfort to them, help to bear the burden with them, and pray for their patience.

For your sakes. Afflictions are the more grievous for friends wrapped therein, so as one cannot well help another. Naomi was greatly afflicted, but the more (she saith) for her daughters' misery with her, who, losing her sons, made also them poor widows. Ahimelech's destruction increased David's sorrows and troubles, Ps. lii.; Elijah not a little grieved for the widow's sorrow with whom he sojourned, 1 Kings xvii. 20, 21; and so was Luther for the Duke of

VER. 14.]   BERNARD ON RUTH.   21

Saxony;* and the reason hereof is true love, which taketh to heart a friend's affliction in their own troubles, as David did Abiathar's, 1 Sam. xxii. 22. This grace of true friendship is much to be wished; for men now-a-days care not much for their friends' misery if they be in prosperity, or if in adversity with them how they themselves may get out, though they leave their friends as a pawn for themselves; yea, such villany is in some men that they will purposely bring their friends into misery to do themselves a pleasure, cozen them to enrich themselves, overthrow them to set up themselves.

That the hand of the Lord. Thus she calleth her affliction the hand of the Lord, because all afflictions come by the power and providence of God as by an hand upon us, Job. i. 21 and xvi. 12, Lam. i. 12, 17, Amos. iii. 6 and iv. 6, 7, 11, 2 Chron. xv. 6, Isa. xlv. 6, 7. For 'afflictions come not out of the dust, neither do troubles spring out of the ground,' Job v. 6. Let, then, all afflictions be acknowledged to be God's hand, not as chance with the Philistines, not of the devil, witches, and ill instruments. If we acknowledge them, with Job, from God, we will go to him, humble ourselves before him, pray for pardon and deliverance by him, as who only can deliver us; yea, this will make us patient under the cross, this will work some contentment, and say, 'It is the Lord, let him do what seemeth him good.' This will make us quiet towards the ill instruments, as David was towards Saul and towards Shimei. This will comfort us under the affliction, when we know it to be God's hand, and that, out of his fatherly mercy, he will lay no more upon us than we shall be able to bear.

Is gone out against me. This good woman applieth the whole cross to herself. The godly in common calamities take themselves to be especially chastised; they put not off the cause to others, but take it to themselves, as David did, 1 Chron. xxi. 17, 2 Sam. xxiv. 27; they think upon their own sins, and not on other men's misdeeds. This is that which humbleth them, and this is it which would humble us; which grace we must labour for.

Ver. 14. *And they lift up their voice, and wept again; and Orpah kissed her mother-in-law, but Ruth clave unto her.*

Here is the event and effect of Naomi's speech again, first jointly in both, which was again their passion, and then distinctly shewed in contraries, in Orpah's valediction, and Ruth remaining still with her mother-in-law.

And they lift up their voice, and wept again. Again their passion of tears is recorded, both alike in passion of affection, but far differing in the truth of the action, the best demonstration of the heart, for in both was a like show of love in their weeping, yet not the like constant conjunction of heart towards Naomi; for the

* Acts and Mon., p. 773 a.
345

one forsook her, and the other abode and went on with her: whence we may see that all outward sorrow giveth not certain witness of the soundness of the heart. This is plain by this example, and by Saul's weeping to David. As this is true in men, so more in women, who have tears at command. Do we not read how the Israelites would weep on one day, and be in rebellion another? Was not Ishmael in his very weeping a very deep dissembler, the like never heard of?* We are not easily, therefore, to be persuaded of inward hearty affection from weeping and shedding of tears. This deceived the fourscore men which met Ishmael, and were most of them slain by him. Some can shed tears at will, and all weeping doth not come from the like cause, though many weep together, and in appearance have the same reason. There be that will weep for company, because they see others to weep, never inwardly moved from the cause, but most from the outward passion of the parties; yet, though there be a weeping not commendable, as that which is counterfeit, that which is upon every light occasion, or which is upon just cause, but in excess, yet it is sometime a matter praiseworthy, when it is from a natural affection, as in Joseph to his brethren and father; from sound love to a friend, as Jonathan's and David's weeping; and when it is from a gracious heart for a man's own sins, as Peter's weeping was; or for the sins of others, as David's, Ps. cxix.; Jeremiah's, chap. xiii; and Jesus Christ his weeping over Jerusalem, Luke xix. 41. Blessed are these mourners, for they shall be comforted; these tears are put into the Lord's bottle, Ps. lvi. 8. And such as be so doggedly hard-hearted, and want natural affection and sound love, so as neither for friend nor kinsman, nor the nighest of blood, they can weep for, are very unnatural, and worse than brute beasts which bleat and low for their own kind; so also they which can perhaps weep for the world, for departure of friends, for loss of parents, children, husband, or wife, yet not for sin, not for God's dishonour, not for the affliction of Joseph, not for the want of the word and the taking away of the righteous; are worldlings, are destitute of divine grace, of the true love of God and goodness; for men can and will mourn for such things as be ever near and dear unto them, and which they, indeed, take to heart.

And Orpah kissed her mother-in-law. As Naomi did by this act, in ver. 9, take her farewell of Orpah with Ruth, so now, Orpah departing, thus taketh leave of her. She wept in love, and kissed her in token of love and as loath to depart, yet voluntarily leaveth her, because she perceived, by Naomi her words, that she could not receive worldly contentment if she should go with her. So here were signs of love only, but not the truth of it. It is easy to make signs of love, but not to shew the true fruits of love. These be

* That is, Ishmael the son of Nethaniah, Jer. xli.- ED.

chargeable, the other cost nothing, therefore they are afforded very cheap ; and where only outward signs of love be, and not a hearty union, their worldly losses, or the fear of such losses, or not the hope to gain the things of this life, will soon separate such friends, as we see in this woman.   Note further,

I. That worldly respects are great hindrances in the course of godliness.   The world keepeth from the entertaining of the truth, Mat. xxii. 5 ; it hindereth in the receiving of it, Mat. xiii. ; it pulleth men from it which have somewhat gone forward in it, as we may see here in Orpah, in Jehu, Judas, Demas, and Henry IV., the last king of France ; and this cometh from the exceeding love of it, and our chiefest care for the body and the things of this life.   But let us take heed of this world, for such as love it, the love of God the Father is not in them, 1 John ii. 15 ; and many for love of the world, forsaking religion, have felt the woe thereof, and have lost that which they loved. Remember Judas, he had the money, but what was he the better ?   It did not comfort him, neither did it continue with him, neither he long in the world.   And yet, wretched caitiffs that we be, like Gadarenes, we will lose Christ rather than our swine ; and with Eve, lose paradise for an apple.

II. That an unsound heart may for a time make a fair show in the way to Canaan, but yet turn back at the last, as Orpah doth here, and as we may see in Jehu, Judas, Demas, Hymeneus, Alexander, Philetus, and many other in all ages, falling back from the truth, which they indeed did never soundly love, and yet will such make so fair an entrance.   And this is by reason, first, of certain general motions of religion, which maketh them in general to approve of the same ; again, the general esteem of the very name of religion ; all holding this, that it is a good thing to be religious, and that none can find fault with a man for that. Further, the working of the word, moving the heart in some sort to entertain it.   And lastly, the desire of praise and good esteem with men : these will make hollow hearts to set on a while to heavenward, but shall not be able to enter.   Therefore we are not easily to entertain men for sincere, because they have made, and do make, fair shows in religion for a time, seeing they may be unsound, and after fall away. And this should make us to examine our own hearts, lest secret hypocrisy lurk therein, and it break out at the length to our shame.

III. That such as want soundness towards God for religion, may yet have otherwise commendable parts in them.   For Orpah is commended for a kind wife, as well as Ruth by Naomi, and for a kind daughter-in-law, ver. 8 ; and she shewed good humanity in going on the way with her mother-in-law, yea, a good natural affection in weeping so at parting.   What shall I speak of Joab's valiant and hardy spirit, of the great wisdom of Ahithophel in all worldly affairs, and of moral men among the heathen ?   Many which had

no part nor portion in Christ have done worthily in the things praiseworthy among men, by a restrained nature, by the power of conscience, from the law of nature written in their hearts, and by the common gifts of the Spirit.   And therefore not to judge ourselves or others soundly religious and regenerate by God's Spirit, for our commendations in mere moral virtues, or common gifts of the Spirit ; for the heathen have surpassed many true Christian hearts herein. And many by a mere civil education, and orderly bringing up in the laudable fashions of men, and good carriage of themselves, as men among men, attain to great commendations in and for their courtesy, affability, discretion, and many qualities in learning and arts, which they affect for praise with men, for their private profit, for advancement in the world ; and not that they do good things for goodness' sake, from the power of grace and godliness in their hearts, which was as yet never engrafted in them, as appeareth by their little knowledge in the word of God, by their demeaning of themselves like statists, indifferently between two religions, by neglecting the examination of their ways by the word, but keeping company with all sorts alike, so far as worldly disgrace come not thereby, by never caring for the growth of religion in themselves or in others, to make the least opposition for it against the common stream.   By all which, and by many good things wanting in them, as a holy zeal, fervency in prayer, the love of the truth for the truth's sake, and such as love it, delight in meditating of God's word, and conferring thereof ; sorrow for the afflictions of God's people, and joy in the overthrow of the enemies thereof (which graces mere moralists are quite destitute of) : we may see that the life of religion, and that heavenly light of true grace is not engrafted in them, which is more worth than all the rest, which yet are commendable ; but these ought chiefly to be our praises, and yet not leave the other undone ; for the one makes a man, but the other a Christian.   And these together, I mean good carriage, and civil behaviour, learning, arts, and other good qualities, make an excellent Christian man.

But Ruth clave unto her.   Though Orpah gave occasion for Ruth to fall off from Naomi, yet her example moved not.   A well-grounded affection is not removed by the inconstancy of others, John vi. 68 ; for true love is fixed upon the thing beloved, and is not tied to any by-respects.   Their love, then, is to be reproved, who fall off for company, their affections were never well settled ; but Ruth's love was most firm ; her person was, as it were, *glued* unto Naomi, as the force of the Hebrew word is, to be knit as man and wife inseparably.   So the word is used, Gen. ii. 24, Mat. xix. 5.   Thus should the love of God's people be one to another, hearty and constant.

Ver. 15. *And she said, Behold, thy sister-in-law is*
346

gone back unto her people, and unto her gods : return thou after thy sister-in-law.

This is Naomi her last trial of Ruth ; and these words shew plainly all was to try her, because she telleth Ruth of Orpah's going back, not only to her people, but also to her gods, which Naomi, a good woman, could not but hate, and could not so ill respect Ruth, and shew so great coldness in religion, and honour of the true God, as to dissuade Ruth from the same God of truth, to return unto idols.

This verse is an exhortation pretended then, but not intended, with the motive thereto propounded, which was the apostasy of Orpah, shewing what she was to Ruth, and whither she returned back.

And she said. Naomi, upon Orpah's departure, for further trial of Ruth, taketh her example, and propoundeth the same to her ; for as she now saw Orpah's inconstancy for all her former resolution and tears, so she had hereby some cause to make further trial of Ruth this one time. The falls of some may justly bring others into the trial, though not wholly to doubt of their constancy. As if none could be good because some are bad ; for some may fall from grace, when other may, through God's mercy, continue to the end.

Behold, thy sister-in-law is gone back. These words shew, as soon as Orpah had kissed her mother-in-law, she went back ; with whom, or with what company, is not mentioned. Of her sister-in-law, Ruth, she taketh no leave, as supposing she would come after ; for we commonly judge others by ourselves, though we be deceived, as Orpah was of Ruth. In Orpah's leaving Naomi upon such light reasons, we see that a feeble heart, not truly settled, with weak reasons of worldly wants, is soon drawn from a right way of well doing. Silly were the reasons which Naomi used to put her to the proof, which sheweth that all her former words in ver. 10 were but a flourish, and were uttered more of a sudden passion than out of any settled resolution ; yet this was not her only weakness, but she left it to posterity. For we may find her followers, such as upon light motions will soon turn from goodness, which shew that they are not settled truly in their affections before they begin, but lightly undertake the way towards heaven, as did Orpah to Canaan, and as easily give it over : a misery to be bewailed, and by a well-grounded resolution aforehand, to be prevented. Again, in this, that Naomi trieth Ruth with this her sister's example, saying, Behold, she is gone back, it teacheth that examples of kindred, friends, and old acquaintance, declining from goodness, are trials of others, to see whether they will abide, and, indeed, no small inducements to pull others after them. Adam was soon drawn by Eve ; Rehoboam's heart was easily led after the advice of his familiars ; the women of Judah, by their husbands, easily fell to idolatry, Jer. xliv. 19 ; which often is done upon foolish affection to those whom they follow, and not of judgment ;

347

sometime of fear to offend, sometime in flattery, sometime through an ignorant persuasion that others do well in that they do, especially if the example before them be of persons of place, learning, honour, and great for outward estate, for they fondly think that such cannot do amiss. Well, seeing examples are so forcible, let them be well examined before they be imitated, be the persons whatsoever ; for precepts, and not examples, are rules to live by. Very excellent persons have often done amiss and gone out of the way ; and as for kindred and acquaintance, we are not to love them before religion, Luke x. 52, 53, and xiv. 26, which should make a division between them and us if they take not the right way, and make us forsake them, remembering that one day God will divide acquaintances, Mat. xxiv. 40, 41, Luke xvii. 34. And if yet men will here stick to them in evil, and not willingly separate themselves, they shall then perish altogether, and too late wilt thou then repent, which wast led away with their company, complaining of thy folly, and curse the time that ever thou didst know them.

Unto her people. That is, to the Moabites, of whom she was, and among whom she was born. She was going to God's people, but she runneth back to idolaters, because she was of them ; there born, as I say, and acquainted with them. It is hard to forsake our native country, where we are born and brought up. This may we see in Orpah, and in the mixed company which came out of Egypt ; thither would they have returned again, though there they had lived in bondage ; and this is first from a natural instinct in every one, even as the heathen man witnesseth.[*] Again, there is better hope, as is supposed, in wants to be relieved among friends, kindred, and acquaintance in their own country, than elsewhere in a strange place. And, lastly, the very thorough acquaintance and knowledge of the country, the people, their nature and conditions, and their own bringing up there like unto them, is a great means to keep the affection and heart towards the same ; but from this, in case of religion, we must labour to wean ourselves, and follow Abraham, Heb. xi. 8, and religious proselytes, Hittai, and Uriah, with many others ; yea, and of later times, blessed exiles from their native countries for the gospel's sake, considering that one day we must bid farewell to all the world.

And to her gods. This is a check unto Orpah : in which Naomi doth closely shew unto Ruth her sister's misery in going back, which was to worship idols and devils, with the people of her country, seeing she now had none to keep her back from the same. Hence note briefly,

I. That to leave God's people, to go to dwell among idolaters, is even to become an idolater ; for the love

[*] Ovid, lib. i. de Ponto :—
   Nescio qua natale solum dulcedine cunctos
   Ducit, et immemores non sinit esse sui.

of idolaters will bring to the love of their idols. See it in Solomon, and in Jehoram, Jehoshaphat's son; for such have daily provocations to that, which, indeed, they be of their own natures prone unto; and therefore the Lord did forbid his people to have any fellowship with the nations, lest they should become idolaters. Therefore let us not come among idolaters, if we would not be like them. We may not presume of our own strength, nor think by our groundedness in religion, to take our liberty to marry with them, to dwell with them, or long to travel among them; for we see daily by experience the vanity of this confidence.

II. That which the idolaters worship, that they take to be God, and so offer divine worship to it. This is plain by Naomi her speech, calling the idols of the Moabites *gods;* and we find that all idolaters gave to their idols the name of God. See this in wicked Jeroboam, 1 Kings xii. 28, and in the Israelites, Exodus xxxii. 8; and, therefore, we may here see the palpable blindness with which God striketh such, to make us avoid them, and yet bemoan them, as also to fear where such be, lest God's wrath seize upon us, for their so robbing the true God of his honour.

III. That idolaters have more gods than one, as these Moabites had Baal Peor, Num. xxv., and Chemosh, 1 Kings xi. The Grecians had thousands of gods, and the heathen Romans not a few; for leaving or not knowing the true God, they wander they know not whither; they have no certainty whereon to rest, they follow what they either imagine, or other do devise, or what by others' examples are practised before them. See it in the Israelites' forsaking the Lord, and in the idolatrous papists at this day; for idolatry is as whoredom, which maketh the adulterer to range abroad in unsatiable lust, not content with one, no, nor with many. No more do the spiritual adulterers rest with one false god, but are mad upon all they see, Ezek. xvi. 24, 25, 28. Oh, therefore, let us praise our God, who hath opened our eyes to see and know him, and hath delivered us from this miserable slavery of idolaters, who serve so many! They must needs be in great fear; for they be as servants serving many masters, all tyrants, and all of several qualities. How should they then ever rest in peace? Note before I conclude, how these Moabites, filthy idolaters, were the children of Lot, begotten in incest upon one of his own daughters in his drunkenness. Whence we may see, that the ill-begotten children of the godly are rather left under the curse of their fathers' sin, than made partakers of any of their virtues, as appeareth both in Moabites and Ammonites, and in Abimelech, the bastard son of Gideon; to shew the Lord's hatred of all filthiness in his people, and to strike fear into their hearts for offending this way. Let parents note this, to take heed they be not fathers of an unlawful issue, if it be not for their own sakes, yet for those they shall beget, whom they bring under a curse for their sin. Let bastards here learn to bewail their

birth, and labour by a new birth according to the Spirit, to wipe out the stain of their parentage according to the flesh.

Turn thee after thy sister-in-law. This exhortation cannot be taken as seriously meant; for would Naomi persuade Ruth to idolatry, and turn her from going to God's people and the true God, to go to the society of idolaters and devils? We may not possibly think so uncharitably of her; and the 18th verse putteth it out of controversy, where it is said, When she saw Ruth stedfastly minded, she left off to speak, as having found out what she sought for, and till then she ceased not to make trial; for where just suspicion of unsoundness is, there trial may be made to the utmost till the doubt be removed: for this is not to beat the parties from goodness, but to see their unfeigned love of goodness, that they, being tried, may be well approved of. Let not any be offended, then, at such trials; for if thou beest sound, the oftener thou art brought to the touchstone, the more purer gold thou wilt appear to be.

Ver. 16. *And Ruth said, Entreat me not to leave thee, or to return from following after thee: for whither thou goest, I will go; and where thou lodgest, I will lodge: thy people shall be my people, and thy God, my God.*

Ruth's answer unto Naomi: wherein is her request unto her, and a reason expressing her full resolution, partly in this verse and partly in the next verse following.

And Ruth said. In this answer following, Ruth sheweth most plainly that she was of a very constant resolution, and not a whit moved with the scandal of her sister-in-law's departure, and leaving of her alone. For the well-settled souls are not to be removed from their resolution to do good, for any lets which Satan and his instruments may cast before them, and in their way. The wrath of Nebuchadnezzar cannot make the three children start back; the plots of princes against Daniel cannot make his heart to faint, neither to neglect to pray unto his God three times a-day; neither four hundred flatterers, nor fear of Ahab's wrath, can make Micaiah dissemble, nor halt in the message of the Lord. A world of wicked ones cannot make a righteous Noah the worse, nor corrupt righteous Lot in the midst of Sodom. They may vex him, but never gain him to their wickedness. What can afflictions work upon St Paul? Surely nothing: they may draw him nearer to God, but never pull such a one from God. Lastly, let backsliders revolt: will Orpah's example move Ruth? Will the falling away of some from Christ make the disciples to leave him? No, no; they are built on the rock, and not on the sand. Therefore we are not to fear their fall; they make God their strength, and he upholdeth them, so as none can pluck them out of his hands, John x. 27, 28.

Entreat me not to leave thee. These words may be read two ways: first, thus, ' Be not against me ;' * and so reading, we learn, that they are against us who use reasons, or do exhort us to turn back from well-doing. Therefore Christ called Peter, *Satan*, that is, adversary, one that was against him, when he gave him counsel to do otherwise than his Father had appointed, and otherwise than according to the end he came for ; and so should Eve have thought of the serpent's counsel, and Israel of Jeroboam's; for such withhold men from pleasing God, from the comfort of conscience, which is only gotten by well-doing, and from the hope of the blessed reward which is promised to well-doing. Let us then hold such for our adversaries, and not think as the men of the world do, who hold all their kind friends which any way pleasure the body, though they be adversaries to their souls, in hindering them in the way to life and salvation, by persuading them to pleasures unlawful, to unjust gain, to a false religion and idolatrous worship, as popery is; but, in these things, because they be blind and see not their harm, they therefore think not that such be against them, when yet there be no greater adversaries than these. The second reading is as it is translated, ' Entreat me not to leave thee;' and thus taking the words, we learn from this godly young woman, that the godly have a desire not to be hindered in a good course. Ruth was going from idolaters to the church of God, and was in love with Naomi, whom she would accompany thither, and would not be entreated to forsake her; no more would Elisha leave Elijah. The godly are like to Ahimaaz, who would not be let for running to David; for, indeed, they set their hearts on the Lord's ways, and have a full resolution to do well, by God's help, and do rejoice in the way of well-doing; and finding therein comfort, like Abraham's servant, will not be stayed, but do hasten home to their heavenly country. This grace let us labour for, to have a desire not to be hindered in a good course, nor to be withdrawn from good purposes, but stand fast in our honest resolutions; which, if indeed we do, then will we shew it: we will pray to God to further us, and to remove all lets that may hinder; we will check such as are against us, Mat. xvi. 23; we will prevent all hindrances, and betimes avoid the occasions which might draw us back, as did St Paul, Gal. i. 15; we will withstand the lets, as Paul also did, Acts xxi. 13; and as David did, when he had a mind to encounter Goliath; his brethren's contempt of himself, the Israelites' fear of Goliath, the words of Saul, nor the Philistine's greatness nor brags, could hinder him, he would follow his resolutions. So should we in all good things.

Or to turn from following after thee. As if she had said, Use no more words to hinder my honest intendment, but go on that I may follow thee; let my sister-in-law go to her people and gods too; her example moveth me not one whit, I will go with thee to thy people and to thy god. I have tasted by thee of true religion, the power whereof and thy virtues so bind me, as I can leave all, country, kindred, and friends, and old acquaintances, to follow thee, my mother. See here,

I. How religion and grace maketh such as be of several nations to love one another; to love foreigners, being religious, better than friends, kindred, and old acquaintance not religious. Ruth is in love with Naomi, a Jew, and esteemeth not of Orpah her countrywoman; for, indeed, religion maketh a more sure conjunction, in a more blessed kindred than nature, having God for our father, the church for our mother, the saints for our brethren, the Spirit of God for the bond of our union, which maketh us to desire to live and die together. Labour for this love, the love of the brethren, before natural love of friends not religious; for this is a true sign of our eternal salvation, and that we be translated from death to life, 1 John iii.

II. A heart truly in love with the godly, will not easily be removed to forsake them, by the falling away of others, as we may see by this example: by Jonathan's cleaving to David, and the disciples' continuing with Christ, though others forsook him, John vi. And this is, because their love is well grounded; for they know the godly to be in their persons honourable; how basely soever the slaves of Satan esteem of them, they know them to be kings and priests unto God. They discern of their graces, and are in love with them for the same; yea, they having the same Spirit, do by the force thereof knit themselves to them, and do know that their end is happiness, Ps. xxxvii. 37, whatsoever their present estate be in this vale of misery. Let us cleave then to these, though others do fall away; and that we may so do, let us not take offence at their weaknesses and frailties, but consider of their love with God, of their excellent graces, and how that Holy Spirit of God dwelleth in them, that they be such as be co-heirs with Christ, and shall reign with him in glory.

For whither thou goest, I will go; and where thou lodgest, I will lodge. This is the reason of Ruth's request to Naomi, from her resolution, which is, not to forsake her company, but to go with her, and to lodge with her, wheresoever she shall lodge; this is her resolution, which made her continue with Ruth,* and not start back. Whence note, that the putting on of a strong resolution will make one withstand all oppositions and hindrances which may lie in the way to be lets from well-doing. This made Micaiah to do faithfully the Lord's message, 2 Kings xxii. This made St Paul to go on to Jerusalem without daunt of spirit, Acts xx. 24, with xxi. 31; for a grounded resolution is such a settling of thy heart as it cannot easily be removed. Let us therefore put on this resolution in making an onset to goodness, and in every good action, seeing there may be many hindrances in the way; and

---

* Trem. Junius, Montan. So in the margin of the new translation.

* Qu. ' Naomi' ?—Ed.

to do this, that our hearts start not back, we must make our resolution strong by these things; we must see that the thing we take in hand be good and lawful, then whether lawful to us, and what calling we have thereto. Thirdly, to weigh the circumstances of time and place, so that it may be done seasonably and fitly. This is prudence, which will much commend the deed. Fourthly, note with ourselves the end, God's glory, public good, discharge of our duty, and beware of sinister respects. Lastly, forecast all rubs which may happen in the way, for such foresight forewarneth, and he which is fore-warned is half armed, and will not repent with an *Had I wist*, neither will be moved with such lets, Acts xx. 14. Note again from hence, that Ruth excepteth not against any condition which may befall Naomi; but will go with her, and take such part as she taketh, whether the lodging be good or bad, whether the place be comfortable or otherwise, whither Naomi shall go. Which example telleth us, that such as truly love the godly both can and will give themselves to them, to accompany them in every estate, not only in prosperity, but in adversity, as did Moses; because they know that God is with them, Zech. viii. 23, they account themselves one, and are of one heart; and having given themselves to the Lord, they cannot but give themselves to his people, 2 Cor. viii. 5. And therefore, if we do love the godly, keep them company, and forsake them not in their adversity.

Thy people shall be my people. She loveth a good woman, her mother-in-law Naomi, and thereby giveth herself to the love of all God's people; for they that love one godly person for godliness' sake, cannot but affect all the Lord's flock; for there is the like reason to all as to one in that respect; and the same Spirit that uniteth the heart of one godly person to another, uniteth the same to all the rest, as being together members of Christ's mystical body. This may try our true love to every godly person, by our true love upon the same ground to all the rest; for else that particular love will not be found to be other than sinister. David's delight was not in one saint, but 'in the saints that dwell upon the earth.' True it is, that by a private familiarity and particular acquaintance with one more than another, the love may more shew itself, as in reason it must and will; yet such a love upon occasion will truly shew itself to all others, which are united in the profession of the same truth, and will be ready to do them good when such are known, as it ever doth wish you well, before there be any acquaintance at all. And if one godly person by a virtuous life may not only procure love to him or herself, but also to all other of God's people, this should make us so to demean ourselves, every one of us, as we may so win others to us, as also the same persons unto the rest which fear God, for the increase of God's kingdom, and so the hastening of Christ's appearing.

And thy God my God. As she leaveth her own people, being idolaters, for God's people, so she renounceth her idols for the true God; for they which truly for godliness' sake embrace God's people, cannot but then entertain the true God and leave their idols, 1 Thes. i. 6, 9, as Ruth did here, and Rahab also; because the love of godliness in men ariseth from the love of God himself, the author of that goodness in his people. The Corinthians gave first themselves to the Lord, then to his servants, 2 Cor. viii. 5; and Zechariah, chap. viii. 23, foretelleth that the heathen having heard of the Lord to be among the Jews, they will then come and desire to be with them. Try our love to the godly by a sound entertainment of their religion, else the love is but carnal, worldly, or counterfeit; for in differing religions, there neither is nor can be any true concord, 2 Cor. vi. 14; and therefore let us not think that either idolaters, atheists, or irreligious persons can be any faithful lovers of the truth. Note again, that godly persons may, by their godliness, draw others unto the embracing of the true God, either by instruction or by a holy conversation, or rather both together, Mat v. 16, 1 Peter iii. 1, and ii. 11. And therefore let us labour by our godliness in doctrine and life, so to set forth the Lord's praises as we may gain others unto him. This is our duty, Mat. v. 16; this is Christian-like carriage which becometh well the saints; this will win souls to God, and so cover the multitude of sins, be an advancement to the Lord's name, and bring comfort to our own souls in the day of Jesus Christ. It may be some will ask, Whether for mere love to the person of any, if one entertain religion, he may be justified in so doing? Surely no. One may occasion another, or be a motive thereto, and so perform a good office on his part; but religion is to be beloved and embraced for itself, and not for man's sake. The person on whom a man relieth may die or turn back from the truth, and become such a ground as the sand, on which a house being built, soon decayeth, and the fall thereof is great.

Ver. 17. *Where thou diest, will I die, and there will I be buried: the Lord do so to me, and more also, if aught but death part thee and me.*

Ruth continueth her speech to Naomi, touching her resolution, which she had begun to shew in the former verse; and in this confirmeth it with an oath, so that Naomi need not doubt of her constancy.

Where thou diest. Ruth speaketh of her mother's death, and also of her own. It is a principle in nature to know and to be persuaded that all shall die, Job xxi. 33, Heb. ix. 27, 1 Kings ii. 1, Joshua xxiii. 14, 1 Cor. xv. 51, Eccles. vii. 2 and vi. 6, for death goeth over all, inasmuch as all have sinned, Rom. 5. Then let all prepare to die at one time or another, which stands in seeking reconciliation with God in Christ, and in endeavouring to keep a good conscience before God and man, Acts xxiv. 16, waiting the time of dissolution, which the men of pleasure, as Dives; the worldly-minded, as the rich man; the drowsy protestant, like the five foolish virgins, and such as go on securely, as those in the old world, and in Sodom, Mat. xxiv. 37–39, do not. All know they must die, yet most neglect to prepare to die, and to provide for themselves a better habitation, which men on earth will do, when they know they must out of their dwellings; they will not be to seek to the very day in which they know they shall be put out.

I will die. I mean to end my days with thee, my mother; I will not return again into my country, but will make my end in what place soever thou shalt die. The true love of the godly one towards another is a continuing and enduring love to death. So was the love of these two, and the love of Jonathan and David, 2 Sam. i. 26, because their love is not grounded upon temporary and mere worldly respects, as the love of others be; nor upon mere nature, as that of parents and children; but upon such reasons as the alteration of outward estate here cannot disannul, or make void. They love one another for their graces in heavenly respects, and therefore by a spiritual bond they are united in heart, and made one. Thus should we love, and thus settle it, that it may abide to death; and that we may so love, let us remember, that we be children of one Father, we be brethren, we be very members of the same body, and Christ Jesus our head, we also are here strangers; and if we love not one another, who will love us? for the world hateth us, John xv. 19. There be which would be held Christians, and yet cannot love such as be so indeed. Cain cannot love Abel, though his brother, nor Esau a Jacob. Some profess to love the godly, but it is sinisterly, not simply for their graces and virtues, as Ruth here loved Naomi, for no other cause of love could there be; for Ruth was young, and Naomi old, and very poor. What power in natural and worldly reason could then lead Ruth thus to love Naomi? Other some love them for their virtues, but their virtues must be such as must make their persons without exception every way pleasing to them, else they will fall off from their love; they cannot, forsooth, bear with infirmities, all must be in perfection. But such do not look into themselves with a single eye, or else with too much self-love behold themselves; for otherwise they would love a godly Christian, as such a one, though accompanied with some infirmities, from which in this life none can be wholly freed.

And there will I be buried. Ruth spoke before of their death, and now of their burial together; so as neither in life nor death she would be separated from her mother. By this it appeareth,

I. That burial was a duty performed to the dead then as now, and therefore she speaketh of it as hoping that it would be performed to them, as men always have done one for another successively: Abraham for Sarah; Isaac and Ishmael for Abraham their father; so Esau and Jacob for Isaac. Yea, we

read how God himself buried Moses; and with what solemnities burials were performed, we may see by the embalming of Jacob, and his carrying into Canaan with such troops, and the mourning there made for him divers days. The godly would not neglect this to John Baptist beheaded, to Christ crucified, and to Stephen stoned. It is humanity, it is an honest and good respect unto the dead, and done by believers also in the hope of the resurrection. It was esteemed a mercy to be buried, and the contrary was threatened as a punishment, as we may see in 1 Kings xiii. 30, 2 Kings ix. 22, and xxii. 20, Deut xxviii. 26, Jer. xviii. Yet we must know, that a Dives may be buried with pomp, and yet go to hell; and a poor Lazarus be exalted to heaven, yea, many saints and martyrs drowned, torn of beasts, and burnt to ashes, yet received the crown of glory, which I speak to shew, that although the godly should want burial, yet that hindereth not their happiness.

II. We may see hence, that the godly and loving friends have an affection to be buried together. Jacob would lie where Abraham was buried; and the old prophet would have his bones laid by the other prophet, 1 Kings xiii. 31. And it was in former times an honour to be buried in the sepulchre of their fathers, 2 Sam. xix. 37. And therefore the loving affection of such is not to be blamed as altogether idle and foolish, which desire to be buried by their beloved friends, especially if they were godly and virtuous.

The Lord do so to me, and more also. When Ruth saw Naomi so earnest to have her to return back, as she thought, for her better satisfaction and assurance, she thus breaketh forth into this speech, ascertaining her that her words came from a true affection and a constant resolution of her heart. This is a form of an oath among the Hebrews; for so it is said that Solomon swore, 1 Kings ii. 23. And thus swore Saul, 1 Sam. xiv. 44; Jonathan, 1 Sam. xx. 13; and Abner, 2 Sam. iii. 9; and David, 2 Sam. xix. 13; but it is not a bare oath, but an execration withal, 1 Sam. iii. 17. Yet is not the curse particularly named, but left unto God. Hence we learn,

I. That it is lawful to take an oath, Heb. vi. 13, Rev. x. 6; it is warranted, Deut. vi., and a part of God's worship which he will give to none other; it is necessary sometime to decide a controversy, as Exod. xxii. 11, and to give satisfaction and assurance to the mind of others, in great and necessary matters which otherwise would not be credited, as here; therefore the anabaptists err, which hold it altogether unlawful; for it is lawful to swear, being thereto called before a magistrate. So Abraham made his servant to swear, Gen. xxiv., and Asa made his subjects to take an oath, 2 Chron. xv.; so Ezra, chap. x., and Nehemiah, chap. xiii. It is lawful to swear for confirmation of a truth in weighty matters one to another, as the spies swore to Rahab; David and Jonathan, one to another; David to Bathsheba; Ruth here to Naomi; and Saint

Paul did often call God to witness, for the glory of God, and the furtherance of the gospel. We may therefore lawfully take an oath, so it be *in truth*, not a lie, not with an equivocation, or mental reservation to deceive; *in righteousness*, that the matter be just; and *in judgment*, knowing well the thing, and upon mature deliberation and settled persuasion of the truth. Beware of common and usual swearing; the custom thereof maketh it worse, and proclaimeth the man to be unreformed in his heart, yea, though the thing be true which he sweareth. A man should be so honest, and his word in such esteem, as his oath should not need in ordinary matters; and as we must take heed of common swearing, so when we are to swear, let it be in truth, righteousness, and judgment; take heed of perjury, which God will revenge, Ezek. v.; yea, he sweareth to revenge it, Ezek. xvii. 16, 19.

II. That the godly, when they swear, they swear by God; if they do otherwise, it is their fault. When the angel sware, Rev. x. 6, it was by God; so was the oath of David, Jonathan, and others. We are taught by God himself to swear by himself, Heb. vi. and this will give satisfaction; for that God can bear witness, and the calling of him to witness, worketh a credit in the party to whom another doth swear: such is the reverence of God's name in men's hearts. He can revenge perjury, and it is his will that we should swear only by him, Deut. iv. 10, Exod. xxiii. We are not therefore to swear by false gods, as did Jezebel by her gods, 1 Kings xix., Josh. xxiii. 7, Ps. xvi. 4, Zeph. i. 5; nor by them that are no gods, Jer. v. 7, Amos viii. 14; nor by the creatures, Mat. v. 35, 36; for such swearers take God's honour from him, and make these things by which they swear idols; they break the Lord's commandment, and provoke God's wrath against them. Ruth, a new convert, would not swear by the idols of her country; for if she had, it would not have satisfied Naomi, and she had shewed that she had not been converted to the true God; whereas now she declared that she worshipped the true God.

III. That every oath is with an execration, either understood or expressed, as here in general terms, and elsewhere they are conjoined, Neh. x. 29; for an oath is a calling of God to witness in a matter, so to bless him if he speak truth, or to plague him if he speak the contrary. This should make men take heed how they do swear, lest they bring a curse upon themselves, as Zedekiah, and Vladislaus king of Hungary, and Rodolphus duke of Suabia, when he rebelled against Henry the emperor, his lord and master, by the instigation of Pope Gregory the Seventh.

IV. That in imprecations and forms of cursing, it is best to pass over with silence the special kind of the judgment, and not to name it, but to leave that to God, as Ruth doth here, and Solomon, 1 Kings ii. 23, Saul, Jonathan, Abner, Eli, and others; and not to say, as now many will, I pray God I may never stir; that I may be hanged; that this bread and drink may never go through me; that I may be damned; that the devil may fetch me; and a thousand of such fearful wishes, too boldly uttered from a presumptuous spirit, not fearing the terror of God, especially when we do consider what dreadful examples there have been of this kind, that even as men have wished, so hath the judgment fallen out,* and therefore let us not be rash with our mouths herein, lest the Lord make us examples of his justice.

If aught but death part thee and me. This is that which she sealeth with an oath, even to be constant to death, and this is the praise of her action. Many can begin well, but they hold not on to death, as did this Ruth. Of constant love I have spoken before. Not further, that though nothing else can, yet death will divide friends asunder; therefore Ruth doth not except against anything but death, which cannot be avoided. This will separate Abraham and Sarah, Jacob and Rachel, Aaron and Moses, Jonathan and David, and this Ruth from Naomi, but nothing else shall, so firmly are faithful friends united and made one. I will not complain here of the levity of this age, of the inconstancy of men's hearts, and how for every trifle they that seemed to be one become two of a sudden; they will prevent death, and sever themselves before. But so much shall suffice for this verse, and the constant resolution of Ruth.

Ver. 18. *When she saw that she was stedfastly minded to go with her, then she left off speaking unto her.*

Here is the force and effect of Ruth's resolution upon Naomi, and withal the very drift of Naomi her speeches to Ruth, concerning her going back, only for trial of her constancy, which, when she saw, she ceased to speak thereof any more unto Ruth. So as here is to be noted, first, the silence of Naomi; secondly, the cause thereof. This is in the first place, the other followeth in the last words of the verse.

When she saw. That is, when she perceived her full resolution, then she admitted of her fellowship, but not before; whence, and from whose wisdom we learn, that the godly wise are wary in their admittance of others into their company, till they well know them. We see the wisdom of Nehemiah, chap. vi. 2, 11, 12; of Jacob, when Esau offered him kindness; and of David towards Saul: though he both wept and spoke him fair, he kept off from him. Neither would our Saviour commit himself to all his followers, John ii. 24, for man's heart is deceitful, and a show may be made of that which is not in the heart indeed. Therefore should we learn Christ's counsel, to be as wise as serpents, with a dove's innocency, lest like a well-meaning Gedaliah, without suspicion of evil in others, because we intend none evil in ourselves, we perish by hypocritical Ishmaels, Jer. xli. 6. Let us in these fraudulent times try, know, and to approve and admit, or dislike and leave men.

* See the book called the *Theatre of God's Judgments.*

That she was stedfastly minded to go with her. This is it which held Ruth's stedfast spirit; she was not of a light and unstable heart. But how saw Naomi this in her? By Ruth's constant abiding by her promise expressing her mind, and by her solemn oath confirming the same promise. So then, words with an oath, and actions agreeing, sufficiently may persuade us of the stedfastness of the heart, and the inward disposition of the mind of such as shew themselves virtuous. And with this should we rest satisfied, as Naomi doth here, as it followeth in the next words, for charity bindeth us to think the best of such testimonies, of promises, oaths and actions concurring. True it is, that all these may be feigned, for wicked men will promise, swear, and in some sort do, but yet not so as they be free from guile therein; they will promise what they truly intend not; they will swear, to be the better credited, and less distrusted, even when they mean to deceive, because they fear not God; and in some things they will be doing, in such things as may rather delude than indeed effect what they pretend, but not what they secretly intend. Such Machiavellians, or rather matchless villains, there be in the world. But I spake before of such as fear God, who are to be believed, when they take an oath to shew the truth of the heart, in that which they do speak. But that we may rest satisfied with an oath, we must observe these things in the party; first, see to his life, whether such a one fear God: then, whether he make conscience of an oath, or be an ordinary swearer, not regarding an oath; and thirdly, what doth make him to swear, whether it be hope of gain, some coming towards him, or fear, or some sudden passion, and not a religious ground; as these concur, so may we believe or doubt. The words translated *was stedfastly minded*, are in Hebrew, *she strengthened herself*, to wit by her oath. By which we may learn that an oath is the strengthening of the mind of him that sweareth, to do that which he hath sworn to do, if it be lawful, and that the oath was not rashly taken. Thus Elijah strengthened himself not to leave Elisha till he was taken up, and Micaiah to perform faithfully his ministry, before and unto Ahab, when he came thither, where he was. And this is lawful sometime in great and weighty affairs; wherein we may fear the fainting of our hearts, then with prayer to God to vow our obedience, and if just cause require, to witness by oath our resolution, as Ruth doth here, and the rest before named. But when we have sworn lawfully, then let us look to it that we do not break it, Ps. xv. Josh. ix. 19, for God will require it at our hand, except it be like Herod's oath; it is then better broken, and to be repented of, rather than kept.

Then she left speaking unto her. To wit, of her returning back again, and of willing her to go after Orpah unto her own country and people; and she left off because she saw that Ruth was resolved to go with her, without sinister and by respects, for that Ruth

could not, by such reasons as she had laid before her, be made to depart from her, being an old poor woman and stranger, albeit Orpah did leave her. So then hence note, that there is no reason to make further trial where an honest resolution is, or may be well discerned; for this were folly, and also uncharitableness, to call still into question that which is out of question, and to suspect an honest mind, which fully sheweth itself as far as it can for the present. Let us, then, learn this wisdom, so to try before we trust, and then to trust after sound trial; for this is the end thereof. Again, where we see the mind settled to well-doing, let us not put it to further trial than need is, lest we do weaken the party's faith, and bring the mind into wavering, but leave him to his honest resolution, Acts xxi. 14, 1 Cor. xvi. 12.

Ver. 19. *So they two went until they came to Bethlehem. And it came to pass, when they were come to Bethlehem, that all the city was moved about them; and they said, Is this Naomi?*

In the sixth verse they took their journey, and after stood parleying by the way; now they go forward till they came to the end thereof; so as here is shewed how long they did journey, and whither, and then what was the event when they came there.

So they two went until they came to Bethlehem. When Naomi had tried her, she took her to her; and so she, poor woman, returneth unto her country, left of all except this one. She was forsaken, but not of all; one goeth with her, and they two poor women go together, and left not off till they did come unto Bethlehem. Whence observe,

I. That they are to be admitted into our fellowship, whom we find to be constant in a good course, and true lovers of goodness, whatsoever they were before. Naomi thus admits of Ruth, no doubt, with great comfort. Thus Paul alloweth of Mark, 2 Tim. iv. 11, though before he had refused him, Acts xv. 38, and willeth others to entertain him, Col. iv. 10, 11. For thus God's angels deal with us; they will account us their fellow-servants when we turn to God, though before we were never so lewd; yea, they will rejoice over us, and will lovingly attend us. Let us then admit of such, as God also himself doth accept of us.

II. That God leaveth not his in distress, or altogether comfortless. Naomi went out with husband and children, and lost them; she returneth not alone, but God sent her one to accompany her, and to comfort her. And where man's company to help and comfort faileth, there God will send his angels, as with Jacob in his travel to Mesopotamia, and with the three children in the furnace; yea, God will stand by Paul, when all men forsake him, 2 Tim. iv., because he knoweth our frailty and weakness, and therefore will not leave his altogether comfortless, that their faith should not fail; which to think upon, is not a small comfort unto God's people in their affliction and troubles.

III. That a true resolution will shew itself in a full execution. She resolved to go with Naomi, and so she did, till she came to Bethlehem. Jacob vowed, and so resolved in his return from Mesopotamia, to build an altar to God at Bethel, and so he did, Gen. xviii. and xxxv. Yet this is so to be understood, if forcible impediments hinder not, as we may see in Paul's will to go to the Thessalonians, which yet he did not then, because Satan hindered him, 1 Thes. ii. 18. By this may we learn to know the difference between solid resolutions and sudden flashes, raw and undigested purposes, between true resolutions and such as be made in show, but in substance prove nothing so, never seen in the effects.

IV. In this their travel to Canaan, and therein to Bethlehem, note three things: their unity, fervency, and constancy. They went together lovingly, they ceased not to go on, they did not linger, they took no by-paths, neither forgat they whither they were going, till they came unto Bethlehem in Canaan. As these thus went to Canaan, so should we unto the spiritual Canaan and heavenly Bethlehem; we must go in unity, 1 Cor. i. 10, and be of one heart, Acts i. 14, and ii. 1, 46, and iv. 24, in a godly fervency, Rom. xii. 11, Titus ii. 14, Ezek. iii. 14, as Elijah, Nehemiah, the angel of Ephesus, Rev. ii. 1, 2, and as our Saviour, whom the zeal of God's house had eaten up. And we must go in a constant spirit, and not be weary of well-doing, Gal. vi., for 'he that continueth to the end shall be saved.'

To conclude the observations from these words, note how Bethlehem, the house of bread, yea, Canaan, a land flowing with milk and honey, and no lack in it, Deut. vii. 8, 9, and xi. 9, 11, 12, and xxvii. 3, was made so barren, as Naomi was fain to go into Moab for relief, and yet now is made fruitful again, answerable to the name. Whence see how the Lord can make a fruitful land barren, Ps. cvii. 33, 34, for the sins of the people, and again can turn barrenness into plenty, of his mercy and goodness, vers. 35, 36. Therefore, to have the continuance of God's mercies, take heed of sin; when we enjoy them, praise him for them, and when we be in scarcity, seek to him, because God can help, Ps. lxv. 10–12, and he hath promised to give a blessing, Isa. xli. 17, 18, 2 Chron. vii. 14, and beware of murmuring in want, 1 Cor. x., remember there the judgment; yet is this a common thing amongst us now-a-days, upon any unseasonable weather, or worldly crosses, to repine, which yet easeth us nothing, but doth the more provoke God to punish us.

And it came to pass, when they were come to Bethlehem. These words are a repetition of the former words immediately before. Thus plainly speaketh the Holy Ghost, declaring the matter not in curiousness of speech, but in evidence of the truth.

That all the city was moved about them; that is, all the inhabitants of the city. A figurative speech, as in Mat. ii. 3, there was a general coming together to see them. Such a moving is sometime for fear, Mat. ii. 3, sometime for joy, 1 Kings i. 45, Mat. xxi. 10, and of a wonderment, Acts ii. 6. All this noteth that Naomi was not an obscure person before, but a woman of fame before she went; and therefore was this observation of her return, when she now was come to Bethlehem. By which we may understand that the more renowned any be in prosperity, the more remarkable are they in a downfall and in adversity. This experience sheweth to be true among ourselves, by very late instances, for the eminency of such in prosperity have the eyes of many upon them, friends, enemies, equals; one sort looks on with love, another with hatred, the last with envy and disdain; and as they be affected in a man's days of prosperity, so will they speak and shew fully themselves in adversity. This should make such as be set out so to the view of men, to behave themselves wisely in every estate, seeing they be so observable.

Is this Naomi? There be three opinions of this, and it may be, that the company being mixed, and of all sorts, they might speak the same words, but with differing minds. Some think the words spoken in contempt, *Is this Naomi!* She was so fair and full, is she now brought down? If this may stand, we see, that poverty bringeth contempt even upon the best. So was Job contemned by base fellows, chap. xxx. 1, 11. So was David of Nabal, of Shimei, yea, our Saviour upon the cross. Solomon speaketh of the poor as subject to scorn and contempt, Prov. xvii. 5, and xix. 4, which cometh through the want of heavenly wisdom, Prov. xi. 12, the want of God's fear, Job vi. 14, and because men in prosperity are proud, and do sinisterly interpret of such as be in adversity. Doth adversity bring contempt? Then let us take heed how by our own prodigality, folly, and wickedness, we bring evil upon ourselves; if it be the immediate hand of God, and not thy fault, thou shalt be censured, as Job was, how much more when the cause is apparently from thyself? Again, let men in adversity prepare to bear contempt, and not be impatient, nor take it to heart, for Job, David, Christ Jesus suffered it patiently. If men learn not patience in this, it will make them lay violent hands upon themselves, as Saul, 1 Sam. xxxi. 4, who could not endure contempt, and therefore would prevent it by killing himself; for impatient proud hearts take contempt in adversity, to be worse to them than death itself. Indeed, to mock or despise the miserable, is an argument of the want of God's fear, and that such are uncharitable, cruel, and void of mercy, for whom there remaineth judgment merciless; yet howsoever the wickedly proud behave themselves, we must in adversity be content.

Some think the words to be spoken with admiration, *Is this Naomi!* as if it had been said, Oh what an alteration is here! And so taking the words, we learn, that strange alterations in men's estates make people to wonder, whether it be in prosperity or adversity, for good or evil in any quality. The wise and learned friends of Job were astonished at the change of his estate. Saul's conversion was wondered at, 1 Sam. x. 11. So the gifts of the apostles and miracles, Acts ii. 7, and iv. 13, and Christ's wisdom and learning, being but twelve years old; for men are more carried away with the consideration of the outward means how things came to pass, than of the power and pleasure of God to make such an alteration. Therefore in great alterations look for wonderings, and take no offence thereat, for it is man's nature so to do at unusual things; yea, it is a certain corruption and folly in the vulgar sort, who consider not the causes of things. It could not but somewhat move Naomi, to see such a concourse of people, to come to wonder and gaze upon them, as people do at strangers, or at others in a changeable estate, even among ourselves. But these follies of people we must pass by.

Some think the words to be uttered from pity and commiseration towards her, as if it had been said, *Is this Naomi?* Alas! what a change is in her? This is that good woman Naomi, whom we cannot yet forget, though in her estate she be much altered. And it is most like they spake in love and compassion, rather than in contempt, because she was the kinswoman of the chiefest man among them, who, it seemeth, esteemed much of her, for he entertained Ruth kindly for her sake, chap. ii. 6, 11, and sent her corn, chap. iii. 17; likewise the women spoke very comfortably to her, chap. iv. 14, 16. Neither doth Naomi tax them for contemning her, but rather answereth to their esteem of her name from her former estate; and therefore this being uttered from their love and pity, and good respect towards her, as being a grace fit for God's people to shew to them which are in adversity, we learn, that good and godly people do nothing less esteem of the virtuous for their outward low estate and poverty. These call her still Naomi, and so acknowledge her; and Boaz esteemed well of her, even in this poor estate. Jonathan did nothing less esteem of David because he was out of the king's favour, neither did Joseph of Arimathea less reverence or honour Jesus Christ because he was condemned and executed as a malefactor among thieves; for outward crosses, afflictions, and miseries of this life, are no stain to true piety, when the crosses fall upon good men for righteousness' sake, or for the trial of their faith and patience, Let us not, then, for outward adversity, like the godly worse when we have loved them, or made show of love in their prosperity, but in adversity shew greater tokens of love; and do not as Job's friends, sit down and censure him, nor as Christ's friends and St Paul's, which forsook them in their troubles. An healthful member of the body is beloved, but when it is in distress, then love of all the rest of the members most sheweth itself; and should

not our love appear to the godly in adversity, which be members with us of the same body in Christ?

Ver. 20. *And she said unto them, Call me not Naomi, call me Mara: for the Almighty hath dealt very bitterly with me.*

This is Naomi her answer unto the multitude flocking about her, calling her Naomi, containing a dissuasion for so calling her, and shewing what name they should give her, with the reason thereof drawn from her present poor estate, which she setteth out partly in this verse and partly in the next.

And she said unto them, Call me not Naomi. This name signifieth *pleasant* and merry, which in her adversity she thought did not befit her, and therefore she did not rejoice in it. Adversity maketh the afflicted nothing to regard worldly names and titles of a better condition and estate, while they be in misery, and have lost their former outward comforts, if they be wise and truly humbled, for such as be humbled indeed are not vainly in love with goodly names and titles to which their estate is not answerable. Which checketh the foolish pride of such as being in a base beggarly condition, living almost of alms, hanging upon this and that friend, yet, forsooth, will brag of their name, their house, and gentility; or rather, indeed, to call it, as they make it, gentilism, through their lewd and vain conversation.

Call me Mara. That is, *bitter*, one in a heavy and distressed estate. The truly humbled desire to be accounted as they be, and not as they be not, as Naomi here is willing to be called *Mara*, because her estate was answerable. She was not proud, she submitted herself to God's hand, and therefore she refused not a name according to the nature of her present condition. Whose humility may check the pride of such as would have better names than they deserve, seeking the name of *goodman*, when goodness is far from them; of *master*, when their gentlemanship did hardly creep out of a dunghill; of *worshipful, esquire, right worshipful*, and many such vain titles, which every upstart now in these days do eagerly affect, not for any desert of virtue, but for that they have gotten some money to put to usury, or procured some office basely by their money, or a little better outward estate by illiberal and base scraping, pinching, and niggardly sparing, or by depending upon some person in authority, by whose countenance they may domineer over their poor neighbours, or by some such way and means whereof this now present age affordeth instances enow; yet are such far enough off from the true causes of gentry, worship, and due honour. This good woman's humility and patience may also check the pride and impatience of such as cannot endure a name like their nature; they can be content to be usurers, but not so to be called; they can live as misers, but will not so be accounted; the denomination from their sinful practices is worse to them than the sins which they do commit, for that they more are touched with the shame of the evil before men than with the offence thereby committed against God. Here, it may be demanded, whether any may be called by any other name than formerly they have been called by? We see here that Naomi would be called *Mara;* Jacob was after called *Israel;* Abram, *Abraham;* Sarai, *Sarah;* and many such instances in Scripture, as Saul called after *Paul,* and Joseph called *Barsabas,* Acts i. 23, which may be to express some grace in them for which they be praiseworthy, as Jacob being called *Israel* because he wrestled and prevailed with God; so Joses called *Barnabas,* 'the son of consolation,' Acts iv. 36, for his rare love to the church, and for giving such an example thereof to the apostles. Simon must be called *Peter* for his constancy; so to express some notorious evil, on the other side Barjesus was called *Elymas,* Acts xiii. 6, 8, and Pashur, Jer. xx. 3, must be named *Magor-missabib.* And we see by ancient practice for greater honour men were called by other names than from their fathers' families, which they purchased as a title of their honour, and for the reward of virtue, to encourage men to noble achievements worthy of honour,* being by others put upon them for the praise of their virtues, without flattery and vain glory; and some names also were invented for disgrace of vice in such as deserved the same, but they also without scorn, derision, malice, and evil will to the party, otherwise than to beat him out from his sin, which may not be for such sin as he committeth of infirmity, but for open and notorious enormities, and from which he will not be hardly reclaimed without some note of infamy.

For the Almighty hath dealt very bitterly with me. The reason why she would be called Mara, because of her bitter affliction which the Lord Almighty hath laid upon her. Whence we may learn these lessons,

I. That the Lord is almighty, Gen. xvii. 1, for he can do what he will in heaven and in earth, Ps. cxv. 3. This should work confidence in his word, for what he saith he will do he can do, his power can effect it. This must make us humble ourselves under his mighty hand, 1 Peter v. 6; he is able to destroy and cast into hell, Mat. x. 28. By this let us be encouraged to do what he commandeth, for he can bear us out in it, and can supply our wants, 2 Cor. ix. 7, 8. Hence may we gather comfort against all that rise up against us for the Lord's cause, for he is greater than all, John x. 29. And we may, to conclude, learn to hope well of others, though they have long gone astray, for God is able to save them, Rom. xi. 23.

II. That the Almighty can alter an estate into the clean contrary, as Naomi into Mara, mirth into mourning, sweet into sour, honour into dishonour; and contrarily, heaviness into joy, disgrace into high esteem, and so forth; as we may see in Job's downfall, and also raising up again; in Haman's honour into extreme contempt, in Mordecai's base estate into great dignity; so in Joseph's exaltation likewise, and in many others; for every man's estate is in the Lord's hand, to alter it at his will, 1 Sam. ii. 7, 8. Let none be proud in their prosperity, for God can cast them down. See it in Haman, Nebuchadnezzar, Belshazzar, and Herod, whom God made spectacles of his displeasure for abusing their prosperity, as we have examples of late among ourselves. And as prosperity should not make us proud, because God can cast us down, so adversity should not make us despair, because God can raise us up, as he did Job, Joseph, and Mordecai.

III. That the godly feel a bitter taste in their afflictions; they are distasteful unto them, 1 Pet. i. 7; for no affliction is joyous for the present, Heb. xii. 11, which maketh infirmities appear in the best in time of their troubles, as we may see in Job, Jeremiah, chap. xx. 12, 14, 15, and Hannah, 1 Sam. i. For none even of the saints of God are perfect in faith, love, patience, and other virtues, which might make us endure afflictions quietly; and therefore we are not to marvel when we hear words of impatience come from weak men, nor sit down and censure them, but to judge charitably, though they cannot bear afflictions altogether with cheerfulness, quietly, and without struggling. For though the spirit be willing, yet flesh and blood are weak, and even the best manifest their weakness, and the bitter taste which they have of affliction.

Ver. 21. *I went out full, and the Lord hath brought me home again empty: why then call ye me Naomi, seeing the Lord hath testified against me, and the Almighty hath afflicted me?*

Naomi goeth on in her speech to the people, so speaking of her as is before noted; first shewing how the Lord had dealt bitterly with her, and then why they should not call her *Naomi,* for that the Lord had testified against her, and afflicted her. Thus she complaineth, and amplifieth the same by contraries.

I went out full. She here speaketh of her former estate, when she went from among God's people. The word is taken from a full vessel; and this is to be understood of her outward estate, in which she felt no want, no more than there is want in a full vessel; for she had an husband and two sons, and no doubt other things sufficient; for the words imply she went not for want, but for fear of want. If the words be understood of her fulness in her husband and children, it noteth that a good woman feeleth no want while she hath a loving husband and obedient children, for she taketh such contentment in them, as she cannot feel want, neither will such an husband and children see her to want. When women are thus happy, let them bless God for their full estate. If the words be understood of fulness for outward things withal, and yet could not abide at home, we may learn that in present

---

* As with the Romans—*Cato Censorinus, Scipio Africanus, Æmilius Macedonicus, Antoninus Pius,* &c.

fulness and plenty there may want contentment, either through a greedy desire which never hath enough, Eccles. iv. 8, or through a distrustful heart fearing to want, with which these were so troubled, as it made them leave God's people for saving of their goods, and to go among heathen idolaters; for whither will not distrust of God and love of riches lead men? They err, therefore, which, being in a poor estate, think contentment to be found in riches and fulness of these earthly things, when Solomon telleth us the contrary, Eccles. v. 10, and daily experience from the rich and wealthy of the world doth apparently shew it.

And the Lord hath brought me home again empty. It is not said that the Lord sent her out full, but she went out of herself, and he brought her home again, but yet empty; she lost what she hoped to keep. This good woman in this speech giveth us to know that she took notice of a fault in voluntarily leaving God's people to save her goods, for which the Lord corrected her, yet in mercy brought her home again, though with loss. Note hence these things:

I. That it is a fault, voluntarily, for safety of goods, through distrust, to leave God's people, and go to live among idolaters; for such love their bodies better than their souls; they expose themselves to great dangers, and deprive themselves of the public and ordinary means of life and salvation. If such have warrant, as the woman had by Elisha, 2 Kings viii. 1, 2, they may have hope; but if they voluntarily, distrusting God, take such a course, they may rather look for a curse than expect a blessing.

II. That there is no certainty in wordly wealth, for here is mention of fulness and emptiness in Naomi; and this may we see in the former examples of Job, of Haman, so in Solomon and his son Rehoboam, in Babylon and Tyre, Isa. xxiii. 9, Ezek. xxvii. 2, 27; for the preservation of outward estates is not in the hands of the possessors, nor within their power, but in God, who is the giver. And again, man in his abundance doth forget God, and so causeth the Lord to take it from them, as he did the kingdom from Saul, the ten tribes from Solomon's house, the government from Jeroboam, and the empire from Belshazzar. We are not then to set our hearts on our outward prosperity, Ps. lxii. 10, neither to glory in our riches, Jer. ix. 23, for outward glory is but as a fading flower, and as the warm sunshine in a cold winter day, soon gone, and all the delight thereof.

III. That oftentimes the way and means which men take to prevent want, by the same they bring it upon them, as it fell out here with Naomi, whose husband left God's people to go into Moab, to save their estate, and there lost all, so as Naomi returneth home in very great want, who went out full. The like befell Lot in leaving Abraham for this-worldly goods, and going to dwell in Sodom, where he left and lost all, and was glad to escape with his life; for if the means we use be not good, it is [so] far from helping or preserving

us, as by God's cursing thereof it turneth to our ruin, for Jeroboam, by his policy, lost his kingdom. Therefore in seeking to uphold or to get an estate, look to the means, whether good or evil, lest we come short of that we do look for. It is ill to leave the means of the soul's safety for these worldly commodities, after which we must not make haste, lest we come to want, Prov. xxi. 5, and xxviii. 22; neither may we use unlawful courses to get them, for the treasures of wickedness profit not, but shall come to an ill end, Prov. xxi. 6, 7, and x. 2; as they are gotten, so in time commonly are they spent.

IV. That such of God's children as go astray he will bring home again, but yet with correction, as he here doth Naomi, and as he did the prodigal son; which he doth in mercy, to make them to know their error, and to walk afterwards more warily. It is comfort that God will in mercy seek up his children, and not lose one of them, Luke xv. 4, John xvii., but yet fear to go astray; for surely he will scourge them for their outroads when he bringeth them home, though it be a David, a Jehoshaphat, or a Josiah.

Why then call ye me Naomi? Hence learn that the humbled and afflicted take no pleasure to be remembered of their former prosperity by names and titles, for it but increaseth sorrow, and affordeth no comfort. What comfort might it be to tell Haman of his former honour, when he was going to hanging? What joy to Herod to hear of his glory and the applauding of him before, when now the judgment was upon him, and he eaten with worms for his vain glory and pride? The afflicted are not hereby comforted, for Naomi taketh no pleasure in that name whilst she is by her estate Mara. It is in vain to mention to the heavy-hearted what they have been, except upon certain hope of recovery to the same again; but their sorrow must be eased by better means of comfort, by shewing them the cause, the end, and benefit of God's fatherly chastisements, and so forth.

Seeing the Lord hath testified against me. Note hence,

I. That man's comfort is nothing able to allay the bitterness of God's discomforts upon us. Their calling her Naomi could do her no good, while she knew herself called by the Lord Mara, and whilst he did witness against her. What can it profit a woman of place, whilst she is in the bitterness of her soul, and afflicted by some grievous cross, to be called *Lady, Madam,* and to be spoken unto with terms of honour, whilst under God's hand! This should make the greatest therefore take more delight in seeking to please God, and to enjoy his favour and countenance, than to be dignified with the most highest titles; for these will afford no comfort when God will not afford it.

II. That afflictions are commonly the Lord's witnesses against us, for something amiss in us; for the first cause of them is sin, and the Lord threateneth them for sin, which the godly in affliction apply unto themselves. In affliction let us search out our ways and repent of our sins, as did David, Rehoboam, and as the parable of the prodigal son teacheth, and the exhortations to repentance upon the Lord's afflicting of his people. We may not be like those in Ezek'el's days, who murmured against the Lord's hand upon them, as not being the guilty parties, but that others had sinned, and they unjustly punished, Ezek. xviii. 2.

And the Almighty hath afflicted me. This sheweth how God did witness against her, even by afflicting her. He witnesseth against us by his word written, by his messengers expounding and applying the word, by our own consciences accusing, and by his corrections and rod punishing. By all which ways God speaketh actually unto us for our amendment, and the godly hear him speak unto them; they together with the correction applying the word unto themselves, for their instruction, do make the affliction profitable unto them. The conclusion which hence I will note is this: that the godly do ascribe all their afflictions to the Lord, as Naomi doth here, and as Job did, chap. i. and vi. 4, and xxx. 11, because they know that nothing is by chance, but by his providence, Amos iii. 6, 2 Chron. xv. 6, Isaiah xlv. 7. Things fall not out by mere natural causes, Job v. 6, but as the Lord will; and therefore should we learn patience, seeing that afflictions come from God. This did work patience in Joseph, Gen. xlv. 7, in Job, chap. i., and in David, 2 Sam. xvi. 11; and so it will in all such as fear the Lord, and submit themselves to his good will and pleasure, as our Saviour did in the garden, saying to his Father, 'Not as I will, but as thou wilt,' Mat. xxvi. 39.

Ver. 22. *So Naomi returned, and Ruth the Moabitess her daughter-in-law with her, which returned out of the country of Moab: and they came to Bethlehem in the beginning of barley-harvest.*

The conclusion of this chapter, and an introduction into that which followeth. This is a brief sum of their journey, shewing who, from whence, whither, and at what time of the year it was.

So Naomi returned, and Ruth the Moabitess her daughter-in-law with her, which returned out of the country of Moab: and they came to Bethlehem. Of Naomi and Ruth, and their loving journeying together, before hath been spoken. Yet note how the Holy Ghost, in naming Ruth, omitteth not to shew again her country, and that she was a Moabitess, and not an Israelitess by birth, and but daughter-in-law to Naomi; yet she came with her to Bethlehem, and that in safety. Whence note,

I. That grace can unite where all outward means are rather hindrances than furtherances thereto, as country, education, and age. Ruth was of Moab; she was otherwise brought up than Israelites were, as a Moabitess woman; she was young and Naomi old, and but daughter-in-law to Naomi, yet she held on to the end. Labour we for grace, which can make

us good and acceptable to God, what[ever] otherwise shall be wanting unto us in worldly respects.

II. That they travel safely whom God conducteth; for Naomi saith before that the Lord brought her home; and here is shewed their country. So Jacob passed well on to Mesopotamia, Gen. xxviii. 15, and returned with safety, because God was with him. So did Israel journey to Canaan, in which they were safely seated, because the Lord was with them. For he loveth those whom he taketh care of; he never slumbereth nor sleepeth, and he is almighty, ever present also to help them. Let us then get him for our guide. And this we shall do if we undertake a lawful journey, if we pray with Moses that the Lord's presence would go with us, and believe, as he hath promised, that he will neither fail us, nor forsake us.

III. That such as be attent to their journey, and desire to come to the end, make no outroads. These came from Moab to Bethlehem, they had no idle vagaries that we read of. Old Naomi desired to see her country, and young Ruth was not wantonly disposed, but constantly kept her company. These two may be types of the believers, Jew and Gentile travelling to heaven, and may teach us to attend our journey, and beware of by-paths and idle outgoings, but to keep on straight, turning neither to the right hand nor to the left, but to remove our feet from evil.

In the beginning of barley-harvest. This circumstance of the time and season doth argue the truth of the story, for shewing the certainty of that which Naomi had heard before, ver. 6, and also to be an introduction to that which followeth in the next chapter. This harvest was in part of March and part of April; for so much sooner is harvest there than here. This harvest time is that which is the time promised to all the earth, Gen. viii., but yet not at one time to all. Now, note here this with ver. 6, and we may see that harvest is called God's visiting his people with bread. Whence we learn, that harvest is God's blessing, in his mercy giving bread to sustain man's life. This is his common blessing, Gen. viii. 22, and promised to the obedient with plenty, Lev. xxvi. 5, 10, for times and seasons are in the Lord's hand; and this time is the appointed time to reap and gather in the corn for food, by which man liveth. Therefore, first, let us acknowledge God to be the Lord of the harvest, as he calleth himself, Mat. ix. 38, and confess this blessing to be from him, Ps. cxlvii. 14. Secondly, to pray to him for it, seeing it is from him, Ps. cxliv. 13. Thirdly, to be thankful when we enjoy this blessing, and to pay the due allotted for the Lord's service in testimony of thanks, Exod. xxiii. 16, and xxxiv. 22. In old time, none appeared before the Lord empty, Deut. xvi. 16, 17. Fourthly, to labour diligently at this time, Prov. x. 5, and vi. 8, seeing it is the appointed time to gather in God's blessings; and be not slothful, the ant will teach thee diligence. Fifthly, to take it as a punishment from God, when this harvest is taken from us, which is done divers ways, as by cursing the fruit that it prosper not, or by sending unseasonable weather to destroy the fruits, Deut. xxviii., Joel i. 11, 12, 2 Sam. xii. 17, Prov. xxvi. 1. Lastly, note hence that it was in the very beginning of barley harvest, which was before their wheat harvest, for they had both wheat-harvest, as Gen. xxx. 14, and xv. 1, and here barley-harvest, and this also first, as 2 Sam. xxi. 9, 10. So that Naomi neglected no time, but took the very beginning, as soon as ever she heard of the Lord's gracious visitation and mercy towards her people. Thus can we provide for the body; let us care also for the soul, that it want not the food which endureth to eternal life. And thus much for this first chapter.

CHAPTER II.

THIS chapter setteth out how Ruth was entertained after she came among God's people, how she behaved herself, and what favour she found at the hands of the chiefest man of the place, where she abode with her mother-in-law.

Ver. 1. *And Naomi had a kinsman of her husband's, a mighty man of wealth, of the family of Elimelech, and his name was Boaz.*

Here is the party set out, whom God in his secret counsel had provided for Ruth, who is described by his affinity with Naomi, and how that was, then by his wealth, next by his family, and lastly by his name. The drift is, to declare what moved so great a man to shew such kindness to Ruth, a stranger and a poor woman.

And Naomi had a kinsman of her husband's. Naomi was not basely married, but to one of an honourable stock, though now grown poor; yet this her affinity brought Boaz to have a good respect unto Ruth, even for kindred's sake, and therefore are these words set down, as is before noted. Here observe,

I. That rich and poor may be nigh of kin. Naomi had a great wealthy man to her kinsman by her husband, and that very nigh too, chap. iii. 1; for diversity of outward estates doth not alter blood and kindred, though it make a change in their persons. Let not therefore the rich disdain their poor kindred, for poverty is no disgrace where there is not want of honesty. Christ was poor, and very poor, living off the alms of others. God chooseth his people of such, James ii. None but have poor kindred, and the best have in some of their forefathers been mean enough.

II. That even kindred either is or should be of force to move kinsfolk to respect one another. This is gathered hence, for that the scope of these words is to shew how Boaz came to respect Ruth, which was for kindred's sake, yet chiefly for her virtues, as after shall be shewed; and for love of kindred, see it in Rahab, Josh. ii. 13, and in the Shechemites, Judges ix. 3, though in other respects, in their choosing of Abimelech, they were not to be commended. See this also in Samson's friends, Judges xvi., in Cornelius to his friends, Acts x. 24. For kindred are bone of bone, as the Israelites spake of David, 2 Sam. v. 1,

and are as the branches from one root, and as members of one body, and therefore must love one another; which reproveth this age, which careth not for their kindred, except they be rich, which is the sin of unnaturalness, 2 Tim. iii.

A mighty man of wealth. Yet also a godly man, as appeareth by his godly behaviour, his speeches, his works of mercy, his praising virtue in others, and his obedience unto God's law in taking Ruth to wife. We see then that a wealthy man may be a godly man some time. Such a wealthy man was Abraham, so Isaac, Jacob, Job, and Joseph of Arimathea; for goods and graces are not in themselves opposite, being both the gifts of God. The one may help the other, grace to guide and dispose well of goods, and goods well used, to declare and set forth the graces of the heart in alms-deeds, in maintenance of God's word, and in doing other Christian duties. Grace humbleth where riches would puff up, yet riches well used bring grace in estimation before men, for they enable men to shew forth godliness, and to pass on their time with the more comfort, Eccles. v. 20, and to countenance and defend their poor Christian brethren in well-doing. Therefore, if grace and goods go together, thou hast great cause to bless God, for it is a most happy estate to be rich towards the world and to God too, to be rich body and soul. But although this is a very rare estate, yet we see that they may meet together, and therefore we may not think that he which is rich cannot be religious. True it is that it is hard for a rich man to enter into the kingdom of heaven, Luke xviii. 24, 25, but it is not impossible. If any ask me why so few are rich which be godly? I answer, Because the Lord chooseth most of such as be poor for his people; these make conscience of getting goods, and will not follow the way of evil men and worldlings to enrich themselves, neither will the Lord make many of them rich, lest they should wax in their wealth proud and forgetful of God, as men in their abundance do. Why, will some say, are most rich men hardly religious? Because God chooseth few of them, 1 Cor. i. 26; they be taken up with the cares of this life, which choketh the seed of the word in them, Mat. xiii.; they set their hearts upon their riches, as they see them increase, and are wholly taken up therewith, so as they cannot set their minds on better things;

lastly, they make riches their god, so as they cannot serve God, because they serve mammon, Mark x. 17.

And of the family of Elimelech. So as Boaz and he were both of one house and stock, and very nobly born both of them, chap. iv. 20, 21, yet Elimelech poor, and his wife in a very mean estate. So as we hence may see, that parents may provide for their posterity; but which of their children shall be rich, which poor, is of God's disposing, and not of man's forecast, as we may see in these two, whose ancestor Nahshon was the prince of Judah, the royal tribe, and ruled over 74,000 men of war, Num. i. 7, 16, and ii. 3, 4, or was fit for it. Thus parents may have a goodly portion, when some of theirs may have nothing left them, Eccles. v. 14, for riches are God's gift; he can bestow them, and he can take them away again, which Job acknowledged. If parents cannot make their children rich, then let them not with too much care vex themselves for them; let them not think that by their scraping together they can make them wealthy after them; that is God's blessing, that is his mercy, for if he bless it not, oh how soon is that consumed by children which parents got with great labour and care, and perhaps with an ill conscience too, which procured the curse, besides much infamy and hatred of men in their lifetime! Is it not madness in parents to damn themselves in hope to make their children great, seeing they cannot effect what they strive for, except God be so pleased to have it? And then here let children look up to God, and learn to fear him, and rest not in their parents' gettings, but rather let them set themselves to honest callings, and learn how to be able honestly and frugally to manage that which shall be given to them, that when they shall have such goods and lands in their hands which their parents shall leave them, they may the better be able to employ them, and so preserve wisely that which is befallen unto them; for let parents get what they can, if they leave their children without callings, idly brought up, to go bravely and to follow the loose ways of most rich men's children in these days, as not knowing anything but how to play the gentleman, as they call it, a consumption will soon seize upon all, and turn them out of all, and they become beggars, as daily experience sheweth.

And his name was Boaz. This is added for more certain knowledge of the party her kinsman; circumstances make histories more creditable, and therefore are they expressed. This name signifieth *strength* or *fortitude.* Whose son he was, and of what house he came, is noted afterwards in the end of the fourth chapter.

Ver. 2. *And Ruth the Moabitess said unto Naomi, Let me now go to the field, and glean ears of corn after him in whose sight I shall find grace. And she said unto her, Go, my daughter.*

This verse is a request made, and sheweth, first, of whom it is made, then to whom and for what, with the grant thereunto, as is apparent by the words. The scope is to shew how great things come to pass by poor and unlikely beginnings, as we may see in this of Ruth, of Joseph coming to be a prince in Egypt. The like may be seen in Moses, yea, in the glorious advancement of Christ's gospel. By all which God's power and wisdom is shewed, man's wisdom cast down, and ourselves encouraged to have faith and confidence in God.

And Ruth the Moabitess said unto Naomi. When Ruth was come into Judah, she and Naomi dwelt together, but yet in poor estate, and now time serving to help themselves by labour, Ruth bethinketh herself what to do in this case. She murmureth not against the God of Israel, as his own people the Israelites did in the wilderness, and were ready to return into Egypt; she minded not Moab; she was not offended with Naomi her poverty, nor with the rest for not affording her plenty; but she resolveth to use her own labour for her help while the time did serve. From which we may learn, that honest hearts truly entertaining religion do not forsake it, or the godly, for worldly wants. Ruth could not for these things be made to start back, nor Saint Paul for all his afflictions, for sincere hearts love religion for itself, and the godly for their virtues, not for their outward estate; they also do know a reward of eternal happiness to be in the life to come, which they set before them, and therefore do not take offence from the outward things of this life, which they least esteem of, and look to have the least share in them; which reproveth those that for the wants of the world bid farewell to the word, like Demases. But the apostles for Christ forsook all, and Moses chose the poor estate of the godly, to live religiously, before the court of Pharaoh, to live viciously. Let this check also those which upon every want murmur against God, and are ready with the rebellious company in the wilderness to return into Egyptian bondage of sin and Satan, for to enjoy some outward and worldly contentment.

Let me now go to the field. Though it was honest, good, and necessary which Ruth intended, yet would she not go abroad without her mother-in-law's leave and good liking; for godly children hold themselves bound to be at the disposing of their parents, yea, in all lawful and necessary things, though their parents also be poor, because such children make conscience of the commandment of honouring their parents. Let children follow this example. Ruth was but a daughter-in-law, yet see her grace and humility, which the Lord rewarded unto her; which justly condemneth the sauciness of children-in-law in these days, who think no duty to be due to father or mother-in-law, especially if they be poor, as was Naomi here. But what speak I of children-in-law? I wish that a just complaint might not be taken up against such as by nature owe themselves unto their parents. Are there not Dinah-like daughters, which will follow their delights till they return home with shame? Do not many marry as their lust doth lead, without any respect to their parents, like the wanton sons before the flood? Gen. vi. I wish the seed of Esaus were not among us, which vex their parents. Children will seek to be nourished of their parents when they are young, or when they be in need. But if parents have need of them, ah how unnatural be they! Will they, like a Ruth, willingly labour for them? or, will they not rather despise them, and get from them, and labour for others? A strange master's commandment shall be obeyed, when a word from poor parents will make stubborn children the more disobedient. But let children know and remember the law against a stubborn son, Deut. xxi. 18, and the curse which is threatened against such as despise their parents, Deut. xxvii. 16, Prov. xxx. 17, that they may fear and tremble, and do no more so wickedly.

And glean ears of corn after him. Ruth asketh not leave to run abroad to see others, or to be seen, to see the country, to get acquaintance, to go to wakes, revels, May-games, morris-dancings, and such heathenish vanities, practised too commonly here, but not known among the ancient people of God. No, no; Ruth desireth to go to labour for her living, and to help also her poor old mother-in-law, yea, she was not ashamed to go to glean. Though she had been the wife of one so well descended, she scorneth not honest labour; for honest minds will stoop to base means (in proud persons' conceits) so they be honest, to relieve their wants in their poor estate. Moses will not stand upon his education, the gifts of his mind, and singular learning in all the wisdom of the Egyptians, but will be content to keep Jethro's sheep in his need; so will Paul work with his hands, and make tents to maintain himself, though he was brought up as a scholar under learned Gamaliel. The humility of these is to be followed as praiseworthy for their virtue and piety herein. It is no shame to labour when men are brought low, whatsoever they be by birth, as they call it, and by their first education. The godly never stood upon these terms, as many now do, who brag of their gentry, and yet are not ashamed to go a-begging or hang upon their richer kindred till they be weary of them, or will run into dishonest courses, and all this forsooth because they hold labour a disgrace. Work they cannot, they will not; but it is no shame for them to live dishonestly and idly, contrary to nature, contrary to God's injunction that men should labour, contrary to the practice of all the godly, and the example of Christ himself, who wrought in a handicraft, as may be gathered by the words out of the Evangelist, Mark vi., and in that it was said, 'He went home and was obedient unto his parents.' Note further how the truly religious will not live idly. This we may see in Ruth here, and in Jacob and others, for they make conscience of the loss of time. Let him or they whoso-

ever, which think themselves religious indeed, make conscience to take pains in some calling, and beware of living idly. What if they can say they have outward means enough for themselves to live upon? Yet they are not to live idly, because idleness is a great sin, the nurse of all vice, as we see in those that live idly; they are made the devil's instruments to all villany. Neither is it enough that a man can maintain himself and be chargeable to none, but he must live to do good to others, as the apostle teacheth, Eph. iv. 28.

Lastly, observe that gleaning, as now, so then, was a lawful means for the poor to get corn for food, as we may read in the books of Moses, Lev. xix. 9 and xxiii. 22, Deut. xxiv. 19. And thus the Lord shewed his care for the poor, and also taught the rich, in the midst of God's mercy and bounty toward them, to be mindful of the needy brethren, and not to forget them. The rich, therefore, must give the poor leave to glean, Lev. xix. 9; they may not drive them out of the field, neither may they glean up their lands themselves and so rob the poor of their due, which is the scatterings of God's mercy towards them. And here let the poor honestly take this liberty to glean, but first let them ask leave of the owner, as Ruth did, ver. 7, then also to acknowledge it a favour, as she did; thirdly, to gather the scattered ears, Deut. xxiii. 24, 25, and not to cut off the ears of standing corn, nor to steal whole sheaves, or out of shocks, as many thievish people do, to the hurt of their own souls, and the hardening of men's hearts against themselves and other poor people more honest than they.

In whose sight I shall find favour. So she went but as unacquainted. She had liberty to glean by law, yet she speaketh as one that would glean with leave, and as she that had hope to find favour somewhere, though she knew not of whom to expect it in particular. Thus she goeth, as we say, at random, or at adventure; but God, as he had decreed, so he directed her by the hand of his providence whither she should go.

One thing note here, that the godly, in using lawful means to live, hope to find favour with one or other for their relief. This Ruth's words here do shew as much; for they trust in God, who hath the hearts of men in his hand, to incline them as he pleaseth, as he did Boaz towards Ruth, and who also hath promised his help to those which, using lawful means, do depend upon him, Ps. xxxvii. 3. And therefore, in doing our part, and using the means, let us in our wants hope well; let us not doubt but that he will bless our labours.

And she said unto her, Go, my daughter. See here how meekly and lovingly this good old Naomi answereth. No doubt but it rejoiced her heart to see her so willing to take pains, whom she, perhaps, would have been loath to have pressed to such a mean business. We may note that requests are to be granted of parents unto children, when they be lawful and fit, as Job did to his children to feast together, David to Amnon his request to have Tamar sent to dress meat for him, 2 Sam. xiii., though yet villany was in Amnon's heart; but the request was reasonable, and therefore yielded unto of David; so was Absalom's desiring to go to Hebron (as he pretended) to pay his vow, which he had made unto God. Caleb also granted his daughter her request, Joshua xv. 19, and Naomi Ruth's here, which is to be followed of loving parents; but yet withal with deliberate consideration of the reasons upon which the request is made, lest a David be deluded, and wickedness be committed by an outrageous Amnon. Another thing may be observed, which is this, that a meek and loving spirit giveth a meek and a loving answer. Naomi saith not, *Go*, as a sturdy speech, but, *Go, my daughter*, for she was not of a sturdy, proud, and impatient spirit, of which a rough and churlish speech is a sign. And therefore let us learn to answer meekly and lovingly, that we may not be justly censured for churlish natures, proud and impatient. Good speech is very graceful to others, and procureth love to ourselves, as the contrary doth provoke unto wrath, as we see Nabal's answer did unto David.

Ver. 3. *And she went, and came and gleaned in the field after the reapers : and her hap was to light on a part of the field belonging to Boaz, who was of the kindred of Elimelech.*

As Ruth craved leave and obtained it, so she now goeth abroad, and by God's good providence lighteth on the field of Boaz. So as here is shewed what she did abroad, 'she gleaned;' then how, 'after the reapers;' where it was,' 'in Boaz's field,' who is here again said to be Elimelech's kinsman, that so the providence of God might herein more clearly appear.

And she went, and came and gleaned in the field. She craved leave to go, and when it was granted her she accordingly went. Honest motions and intendments to well-doing are to be put into practice, else they be nothing worth. Paul had a mind to visit the brethren, and so he did, Acts xiv.; the prodigal son had a purpose to return home, and he returned; Moses thought of going out to visit his brethren, and so he did, Exod. ii. If motions be good, it is good to put them in execution, and that speedily, if cause so require, as Ruth doth here, and not to mind, purpose, and will to do well, and yet never to do as they so purpose, losing the fruit of good thoughts. Again, note from this her bold adventure, and going forth in such perillous times, that whom necessity moveth, and confidence in God encourageth, they do fear no danger. Ruth went abroad among strangers; she was a stranger and a young woman, yet trusting in God; and being urged of necessity to use honest means to live, she feared no peril, though in those days every one did what they listed, because there was then no king

in Israel, Judges xviii. Of such an undaunted spirit was Ehud, in setting upon Eglon; Gideon, in destroying Baal's altar; Elijah, in seeing the face of Ahab; and Micaiah, in telling the truth before two kings, contrary to the word of four hundred false prophets; for when men have faith in God, when the duty of their calling warranteth them, they grow courageous and bold, and do put on a resolution without fear. Therefore, in our affairs to remove fear, let us have an honest calling to that which we go about, and have confidence in God, who is able and will stand by to help us.

After the reapers. She followed such as cut up the standing corn. She thrust not herself in before, or among them, as an impudent, bold housewife; but followed after them, to gather up the scattered ears which they did leave; and neither this did she neither without leave, see verse 7; all making to the commendation of the honesty, modesty, humility, and good behaviour of this virtuous young woman, that her example might be for others to imitate.

And her hap was. That is, though she went at unawares, making choice of no place, but where she should find favour, yet she light well, by God's good providence, which is here to be understood in her good hap; which word is spoken according to men, when things fall out besides a man's purpose, or otherwise than was intended, and whereof a man is ignorant, before the thing come to pass, then it is counted hap, or luck, Deut. xix. 4; or, as the heathen used to speak, fortune. It is not unlawful to speak according to men thus, It happened, it chanced, it was my luck, Luke x. 31; so it be we understand thereby that which happeneth beyond our purpose and expectation, but yet guided by God's hand and providence, Mat. x. 29, 30; and also that we know and hold no mere chance and fortune, as the heathen have imagined, Acts xxvii. 34, without the hand of God acknowledged therein, as the idolatrous priests and diviners of the Philistines once spoke, 1 Sam. vi. 9, if we understanding ourselves in this wise, there is no scruple to be made of speaking as aforesaid, always excepting in clear case, where the apparent hand of God is seen, for thus offended the Philistines.

To light on a part of the field belonging unto Boaz. God doth so govern men's actions, as things fall out beyond expectation as they were to be wished. See it in the success of Abraham's servant, Gen xxiv., sent to fetch a wife for Isaac; in Elijah his coming to the poor widow of Sarepta in a most fit hour; and in Saul's coming into the cave where David and his men were, by which David took occasion to clear his innocency to Saul, which otherwise could never have been so well demonstrated. And this God doth, as foreknowing and determining everything, and ruling the same by the hand of his providence, as himself hath determined to bring things to pass. This should make us to rely upon God's providence, as Abraham did in that thing, which was to his servant uncertain, Gen. xxiv. 7, and also to acknowlege his providence in everything, in a work of mercy to be thankful, and in any other trial to learn patience. Note again hence, that God will prosperously direct the well-minded, which will use honest means to relieve themselves. So hath he promised, Ps. xxxvii. 3; for their way is well-pleasing to God in such a course and case. Let us therefore depend on God, and use honest means to sustain our wants; so shall we assuredly have experience of God's goodness towards us.

Who was of the kindred of Elimelech. These words are again mentioned, to shew that it was the same Boaz mentioned before, and also to shew why Ruth had so quickly obtained leave to glean there, and why Boaz did so much respect her afterwards, and that of a sudden, upon so small acquaintance, and to give us to know what a way hereby was made to further the Lord's intendment in matching Boaz with this Ruth, Elimelech's daughter-in-law, and the wife once of Mahlon, one of his sons, which being dead, the next kinsman was to raise up the name of the dead, and to take the widow for his wife; so that Elimelech might not want one for his inheritance amongst God's people.

Ver. 4. *And, behold, Boaz came from Bethlehem, and said unto the reapers, The Lord be with you. And they answered him, The Lord bless thee.*

God bringeth Ruth by his hand unto Boaz's field, and then he by the same hand draweth Boaz to come thither while she was there, that so the one might be known to the other; that by seeing and liking the match might be made which God in his mercy intended for his daughter, this young woman. Here in this verse is Boaz going into the field to his reapers, then his saluting of them, and their resaluting of him.

And, behold. This is used to set out a remarkable thing; and is here as if it had been said, Take notice of God's providence herein, as a thing worthy observation, that Boaz should now come into the field at this time unto his reapers; and in willing the reader to behold this we may learn, that the provident hand of God is in all things to be diligently marked and observed. For hereby we shall see God in everything, and so acknowledge his ruling hand in and over all. We shall see his favour and help in delivering his children and servants, as he did David from Saul, 1 Sam. xxiii. 26, 27; in furthering them to their honour and welfare, as here Ruth; and so Mordecai, when the king must in reading light upon that place in his chronicles which concerned him, Esther vi. We shall, then, hereby see his wrath against the wicked, in bringing Jezebel to Jezreel, with Jehoram and Ahaziah, to cut off at once the house of Ahab, as he had threatened, 2 Kings viii. 29 and ix. 15, 16. Let us, then, observe wisely the hand of God's providence, that he may have the glory in all things, when

363

we see his rule and power either in his works of mercy or works of judgment.

Boaz came from Bethlehem unto his reapers, who were reaping in his field, and so like a good husband would have an eye unto them; for good householders do oversee the affairs of their house and family, and such also as they set on work: 2 Kings iv. 18, the Shunamite would be with his reapers, as Boaz was here. This is Solomon's counsel, Prov. xxvii. 23. And the praise of a good housewife also is, to look well to the ways of her household, because riches are uncertain, Prov. xxvii. 24; they abide not for ever. And it is no less a virtue to keep what we have gotten, than to get what we had not.* Careful vigilancy over our family is a good means to preserve our estate. By this shall we see who is faithful and painful, to commend and reward them, and who is negligent and faithless, to reprove and correct them, or else to remove them. Let us therefore learn to play the good husbands, as men say; for it is no fault for a man to be thriving, or for the greatest to look well to their charge. If any fault be, it is in covetousness and niggardliness, and not in provident circumspection, and in a watchful eye over the family, to keep them in honest labour, and to prevent wastefulness. Negligent masters in this point are worthy reproof, they spoil their servants, they undo themselves. And here such must know themselves to be in error, who think it a disgrace for men of worth to see to their servants and to be among their workmen. Indeed, if servants were like unto Jacob, faithful and painful, Gen. xxxi. 38–40; or like Joseph, to be trusted with all that men have, Gen. xxxix. 23; or like the faithful workmen in Joash's and Josiah's days, 2 Kings xii. 15 and xxii. 7; the eye of the master might be spared. But many servants be rather like false Ziba, filching Onesimus before his conversion; riotous like those in Mat. xxiv. 49, or runaways like Shimei's servants,† so that masters had need to see to them; yet must masters beware of a greedy mind, as thinking that servants never do enough. They must take heed of distrustful minds, without just cause; charity thinketh no ill. Neither must they keep their servants to work so hardly, as that they cannot afford them any time to serve God; for such masters are more like Turks than Christians, and use their servants rather like beasts than like men endued with reason, and having souls to save. If masters take time also for the soul and for the service of God, and then be provident for the world, it is praiseworthy, and the fruit thereof will appear in God's blessing falling upon the work of their hands.

And said unto the reapers, The Lord be with you. Thus Boaz speaketh to them, when he cometh into the field; this was his manner of saluting them, and likewise of their resaluting him again; so that the

---

* Non minor est virtus, quàm quærere, parta tuerc.
† 1 Kings ii. 39.—Ed.

form of saluting is not one and the same, as we may see in Ps. cxxix. 8, Mat. xxvi. 49, Joshua xx. 26. Now, salutations are not only words of courteous and civil behaviour, but prayers made unto God one for another; and therefore we may hence learn,

I. That it is a commendable thing for one to salute another when they meet. This our God and Saviour did, John xx. 26; this angels have done, Judges vi. 12, Luke i. 28; and this we see good men have done. It is among men civility and courtesy, especially of the superior to the inferior, as here; it also procureth love, as we may see in Absalom's courteous saluting the people, by which he stole away their hearts after him; but this was the abuse of this commendable practice. We must beware of hypocrisy therein; we must not salute like Judas, Mat. xxvi. 49; not like Joab, with fair words, and foul hearts and hands, 2 Sam. xx. 10; neither must any neglect this, of pride and contempt of others, as too many now do. If this be commendable, then surely the Anabaptists do err, who hold it unlawful to salute such as they meet, objecting certain places of Scripture, as 2 Kings iv. 29, where the prophet commandeth his servant not to salute or resalute any that he met. But this place is to be understood only to express the haste he should make, as the commandment to gird up his loins doth shew. It doth not simply forbid to salute any at all other occasions or times. Another place is in Luke x. 4, where our Saviour Christ forbiddeth his apostles to salute any man by the way. Neither is here forbidden to salute any, for in verse 5 he teacheth them to salute others. But this speech was to shew that they should make speed in that whereabout they were sent, and to avoid the least hindrance that might stay them from performance of their duty; for by saluting one another sometimes occasions are taken of staying, which here he seemeth to have relation unto, and not that he would have them neglect common and commendable courtesies. The third place is 2 John 10, where he forbids to bid God-speed to some; which is to be understood of not allowing of such as were heretics and false teachers, as far forth as they were such, and therein not to wish them prosperity, which is nothing to ordinary salutations.

II. That masters are to pray that God may be with their household, family, and workmen. So doth Boaz here pray, and there is good reason for it; for if God be with them, they shall prosper; as did Jacob and Joseph in their services, and Abraham's servant in his business. It is he that giveth them strength to labour, and without his blessing nothing can go forward, Ps. cxxvii. 2; for he giveth power to get wealth, Deut. viii. 18. And therefore let masters remember this duty to God for their family and servants.

And they answered him, The Lord bless thee. Thus they religiously salute him again; so as they which do salute are to be resaluted. The Scripture teacheth humanity, and commendeth the same to us in godly men's practice; as here in saluting one another, so in comely gestures, in reverencing our betters, as Abigail did David, and Joseph Jacob, Gen. xlviii. 12. Indeed the Scripture, besides other things, is a school of good manners, and therefore checketh such as be uncivil in their carriage and behaviour, when civility and good manners are a grace to a Christian profession. Again note, that servants are to pray for a blessing upon their masters. It is a rare grace to play the part of an Abraham's servant, Gen. xxiv.; but thus to do, argueth true love in a servant; and if a master be blessed, he is the better enabled to do for a good servant. But where are such servants now to be found?

Ver. 5. *Then said Boaz unto his servant that was set over the reapers, Whose damsel is this?*

This is an inquiry after the young woman. Wherein is to be observed, who maketh the demand, of whom he inquireth, and concerning whom the demand was made.

Then said Boaz. He no sooner came into the field, and had saluted his reapers, but his eye was upon Ruth; of her he took special notice, and demanded who she was, and to whom she did belong. Which sheweth a guiding power of God herein, and also that afore this time he had not seen her. Old Naomi had not sent her, it may seem, to his house, nor abroad to be gazed upon, and yet was she famous for her virtues, chap. iii. 11, which will spread themselves abroad well enough, though the party in person be known to few.

Unto his servant that was set over the reapers. Boaz had placed one as overseer to the rest, and of this man doth he demand the question. Hence note, that it is a point of wisdom in great families to appoint an overseer over the rest in the master's absence. Thus Abraham had Eliezer his steward, so had Ahab his Obadiah, and here Boaz, the bailiff of his husbandry; for masters cannot always be with their servants, and therefore it is necessary to have such a one, to set every one to their task, to see what is done to be done with diligence, and also well and orderly, and to prevent falsehood and deceit as well as they can, and further to acquaint their master with his affairs, with the pains and labour of such as be diligent, and contrarily to give notice of such as be not for his service, that so the one sort may be rewarded as they deserve, and the other put off, after their wages be paid them, for the hire must not be kept back; which a good steward must have care of for his master's credit, and his own discharge. But yet here let masters, in setting one over the rest, make a good choice, and see that the man be, first, wise and skilful in that he undertaketh; secondly, one diligent and painful in his own person; thirdly, a man fearing God, as was Abraham's servant, and Ahab's steward; for such a one will be honest towards his master, careful to make others religious, and so procure a blessing to the whole house. Such an one may be trusted, as Potiphar did Joseph; and to such an one authority may be committed to command others, and to order matters among servants; but yet ever so as that he be ready to give an account of his stewardship. Now also hence we may infer, that if one may be set over another in a family, then also in a commonwealth, for without order of superiority and inferiority no commonwealth can stand, 1 Chron. xxvii., which being true, overthroweth the anabaptistical anarchy. Moreover, in that the overseer is asked concerning this damsel by Boaz, and not the rest, we learn, that servants who are betrusted with the care and charge of business, are to give account touching any thing or person within their charge; to them the question is to be made, which will make such to look to their charge, to be ready to answer according to the trust committed into their hands.

Whose damsel is this? This sheweth that Ruth was yet but young, and therefore the more commendation to her, that came to be so famous for virtue; and in that Boaz asketh not *what*, but *whose* damsel she is, it giveth us to know that he thought her to belong to some, as one of the maids of Israel, and that she was not (as now vain young women desire to be) at their own hand, which is the next way to lewdness and all looseness. Such mistressless maids were not then as now too common, which maketh them also to become common. An evil not sufferable in a well governed state, to have masterless men or mistressless women. It is fit to ask young people till they be married, Whose they be? to whom they belong? and whom they do serve? Before I conclude this verse, another thing may be noted from Boaz; that it is a wise part of a householder to know who they be which come to his house or into his grounds or field to take commodity by him; as he doth here, finding her in his field with his reapers; lest a man give countenance to the unworthy, 2 Thes. iii., for men are to be merciful, but yet in wisdom, because some are not to be relieved; therefore let men well know to whom to give. In former times, amongst us, men have been commended for good housekeepers; but if their housekeeping were examined by God's word, we should find it nothing less than good housekeeping, but rather such houses of riot, excess, prodigality, gluttony, and drunkenness, suffering all sorts of idle, lewd, and licentious mates to come in to eat, drink, card, dice, riot, and revel under a lord of misrule, especially at Christmas, a time pretended to be spent in joy and rejoicing in the honour of Christ, but was indeed abused to his great dishonour, to the increase of sin, and the pleasing of Satan.

Ver. 6. *And the servant that was set over the reapers answered and said, It is the Moabitish damsel that came back with Naomi out of the country of Moab.*

The servant's answer unto his master, briefly and fully, in which he here and in the next verse praiseth

Ruth also. He telleth here what she was, whence she came, and with whom, and so sheweth whose she was, and to whom she did belong.

And the servant that was set over the reapers answered and said. By this servant's ready answer unto his master's demand, it appeareth that he had made inquiry of her what she was. Faithful servants which have charge committed to them, should be able to answer to their lord or master concerning any person or thing which fall within their charge, when the question is asked. This doth argue the care and diligent circumspection which is to be used of all such as be put in trust, and it will commend their faithfulness and honesty; and the contrary sheweth faithlessness and dishonesty.

It is the Moabitish damsel that came back with Naomi out of the country of Moab. This servant very briefly telleth to the full what she was; and here it is not a bare declaration, but also a commendation of her, who being but a young woman, would come with an old poor woman from her own country, into a strange land, which indeed was a great praise to her, as I have afore noted; and if the servant spoke this, as some learned think, in the way of commendation, we may learn,

I. That as the master was a lover of virtue, so was the man; so like happy master, like happy man. For as this praised her to the master, as it better appeareth in the next verse, so the master greatly commendeth her, after he took notice of her, by which the love of goodness in them both appeareth. Which may set out their happiness; and on the contrary it is unhappiness to an Obadiah to dwell with wicked Ahab, or a Jacob with a Laban; so to an Hezekiah to have his Shebnah, or an honest Mephibosheth his wicked Ziba.

II. We may see that the godly and well-disposed will praise virtue in whomsoever they see it, whether in strangers or home-born, in poor or rich, noble or base persons, friend or foe, as David did in both Saul and Abner; because honest and virtuous minds love virtue truly in every one, they are not transported with an ill-disposed heart, either through pride or envy, to disdain or malign graces in other, but to speak the truth, and to praise them for whatsoever is good in them. This mark of true love let us shew forth; this will preserve goodness and virtue in others, procure respect to ourselves, and good favour to such of them as be poor, as we may see here from Boaz towards Ruth. This condemneth such, first, as cannot praise other for well-doing; which argueth pride, or envy, or malice, or all of them, and by which they shew too much self-love in themselves, and little love or none at all to their neighbour. Secondly, those which are so far from praising men, as they lessen their virtues, and blazon their infirmities, and so seek to disgrace them, contrary to true love and charity; and yet a common evil in these days in most. Thirdly, those that will commend perhaps others, but not before better than themselves, not to the full, but with their *ifs* and *ands*, with words of exception, shewing plainly they be loath to give men their due, falsely supposing the praises of other should derogate from themselves, and from their own worth; so vainly jealous are we of our own reputation.

III. We may observe that, in praises, religion is to have the first place; for here is Ruth set out as one forsaking her heathenish acquaintance to keep company with a virtuous woman, and leaving her idolatrous country for to dwell in Judah amongst God's people; and thus is Job set forth, Job i., and Cornelius, Acts x. 2. For religion and virtue is that which is in man most excellent, making him more than a man, forasmuch as he becomes a spiritual man of a carnal. Therefore, here let our commendations begin, and not dispraise men for profession of religion, an argument of the want of religion, nor judge them worthy commendations which are altogether without religion. True it is that many may have such gifts of nature and art as may much set them out with men, but if they want religion and virtue, their praise is more heathenish than Christian; and therefore they have no cause to rejoice in abilities of nature or art, seeing Satan, the enemy of all mankind, may therein be preferred before them. And in nothing can man be said to be more excellent or happy than a very devil, except in the right use of true religion; in nothing else can he go beyond him, nay, in no other thing can he equal him. Let, therefore, true religion and undefiled before God the Father, which is, to visit the fatherless and widows in their adversity, and to keep ourselves unspotted of the world, be our chiefest praise.

Ver. 7. *And she said, I pray you, let me glean and gather after the reapers amongst the sheaves: so she came, and hath continued even from the morning until now, that she tarried a little in the house.*

The bailiff proceedeth still on in the commendations of Ruth, from her humility and modesty in not presuming without leave, and then from her diligence and constancy in her labour and painstaking.

And she said, I pray you, let me glean and gather after the reapers amongst the sheaves; that is, the ears of corn which lie scattered by the sheaves which yet lay abroad, and not that she did desire to be meddling with the sheaves. This she desired, and Boaz alloweth, ver. 15, which seemeth, therefore, to be a special favour to her. It was lawful for strangers, fatherless, and widows, to glean, by God's allowance and commandment unto his people, Deut. xxiv. 19; yet she entereth not boldly upon that liberty, but asketh leave humbly and modestly. Whence we may learn, that although God do bid the rich to relieve the poor, and to give leave in this case for them to gather scattered ears, yet is the same to be obtained by leave

and the good will of the owners, as Ruth here hath leave. For though the rich be commanded to give by God's precept, yet before men they have right to all they have, and it is at their liberty to dispose thereof in that respect; and they may make choice of their poor as they see them to need, and to be worthy of relief; and therefore, albeit a man be poor, he may not (because God commands the rich to relieve him) be his own carver, he may not take from the rich anything but as it shall be bestowed upon him. Let the poor learn humility and modesty, and not be insolently bold and unthankful, or false and deceitful, as many be, who make no conscience to filch and steal, and think their poverty a reason sufficient to excuse them, especially if it be but in trifling things, as they account them, as is the picking now and then ears out of sheaves, or shocks of corn, or breaking hedges for firewood, or robbing of orchards, or the like. But let them know that poverty excuseth not their sin; it is theft in them, and the thief is cursed, Zech. v.; and thieves shall not inherit the kingdom of God, 1 Cor. vi.

So she came, and hath continued even from the morning until now. After leave, she set herself to work, but before, as it may be seen, she went home again, and stayed a little; so as her first coming was but to know where to get leave, and then forthwith after to fall to her labour; yet she made not her mother acquainted with anything till night, as apparently by ver. 19. The chief point commended here to us is, that painfulness in our labour, with constancy, is praiseworthy; so is it here in Ruth, as it was in Jacob, and blessed in them both; for this is commanded, Eccles. ix. 10, and the contrary forbidden, Rom. xii. Let us, then, be diligent in our labour, and be constantly painful. So shall God be obeyed, Eccles. ix. 10, Prov. xxvii. 23, who hath promised to bless such, Prov. xxviii. 19, and xx. 13. So it is gainful, to the body healthful; it doth procure favour, Prov. xi. 27, and honour, Prov. xii. 24, and maketh rich, Prov. x. 4, with God's blessing, Prov. x. 22. Beware, then, of sloth, which is forbidden, Rom. xii.; it bringeth men to follow vain company, Prov. xxviii. 19, gaming, Prov. xxi. 17, as experience sheweth, and so hasteneth poverty, Prov. x. 4, as being the punishment thereof; for God threateneth such with scarcity, Prov. xix. 15, and xii. 24, and vi. 6; and we see that such become wasteful, Prov. xviii. 9, and their house decayeth, Eccles. x. 18. There be which labour, but not cheerfully, not constantly; and therefore these may here learn to amend by the example of this Ruth, and the good housewife in the Proverbs, chap. xxxi. 13, which putteth her hands willingly to work; for it is a hateful thing to be slothful in our business, and forbidden, as before is shewed, Prov. x. 26, xxviii. 9. In this, the servant or day-tale-man may rob their master; they are brethren to great wasters, saith Solomon, and are a consumption to the estate of such as keep them. Yet such make no conscience of this deceitful working, though perhaps they have a good measure of knowledge, and would be held more conscionable than some others be. But here it will be asked, perhaps, Who may be called slothful? Solomon will tell them that such be slothful, first, which refuse to work, Prov. xxi. 25, 26; secondly, which make idle excuses to keep them from daily labour, Prov. xxii. 13, and xxvi. 13; thirdly, which be subject to much sleep, for sloth causeth sleep, Prov. xix. 15; fourthly, which love their beds too well, Prov. xxvi. 14, and xxiv. 33; fifthly, which suffer their ground to lie unhusbanded, and their house to decay, Prov. xxiv. 30, 31, Eccles. x. 18; sixthly, which for a little cold will neglect their profit and doing of their duty, Prov. xix. 4; seventhly and lastly, which go lazily, as if they went upon thorns, and loath to hurt themselves, Prov. xv. 19. These be Solomon's marks of the slothful.

Save that she tarried a little while in the house. Thus this servant is careful to speak the truth in his relation to a small circumstance of time, that he might not be disproved. Honest minds and lovers of the truth are careful to speak truly every way, in every circumstance, that they may not be taxed in the least degree of untruth. For he hath an high esteem of the truth, whereupon he weigheth his words, and is careful in speaking only the truth. Oh that this care were in every one now-a-days, as it should be! We are commanded to speak truth, Eph. iv. 25, and not to lie one to another; and God, whom we worship, is the God of truth, Rom. iii. 4; Christ is truth, Mat. xxii. 16; and the Holy Ghost is the Spirit of truth, leading into all truth, John xiv. 17; the gospel, by which we believe, is the word of truth; and, lastly, it is a mark of one that shall dwell in God's tabernacle, and rest on his holy hill, to speak the truth, and that from his heart too. If we have such motives to press us to this duty, then, first, justly are they reprovable which do make no conscience of speaking truth, but are notorious liars; such be of the devil, John viii. 44; they live in one of those sins which made the Lord to have a controversy with the inhabitants of the land in the days of Hosea, Hosea iv. 2, and the liar shall be cast into everlasting destruction, Rev. xxi. 8. There are such as seem to make conscience of common lying, but yet will slip in the tongue now and then, as, first, to flatter others; so did the four hundred false prophets lie to Ahab, so did Doeg to Saul. Secondly, they that utter an untruth to do another a pleasure, which is called an officious lie, as the midwives in Egypt did, and Michal when she preserved David; but we may not do evil that good may come thereof, we may not lie for God himself, Job xiii. 7, 10. Thirdly, they that by lying make others merry. In all the Scripture I find not an example hereof. It may be, though many then were wicked, yet it seemeth not one was so lewd as to abuse his tongue with lying to make others

sport; it is wickedness to make a sport of sin. Fourthly, they that lie for gain now and then, like Gehazi, or as Ananias and Sapphira, whom the Lord fearfully punished; and yet it is too common for men now to lie for gain, it is almost a mark of a tradesman. Fifthly, such as lie of ill-will, maliciously, and of envy, as Haman against the Jews, scribes and pharisees against Christ, and Potiphar's wife against Joseph. Hence arise slander and backbiting, which Christians must carefully avoid; and not only the hateful kinds of lying, but the other also, and every untrue speaking in any degree; and to do this, speak ever with understanding, deliberately, without hasty passion, without by-respects; also avoid levity, and beware of too many words.

Ver. 8. *Then said Boaz unto Ruth, Hearest thou not, my daughter? Go not to glean in another field, neither go from hence, but abide here fast by my maidens.*

Boaz having heard of his servant who she was, and then also taking notice of her from that which he also before had heard of her, as it appeareth in ver. 11, he now turneth his speech unto her. Where note, who, to whom, how he speaketh, and what, even words of love and kindness, forbidding her to go any whither else, but to abide by his maidens.

Then said Boaz unto Ruth. This noble rich man sheweth great kindness unto the poor woman and stranger; when he knew what she was, he vouchsafed to speak to her and to comfort her in her poor estate. The rich and the mighty are to shew themselves respective to the poor which be godly, though strangers, when they be rightly informed of them, as Boaz sheweth himself to Ruth here. It is a sign that they are godly which love godliness in others, especially the poor, themselves being rich. It greatly comforteth the afflicted spirit, and lifteth up the heart of such poor, and doth in some sort strengthen them in their well-doing. Those rich men do not well, then, who do in their high esteem of themselves despise the poor, and hold them very dissemblers in their profession, supposing without charity that the poor cannot be religious, when yet of the poor for the most part God chooseth his people, James ii.

Hearest thou not, my daughter? Thus lovingly he speaketh unto her. And we find in Scripture that two sorts of persons thus spoke unto others: the elder unto the younger, as Eli to Samuel, Boaz here to Ruth; and men of authority to inferiors, so spake Joshua unto Achan, Joshua vii., and Joab unto Ahimaaz, 2 Sam. xviii. 22. From this courteous speech of Boaz, both as an old man, and also indeed as a man of authority, as appeareth in ver. 1 and chap. iv. 1, we learn,

I. That an humble and merciful man speaketh kindly where he wisheth well, as also Joseph did to his brethren, Jonathan to David in distress, and Job to the poor. Humility is not high-minded, and mercy is compassionate, love cannot be rough-hewed, and therefore such as have these graces will be courteous, and cannot but use good terms, especially to the poor and needy; which condemneth those as void of humility, mercy, and love, which are like churlish Nabals, and not like blessed Boaz unto the honest and painful poor.

II. That the ancient in years, and men in authority, are to behave themselves as fathers unto others, for so are they called, 1 Sam. iii. 6, Joshua vii. 19, 1 Sam. xxiv. 11, 2 Kings v. 12; and this must be in instruction and good example; and the magistrate in correcting, not with rigour, but as a father with mercy and compassion, punishing the sin but loving the person as a father doth. It is a foul fault for the grey-headed to be more child-like than father-like, and for a magistrate to shew rather cruelty than compassion. It were good for such to remember that they are as fathers, that the world is unstable, that their turn may come to stand in need of mercy, and they should think that God made the one as well as the other. This made Job to carry himself gently and humbly towards his inferiors, Job xxxi. 15. And here let such as be in authority be reverenced and loved as fathers; and beware that the ancient in years be not despised, but rather do them honour, Lev. xix. 32, for old age is 'a crown of glory when it is found in the way of righteousness,' Prox. xvi. 31. Let the children devoured which mocked the old prophet Elisha be a warning to all such to take heed; and remember Korah his rebellion against authority, and how the Lord punished it.

Go not to glean in another field, neither go from hence, but abide here fast by my maidens. In harvest all work that can; men and women are here sent into the field, and continued working. It is the time of reaping and carrying in God's blessings given, and therefore may none be idle. To come to the matter between Boaz and Ruth, we see how before he in a loving term spake to her; here he expresseth his love in deeds, both in these and the words following in the next verse. Note, that the goodness of a merciful good man stands not only in loving terms, nor in fair words, without good deeds; both words and deeds are necessary to comfort the afflicted, with both which Boaz declareth his love to Ruth. He alloweth her to glean amongst the sheaves, he warneth her not to go any whither else, he willeth her to keep with his maidens, and to follow his reapers, to eat victuals with them. Thus let men shew mercy in word and deed, 1 John iii. 18; we may not do well and speak uncomfortably, neither may we give good words and neglect good deeds, as some in St James's time did, James ii., and too many now do. Another thing may we hence note, that women are to keep with women. This is Boaz's advice to her, and it is most fit for sex, for safety, for preservation of chastity, and a note of woman-like modesty, from

which such be far as delight rather in men's company, a note of wantonness and of an unchaste heart. Women must company with women, and yet some not with any * of that sex. Ruth must keep with Boaz's maidens, the servants of a godly man. It is dangerous for a Dinah to go to the daughters of the land, a chaste maiden to go amongst wanton, idolatrous women, or a virtuous woman amongst vicious wantons and unchaste persons. Therefore let her which loveth her honesty walk wisely towards both; avoid altogether the one, and be wise to judge of the other.

Ver. 9. *Let thine eyes be on the field that they do reap, and go thou after them: have not I charged the young men that they should not touch thee? And when thou art athirst, go unto the vessels and drink of that which the young men have drawn.*

Boaz goeth on expressing his love to Ruth more and more; and this is here shewed in three things: first, in willing her to follow the reapers into every field; secondly, in his care for her safety, in charging them not to touch her; thirdly, in allowing to drink when she was dry of that which was drawn for them.

Let thine eyes be on the field that they do reap, and go thou after them. Boaz had, it seemeth hereby, a great harvest; for this implieth they were to pass from field to field, and he willeth her to go after whithersoever, and not to lose their company, as desirous to do her good this way, and so to be beholden to him as she should not need to go to any other place to glean. See here how bountiful a merciful and loving man is. So is true love in whomsoever it is, 1 Cor. xiii. 4, and mercy is not miserly, as appeareth in Job, chap. xxxi., and in Cornelius, Acts x. 2. See this also in the Lord's love towards his beloved, his church, fetched from the love of a lover to his beloved, Ezek. xvi. 8, 10–12. Let then our love and kindness appear by our bounty and mercy, as Joseph shewed to his brethren and father, Gen. xliii. 34, and Pharaoh did to them for his love to Joseph, chap. xlv. 17, 18. Love where it is cannot possibly be barren; they therefore which shew it not in works of love and mercy, as need is and their ability will give leave, they are no true lovers of their brethren. People are now most in saying, nothing in doing; they are like the adamant, drawing all to them, and as the lion's den, admitting in all but suffering nothing to go out. It is rare to hear of a Macedonian-like bounty, freely to give beyond ability; or of any like a poor widow which gave her two mites, all she had. If men would give of their superfluities, it were well. Oh that we loved as well the works of mercy, and our poor brethren, and the ministry, yea, but half so well as we do dainties for our bellies, brave clothes for our backs, and titles to bring our persons into reverence with men. But thus much for this.

Have not I charged the young men that they should

* Qu. 'with some, not any'?—Ed.

not touch thee? To *touch*, is in any way to wrong another, Gen. xxvi. 11, Ps. cv. 15, Zech. i. 8. By which kind of speaking used by the Lord, we are taught that the least wrong is not to be offered to any, not so much as to touch them as by way of offering thereby injury. This care had Boaz for Ruth, who not only doth her good, but preventeth evil from her, in laying his command upon them not to touch her. And in speaking by an interrogation, it is not only to assure her of the truth, but it implieth his authority over them, so as they durst not offer her any wrong, but would quietly suffer her to be amongst them. Whence note, I. Young poor women and strangers even then were subject to abuse, and young men too wantonly given towards such. This Boaz knew, and therefore gave them this charge. For youth is vanity, as Solomon speaketh, and lust is as a commanding law over their hearts, except they have grace to restrain the same; and that must be by ordering themselves according to God's word, Ps. cxix. 9. Let youth take notice hereof. II. That Boaz had a command over his servants, so as they stood in awe of his word, else what had this been for Ruth's safety? Neither would he have thus spoken, 'Have not I charged them?' but that he knew his word to be a law to them. And such authority should masters have over servants, who should be subject to their masters, and not stubborn and gainsaying, without care to shew obedience, as too many be. III. That Boaz taketh care of her safety; for love doth not only good, but seeketh to prevent ill from such as they do love and entertain. Such care was in Lot towards his guests, Gen. xix., and in the old man of Gibeah towards the Levite, Judges xix. 16, 23; for this is a fruit of love, and also of faithfulness, when any one hath taken another into his protection, and admitted among such as he hath authority over. This is an use for magistrates, they should care for the preservation of others by their authority, Job xxix. 12, 17, for therefore are they set in such a place, Ps. lxxxii. 3, 4; and if they have not this care, it is their sin, Prov. xxxi. 8, 9, xxiv. 11; and as they must see to all, so especially to the fatherless, widows, and strangers, and poor labourers, Exod. xxii., Mal. iii. 5, for wrong offered to these greatly displeaseth God, which he threateneth to revenge. And this should teach governors of families so to rule and order their families, as they suffer not one to wrong another; that their eyes be upon them so as they should not dare to offend against honesty and chastity, by sitting among and dallying with young women, by filthy and wanton songs, by any other allurements to sin, which young women are to avoid as they have a care to preserve their chastity; and young men's vanity and wickedness herein must be restrained by their parents and masters. Yet are there some so far from this, as they can take pleasure in the light behaviour and wanton speeches of servants and others, especially in reaping their harvest, allow-

369

ing them thus, as they account it, to be merry with their tongues to make their hands to work the faster; but this is in comparison a light fault (though also a foul sin, Eph. v.), for some masters are authors of uncleanness, and deflower maidens themselves, like lustful and foul adulterers; but let such remember the wrath of God against them.

And when thou art athirst, go unto the vessels, and drink of that which the young men have drawn. Thirst will come upon the painful labourer, and it must be quenched. Boaz therefore had provided for his servants vessels for water, which the young men drew; of this he giveth Ruth leave to drink. It may seem a very small kindness to vouchsafe her liberty to drink of the water; but we must know that it was common drink for the best as well as the worst. Saul drunk water, 1 Sam. xxvi. 11; Sisera called for water, Judges iv.; Abraham gave a bottle to Hagar for Ishmael his son, Gen. xxi. 14; and his servant drank water at Rebekah's hand, Gen. xxiv. It was not easy neither to come by in such an hot and high country, water was not everywhere so plentiful, as appeareth by the strife of Abimelech's and Isaac's servants, Gen. xxvi. 19–21; by Hagar's lamenting for want of water; by the miracle wrought for Samson, Judges xv.; for the country was hot, and the waters above the earth soon dried up, the springs were hard to be found, and wells were very deep, John iv. So as this was a very good favour of Boaz to Ruth; and Ruth, we see, in the next verse, took it to be a great kindness, and was very thankful in all humility. By this we see that a work of mercy and love may be shewed in a small matter, as in a cup of cold water sometime, Mat. x. 42, which shall not lose the reward; for it is mercy to supply the want of others for an hearty compassion, how little soever the thing be. This may teach men to be thankful for supply of their want, though the matter be but little, and not to think mercy and kindness to consist in great gifts, and good turns to be done in things of weight only.

Ver. 10. *Then she fell on her face, and bowed herself to the ground, and said unto him, Why have I found grace in thine eyes, that thou shouldst take knowledge of me, seeing I am a stranger?*

Ruth's thankfulness to Boaz, set out by action and speech. The action was a most humble and lowly gesture; the speech was an acknowledgment of favours with admiration, with a reason thereof, for that she was a woman of another nation.

Then she fell on her face, and bowed herself to the ground. Thus Ruth beginneth to shew her thankfulness in a most respective fashion, which commendeth to us her good manners, to so great a person. This manner of behaviour was much used in those eastern parts, as we may see in Jacob to Esau, Gen. xxxiii. 3: Abraham to the Hittites, xxiii. 7, 12; David to Jonathan, 1 Sam. xx. 41; Abigail to David, and the servant to his Lord, Mat. xviii. 26. The Scripture often noteth the civil gesture and comely behaviour of his servants, as worthy imitation, and as a just reproof to the rude and uncivil. But yet here is a caveat first to them which use such outward courtesies, that the same be done in humility of heart; that it be not a foolish affection, an apish imitation, or mere courtly complimenting, being but all shadows of humility, and yet indeed nothing less, as appeareth in the lively colours and public ensigns of pride in such persons, if they be observed aright. Then, next, that such as have these reverent gestures given them do consider whether they deserve them, for their place and person; if they do not, receive them not; if they do, yet not to wax proud in heart thereby.

It may be some will here make some questions; as, first, whether it be lawful to give honour thus unto man, in such an adoring manner? This is answered before; for the Holy Ghost recordeth it as commendable. Secondly, then, what difference between this which is done to men, and that which is done to God almighty? Surely, in respect of the outward act, no difference is there at all, but of the mind, which doth conceive of God herein as God, and so this outward humiliation becometh divine adoration; and of man, but as man, worthy of reverence and honour for his place, his age and gifts, and so the worship and reverence done him is only civil. Thirdly, some perhaps will ask, Whether this may be given unto wicked men? Yes, without doubt, as we see Jacob's reverence to profane Esau; David's, to wicked Saul; and Abraham's bowing of himself to the idolatrous Hittites; for men and their places are to be distinguished. True it is, that Elisha shewed little respect unto Jehoram. and Mordecai would do no reverence to proud Haman, but these had (no doubt) some extraordinary warrant so to do, and are not therefore for ordinary imitation. The reasons alleged for Mordecai are known, and therefore I will not trouble here the reader with them, because they be but weak conjectures.

Why have I found grace in thine eyes, that thou shouldst take knowledge of me, seeing I am a stranger? This humble soul wondereth at his so great kindness, though it was but to have leave to glean, and to drink water out of the vessels. She thought it strange, that so great a personage should speak thus respectively to her that was but a stranger. From hence may we observe, first, that the virtuous and thankful persons take most kindly such favours as be shewed them, and do wonder rather thereat than make light thereof, though but in common and mean things, especially if the favours be done with cheerfulness, as this virtuous woman Ruth doth here; for such do look into themselves, and their unworthiness, thinking with themselves what might rather withdraw men's affections from them, than win them to them. They also look up to God, and behold him in the giver, he being as God's hand offering his mercies to them. These things make them to be very thankful, and to express it fully. This example of thankfulness is to be imitated of every one beholden unto others, and justly reproveth the ungrateful, of which there be these sorts: first, such as receive favours, and will not acknowledge them; like the nine lepers, Luke xvii. 18; secondly, such as scornfully refuse kindnesses offered, as they that will not be beholden unto others, because they think they can live of themselves; thirdly, which will not requite a good turn done them, but rather churlishly reproach the party, as Nabal did David; fourthly, which will not help in need such as put their very lives in their hands for them and for others: thus dealt the men of Succoth with Gideon; fifthly, which in prosperity forget their friends, and what pleasure was done them in their adversity, as did Pharaoh's cup-bearer, Gen. xl. 23; sixthly, which recompense evil for good, Eccles. ix. 15; as Joash did to Jehoiada his son; Hanun to David's messengers, 2 Sam. x. 4; or which love a man less, because of his love to them; and so the Corinthians to Paul: the more he loved them, the less was he beloved, 2 Cor. xii. 15. All these are ungrateful. Now, ingratitude is a foul sin, it is a stoppage to all favours, and drieth up the affection of men's hearts; and God punished it in Joash, 2 Chron. xxiv. 25, and revenged it upon the Shechemites, Judges ix. 16, 20, 56, 57; and therefore let us not be guilty of a sin so hateful to God and man.

II. We learn, that it is a great favour and grace for a rich inhabitant to take knowledge of one poor, and a stranger too. This Ruth in her words here confesseth and admireth. For indeed nothing but goodness in a man maketh him kind to strangers, especially poor ones; it is not nature, nor worldly reason. And therefore when strangers find favour where they come, let them acknowledge it a great kindness, and a mercy of God, and a work of his grace.

III. That a godly man, as Boaz, will be good unto the godly poor, though a stranger. And so should we, as the apostle commendeth it to us, Heb. xiii. 2, and our Saviour in the parable of the Samaritan; and we must consider, that we come into strange places ourselves, and need favour; remembering, moreover, this, that if such strangers be Christians, they be our brethren and sisters in Christ, for in him there is neither Jew nor Greek, but we are all one, Col. iii. 11, Gal. iii. 28. Which condemneth the ill disposition of such as cannot abide that strangers should come among them, and that not such as Ruth, of another nation, but such as be born in the same kingdom, yea, in the same country, if they fear any charge to come to them thereby. Oh how would they take on in our uncharitable days, if a poor Naomi should, after many years, return to the place of her former abode, and bring a poor woman with her, to charge the parish! Well, good Boaz did not so, neither the inhabitants of Bethlehem.

IV. Note, how shamefacedness, wisdom, and humility are excellent ornaments of praise in a woman, as they are here in Ruth. She cast down her eyes, not looking impudently upon him; she bowed to the ground, and shewed humility; and her words were effectual and few, and therein was her wisdom. These three, shamefaced countenance, humble gesture, and fewness of words do grace a woman highly, and do win her honour, though never so poor. And therefore let women labour for them, more than for a fair face, gay clothes, and a great portion; these make them saleable with wantons and worldlings, but the other with the wise and virtuous. This reproveth such as be of a proud and haughty carriage, Isa. iii. 18, which are costly dames, commanding mistresses, but hardly obedient wives; such also as be great talkers, reproved by the apostle, 1 Tim. v. 13; these be shrewd dames, often they breed contention abroad, and some disquietness at home, for want of the government of the tongue; such women as be bold without blushing, impudent dames, which will not cover their faces with Rebekah for modesty's sake, but will go naked so far as modesty crieth shame upon. But they which have to sell think they may be allowed to set open their shop windows. But chaste minds, seeing the deformity thereof, will frame themselves to a more decent and modest behaviour; such as would hold the name of the virtuous, will not so much labour in the outward show, neither go after the fashion of vain persons. Chaste Penelope, a heathen, will stand covered before her suitors. And will Christian women shew themselves so naked, as some do, to the view of all! Oh impudency! Oh immodest show of lightness and vanity!

Ver. 11. And Boaz answered and said unto her, It hath fully been shewed me all that thou hast done unto thy mother-in-law since the death of thine husband; and how thou hast left thy father and thy mother, and the land of thy nativity, and art come unto a people which thou knewest not heretofore.

Boaz his reply unto Ruth, giving her the reasons of his kindness towards her, a stranger, which was by relation made to him before this of her virtues shewed in her love to her mother-in-law, and in her grace and godliness, leaving her own country to come and dwell among God's people, though unknown to her aforetime.

And Boaz answered and said unto her, It hath fully been shewed me all that thou hast done. A good report, and that to the full, was spread abroad of Ruth, of which Boaz had taken notice, and for which he was so kind to her, as he here acknowledgeth. Whence note, I. That virtue shall not want trumpeters to sound out her praises to the full, Ps. xxxvii. 6. Ruth was made renowned among all the people, and Joseph at length throughout all the land of Egypt, which is God's mercy for encouragement to virtue; and this will those do which love virtue in others. Therefore,

let such as would be renowned strive to be virtuous; it is the worthiest matter of praise and commendation; it procureth love, and that true love of such as never see us, as did Solomon's fame, and so Christ's. It causeth an honourable remembrance after death; * it is such goods as cannot be lost; † but beauty may with sickness and age be defaced, strength also may decay; so Haman may lose his honour, and Job may be dispossessed of all his riches in a moment, but virtue abideth for ever. Lastly, this is pleasing to God, to all good men, yea, and makes the angels to attend upon us, as the Lord hath put the charge upon them. And yet the praise hereof is least respected, but men seek praises which be after man's wisdom, earthly and sensual: as Absalom's, for beauty; Haman's, for favour with a king; Ahithophel's, for worldly policy; others, for riches and authority over their brethren; which yet they are no lasting praises, soon lost, and never afford true love in the hearts of men, as virtue doth; which may minister comfort to such as be virtuous, who deserve true praises, and they shall not want them; they shall not need to brag, as the proud hypocritical pharisee, of their well-doing. Grant that many now will not give them their due, some of pride, other through envy, and a third sort of ill-will cannot speak well; yet, when they be dead, even such as did dispraise them will then praise them; but howsoever, they shall at the last day receive praises of Jesus Christ before the angels and all the world, and be everlastingly rewarded for the same.

II. That well-doing procureth favour to the poor, though strangers, at the hands of the virtuous; for this was the cause of Boaz's love to Ruth, as here he acknowledgeth; and this is true godliness, to love others for their goodness. Would you poor find favour? Labour to be virtuous, for God will procure the liking of others, and move them to do you good, as God did Boaz's heart towards Ruth. This is the way to do you good, and not to live idly, lewdly, and by flattery and tale-bearing to think to prosper, which is the trade of too many poor ones. With some for a while they may find favour, but in the mean space they procure hatred of some others, and at length will be abhorred of all. And here let the rich learn upon whom to bestow freely their kindness, and whom to love and respect; even the godly poor, such as be of the household of faith, Gal. vi. 10, for in them Christ is relieved, and such shall not lose their reward, Mat. xxv. 10. If you ask, Who are these godly poor? I answer, Even such as Ruth, which get a good name by their virtuous lives, their duty done to their betters, their painfulness in labour, their conscience of religion; these be the godly poor, and not the stubborn, the idle, the irreligious, swearing, fighting, railing, drunken poor, who are more worthy of punishment than relief.

Unto thy mother-in-law, since the death of thine hus-

---

* Vivit post funera virtus.—*Bias.*
† Omnia mea mecum porto.

band. Thus Boaz beginning to particularise her virtues; and the first here is her loving carriage and praiseworthy behaviour unto her mother-in-law, not only while her husband lived, but ever after, not ceasing to love because he was dead, for whose sake she first was occasioned to love her. Due praises can be shewed in particular virtues. See it in the praises of Job, Job i.; Cornelius, Acts x. 2; the angel of Ephesus, Rev. ii. 1, 2. And, therefore, in praising any, we must be able to instance in those things which deserve such praises, else it is sottish ignorance, or gross flattery, or both. Again note, that whom we love for our friends' sake being alive, if love be unfeigned, it will appear when they be dead. This is Ruth's love unto Naomi, David's to Mephibosheth for Jonathan's sake. True love is a fountain that never can be drawn dry. This reproveth the loose love of many, who can love and lightly turn it into hatred of the same person upon small occasions; such also as can love their friend for his time, but when he is dead, will neglect all respect to every one of his, whom in his days they pretended to love.

And how thou hast left thy father and thy mother, and the land of thy nativity, and art come unto a people which thou knewest not heretofore. This was rare love, and a very great measure of grace, for religion's sake to forsake natural parents for a mother-in-law, her own country for a strange nation and people; she must needs be endued with a strong faith, and an extraordinary measure of love to religion and the worship of the true God. By which we see that faith and fervent love overcome all difficulties, even nature itself; as here in her, so in Abraham, Heb. xi., when leaving his country, he travelled he knew not whither, Gen. xii., and did offer up Isaac at God's bidding, Gen. xxii, and put away Ishmael, Gen. xxi., and all three without gainsaying, cheerfully. These overcame carnal reason, and this desire of pleasing God, Gal. i. 10, made St Paul a zealous professor; faith made Gideon to leave thousands behind him, and to be content to enter the battle with three hundred against many thousands,* Judges vii. 7, 12, and viii. 10; so did Joshua by God's direction command seven priests to go seven times about the walls of Jericho, to beat them down with sound of rams' horns, Joshua vi. This faith and love made many proselytes and heathen to become Christians, and Christians in the time of bloody persecutions to forsake all for Christ's sake and his gospel, as the apostles spake of themselves unto Christ. This faith and love of God will vanquish the world, 1 John v. 4, 5, and will make Moses leave the court of Pharaoh to be with God's people in affliction, and will make Amaziah to separate himself from the wicked, and make light of an hundred talents of silver, 2 Chron. xxv. 6, 9, 10; yea, so powerful is faith and love of God, as they will overcome ourselves, even to make light of ourselves and our lives for the Lord's sake, as we see in

* 135,000.

the blessed martyrs, suffering cruel torments for the truth's sake, for the power and faith of spiritual love is supernatural, and is wrought and so assisted by God's Spirit, as no worldly or fleshly impediments can hinder them in the way to eternal life. Therefore must we labour for these graces above all things, if we would be masters over ourselves, if we would prevail against all hindrances of our salvation. These will bridle lusts, contemn vain honours, resist Satan and his temptations; and seeing they are so powerful, hence may we see whether we have this faith and true love, if we can overcome our corrupt nature, carnal reason, and this evil world; but if these overmaster us, then want we this faith and love; from which those be far off, who are led like beasts by nature, like sensual men by lusts, corrupt reason, and by this unconstant world, and the vanities thereof. Though they do bear the name of Christians, yet Christ's power is far from them. Note further, hence, why he speaketh thus to Ruth; even to give her to know the true cause of his kindness and good respect towards her, even her godliness and grace. Which may teach, that virtue and grace are the greatest motives to incite great men, which be also good men, unto the works of mercy and bounty to the poor, as we here see by Boaz's speeches; for virtue is lovely to them which are virtuous, though the parties be never so poor. Let, then, the poor labour for grace and godliness, that they may find mercy at the hands of the wealthy, for if they fear God he will be their spokesman, he will move the hearts of others to do them good. Though this be the way to procure favour, yet commonly we see the poor idle and too lewd of life, and yet they murmur, curse, and rage if they be not relieved; for they think they ought to be relieved, even because they be poor, though never so wicked, though they will hardly labour to take any pains to live, when of such the apostle speaketh that they should not be relieved: 'He that will not labour, let him not eat,' saith the apostle, 2 Thes. iii. As this is for instruction to the poor, so the rich, from Boaz, may learn on whom to bestow their favours and works of mercy; even upon the godly, the household of faith, Gal. vi. 10; for in them Christ is relieved, Mat. xxv. 10; in them they do lend unto the Lord, Prov. xix. 17, who will repay them to the full, and greatly reward them, Ps. xli. 1–3. But of this a little before in the beginning of this verse.

Ver. 12. *The Lord recompense thy work, and a full reward be given thee of the Lord God of Israel, under whose wings thou art come to trust.*

These words are a prayer and blessing pronounced out of the mouth of Boaz upon poor Ruth, which doth marvellously set out the piety of this man. Here may be noted, who makes this request, to whom, for what, for whom, and why.

The Lord recompense thy work. This rich Boaz

prayeth for poor Ruth. Whence note, I. That there is a recompence of reward from God, even to the poor, for well-doing. This the prayer of Boaz sheweth, who else would not have begged it at God's hand; and we must know, that the Lord in promising to reward well-doing, excepts against none, rich nor poor, but will recompense the well-doer, be he whosoever; with him is no respect of persons, but he that worketh right-eousness is accepted of him, Acts x.; and godliness (in whomsoever it be) hath the promise of this life and of the life to come, 1 Tim. iv. 8. Let this comfort the poor in their well-doing and in their works of virtue and godliness.

Quest. Here it may be demanded, what good works can the poor do, to expect reward from God, seeing they have no riches?

Ans. A good work is not, nor stands not only in giving alms and such like things, for then should only the rich be doers of good works; but many other things are good works and approved of God, and which he will recompense, which the poor that have not one penny may do: as to do the duty of love and obedience to their parents, or to others to whom they owe it; to forsake idolatry for the true worship of God; to leave their country for the Lord's sake and for his people; to forsake their old heathenish acquaintance and kindred; all which Ruth did. And these may the poor do, which works God will recompense; and all other duties which one oweth to another, in any sort, being done in faith, in love, and in obedience to God, they are good works, and the Lord will reward the same; even the honest and painful service of a poor servant, as the apostle teacheth, Col. iii. 24. We see then that the poorest may do good works, though not such as commonly are so called, to the doing whereof the world's wealth is required; and yet herein a poor soul's two mites are more acceptable to God than the superfluities of the rich.

II. The rich, from the example of Boaz, may not think scorn to pray, and that very heartily, for the poor. It is a very rare example to see so mighty a man of wealth, and so high in authority, to be so much taken up in his affection, in considering the poor wo-man's virtue, as to break forth into so vehement a prayer as this was, as appeareth by the doubling of the words; and yet this ought rich men to do, if they think that the poor are not excluded out of the com-munion of saints, and that they be the children of God with them, as they are taught in the Lord's prayer. This would shew a great measure of grace, this would encourage much the poor to go on in well-doing. But, alas, this comes not once into the thought of a rich man; he thinks the poor bound to pray for him, but himself not at all, upon any occasion, for them, be-cause he thinks he can pleasure them, but they can no way pleasure him; so he considereth only outward and personal benefit, and not the excellency of virtue and fruit thereof to them and others, as Boaz did.

373

And a full reward be given thee. A good man thinks his mercies and kindness are not enough to recompense and reward the virtue and works of well-doing in others; for he valueth virtue above wealth, and above the price of all these transitory things. Again note, that there is to be expected a full reward for a good work; I say, first, a reward, yet so that it be looked for in mercy and not in merit; for God hath promised a reward, and that in many places of Scripture; and then it shall be a full reward, which Boaz prayeth for here to be given to Ruth: which shall be certainly accomplished in the life to come, and here sometime in a great measure, as it was to Ruth, in giving her Boaz for an husband, which he little thought of in this prayer, that he should be the reward of her godliness and grace. This is an excellent encouragement to virtue and good works.

Of the Lord God of Israel. Israel was Jacob's name, and now applied to all his posterity, the people of God. Thus was the true God called by the name of *God*, noting the persons in the Trinity; and of *Lord*, noting his substance and being of himself, as the original words to the learned do shew; and he is the Lord God of Israel, because he chose the Israelites to be his people before all nations of the earth, Deut vii. 6, a type of the elect number called 'the Israel of God,' Gal. vi. To this true and everliving God doth Boaz make request for a full and perfect reward, shewing that it is not in man, but it must be God that can make a full payment to godliness; the full reward is to be given of him, and therefore from him it is to be expected, who hath the recompence in his hand in full perfection.

Under whose wings. A figurative speech, usual in psalms, to express the love of God, and the protection of such as be his, Ps. xvii. 8, and lvii. and xxxvi. 7, and lxi.; for as a hen nourisheth and defendeth her young ones under her wings, from the kite and other ravenous birds, so doth the Lord care for his people, to keep them in safety from dangers, Deut. xxxiii. 29. They are safely protected who come to the Lord and trust in him, Ps. xci.; for God hath undertaken to protect such, and he is able to defend them, and he will do it, because he loveth them, Zech. ii. 8. Oh then, let us labour to be of the Lord's people, to go unto him and to trust in him. Men being in danger here, get into great men's service for protection; and we being in greater danger, yea, in such dangers every day, on the right and left hand, from which none can deliver us but God, should not we seek his service for protection! And being in it, let us be comforted as sure of his aid; let us trust in him as did David, Ps. lxi. 4, for he saveth all them that put their trust in him, Ps. xvii. 7, and lvii. 1. Let us in need run to him for aid, as did David, and desire to be saved by him, Ps. xvii. 8, and cxix. 94; and let us rejoice under the shadow of his wings, Ps. lxiii. 7; for his angels shall guard us, and pitch their tents about us, Ps. xxxiv.

and xci. ; he will make a hedge about us also, Job i. ; and if this will not be defence enough, then will he be a wall of fire, Zech. ii. 5, so sure and safe shall we be from all our enemies.

Thou art come to trust. Boaz taketh it for granted that she had faith; for they that come to God must believe that he is, Heb. xi. This draweth us to God, this keepeth us with him when we be come unto him. Now, that we may know what is here meant by faith, we must understand that there be degrees hereof; as to believe there is a God, against all the atheists which deny this principle in nature. 2. That that which we believe to be God, be the true God, even God by nature, and none other; and that he is not many, but one God only, against all idolaters and worshippers of false gods. 3. That he be such a one as he revealeth himself in his word, and so conceived of, and no otherwise, a spirit, true, just, merciful, almighty, and so forth, against all carnal conceits and fleshly apprehensions of God, as is in the ignorant multitude and the blind papists our adversaries. 4. That we have sure confidence in him, wholly relying upon him and commending ourselves so to his protection, as unto a safe place, where we think to be sure; and so the word in the original* is here used. The knowledge hereof should make us to examine our faith, whether we thus trust in him and have the saving faith which maketh not ashamed. Such a faith is, first, without hypocrisy, being faith unfeigned, 1 Tim. i. 5. Secondly, it is accompanied with the Spirit of God, Gal. iii. 14. Thirdly, Where it is, there is inward peace of conscience, Rom. v. 1, and freedom to draw nigh to God with boldness, Heb. iv. Fourthly, It sheweth itself in a godly conversation, Eph. iii. 12; for the heart is purged and pure, Acts xv. 9, and a good conscience is joined with it, 1 Tim. i. 5; it worketh also by love, Gal. v. 6, and sheweth itself by works, James ii. 7, and so causeth obedience to the good pleasure and will of God, as we may see in Noah building the ark, and in Abraham offering up Isaac, Heb. xi. Fifthly and lastly, It maketh us to rejoice in the means of salvation, Acts xiii. 48, and to be of one heart and soul with the believers, and such as we perceive to fear God, Acts iv. 32. By all which, our faith may be examined; and by these may we know how little there is in men in these days. Where and when there is such hypocrisy, so little true love of the word, or of them that love it, and so much wickedness and lewdness, they make open proclamation that this grace of true saving faith was never grafted in their hearts.

Ver. 13. *Then she said, Let me find favour in thy sight, my lord; for that thou hast comforted me, and for that thou hast spoken friendly unto thine handmaid, though I be not like unto one of thine handmaidens.*

Ruth's speech unto Boaz, acknowledging his favour with great humility, shewing what it wrought in her,

* חסה, *recepit se in locum, ubi sit tectus ab injuria.*

and the reason also thereof, with a debasing of herself as inferior to his servants.

Then she said, Let me find favour in thy sight. These words may be read two ways: either thus as here, and then they shew Ruth's desire of the countenance of his favour. For the poor do not only desire to get the rich man's good will, but would gladly have it continued. And a thankful mind seeketh the continuance of undeserved favours, and not Hanun's part, 2 Sam. x. Or the words may be read thus, 'I do find favour in thy sight.' And it is then as if she had said, 'It is enough that I, a poor stranger, find this favour in thine eyes.' So are the words to be taken, Gen. xxxiii. 15, and so in 2 Sam. xvi. 4. She did not expect so much at his hands, and therefore, knowing herself to have deserved nothing at his hands, she rests very thankful for this so great a kindness; for where nothing is deserved, and nothing owing, there to find special favour deserveth great thanks, which here she acknowledgeth, and in the like case so must we. The choice of the reading I leave to men's will; either may stand, and the learned in the tongue use either, and our last translation in the margin leaveth it free. The thing she either asketh or acknowledgeth is favour or mercy, compassion and good will (all which the word* signifieth) in his eyes. By which word she confesseth all his kindnesses in word and deed shewed to her to be of his mere goodness and good will; and so should works of mercy come from the rich to the poor. The eye of the rich looking upon the poor should work compassion in the heart; then do such find favour in their eyes, when they are beheld and looked upon with respect to do them good. This favour in the eyes is not in every rich man when he beholdeth the needy. It must be a good Boaz that hath such eyes, for a Nabal wants them.

My lord. A title of reverence she giveth him. The word † signifieth such a one as beareth up the family or commonwealth as a pillar. This the name *lord* importeth. I wish this title to be remembered of the great ones, that they may shew themselves pillars and upholders of the commonwealth and of their houses, and not destroyers of them. The thing I note is this: It is lawful to give honourable titles unto men as befitteth their place. So did Aaron to Moses, Num. xii. 11; Hannah to Samuel,‡ 1 Sam. ii; Obadiah to Elijah, 1 Kings xviii. 7; and Hazael to Elisha, 2 Kings viii. 12; and so did the Hittites to Abraham, Gen. xxiii. 6. So as both such as were in and such as were out of the church used such terms of reverence, and therefore may they be used, as St Luke did, Luke i. 3, and also St Paul, Acts xxvi. 25, herein taking heed of unjust titles, of base flattery, and the excess in giving even just titles. Note again another thing: that the more humble men of good place and wealth shew themselves to be, the more honour they get, as we see

* חן *Misericordia, compassio, benevolentia, gratia, favor, &c*
† אדון   ‡ Qu. 'Eli'?—Ed.

here. She did him reverence before, verse 10, in a most humble gesture, when she saw his worldly kindness; but now perceiving the ground to be the love of her virtues, and so himself to be a lover of virtue, she calleth him *lord*, increasing in her honouring of him, as she took knowledge of his worthiness, the more for his love of virtue and godliness than for the outward and worldly kindness. Here is wisdom, and an excellent example, teaching how to honour men truly, how far, and especially for what. This instructeth men to carry themselves lowly which are of place, and to express their love of virtue. It shall not make them be less but more esteemed by much of those that be godly and wise, else were they reprovable. Jonathan's humility and goodness lost him no reverence with David, 1 Sam. xx. 41. They be counted clownishly base, or foolishly proud, or ill-mannered, which will give less honour to a man for his virtues and humility, whenas he is to be esteemed for that cause more worthy of increase of honour with men of wisdom and understanding.

For that thou hast comforted me. To wit, a stranger, a widow, and poor, even me hast thou comforted by such gracious speeches, so full of mercy and piety. The word* *comforted*, by an antiphrasis, signifieth a freedom from grief, which implieth that before she was not without heaviness in this her poor estate; for a widow, poor and a stranger in the place of her abode, how can she not be sad and pensive? Afflictions are not joyous to any for the present; they will make sad the heart of the best for a while, so long as we carry about this corrupt heart and nature of ours; and therefore let men look upon the afflicted with compassion to comfort them. Many ways did Boaz comfort poor Ruth. First, by a loving appellation, calling her his daughter, ver. 8. Secondly, by allowing her to glean in his fields, and willing her so to continue with his maidens, vers. 8, 9. Thirdly, by charging his servants in her hearing not to touch her, ver. 9. Fourthly, by granting her freedom to drink with his servants when she should be thirsty. Fifthly, by commending her virtues, and making mention of her former well-doing. And sixthly, in heartily praying for her. Thus may the poor afflicted be comforted by the wealthy and persons of authority, and especially in praising their virtues and praying for them, for the godly esteem highly of the prayers of the godly, for they know that God heareth them. The prayer of faith and fervency of spirit availeth much, James v. 16, and God hath promised to hear one for another, Gen. xx. 7, Job xlii. 8; and it is a sign of the Lord's great displeasure when he will not have one to pray for others, 1 Sam. xvi. 1, Jer. vii. 16, and xi. 14, and xiv. 11. Therefore, let us make much of the prayers of the godly, for they are comfortable. St Paul besought the saints to pray for him, and that very often; and this he doth almost in every epistle, he entreateth

the Romans, Rom. xv. 30; Ephesians, Eph. vi. 18; Philippians, Philip. i. 19; Corinthians, 2 Cor. i. 11; Thessalonians, 2 Thes. iii. 1, 1 Thes. v. 25; Colossians, Col. iv. 3; the Hebrews, Heb. xiii. 18, 19; all but the backsliding Galatians, a thing worthy of note.

And for that thou hast spoken friendly unto thine handmaid. This sheweth wherein she took the greatest comfort, even in his last words, in praising her virtues, and praying for her, which sheweth what it is wherein the godly poor take special comfort, even in their good name for well-doing, and in the prayers of such as be godly. To be praised of the godly for well-doing is great comfort, for they be the best judges thereof, and they be the best men, and their prayers, as before is noted, are available with God. Let us, then, strive to get a good name with them, and to have their prayers and requests to God for us; and when we get these let us be comforted therein. The word translated *friendly* is in the Hebrew * *to the heart*, and so the Septuagint translate it, The heart is affected with comfortable words. Thus Joseph also spake to the heart of his brethren, Gen. l. 21, for the heart in adversity wisheth comfort, and when the same is offered it rejoiceth therein. Therefore must we so speak to the afflicted, as we may make glad the heart of the oppressed. So doth the Lord speak to his people, Hosea ii. 14, and so commandeth he his prophets to speak unto them, Isa. xl. 2. Now, to speak to the heart of another is thus, first, when we speak with a feeling of their afflictions from our own hearts; thus the Jews comforted Mary and Martha, John xi. 19. The Syriac there is, they spake with their heart; and so spake St Paul to the Thessalonians, 1 Thes. ii. 11. And secondly, to speak such things as tend to their comfort, and what we know in their case may comfort them, as Joseph did to his brethren, Gen. l. 21; and as the prophet Isaiah sheweth in chap. xl. 2. If this be our duty and our mercy to the distressed, then they offend against mercy and charity who speak uncomfortably unto the afflicted, as the Jews did to our Saviour upon the cross, and the friends of Job unto Job, which much displeased the Lord, and kindled his wrath against them. Boaz before called her his daughter, but she nameth herself to be his handmaid, a term of humility, and a note of modesty in herself, who was nothing lifted up with a proud conceit of herself for all his favour and commendations; for godly and humble persons are in themselves no whit the higher minded for the good that is spoken of them, nor for the countenance of great persons towards them, for they truly know themselves to be nothing, and that all is from God, the fountain of goodness. Therefore there is no danger to praise these upon just cause to their faces for their comfort, as Boaz doth Ruth here, especially being in a low estate and in affliction.

Though I be not like one of thine handmaidens. Thus

* נחם Gen. xxiv. 67.

* על לב ἐπὶ καρδίαν.

doth Ruth debase herself, for such as be truly religious have a low esteem of themselves. The examples are pregnant; in Moses, Exodus iii. 13; Gideon, Judges vi. 15; Abigail, 1 Sam. xxv. 24; and the centurion, who held himself not worthy that Christ should come under the roof of his house, so lowly thought he of himself. Because they know and feel their infirmities, they have overmastered pride and self-love, they acknowledge that in themselves, that is, in their flesh, dwelleth no good, and therefore they think and speak of themselves very humbly. Which grace we must labour for, for it will procure love, yea, honour; for he that humbleth himself shall be exalted, Prov. xxii. 4, and xv. 33. Now, the true signs of such as be lowly in their own eyes are these: First, they think better of others than of themselves, as Ruth doth here, and as men should do, Philip. ii. 3. Secondly, they be loath to undertake great and high matters, as Moses to go to Pharaoh, and to bring Israel out of Egypt, Exod. iii. 11; and David to be Saul's son-in-law, 1 Sam. xviii. 23. Thirdly, if they be advanced, they receive honour with great humility, as Abigail did, 1 Sam. xxv. 41. Fourthly, in their high place and prosperity they be not of a proud and haughty spirit, as we may see in Joseph, Moses, David, Esther, ruled by Mordecai, and in the apostle St Paul. Fifthly, they scorn no duty, though mean, if it be a duty for them to do, Gen. xiii. 8. Abraham, the uncle, will entreat peace at the hands of his nephew Lot; if Dathan and Abiram scorn to come to Moses, he will go to them, Num. xvi. 12, 25. They stand not upon their place, so as they neglect what is fit to be done. Which justly reproveth those which have too high an esteem of themselves; which pride ariseth, first, of an overweening of themselves, of their own gifts, or what they think to be good in them. Secondly, by only looking upon the good in them, and what by their place and birth they may claim, but not at all of the evils in themselves, by which they have cause to be cast down. And thirdly, by comparing themselves either with their inferiors or with their equals, upon whom yet they cannot look with an equal eye, but with some better esteem of themselves, by some one thing or other wherein they would find themselves to excel them; but they never look upon their superiors, except with the eye of envy, nor upon any in that wherein they be overmatched, which maketh them so proud. The true signs whereof are these, First: they highly esteem of themselves, and very meanly of others, and that often of their betters, as did Gaal, Judges ix. 28, 29. Secondly, they have aspiring spirits, and think themselves worthy of higher places, as Adam and Eve, Absalom, with Korah and his company. Thirdly, they are in prosperity impatient, and cannot endure the neglect of duty towards them, which they look for, as Haman, Esther iii. 5 and v. 9. Lastly, they disdain to be at command of their betters, as did Dathan and Abiram, Num. xvi. 12, and Hagar to be in subjection

to her mistress, Gen. xvi.; for they think themselves as good as others.

Quest. Here it may be asked, how Ruth was unlike to Boaz's handmaidens?

Ans. It is thought she so spake, because she was not an Israelitish born, one within the covenant and of God's people, but a Moabitish woman, of an idolatrous kindred and incestuous race. In which respect she might well think herself inferior to them; for the children of the church are more excellent than any other people whatsoever. David therefore held it better to be a door-keeper in God's house, than to dwell in the tents of the ungodly; and Moses judged the Israelites in affliction more happy than the Egyptians and himself in Pharaoh's court; for the church's children are God's children, when all other are but his servants; they are in the covenant of God, the other strangers; they have spiritual gifts communicated to them, the other enjoy but temporal favours; they are highly esteemed of God, and bought with a price, when the other are accounted but as whelps, as Christ spake to the Canaanitish woman, and are left in their spiritual captivity; they have angels for their guard, and commanded to attend upon them, the other have not so; lastly, they have inheritance in heaven, but the wicked shall go into hell, and all the people which forget God. And therefore in this respect Ruth might speak truly, though now she was become a proselyte, and so was to be held as one of the Lord's people.

Ver. 14. *And Boaz said unto her, At meal-time come thou hither, and eat of the bread, and dip thy morsel in the vinegar. And she sat beside the reapers: and he reached her parched corn, and she did eat, and was sufficed, and left.*

The last words of Boaz in this first conference with Ruth, still expressing more and more his love unto her: first, in calling her to their victuals; then, in giving her some himself, even so much as was sufficient for the present, and more also, for she left thereof. So here Boaz inviteth her to dine with them; then she sitteth down, he welcometh her, and she eateth and is sufficed.

And Boaz said unto her. The more thankful she shewed herself, the more favour she found; for thankfulness and humility increase favour, as we see here. Which two virtues are so lovely, as they draw the liking of all men unto them. Humility graceth a man's person, and another thinketh himself honoured by a humble carriage towards him, and thanks is the praising of his goodness, and an acknowledgment of being beholden, which do much move men's hearts unto kindness and favour. Very thankful was St Paul, Philip. iv. 15, and so was David, 1 Sam. xxx. 26, to them which did them good, whose examples we must follow.

At meal-time come thou hither. Boaz knew her to be poor, and therefore he helpeth every way to supply her wants ; in the field for the present, but he leaveth her to her labour, to provide for afterwards. And thus the poor are to be sustained in their present wants, so as they may yet follow their calling, and labour therein. In saying 'at meal-time,' it noteth that there were set times to eat, and preparation made for it. And so indeed do good householders, as we see in the commendations of the good housewife, Prov. xxxi. 15, for this argueth a care and love to servants, and also preventeth their lingering in their labour, when they need not murmur for their diet, nor long wait for it. This care should be in the governors of families, which reproveth, first, such as can call upon their servants to set them to work, but are too negligent in preparing food for them, wholesome and sufficient; secondly, such as do provide, but not in due season; thirdly, such as will provide in time, but will hardly allow them time to eat, for hastening them to their work. But these cause servants to pocket, to steal, to have their secret meetings, to the great damage of the family, and so make good that which Solomon saith, Prov. xi. 24, 'There is that withholdeth more than is meet, but it tendeth to poverty.' This also is contrary to that precept in some sort, Deut. xxv. 4, 'Thou shalt not muzzle the mouth of the ox which treadeth out the corn.' And it is contrary to the condition of such as be godly; for such a one is merciful to his beast, Prov. xii. 10, then much more to his servant.

And eat of the bread, and dip thy morsel in the vinegar. Here is their household fare and harvest men's feeding; they had bread of wheat, 1 Kings v. 11, but the usual was of barley, being most commonly mentioned, Judges vii. 13, 2 Kings iv. 42, Joshua vi. 9, as the ordinary bread. Vinegar was used in hot countries, both to stir up appetite and to quench thirst ;* they used also oil, 1 Kings v. 11. In Italy they used in harvest to mingle vinegar and wine and water together. This fare, provided for Boaz's family, he allowed Ruth to eat of; for a merciful man will not only relieve the poor abroad, but sometimes at home with the food of his family, as Job did, Job xxxi. 17, 18. He limits not his goodness, but is ready to help as he seeth occasion, and as the poor shall stand in need, Neh. v. 18. Let the rich, then, this way relieve the poor, Luke xiv. 13, 14 (and not play the Nabal's part, 1 Sam. xxv. 11), if reason so require. Note again here, what homely and plain fare the godly in former times were contented to live with usually. See this in Abraham his entertainment, bread, butter, milk, and veal; he runneth to fetch the calf himself. Sarah bakes the cakes, and the man dresseth the calf, for which the strangers stay. Poor feeding had the prophets; though Elisha bade set on the great pot, 2 Kings iv. 38, it was but homely fare. They were not so dainty-toothed as now men be, which can eat nothing but what is finely cooked. The first sweet tooth that

* Lavater *in hunc locum.*

in Scripture I do read of was old Isaac, Gen. xxvii. 4; he loved savoury meat which Esau provided for him, in whom he took such pleasure for his venison and sweet meats, that he would have turned the blessing due to Jacob upon him, which that profane Esau had formerly sold for a mess of pottage, in the sale of his birthright. The godly should not eat for the palate, and to please appetite, but to preserve nature, which is contented with a little, and wholesome, though it want the dainty cooking. Hungry stomachs, and bodies well laboured, will not much care for sauce; this daintiness ariseth of idleness, and too much plenty, which do breed diseases, and shorten life in many. Let these nice stomachs know that Esau who, no doubt fed daintily, that could provide so well for his father, yet, when he came once home hungry, could be glad of a hunter's fare, and sup up a mess of pottage; such a delicate cook is hunger, which can season and make savoury very homely cheer. They that despise plain feeding, and love to fare delicately every day, must remember that it was the practice of him that went to hell, he fared deliciously every day, Luke xvi. 19. This hardens the heart of such, not to regard the poor, as it did his. This is chargeable, and bringeth unto poverty, Prov. xxi. 16, and withholdeth men from doing good works; for three things have destroyed charity among us in rich men and gentlemen, as they be called, to wit, costly buildings, costly raiment, and costly fare. Lastly, this engendereth lust; whence follow many enormities in them which follow idleness, one of the sins of Sodom, Ezek. xvi. This moderate feeding, and homely wholesome fare, which formerly men were content to feed upon, may reprove the daintiness of servants, which now-a-days will hardly be content with such fare in their master's service, as when, after coming to their own hand, they would be glad of the worst bit thereof; but thus it is when men know not when they be well, neither understand what it is to be maintained of others, till they come to find themselves.

And she sat beside the reapers. She did not impudently thrust in herself amongst them, but modestly took place somewhere beside them; whose example teacheth, that free favours are to be modestly received of the poor. It is civility, it is a virtue praiseworthy. And therefore let the poor learn modesty, learn to carry themselves as they ought; they shall procure more favour than the impudent and the unmannerly beggars.

And he reached her parched corn. That is, corn steeped and dried, and made for to eat. This we read of elsewhere also as a common food, 1 Sam. xvii. 17, and 2 Sam. xvii. 28, Lev. xxiii. 14. This was of the best food at the table. This kind of food was presented to David and his followers, 2 Sam. xvii. 28, and the same carried by him from his father to his brethren, 1 Sam. xvii. 17, an ephah of it; so Abigail brought to David five measures hereof, 1 Sam. xxv.

18, and of this Boaz giveth to Ruth, noting his kind courtesy to her; for it is a note of respect when the master of the table reacheth of that which is before him unto others. So did Elkanah to Hannah, 1 Sam. i. 4, whom he specially loved; yea, some time thus did our Saviour to his disciples, Luke xxiv. 30, John xxi. 30, which men do now follow, but oftener therein shewing their own good manners, as it is accounted, than making it the token of love, which by these things now in this complimenting age cannot be discerned. Observe hence further, that a godly rich man can be content that the godly poor taste of the best of that which is before him, for such he knoweth are near to him in Christ, and dear to God his Father. He gave not to Ruth what he would have given to his dogs, or what is hardly fit for dogs, or good for none but for dogs. Many, indeed, give to their dogs what might be fit for the poor (an evil sin under the sun, which may cause them or theirs to want), and others give only to the poor what else they would give their dogs, by a too base estimation of their poor brethren. Such gifts are not esteemed of God, though he say that what is given to them is lent to him; but it must be an alms beseeming them, and fit for a Christian to give to a man, and not unto a dog.

And she did eat, and was satisfied, and left. As she sat down to eat, being bidden, so she did eat as much as did suffice, and left. Which sheweth, first, her plenty, which is a blessing of God to have enough to suffice nature, for so God promiseth to his, Deut. xi. 15, Lev. xxv. 5, Ps. xxxvii. 3. Now this blessing stands in three things: first, in health, with a good stomach, that nature may receive food for nourishment; secondly, in competency of food, and wholesome withal; thirdly, in God's blessing of the same received, that it may strengthen us. None of these can be wanting to the necessary preservation of life; for stomach without food, food without health and stomach, and both without God's blessing, are not able to save life. Where, therefore, they concur, men have cause to bless God so much for the plenty. In the next is shewed her moderation: she ate not to satiate, but what was sufficient, for moderate feeders eat only to content nature; and that is sufficient which refresheth the body, and keepeth it apt for labour, and not that which satisfieth the unruly appetite, but overchargeth nature. This teacheth us to eat what may suffice, and be thankful to God. Two extremes are to be avoided; the one is such abstinence whereby sufficient food is not received to sustain life, either of a foolish devotion, as some formerly have done, or else of a desperate neglect of life, which is the murdering of a man's self. The other is excess, which is the sin of gluttony, overcharging nature, which sin is forbidden in Scripture. It breedeth security in the heart, Luke xxi. 34, Rom. xiii. 13, and diseases in the body, and so shorteneth life. Such a one as is so given to this sin is a belly-god, Philip. iii.; he is like the horse-

leech, which sucks till it can draw blood no longer, but is ready to burst. He is like the fish called *onos*, or the ass-fish, which hath the heart in the belly; so is this man set all on his paunch. He is like the beast called *gulon*, a name answerable to his nature, which eateth that which he preyeth upon, if it be a horse, till all be devoured,* ever filling his belly, and then emptying it, and then falling to it again, till all be consumed: such a delight hath he in his appetite. And such beast-like men there have been, who, having filled their belly, have, for the greedy desire and unsatiableness of their appetite in variety of dishes and delicacies, wished their back a belly. Such *gulons* may from this beast behold themselves how like him they be; but I may say how worse they be; for he is a beast, and doth but like himself, but these be men having reason to guide, and should have religion to bridle their devouring nature and brutish appetite. Lastly, note that Ruth left of that which was given her, which she also reserved to give unto her mother-in-law, as it follows after in ver. 18.

Ver. 15. *And when she was risen up to glean, Boaz commanded his young men, saying, Let her glean even among the sheaves, and reproach her not.*

Ruth's return to her labour is here set down, and her encouragement in the same by Boaz his love, who charged his servants to give her leave to glean, and that among the sheaves, and not reproach her for so doing.

Before I come to the words, here it may be demanded, whether there was giving of thanks, seeing their sitting down and their rising up to labour is mentioned, but not this duty of thanksgiving and prayer to God for a blessing upon their food?

Ans. We are to think they did, though not here noted, for everything is not written which there was done, as Ruth's thanks for her food, which we cannot think she omitted, who before did shew herself everyway so thankful. And there are such reasons to persuade us that Boaz would not neglect this duty, as we may easily admit his giving of thanks. First, his own godliness and knowledge of his duty, and then the commandment of God, Deut. viii. 10, which he could not be ignorant of, and of which no doubt he made conscience. Therefore let not any from hence gather a loose liberty to neglect this duty, because the holy writer mentioneth it not, but learn from other places to know it to be their duty. It was a custom among Christians, as at this day with us. There is a commandment to glorify God in eating and drinking. The creatures of God are to be received with thanksgiving, and are sanctified by the word of God and prayer, 1 Tim. iv. 3, 5; and holy men have used it; Samuel, 1 Sam. ix. 13, St Paul, Acts xxvii. 35, yea, when he and the people had long fasted, yet ate he not before grace. Our blessed Saviour, the innocent

* Gesner.

Lamb of God, spotless and sinless, yet ate not but first gave thanks, John vi. 11, 23. It therefore is our duty, and befitting all, before they receive food, to give thanks; for what can our meat do without God's blessing? How soon have some been choked, and have ended their days suddenly! And do we not remember that the Israelites perished with meat in their mouths! Neither let this duty be put off to children, as if it were too mean a duty for the master of the table. Were it not grossly ridiculous, and a very scornful part, for a man to receive a favour from a king, and then call his child to give him thanks! Our Saviour put not this off to another, nor Samuel, nor Paul: are they not worthy imitation?

And when she was risen up to glean. The history turneth again to Ruth, and sheweth what she did after her repast, and the liberal feeding allowed her by Boaz; she betook herself to gleaning again, and returned to her former labour. Whence we may learn, I. That the godly poor, by their favours received, and helps in their need, are not the more negligent, but the rather the more painful in their labours, as may be seen here in Ruth; for they know that such helps are for to stir them up to well-doing, which use they make of them, and not to live idly, as many do, who are not worthy to eat, 2 Thes. iii. The poor are to follow Ruth's steps, and learn, for the mercies of men towards them, to continue painful in their calling. II. That the true use and end of receiving food is to strengthen our bodies, to preserve them in labour, Eccles. x. 17. Ruth eateth to suffice nature, to return to work. The apostle joineth eating and labour together, 2 Thes. iii. 10, neither would he eat the bread of idleness, 2 Thes. iii. 8, nor the good woman commended in the Proverbs, Prov. xxxi. 27. God would not allow the sole monarch of all the whole earth, no, not in innocency, when the earth brought forth without labour, to eat without painstaking; he must dress the garden. Food is the reward of labour of such as be able, and it is a blessing to eat the labour of our hands, Ps. cxxviii. 2. Therefore such are here reproved which rise up to eat and drink, and do eat and drink to rise up and play, or prate, or sleep, or to run to plays, to fulfil their lust; to deck themselves like wantons, the sons and daughters of Belial, of Jezebel; some be Cain's race, and eat to be vagabonds, going up and down begging; some of Esau's race, and eat to hunt and hawk, till they have sold their inheritance for a mess of pottage, and themselves be less worth than one meal which they before bestowed upon their dogs. These should know that they are born to labour, and that godly men and women have so bestowed their time; yea, Jesus Christ himself lived in a calling painfully.

Boaz commanded his young men, saying, Let her glean even among the sheaves. What Ruth desired, ver. 7, here Boaz alloweth her, when he saw her so well given and so painful. So we see how the godly diligent hand obtaineth favour and a blessing, Prov. xiii. 4, as

appeareth in Ruth here, and in Jacob, Gen. xxxi., whose pains the Lord rewarded abundantly. This is taught in the parable of the talent, Mat. xxv., in which the stock of the diligent is increased, for God hath thus promised to do, Prov. xiii. 4; and labour is a means appointed of God to get his blessings, who also openeth the heart of the rich to do good to the poor, which labour painfully. Would we have supply of our wants? would we have earthly blessings? then must we labour and take pains. Of gathering among the sheaves, see verse 7. Boaz here is not only content that she should gather by, or besides, but between the sheaves, where more plentiful gathering was of ears and scattered corn; it was more than a common favour, an argument of his special love. The rich are to be merciful, yet may they extend their bounty, as they shall like, to one more than to another, as they shall think fitting. Of which before on verse 7.

And reproach her not; or, as the marginal reading is, *shame her not.* From these words note, I. Young men are apt to offer injury, and to reproach the poor women, widows, and strangers; else Boaz would not have given them this charge, but that he knew their wanton behaviour by nature, and how the Jews took liberty to use their speeches against such strangers, especially, perhaps, when they saw her better respected than their own countrywomen. II. That reproaching is to put shame upon one; therefore is such a word* here used, as may be translated either way. III. That goodness and mercy stands not only in doing good, but also in preventing evil, as much as lieth in us; both is here done by Boaz, as is also before noted out of verse 9.

Ver. 16. *And let fall also some of the handfuls of purpose for her, and leave them, that she may glean them, and rebuke her not.*

Boaz's speech, continued to his servants, touching his liberality towards Ruth, who thought it not enough to let her glean among the sheaves (for that he knew she would not filch nor steal out of them), but he commandeth his servants, that they should of purpose let fall handfuls for her to gather, and not rebuke her for so doing. So here is Boaz's charge, with the end why, and also a forbidding of them to rebuke her.

And let fall also some of the handfuls of purpose for her. As they reaped, they cut by handfuls, and thereof made sheaves, of which handfuls they should let some fall, as they were reaping, or else some of them, as they were binding up the sheaves, which is the more likely. Howsoever it was, we may note, I. That a merciful man and a godly man is frank-hearted to the godly poor, such as be painful and deserve love. This is evident in Boaz, whose merciful kindness is many ways set forth; he spake to her in a loving appellation, calling her daughter; he admitted her to his table as one of his family; he praised

* תכלימוה

her virtues, and prayed for her; he bound his servants to the good behaviour towards her, to prevent injury which might be offered to her; and he also did give to her, and that both freely without asking, and largely without niggardly sparing. Now a good man is moved, as Boaz, to this, because he conceiveth the misery of another with a fellow-feeling; he placeth himself in their stead, and considereth his own frailty, the world's mutability, and that he may stand in need if God should lay his hand upon him; lastly, he knoweth that God loveth a cheerful giver. Therefore, here let us in our charity towards the godly, imitate this blessed Boaz; shew our love in words, in deeds, in doing good, in preventing evil every way; and what we do, to do it freely and bountifully. Many will not give, as being altogether merciless; but let them remember the threatening of James, chap ii. 13. Many will give, but not largely, nor freely, without importuning, though they be able, and their brethren stand in need. II. Note that servants are not to give what is their master's, without his warrant: for Boaz here alloweth them to give her; and without this warrant it had not been lawful for them to have thus left her handfuls of corn; for servants are but trusted with, or amongst their master's goods: they are not disposers of them; the disposing is at the pleasure of the owner, and not of the servants, which have no right in them at all. Those servants, therefore, which will take upon them to give of their master's goods, under pretence of charity, or what else, are to be reproved; for it is theft so to do without the will of the owner, Gen. xxxi. 32; and the gift so given, under what show soever, is not acceptable to God; for men must give of their own, and not be liberal upon other men's estates.

And leave them, that she may glean them. Here it may be asked, Why did not Boaz rather give her a quantity of corn, and so send her home, rather than to let her abide in the fields to glean? Because he would so relieve her, as yet he would keep her in labour, and not maintain her in idleness. And this is the best charity, so to relieve the poor, as we keep them in labour. It benefits the giver, to have them labour; it benefits the commonweal, to suffer no drones, nor to nourish any in idleness; and it benefits the poor themselves, it keeps them in health, it discovers them to be idle or painful; if painful, it procureth them favour; and lastly, it keepeth them from idleness, and so from a sea of wickedness, which the lazy persons are subject to, and run into, as the vagrant poor giveth us sufficiently to know, which dwell among us, or rather rogue up and down without dwelling or certain abode. Let, therefore, men thus relieve the poor with Boaz; and if men would spare from excess of apparel, dainty fare, idle expenses in keeping hawks and hounds, in following unthrifty gaming, and such like, and lay up that to charitable uses, to set the poor on work, what singular good

might be done! The poor would cease to complain, and the rich themselves would be better for it.

And rebuke her not. This caveat he addeth, that they might not think his command, to let fall handfuls, was for trial of her, but that she should carry away what they should so let fall, without check. Before he warned them not to reproach her, by giving her ill language; and here he would not have her to suffer rebuke at their hands, for taking what he shall allow her; for the servant is not to find fault with any person for receiving his master's kindness: he may dispose of his own, and the servant is not to dislike with it, in checking the receiver, in whom there is no cause of rebuke, but rather in the evil eye of the servant, as our Saviour sheweth in the parable of the vineyard, Mat. xx. 15.

Ver. 17. *So she gleaned in the field until even, and beat out that she had gleaned; and it was about an ephah of barley.*

This sheweth the continuance of Ruth in her labour till the end of the day; then, her beating out the corn, and what it by measure came unto; the scope to set out God's blessing, her painful travel, and Boaz's furtherance thereof, as is noted in the former verses, by allowing her to glean amongst the sheaves, and commanding his servants to let fall handfuls for her to gather up.

So she gleaned in the field until even. Ruth abode in that same field, as Boaz advised; there she found kindness. It is good abiding there where we do well. It is wantonness to be removing from thence, and not being in want, as many light servants do, who, as rolling stones, which can never gather moss, feel want ere they be aware. Ruth kept herself there where she was well; and so should others do, and reap the fruit of wisdom and constancy; both which appeared in Ruth herein. Note again, from her example of sedulity, that such as love labour take pains so long as they may, all the day till night; for the day is the time of labour till the evening, as the psalmist speaketh, ' Man goeth out to his labour until the evening.' Ruth rested not till the time of rest; for they that love labour do strengthen themselves to it, as Solomon speaketh of the good housewife, Prov. xxxi. 17. And this strengthening is thus: when they labour to come with a good will to work; when they force their own consciences thereto from the commandment of God to labour; when they do consider labour as the ordinary means appointed, both to get an outward estate, and to preserve the same; and, lastly, when they joy in the fruit of their labour, and reap the profit of their hands, Prov. xxxi. 18. Thus should we strengthen ourselves to take pains, as Ruth here did. So shall we eat the bread of our own hands, as the apostle exhorteth, 1 Thes. iv. 11, 2 Thes. iii. 12; which, as before I have noted, is a blessed thing, Ps. cxxviii. 1; and we shall not eat the bread of idleness, the bread which the good woman would not taste of, Prov. xxxi. 27; it is unsavoury to all that truly fear God, and walk as they should, in an honest calling. This diligence and constant labour of Ruth, checketh those which will not work on the day, to have the sweet labouring man's rest in the night; not in health, to relieve themselves in sickness; not in youth, to maintain old age; not in summer, for heat; not in winter, for cold; but rather as drones, desire to live upon the sweat of other men's brows, not upon the labour of their own hands, as God spake to Adam, Gen. iii. They also are here reproved, which will not be constant in labour, but work only by fits to supply present wants, and to have money to spend, not setting hand to labour while they have one penny, never providing for the time to come, but do rest upon their present strength, to labour for supply of present wants, and no farther; whereby it cometh to pass, that in sickness and old age they must either be relieved of others, or perish for hunger.

And beat out that she had gleaned. She was both the gleaner and the thresher. Corn was beat out sometime by oxen or horses treading, or by a wheel running upon it, or by a staff, as here, or by the flail, as now everywhere with us. It was a mean course to glean, but a meaner for herself to sit down to beat out what she had gleaned; and yet this she did before she went home to her mother-in-law, whose house she would not cumber, nor trouble her old head with the noise of the beating; she would bring home all ready with her. She laboured more like a servant than a daughter-in-law, and yet she in love was more than a daughter-in-law. Her service was beyond a servant in labour and travel, with diligence and faithfulness, and her love surpassed and exceeded the love of many natural children. The thing principally here to be noted is that the godly, which indeed be truly humble and painful, refuse no honest kind of labour: Abel will keep sheep, Jacob will do the like; Sarah will bake cakes, even ordinary bread, not like the apothecary's stuff, such as our ladies perhaps will put their hands unto, if their fingers be yet not too fine; Rebekah will take a pitcher and fetch water, yea, more, will draw for the camels of a stranger out of courtesy; yea, Gideon will thrash, Boaz will lie by his corn-heap, Ruth will beat out her corn, and the honourable woman will put her hand to the distaff. The reasons are, because such have put on humility, which will refuse to do nothing that is honest and lawful; they know no dishonesty therein, and that it was held a virtue aforetimes to labour in such things as the pride of our times judge base and contemptible, and themselves disgraced therein.* By no means many in our age will labour upon any occasion in any common thing; they have (forsooth) their reasons; they allege birth: but who better born than Cain and Abel, the sons of the sole monarch of the whole world? Christ

* *Vide* Martin Bucer, *De Regno Christi*, lib. ii. cap. 48, 49.

381

Jesus, by birth as man, descended of kings and the king of Judah, yet was a carpenter, Mark vi. 3; he had birth to have boasted on, and he had power divine to have exempted him from labour, yet he would not do so. King Alphonsus, doing something with his hands, and labouring so as some which beheld him found fault, smiled, and said, Hath God given hands to kings in vain? Yea, the Grand Signior* by his law, as I take it, is to do daily some bodily work with his own hands; and that law they do observe to grace labour, and that labouring men should not become contemptible. They will allege, I mean our gentlemen idlers, that they have rich parents to maintain them, that they need not work. Yes, if not for maintenance, yet to prevent a world of wickedness which cometh by their idle life. For who set out the ensigns of pride in apparel but these? who prove so prodigal? who live so much in filthy lusts of uncleanness? who maintain play and playhouses? who are the tobacconists, the drunkards, the riotous persons? who of the roaring boys and damned crew, but commonly these? Behold, you rich parents, the goodly fruit of the idle education of your children! But grant they prove not ever such as be here named; may they yet live without callings, and only live idly and do nothing, because their parents can maintain them? Did rich Abraham so bring up Isaac, or he so Jacob, and this man so his children? or did Jesse thus train up David? If he had, surely he had never been king of Israel, for God never made choice of any man to advance him but such as were in their callings. God calleth Moses keeping sheep, so David;† and Gideon when he was threshing, and Elisha when he was ploughing, Amos when he was with his cattle. What shall I speak of the apostles when Christ did call them? Was not some mending their nets, other fishing, another sitting at the receipt of custom? none idle or out of a calling. So long as the prodigal son lived out of a calling, yea, till he kept swine, as base as it was, he never came to himself, he never had grace to repent. These idlers and loose livers yet say for themselves that it is a disgrace for them to mind so mean things, as the men of old time did. Disgrace! Who can hold that to be a disgrace which better men have done? Better for piety to God, better before men, for nobleness of birth, for greatness of state, and for name of renown in the world. Again, who do make that a disgrace now, which God in his word sheweth to have been their praise? This conceit of disgrace ariseth from the spirit of pride and vanity in the sons of Belial. But if conceit of disgrace make them avoid labour in some calling, whether of the mind or body, then would I fain know why they avoid not those things wherein disgrace is indeed, and why they shame not to live idly, prodigally, lasciviously, in riot and excess, in

* The great Lord of the Turkish empire.
† See what David was when he yet kept sheep, 1 Sam. xvi. 12, 18, 19, and xvii. 40, 42.

foolish pride and vanity, and lewd courses, unbe-
seeming the name of Christianity. Lastly, these unprofitable members will say they have better been
been brought up than to take pains. What is this
better bringing up? It is to follow fashions, or to
drink and whiff the tobacco-pipe, or to congee and
compliment, or to hunt and hawk, and then curse
and swear as the furies of hell; or else to handle a
weapon to strike and stab, and upon a word to challenge, and so into the field to play the devil's com-
panion, or to play at dice and cards, or to read
amorous books, to court a courtezan, I should say
a gentlewoman or a young gallant, to vanity and
wantonness? How much more commendable were it
and profitable to be employed in some good literature, as in the knowledge of tongues and arts? And
will their bringing up allow them to live idly? Was
not Paul brought up at the feet of Gamaliel, a great
statesman among the Jews? and yet he laboured with
his hands, and never lived out of a particular calling? And was not Moses brought up in Pharaoh's
court, and in all the learning of the Egyptians?
Yet did he live in a calling, and would be a shepherd rather than live idly, or in Pharaoh's court
wickedly. He pleaded not his birth, his gentry, his
better education, as these do. It is enough to be a
gentleman, as they speak now-a-days, to countenance
him in sin, in sloth, in bravery, in contempt of a strict
life, to live out of a calling, saving the calling of a
gentlemen, a profession so abused to advance sin and
Satan's kingdom, as nothing more; yet never read I
nor heard I of in holy writ, or elsewhere, that the
title and name of a gentleman should be a calling to
exempt men from all callings, from all honest labours,
and to leave them loose as wild colts without bit or
bridle, to their own lusts and licentious liberty, and
finally to their ruin and destruction. This is not
gentry, but rather gentilism, to be hated of a Christian,
the practice whereof was odious even in the commonwealths of heathen men.

And it was about an ephah of barley. Thus much
her day's labour came unto, which was almost a bushel
after our measure. An ephah was ten times as much
as an omer, Exod. xvi. 86, which was the measure
for gathering manna, ver. 16, and this was as much
as would serve one man bread for a day. So Ruth
had gathered so much in one day as might serve her
many days. Thus the Lord blessed her labour; whence
we may learn this, that the Lord can and will give
sometime a plentiful blessing to the diligent hand.
Thus he blessed Jacob in his painful service, so as he
was able to give to Esau a present of five hundred
fifty head of beasts and cattle of one sort and other,
Gen. xxxii. 13, 14, for all things are in his hand and
at his disposing. How soon did he enrich again Job?
It is nothing with the Lord to make a poor man rich.
And therefore in our labours let us have recourse unto
God, because he giveth power to get wealth, Deut.

viii. 18. Without his blessing our labour is in vain,
Ps. cxxvii. 2, Haggai i. 6; but with his blessing our
labour shall take good effect, John xxi. 6.

*Ver. 18. And she took it up, and went into the city;
and her mother-in-law saw what she had gleaned: and
she brought forth, and gave to her that she had reserved
after she was sufficed.*

Ruth's comfortable return out of the field, with what,
whither, to whom, with her kindness in giving what
she had reserved at meal-time from Boaz's table, so
as she had a double witness to shew her mother his
kindness: the ephah of barley and the food of his
table, both which did (no doubt) greatly comfort the
heart of Naomi, as appeareth by her hearty prayers in
the next verse.

And she took it up, and went into the city. She
beareth the burden herself. And this is noted to
shew how the Lord taketh notice of the burdens of
his children, which are of two sorts, either such as be
voluntarily undertaken, and willingly for discharge of
their duty, as Jacob in his service to Laban, Gen.
xxxi. 12, or Ruth here for her honest maintenance, or
else imposed upon them, as the burdens of Pharaoh
upon the Israelites, Exod. iii. 7. On both the Lord
looketh, approving the one and pitying the other,
which may give comfort unto the painful, in bearing
the burden of their calling, or of oppression; for the
Lord knoweth their troubles, their labour, and travail,
and will do them good in the end, if they wait with
patience.

And her mother-in-law saw what she had gleaned.
By this it appeareth that Ruth did hide none of her
gleaning from Naomi, but shewed her all, and this for
three causes: to manifest God's mercy towards her,
that she might praise God with her; to shew that she
had been painful in her absence, and not spent her
time idly; and to shew her faithfulness, that she kept
nothing from her. And thus should children and servants do to such as depend upon their labour; approve
their labour by the fruits thereof, and their faithfulness
unto their parents and masters. They may not be
faithless, as some servants be, nor careless and idle, as
be too many children, who under their parents take
liberty to be lazy, when yet they have more reason
to be painful and careful than servants, as nature,
better maintenance, and the hope of portions and inheritance bind them.

And she brought forth, and gave her. After that
Ruth had shewed what she had gleaned, she took out
some victuals, and gave to her mother-in-law also.
Godly children are kind and loving to their parents.
If this be in a daughter-in-law to a mother-in-law,
much greater is the bond of duty of natural children
to their natural parents, see chap. iv. ver. 15, if they
be truly religious, as may be seen in David to his
parents, 1 Sam. xxii. 3, and Joseph to his, Gen.
xlv. 11. And good reason is there why they should

do their parents all good; nature binds them, also the commandment of God, to honour them, Exod. xx., which comprehendeth love, reverence, obedience, and relief; and the example of godly children, yea, of Christ himself unto his mother, moveth them, John xix. 26, 27. There be also rare examples for this among the heathen,* the rather to persuade Christians hereunto, lest they rise up in judgment against them. Let children, therefore, learn to be kind and merciful to their poor parents, and not be like the unnatural imps whereof there be these sorts, such as care not to provide for them, but to get all they can from them; they are not willing to do them good, but grudge to relieve them, and are sick of their lives, wishing their death, to be eased of the burden. Other there be which will rob their parents, and steal from them what they can get, yea, and think it no sin, as Solomon telleth us, Prov. xxviii. 2, 4; yet are they the companions of a destroyer. The third sort are those hellish monsters who rise up to murder their parents; but the Lord revengeth it, as we see in the example of Absalom.

That she had reserved, after she was sufficed. It is meet to eat to suffice nature for the preservation of life, and the better enabling of us to walk painfully in our calling, of which before in ver. 14. Note further hence, I. That such as have true love, will spare from themselves to relieve others, yea, though they themselves be but poor, and have nothing but from hand to mouth, as we say. Of this we have here an example, and in the poor widow which gave her two mites, Luke xxi. 2; yea, our Saviour, who was relieved by others, yet kept a bag for the poor; he spared of his gifts to give unto others. For true love cannot but pity the want of others; and such as so love will not hoard up for themselves, and let their poor brethren remain in want, when for the present they have sufficient; they live in hope of supply, and doubt not of God's providence for the time to come, when they give charitably what they may spare for the present. This condemneth the cursed covetousness of such as have laid up in store for many years, and yet will not bestow anything upon such as do need; and also it checketh such as excuse and exempt themselves wholly and always for giving anything, because they be poor. If this plea had stuck in the heart of the poor widow which cast her mites into the treasury, she would have reserved them to herself, but so should she have lost her eternal praises.

II. Such as would thrive, spend not all at once, but reserve somewhat both for themselves and for others. Ruth ate, she was sufficed, and reserved some for afterwards for her mother and herself; she was not riotous and wasteful because she had more than did suffice for the present: for such as be painful know how they come by that which they have; they also know it to be a virtue to spare and keep what necessity causeth not to be laid out, neither

* See Val. Max., lib. v. cap. 4.
383

charity nor pity to be spent; they know that what they have is so their own before men, as yet before God they are but stewards thereof. Therefore from this, and Ruth's example, we must learn frugality, to use God's blessings to do ourselves good; but we must beware of waste, and not let anything be lost, as our Saviour commanded, John vi. 12, 13, when he had fed so many thousands. They then here are worthy of just reprehension, who wastefully consume God's blessings: some on their belly, as do drunkards and gluttons; some on their fleshly delights, bringing themselves to a morsel of bread; others upon play and gaming, idle and prodigal unthrifts, such as this our nation now is too much burdened with; others upon too costly and often fantastic attire, the ensign of pride and vanity, to whom if any speak for their reformation, they reply with words of contempt of others, and careless neglect of their own estate, saying, They spend but their own, what have any to do with it? But these must remember that they must give an account unto God, whose blessings they waste; they must also know that God's gifts are not given them to consume wholly upon themselves after their lusts, but to be stewards thereof for God, and in his stead to do good to others, as need shall require. This prodigality the Lord often punisheth with poverty, Luke xv., and sometime with imprisonment, yea, with shameful deaths in some, whom God giveth over to fall into the hand of the magistrate, for some evil committed and deserving death.

Ver. 19. *And her mother-in-law said unto her, Where hast thou gleaned to-day, and where wroughtest thou? Blessed be he that did take knowledge of thee. And she shewed her mother-in-law, with whom she had wrought, and said, The man's name with whom I wrought to-day is Boaz.*

Here is Naomi her question to Ruth, with her hearty prayer to God for him that had so mercifully dealt with Ruth; and Ruth's answer to her again, shewing with whom she had gleaned, and naming the name, even Boaz her kinsman.

And her mother-in-law said, Where hast thou gleaned to-day, and where wroughtest thou? When Ruth went out in the morning, she asked leave of Naomi to go to glean, but whither she knew not; therefore now being returned with so much corn and such food, she asketh Ruth where she had been, not doubting of Ruth's honest dealing, but in admiration of God's mercy, and in desire to know who was the instrument of that hand of God upon her. For favours bestowed do win affections, and cause a longing after the party to know who it is, if we know not his person, as here, and also what his name is, and of what kindred, though we look upon the man as Saul did, 1 Sam. xvii. 55–58, that so we might see the reason thereof, and might shew particularly our love unto such a one, praise God, and pray also for him. Now, if this be the force of benefits from man, how much more from God, from whom we receive so many and daily blessings! These should win our affections to him, and work in us a desire to know him, who he is, and why we should receive such kindness, that so we might love him, praise him, and in all thankfulness yield him all obedience. But, alas, upon whom do his blessings thus work? I wish that his mercies made us not forget him, and to forsake him, when we have known him. In this that Naomi suspecteth not Ruth, but rather admireth God's mercy towards her, we may also note that the godly are not uncharitably suspicious of them that be poor, when they know them to be godly. Naomi did not think of any unjust dealing of Ruth, as if she had stolen this corn, nor that she had gone a-begging to get it, or this other food: for she asketh where she had gleaned and wrought, not where she had stolen and begged; for love is not suspicious, it 'thinketh no ill.' Naomi was persuaded that some had bestowed this favour upon Ruth gleaning and working in the field. This grace of charity must we labour for, even in thinking not amiss of others in getting goods, though much in a small time, so there be not apparent tokens of the ill means used in getting the same; for God can suddenly enrich a man, as he did Abraham and Lot, so Jacob in the service of Laban, for 'the blessing of the Lord maketh rich,' Prov. x. 22. Yet if the man be wicked, and hastily is made rich, except an apparent cause be seen, and the means also, he may be suspected; for of such Solomon speaketh in the Proverbs, chap. xxviii. 20, and xx. 21, that they shall not be innocent, and goods so gotten shall not be blessed in the end. Some from hence teach, because Naomi asketh Ruth where she had gleaned and wrought that day, that parents are to take an account of their children, how they spend their time, where they have been, and with whom. Indeed, this will make children to take more heed to their ways; it will discover to parents their nature and conditions the better, and it may prevent many evils, through fear to be called to an account for the same. As on the contrary, this neglect in parents gives children the rein, and so they take liberty to sin, presuming of parents' indulgency, as did Adonijah, to whom David never said, Why hast thou done so? 1 Kings i. 6, which made him proud and presumptuous to his own destruction.

Blessed be he that did take knowledge of thee. To wit, to shew thee this mercy and kindness; for he taketh knowledge of another, who considereth so of him, as his estate and condition requireth, and thereafter doth him good, as Boaz did to Ruth, when he knew what she was, as is before noted out of vers. 8 and 9; for which here Naomi is thankful, before she knew the name of the man, and here heartily prayeth for him. Hence teaching that benefits received provoke the godly to be thankful, though they know not the parties, and also to pray for them, as Naomi doth here, which serves to encourage men to do good to the godly, though their persons be not known; they shall not lose with them the fruit of their well-doing; for such will be thankful, and will pray for them that God may bless them. And this teacheth such as receive favours to shew themselves thankful to them which bestow them. Now, thankfulness appeareth, first, in acknowledging of benefits received: the contrary is ingratitude, and a note of pride withal; secondly, in praying for them, as Naomi doth here, and St Paul, for his friends, 2 Tim. i. 16; thirdly, in requiting the kindness, as we shall be able, and occasion offered, as David to Barzillai, 1 Kings ii. 7; the spies to Rahab, Josh. vi. 23; Elisha to the Shunamite 2 Kings iv. 13; and the great emperor Ahasuerus to poor Mordecai, Esther vi. 3, which is a reproof to the ungrateful, such as will not acknowledge a benefit, or lessen it when they confess it; they that never care to requite it, though it be in their power so to do it, yea, and need on the other side require it; lastly, such as do requite evil for good. Here we may further note, that a good heart rejoiceth in the welfare of another. For Naomi blesseth God for Boaz taking knowledge of Ruth, and for doing this kindness unto her; so do the Macedonians for the Corinthians' kindness unto the saints at Jerusalem. For such have loving hearts, and are void of envy, therefore can they rejoice and bless God, yea, and pray for a blessing upon those which do good unto others, which grace we must strive for.

And she shewed her mother-in-law, with whom she had wrought, and said, The man's name with whom I wrought to-day is Boaz. As Naomi did demand of her where and with whom she had been, so Ruth answered plainly, telling her that the man's name in whose field she gleaned that day was Boaz; by which Naomi perceived the good hand of God's providence conducting her into the kinsman's field, whose favour made her afterwards to counsel Ruth to go into the threshing-floor to Boaz, as it followeth in the next chapter. Ruth calleth gleaning *working*, as Naomi did before; for the diligent hand worketh even in that, which otherwise may seem to require no great labour. She saith she 'wrought with him,' not that he laboured with her, neither that she did work for him, as the phrase in our speech doth intimate; but her meaning is, that she wrought in his field with his leave and good liking. In telling his name to her mother-in-law, it seemeth she learned it in the field; no doubt she did ask after it, that so she might speak of his goodness unto her mother-in-law when she came home. And we must know that it is our duty to take special notice of such as do us good, to know them by name, that so they may be acknowledged as occasion shall be to meet with them, that they * may in particular pray for them, and to give them their due

---

* Qu. 'we'?—ED.

praises to others. For either to neglect to know them, or easily to forget our benefactors, is a fault.

Ver. 20. And Naomi said unto her daughter-in-law, Blessed be he of the Lord, who hath not left off his kindness to the living and to the dead. And Naomi said unto her, The man is near of kin unto us, one of our next kinsmen.

This is Naomi her speech again unto Ruth, wherein she first earnestly prayeth for Boaz, with the reason why she was so moved thereto, and then sheweth her what he was to them, even a very near kinsman.

And Naomi said unto her daughter-in-law, &c. When she heard who it was, and calling to remembrance what he was to them, and what mercy he had formerly shewed unto her husband and children, she breaketh forth into prayer for him. Whence we may learn that new kindnesses added to the old do the more inflame the affections to love and hearty well-wishing, as may appear here by Naomi; for new favours call the old to remembrance, and testifieth the continuance of love. This is an encouragement to such as have been kind, still to continue so to the thankful; the latter favours shall keep up the affection of love, and be the remembrancer of what is past, and to bind the parties the more unto them. Now, if this be so with men, how should we be inflamed in love towards our good God and Father, who daily reneweth his blessings upon us! Ought we not to increase in love according to his mercies? But, O ungrateful man, what stupidity possesseth thine heart! Do we not receive his blessings with one hand, and shew our unmindfulness of him by the other? If the keeping of his commandment be the mark of our love, as it is, 1 John v. 2, then surely our waxing wanton against him, by abusing of his blessings, openly proclaim rather hatred than love unto him. This is our unthankfulness, of which we must repent.

Blessed be he of the Lord. This is her prayer made to the Lord to bless him. From this note many things. I. That prayer in and by every true member of the church hath been only made unto God. This the examples of all the godly do confirm, and thus are we commanded to do; and therefore the prayers made to saints, angels, yea, or to the Virgin Mary, are abominable and cursed idolatry. II. That it is the Lord that doth bless and make happy, for what is begged of God, that is acknowledged to be his gift. And what happiness, corporal or spiritual, can man attain unto but by the Lord? Therefore, if we want blessings, let us beg them of him; if we have them, acknowledge him the author, and be thankful in cheerful obedience for the same, as we be exhorted in the word of God, Deut. x. 12, Rom. xii. 1. For who can think himself blessed of God, and not be thankful and obedient unto him, but such as be void of all grace! III. That the Lord will bless the merciful. For she prayeth for that which she had warrant to ask; and

385

we find that the Lord hath so promised to do, Ps. xli. 1, 3, Mat. v 7. And therefore let the merciful look for a blessing, and let us pray for that blessing upon their heads which shew mercy unto the poor and needy, that they may be encouraged in such works of charity. And to move them hereto, let them consider God's promise to them, how they be under God's protection, Deut. xxiv. 13, how others pray for them when they do little think thereof, and do bless them, as Naomi doth Boaz here; and if the poor fail of their duty, yet the almsdeed ascendeth up to God, Acts x. 4, and the work done shall bless them, even the back and belly of the poor, Job xxxi. 20. Let these things move the rich to do works of mercy, and to rejoice therein. IV. That the poor's reward unto the rich for their works of charity is only their prayer to God for them. Naomi had no other recompence for Boaz but this; and this is a great requital, when it is a fervent prayer from faith, for such the Lord doth hear, and will himself reward their works, he becomes bound for them, to make good what on their behalf is wanting, which may greatly comfort such as be merciful. And seeing the poor have nothing else to repay back but their prayers, let them not fail in this, not only when and while the benefit is in receiving, but even when for time the favour may seem to be forgotten, so often as their benefactors come to their remembrance, not to fail to lift up a thought to God for them.

Who hath not left off his kindness to the living and to the dead. The reason which moved Naomi to pray so fervently for a blessing upon Boaz was his constant favour towards them alive, as before to her husband and children then dead; and it is as if Naomi had said, He continueth still in his former kindness to us that be now alive, to thee and me, which he shewed to my husband and children now departed this life. The papists * prattle, I know not what, of benefiting the dead by works of charity, out of this place, by wresting the sense thereof to maintain their error, which I leave as idle and unprofitable, and come to more sound and profitable instructions for ourselves. Hence may we observe, that true love in good men dies not with the dead, but is shewed to those they leave behind them, as Boaz doth here to Ruth and Naomi for their husbands' sake; so did David to Mephibosheth for Jonathan's sake, 2 Sam. ix. 1; for a true friend loveth at all times, Prov. xvii. 17. David received kindness of the king of Moab, 1 Sam. xxii. 4, and being dead, he sent to comfort his son Hanun, if it had been so taken, 2 Sam. x. 2; for a true friend seeth his friend alive in his children and posterity. Let us then, if we love one truly, not bury our love with him in his grave, as the manner of the world is now, which is full of counterfeit love; but let us imitate our heavenly Father, who loved Abraham, Isaac, and Jacob, and their seed after them, and promiseth

* Feuardentius *in hunc locum.*

mercy unto thousands of the posterity of such as love him and keep his commandments, Exod. xx. This reproveth such which let their love die with their friends; also such as love their friend's posterity, if they be rich, but not if they be poor, as Boaz doth here. But true friendship maketh no difference of a friend by riches and poverty; for if this make the difference, the friendship is certainly counterfeit. Thirdly, this condemneth such friends as love such as remain of their friends departed, so as under colour of kindness they rob their children committed by the will of their dead friend to their custody; such villany there is in the world, and falsehood masked under the shadow of love.

Besides instruction, here is also matter of consolation, if we consider how God raiseth up constant friends to poor posterities. Though this be rare, yet we have in this place an example, that God is the same in power and mercy to do the like still for his children; but be it that men fail to be faithful in their love, let us be comforted in this, that the Lord is faithful. If he love Abraham his friend, his posterity in Egypt after four hundred years shall reap benefit thereby; if the Lord choose a David, he will for a long time for his sake shew kindness to his posterity. Let this, this I say, settle the hearts of careful parents for their posterity; for if the Lord love them he will not fail them, nor forsake their posterity that shall depend upon him; he is the sure and constant friend, and will not leave off his kindness to the living and to the dead, as Naomi speaketh here of Boaz.

And Naomi said unto her, The man is near of kin unto us, one of our next kinsmen. It may seem by this, that before now Naomi had not told Ruth of Boaz her rich kinsman, but at this present, as occasion had now offered itself, now she telleth her that he was a very near kinsman, one of her redeemers, which had a right to redeem the inheritance, and so to marry her and raise up seed unto the dead, as the law required, Deut. xxv.; and this Naomi tells her of, to shew how natural affection did in some sort bind him to this kindness which he had shewed her, and also to comfort Ruth in this poor estate, in hope of a better condition, as it afterwards fell out. Observe, hence, I. That the godly wise poor are not vainglorious boasters of their rich friends and kindred. Naomi made not him known before this to Ruth, both for that she would not entice Ruth to come and embrace her company for any outward respect of worldly friendship, and also because she knew it to be folly to boast of rich friends, except they were sure to find them good and kind. Naomi was not as some poor be, which foolishly brag of rich kinsfolk, while yet they find them not true friends, such as will hardly acknowledge them to be of their kindred, either do them almost any good at all. II. That it is then a comfort to the poor to speak of rich kindred, when they shew themselves kind, as kindred ought to do, for *kindred* may so be called from

kindness in them, and by shewing themselves *kind* to their *kinsfolk* as Boaz doth here; and therefore Naomi now, but not before, telleth Ruth of him, what he was to them. The poor may hence learn when fitly to speak of such kinsfolk, and the rich may see how to open the mouths of their poor friends to speak of them, and to pray for them, even by shewing the true tokens of love and kindred. III. That near kinsfolk are to be kind to their poor kindred, for Naomi giveth this as some reason of Boaz his so great favour towards them; and this natural bond of love hath both reason and religion to strengthen the same, and therefore such as be so bound, and will not be kind, do against nature, reason, and religion, as when parents neglect children, these their parents, so brethren and sisters one another; and yet this unnatural affection is common in these our days, which the apostle condemneth, Rom. i. 31, and also foretelleth it to be a sin in the last days, 1 Tim. iii. 3. Lastly, in calling Boaz one of the redeemers, as the word translated *kinsmen* sheweth, it may put us in mind of this, that the Lord hath great care over the poor, who appointed by his law the redemption of lands to the family again from which it was sold, Lev. xxv. 25, Deut. xxv. 5, 6. And this care hath ever the Lord had, as may appear by commanding to relieve them, by promising to reward the good done unto them, by blessing such as have been merciful, and leaving their praises in the Scripture by publishing their reward at the last day, and by ordaining a law for the redemption of their estate among the Israelites. The consideration whereof may move the poor to be thankful and rest in God; and the rich to be good unto the poor, and herein to imitate the Lord, who so careth for them, as we see.

Ver. 21. *And Ruth the Moabitess said, He said unto me also, Thou shalt keep fast by my young men, until they have ended all my harvest.*

Ruth here relateth Boaz's further kindness, both what, and how long, to glean in his field after his reapers, as in the eighth verse, and that unto the end of harvest.

And Ruth the Moabitess said, He said unto me also, Thou shalt keep fast by my young men. When Ruth perceived the joy of Naomi for this kindness of Boaz, she goeth on to relate further testimony of his love; and it is as if she had said, Boaz did not only thus with me, as thou my mother hast heard and seen, but which is more, he willed me to continue with his servants till harvest be ended. Where we see, that where praises of others are well taken, it maketh the relater to express more fully their goodness. And therefore, to encourage men to give others their due praises, let us receive willingly the relation of their virtues and graces; for such is our corruption, that we can attend to ill reports, which makes many so ready to speak ill of others. I wish our ears open in the other respect, but in this I would we were more dull of hearing.   Three reasons may be given of the relation of this kindness to Naomi.   One may be this, to set out Boaz's praises, and to shew his kindness to the full even as she found it.   If so, then we learn, that thankful persons conceal nothing of others' kindnesses, either in word or deed, that may tend to their just commendations; and thus thankful should we be.   This thankfulness is an excellent virtue, commended in Scripture and practised of the godly, as before is noted; and on the contrary, ingratitude is odious, and causeth uncharitableness in giving, because the poor take not thankfully their alms; in lending also, and that either not at all, for that men be so dishonest, that they will not repay what they owe, or defer to pay in due time; or not freely, but for gain, because men would benefit themselves by other men's money, but will not willingly requite it without compact aforehand.   And thus we see the evil of ingratitude.   The other reason may be, to know her mother's pleasure therein, and how she liked of it to go still into Boaz's fields.   If this, then we may learn, that children are to take advice of their parents in their courses, so servants of their masters, for this is to give them honour; also an acknowledging themselves to be at their disposing, and not their own men, and it will free them from blame, when things, perhaps, fall out crossly.   It is a fault for such to run on ahead as best pleaseth themselves; this is disorder and unruliness not sufferable; this is 'headiness,' condemned by the apostle, 2 Tim. iii. 4, and much evil hath come hereby.   See it in Esau his marriages, Gen. xxvi. 35; in Dinah her wandering, Gen. xxxiv. 1; in Simeon and Levi their cruelty; in Abimelech's contentious servants, Gen. xxi. 25, 26, and Lot's servants; those might have bred heart-burning between Abimelech and Abraham, as these divided Abraham and Lot asunder.   Heady and unruly children and servants may do a great deal of mischief; they are therefore to be advised and to follow advice.   The third reason may be to shew her mother-in-law where she might with good profit continue to glean, and also of her willingness therefore to continue in that labour.   If so, then we see that the fruit of our labour, gain, and commodity, doth spur on the diligent to continue therein.   Therefore pray for a blessing to be encouraged in painstaking, and feeling the fruit, continue therein.

Until they have ended all my harvest.   They had a barley and wheat harvest, both here meant, as is plain in verse 23.   These words, *until they have made an end*, shew some length of this harvest, and his conceit of Ruth's painfulness, that she would continue to the end, and not give off after a day or two; they note also his love and mercy to the poor widows; and lastly, they set forth his equity and true liberality, that granted her freedom in his own, and not in other men's fields.   What further may be observed from hence, see before in the eighth verse, where the matter is handled; here only is the relation of her liberty

unto her mother-in-law.   In all which speech it is worthy the noting, that she speaketh not a word of Boaz's great commendation of her own self, ver. 11.   Which commendeth to us in her modesty, that is, to pass over our own praises, which is an example for our imitation, that we might not be condemned of vainglory, and to be such as be in love with themselves, as those be which love to tell of their own virtues.

Ver. 22.   *And Naomi said unto Ruth her daughter-in-law, It is good, my daughter, that thou go out with his maidens, that they meet thee not in another field.*

Naomi her good counsel, with the reason, drawn from peril and danger, if Ruth should not follow it.

And Naomi said unto Ruth her daughter-in-law.   Here note once for all, that plainly the writer of this history setteth down this conference, repeating again and again *Naomi*, and *mother-in-law*, and *Ruth the Moabitess*, and *daughter-in-law*, which I note to tax curious ears in these times, who can away neither with speech nor writing except all be very sententious, brief, without repetitions, or one word more than they conceit to be needful.   God's Spirit, the author of every good gift, be it ever so excellent, taught not this penman to be so curious; not that he would have holy things carelessly and rudely set down, as men censure it, but to humble proud wits given over to a light esteem of holy writ, not caring to read therein for the plainness of style,* that so through their own pride they might perish, as, alas! many of our high wits do, who cannot, in the haughtiness of their own hearts, descend to so low a pitch, nor vouchsafe to spend any time in such homely histories as be in the Scripture, because, as they profanely judge, the style is not stately enough for their carnal hearts.   And as this taxeth these proud and profane persons, so also doth it such as do despise or carelessly neglect many good men's labours, only for the plainness of the speech, as if all writings were weak which are void of strong lines.   These dainty palates can away with nothing but what is finely cooked, because they come not with hunger after good things, but are carried away more with the manner than with the matter, and so more with shadows than substances, as in likelihood it would appear if they should come to the trial of religion and suffering for the name of Christ.

It is good, my daughter, that thou go out with his maidens.   This is Naomi her advice to Ruth.   From whence, note, I. That parents are not to be wanting in giving good counsel to their children: as here a mother-in-law to Ruth, and Jethro, a father-in-law, to Moses, Exod. xviii.; David to Solomon, 1 Kings ii.; and Eli to his sons, 1 Sam. ii. 23–25.   It is their duty so to do, and the younger years need it, wanting the expe-

---

* Albeit, what human eloquence could ever attain to the sublimity of style used in the prophetical books of sacred Scripture, as in Isaiah, Jeremiah, and others?

rience of the aged. Let parents perform then this duty, shewing their children what is good, what duties they owe to God and man, and how they should demean themselves well every way. Contrary to these do they which take no care to advise their children, but do let them follow their own swing. Such also as counsel for the body, as the heathen may do, but not for the soul, as Christians should do, Eph. vi. 4, Deut. vi. 7. Thirdly, those wicked parents which counsel their children not to do well, but to do ill, to lie, swear, steal, as many poor do; or to dice, card, drink, or to do worse, as men desiring to be counted of another rank wickedly teach their children by their lewd examples, to their shame and their children's ruin, the infecting of the commonwealth, and the destruction of their house many times. Whereas, such parents as do advise well their children, do discharge their duty towards God and their country, and acquit their souls from the blood of their children, Titus ii. 3, 4. II. That it is good for women going abroad to associate themselves to those of their own sex; for they are subject to be tempted, to be deceived, and abused, being weak in temptation and easily overcome. Let women learn here of Naomi her advice to Ruth, and follow it; let them beware of being alone, as Dinah, or in suspected places with lewd women, or in light and wanton company. It is no good sign of a maiden's chastity to seek to be in men's company, as many do, till shame come upon them.

That they meet thee not in another field. Meaning some lewd and lustful men, whom Naomi will not so much as make mention of. Though Ruth named in verse 21 young men, yet her mother-in-law will not name them; she avoids the mentioning of men to her, as teaching her, and so all others, that women should avoid, in their private conferences, unnecessary talk of men. Note, moreover, that it is wisdom to prevent dangers, and not expose ourselves into peril when we may avoid it, Num. xiv. 42, 43. Naomi knew the danger of those times, and how wickedly many were bent, and ready to abuse a poor young woman and a stranger, and therefore she teacheth Ruth to be wise to prevent the same; for if we unnecessarily cast ourselves into danger, we do tempt God, which we may not do, Mat. iv. 7, Deut. vi. 16. It is not 'our way,' and therefore we have no promise of protection, Ps. xci. 11; and God hath punished his own people for so doing, as we may see in the Israelites, Num. xiv. 42, 45; and in good Josias, who escaped not correction, 2 Chron. xxxv. 22, 23. And therefore let us learn to be wise to prevent dangers, and not carelessly expose ourselves thereinto. Nature teacheth this to beasts, much more reason should persuade man unto it; and religion alloweth it, and commendeth that prudent man that seeth the evil and avoids it, Prov. xxii. 3, when they have no just cause to the contrary. I mean the evils of trouble, crosses and such like; for the evil of sin is ever to be avoided, of which it may be Solomon

doth speak; yet is it wisdom to avoid unnecessary crosses, and troubles of this life, and such dangers as may procure our hurt, as Jehoram did by the advice of Elisha, 2 Kings vi., discovering the armies of the Syrians unto him, that he might not be endangered by them. If here any object the certain danger that Micaiah willingly did run into, when he went to prophesy before Ahab, who hated him, and such like, I answer, that men cast themselves into danger two ways: first, by the virtue of their calling, either ordinary or extraordinary, as did Micaiah, which men may not forsake for any trouble or danger whatsoever. The other is without a calling. Such fool-hardiness hath no assurance of a blessing; if they escape the peril, it is God's great mercy, and not their deserving; and if trouble come upon them, they can have no comfort in it, but must take it as a rod of correction, to teach them to be more wise afterwards.

Ver. 23. *So she kept fast by the maidens of Boaz to glean unto the end of barley-harvest, and of wheat-harvest; and dwelt with her mother-in-law.*

The obedience of Ruth, in following Naomi her advice, and her constant love unto her, in not departing from her.

So she kept fast by the maidens of Boaz to glean. Concerning Ruth here we may learn, that children are to take the good counsel of their parents, and to follow the same; as Ruth doth here, and as did Jacob, yea, Moses the advice of Jethro. It is the note of a wise child, and a child's duty, if the counsel be wholesome and good, Prov. xiii. 1, and i. 8, 9, and xxiii. 22. And it is a reproof to rebellious children, which will not learn nor obey, like the sons of Eli, and of Samuel; but they paid for it, as ever such shall do.

Unto the end of barley-harvest, and of wheat-harvest. All this time Ruth applied herself for profit, as being the time of gathering food for winter. She played the ant, and not the grasshopper, Prov. vi. 8; for it is good thrift not to slack the time of our profit, which God in mercy affordeth to us. This may we learn of the ant, to which the Lord sendeth the sluggard, Prov. xxvii. 24; for riches are not for ever, nor the like time to get them, and therefore must we take the season offered, especially in harvest, which calleth forth every one to take pains to gather in God's blessings for their life and maintenance. Perhaps some will say, that Christ willeth us not to take care, Mat. vi. 31, 34. But doth he will ever any man not to labour? The care which Christ speaketh of is immoderate care, care without faith, or care full of doubting, and little faith, ver. 30; and that which is without care of religion, the mind being taken up wholly with the world, ver. 33; else men may, yea, and ought, to labour for the things of this life, to be provident for the time to come, and frugal in expenses for the time present.

And she dwelt with her mother-in-law. That is, all that time of harvest and after. This is noted, to shew

Ruth's love and constant affection towards Naomi, that no favour abroad, or gain reaped by the labour of her hands, could make her forsake her mother-in-law. Hence riseth a good lesson, that children's favour abroad and good gettings should not draw them from their poor parents, so long as they stand in need of their help. For how can children ever shew themselves thankful better than in such a case, where what they get they can willingly bestow it upon their poor parents, so maintaining them, who were the authors of their being, and instruments of God for their education? But, alas, the case is otherwise now. This Ruth the Moabitess, a heathen by birth, may rise up in judgment against such as should be natural children, who having gotten from under their parents, when they see they can live of themselves, they make no reckoning of them, being altogether unwilling to live with them, and most of all to relieve them.

CHAPTER III.

IN this chapter is Naomi her care to provide a match for Ruth, to requite her labour and love towards her; wherein may be observed her advice, the execution thereof, and the good event of the same.

Ver. 1. *Then Naomi her mother-in-law said unto her, My daughter, shall I not seek rest for thee, that it may be well with thee?*

This is Naomi her resolution, to provide a marriage for her daughter-in-law. It is propounded with an interrogation, to shew her full determination. Here note who resolveth, for whom, and what it is, and the end why.

Then Naomi her mother-in-law said unto her, My daughter. Here Naomi deviseth how to requite Ruth her love and labour, which is by resolving to get a match for her; and this she doth, as a mother doth for her daughter, after that Ruth had so laboured, and now was at rest with her in the house. Of the term *daughter* before, and also of thankfulness, how good turns should be requited (which here is Naomi's purpose), I have spoken at large.

Shall I not seek? As if she had said, Know it, my daughter, that I am resolved to seek rest for thee. It is the parents' duty to provide matches for their children, 1 Cor. vii. 36. So did God, the general Father, for his son Adam, Gen. ii.; Abraham for Isaac, Gen. xxiv.; and Isaac for Jacob, Gen. xxviii. For children want judgment to make their choice, and are led more by fond affection, or by strength of lust, which is worse, than by reason and good discretion. But yield they were wise in their choice, yet are they not so to do it without consent of parents; but should do as Samson did, Judges xiv. 1, 2, who entreated his father and mother to get him for a wife the maid which he liked. Let therefore parents have a care of this duty, and betimes provide for their children, as they shall see just cause, and so make choice, as one may be a mutual help to another. For this end let them observe their natures, like somewhat in years, in conditions, and body in some sort, that one may be pleased with the other. Then know their religion and virtues, that they may be of one heart towards God; so shall they love one another much better, pray for one another, and have a fellow-feeling in every condition; yea, this will sweeten their estate unto them. When they have noted well these two, if with good natures and graces they can procure goods, it shall not be amiss, to help to bear the burden of marriage. Such parents are here to be reproved which neglect this duty, either of carelessness, wanting true love; or of wicked covetousness, for that they are not willing to spare anything from themselves, though they yet have sufficient.

Rest for thee? So she calleth the married estate. The word* is a place of rest to settle in. Marriage estate is an estate of rest; so here called, and in chap. i. 9, in respect of the mind of all such as desire marriage, and have not the gift of continency, they are restless. It is called therefore *portum juventutis;* because youth are tossed by lustful thoughts, as the ship with the waves of the sea, till they be married. *Mulieri* (saith one) *nulla est requies, donec nupserit.* It may also be called rest, for the contentment and delight which one ought to have in the other, and in the blessing of posterity, by the mercy of God. Seeing it is so called, let the married parties labour to make it an estate of rest and peace. And the means be these: first, to love one another entirely. To work this, see the good things in one another, and cover the evil, and wink at defects, and be as blind that way after marriage as they be before. Secondly, to perform duties of love one to another cheerfully; so they have promised, so God commands them, and so the mutual good of both requireth it, and true love will do it. Thirdly, to bear one another's infirmities patiently, for they be one, else this will make them two, if they cannot bear with one another, and forbear too, to keep peace. Fourthly, to take their outward estate of God thankfully, and live in this respect contentedly, let them not think how better they might have been; for such discontented thoughts breed but sorrows, and help nothing at all to quietness, but rather to increase discord. Fifthly, to pray daily one for another, and that fervently, that God would remove the hindrances of love, or give wisdom and patience to bear the same. Sixthly, and lastly, in every discontentment to lay the fault rather upon ourself, than to cast it upon the other. Let the husband think rather

* נוח of מנוח, *placidè quievit.*

389

the cause to be in himself than in his wife, so the wife is rather to blame herself than her husband. If thus the married would do, faults would be soon amended, and jars prevented; and the failing in these things is the cause that marriage is not the estate of rest, but a miserable, restless condition, and that through their own sins and corruptions.

That it may be well with thee. Marriage is for the well-being of such as enter into that holy estate. The husband is for a guide to the woman, and the woman is ordained for a meet help for the man, Gen. ii. 18. And therefore this is for confutation of those which simply prefer single life before marriage; nay, doth not God say, 'It is not good for man to be alone'? Marriage is called an honourable estate, and is commended far before the other life in Scripture. It maketh two one; it is the holy means of a lawful posterity, and it is the estate in which the most holiest have lived, and in which Christ himself would be born, though conceived by the Holy Ghost, and born of his mother a virgin. Saint Paul indeed commendeth single life; but not simply, but with respect unto the then present times, full of troubles and persecutions. If marriage be then for well-being, let parents take care to provide for their children matches fit and commodious, for religion, for conditions and means of maintenance, for so shall it be well with them. And let such as be married, so make a right use of marriage, that it may be for their well-being, and the bettering of themselves, which stands in three things: first, in the mutual society and near fellowship of one another, for 'two are better than one;' secondly, in preventing thereby incontinency, and the sinful lusts of the flesh; thirdly, in begetting an holy posterity, training them up in the instruction and information of the Lord, in whom their parents do live, after they be dead.

Ver. 2. *And now is not Boaz of our kindred, with whose maidens thou wast? Behold, he winnoweth barley to-night in the threshing-floor.*

Naomi propoundeth to Ruth the party whom she desireth to match her with, giving a reason, and shewing the opportunity of time and place where to break the matter unto him.

As Naomi affected to do Ruth good, so she devised the means; for a true friend is not in show only, or in well-wishes, but in devising how to bring to pass what they desire, and to effect what truly they do affect. Jonathan wished well to David, 1 Sam. xix. 2, 3, and xx. 12, 13, and he devised means for his safety. Abraham wished well to Lot, Gen. xiv., and therefore endeavoured to do him good, and to recover him when he was led away captive. Where we then wish well, let us shew it, in counsel, in help, in countenance, and not be as such, which will not advise their friends of their own accord, nor help them in adversity, hardly countenance them when any of note frown upon

them. Some are friends like Peter, in the time of his weakness, who followed his Master in trouble afar off; some like Paul's friends, who forsook him wholly in peril; some like Jehoshaphat, who can speak well a word or two for a Micaiah, but not stand out for him, when he is sent by Ahab to prison most unjustly. Many friends there be, but yet few friends indeed.

And now is not Boaz of our kindred? How akin to them, see chap. i. 1, and ii. 1. This kindred she nameth, because of the law in Deut. xxv. 5, 6, of which afterwards in chap. iv. Here we do see what ground she had to seek this match for Ruth, even the law of God, as she thought. Her ground in thus making choice was from God, and therefore there was more hope to speed, though in man's reason most unlikely. Note, that godly parents seek to match their children where God alloweth. Abraham will not match with the Cananites, Gen. xxiv., but sends into his own country, and thither Isaac and Rebekah send Jacob; for as in other things, so in this they set God before them, looking to his liking and approbation, that they may expect his blessing. Therefore, let such as intend to marry, marry in the Lord, have his consent, and pray for his presence at the marriage-making, at which he will be, if it be after his will, that is, when parties marry lawfully, and in the fear of his name. Other marriages he will not countenance; as these; first, such as be made within degrees forbidden, though allowed by the usurped authority of the pope's forged vicarship; secondly, with infidels, as did the Jews, Neh. xiii. 25, 26, and into which sin fell Solomon, 1 Kings xi. 1; thirdly, with idolaters, though they profess the true God, and yet worship idols, as did Ahab; and therefore Jehoshaphat his marrying of Jehoram his son with Athaliah, was unlawful, and punished heavily by God: such is the marriage of a protestant with a papist; fourthly, with wretched worldlings, and such as be without religion in truth and sincerity, 1 Cor. v. 10, 11; for if we have not ordinary familiarity with the wicked, with such as be fornicators, covetous, extortioners, railers, drunkards, inordinate livers, idle without callings, and disobedient to the word, blasphemers, ungodly, despisers of those that be good, lovers of pleasures more than lovers of God, and such like; if, I say, we may not keep familiar company with such, then certainly we may not marry with them; their birth, wealth, and conceited hope to win them, cannot make way for such marriages to them which fear God, and love their own souls. Fifthly, with such as be unjustly divorced; for that is to marry another man's wife, and to commit adultery. These marriages are made after the flesh, where the devil danceth, but God is displeased, and good angels, and good men offended.

With whose maidens thou wast. These words are added, to shew what Boaz she meant, and also to give Ruth some hope of good success. For Ruth might object three things, which Naomi in this verse preventeth. She might have said, Alas, I am poor, what hope of one so rich ? To which Naomi answereth, He is thy kinsman, and therefore by law bound to marry with thee ; though herein she did somewhat err. Again, if Ruth had said, I am not known well to him, and I fear his dislike, Naomi here putteth her in mind with whom she had been, even with Boaz, who had taken notice of her, and had been kind to her, and had spoken well of her ; yea, in this she calleth a particular kindness of Boaz to her remembrance, who willed her to abide with his maidens. Thirdly, if Ruth had objected the want of opportunity and fit occasion to speak to him, 'Behold' (saith Naomi) ' he winnoweth this night barley in the threshing-floor.' So then note, that warrant from God, experience of the love of man, and fit occasion to effect a matter, are strong inducements to attempt the same. These made Esther to adventure to go unto Ahasuerus, her calling from God, her experience of former favour, and the present cause requiring, and occasion offered to make trial ; and where these concur, let us boldly do our endeavour, with hope to effect what we go about.

Behold. That is, see and consider the providence of God ; it is as one would wish, it falleth out opportunely, as if God had decreed to bring it to pass. So Naomi observed God's providence plainly, for it appeareth manifestly, where and when he decreeth to bring things to pass, so as we may say, Behold, the hand of the Lord ! And this either for good, as in preventing Mordecai's destruction, Esther vi. 1, 3 ; the widow of Sarepta her famishment, 1 Kings xvii. 10–14 ; David from the hand of Saul, 1 Sam. xxiii. 27 ; Moses from drowning, Exod. ii. 5 ; and Joseph from perishing in the pit, Gen. xxxvii. 24, 28 ; or for evil, to bring judgment upon the wicked, as upon Jezebel and Jehoram, 2 Kings ix. 15, 21, 25, 30, 36, as God had threatened, catching them as it were in a trap, the one in the portion of Naboth, and the other in Jezreel. For the Lord seeth all things, and his eyes are upon the ways of men, to bring his decree to pass by his power and providence, Job xxviii. 24, xxxv. 21.

Let us, then, cast our eyes about us, and observe God's providence ; for so shall we see both his mercy and justice to praise him ; it will make us patient and contented under every cross, and carefully to rely upon him, when we see how his providence waiteth upon his promise, good will, and pleasure. Yea, this will comfort us, and make us not to fear what man can do unto us, seeing his hand is ready to help.

He winnoweth barley to-night in the threshing-floor. For the threshing-floors in those times, it seemeth, from the first of Samuel, chap. xxiii. and other places, that they were abroad in the fields, as the wine-presses were ; and this place sheweth that Ruth went out of city thither. In such a place, David built an altar to the Lord in the threshing-floor of Ornan, 2 Chron. iii. 1. Of the manner how it was made is not expressed in the Scripture. It may also seem that the winnow-
391

ing was towards the evening in those hot countries, when the wind did arise called the wind of the day ; or as in Genesis it is translated, ' the cool of the day,' Gen. iii. 8. Boaz, though he winnowed not himself in person, yet he may be so said to do, in commanding his servants, he there being a diligent overseer, and a helper forward of the work with his presence. Howsoever, this may we learn, that it is no unseemliness for men of birth, of place and wealth, sometime to follow in their own persons mean labours of their calling ; as he doth here winnowing of corn, Gideon his threshing, Judah his sheep-shearing, Elisha his plough. This they did not of base niggardliness, as loath to keep servants to do it, but to exercise themselves in labour, which is healthful, to prevent idleness and ill fruits thereof, to be an example to others, as was Julius Cæsar, who would go bare-headed, and on foot, both in hot sunshine and in foul weather often before his soldiers ;* and as the Lord Lacy, chief-justice in Ireland,† who took up stones to bear them to the building he had in hand, to provoke the lazy Irish to take pains. Which reproveth those which do condemn them that so take pains, being persons of worth, as if it were discredit to them, and to be basely accounted of for so doing ; when yet we see out of the Scripture, men (as these proud fellows hold them) of mean callings, chosen to high places ; as Moses from keeping sheep, to be ruler of God's people ; so David to be king ; Gideon from threshing to be captain over the host of Israel ; Elisha from the plough to be the Lord's prophet ; so Amos from the herd ; Peter from a poor fisherman's estate to be an apostle. And the like we find in heathen history of one L. Q. Cincinnatus,‡ who was fetched from the plough to be made dictator in Rome, and after returned to husbandry again. Thus we see how great men did set themselves to callings (now held base and mean by proud and riotous spirits), and also many highly advanced from mean places and low estate of life, for their worthiness and virtuous industry for which they were honoured, how mean soever by birth or education. Such were these emperors, Pertinax, an artificer's son ; Diocletian, a scrivener's son ; Valentian, the son of a shoemaker ; and of a gardener came Probus. Let our lazy and lewd roysters, upstart gentry, or such as come of worthy ancestors, yet having no worthiness in themselves, behold these, and learn to do as Maximinus Senior did, who, when he was general, did take such pains in mean matters as others found fault with him. But he answered them, *quò major fuero, tantò plus laborabo,* the greater I am, the greater pains will I take. If our youngsters would think hereof, they would not scorn to take pains as they do, and yet scorn not to live in a more base course, unworthy their gentility of which they so much stand, and most unworthy their Christianity, which they too little regard. Whatsoever men's birth and estate be, yet ought they to labour in a calling, because

* Sueton.   † Irish Chron.   ‡ Eutrop. Val. Max.

God so commandeth, Gen. iii. 19, to avoid idleness, to prevent much evil, which cometh from idleness, to live not as caterpillars, but as profitable members in the commonwealth, to be an example of well-doing to others, and to be the better able to maintain their estate and place, both to themselves and to their succeeding posterity also.

Ver. 3. *Wash thyself, therefore, and anoint thee, and put thy raiment upon thee, and get thee down to the floor; but make not thyself known to the man until he shall have done eating and drinking.*

Naomi her counsel to her daughter-in-law, Ruth, shewing whither she should go, what to do before in preparing to go thither, and how warily she should carry herself for being known till after supper.

Wash thyself, therefore. That is, because I would have thee to go to him, make thyself ready, and first wash thyself. Washing is double: first, inward, which the apostle exhorteth unto, 2 Cor. vii. 1, Titus iii. 5; and this is it David prayed for, Ps. li., and without which none can enter into the kingdom of God, John iii. With this washing are we to approach nigh unto God, as Ruth by her washing went unto Boaz. The second is outward, and this is threefold: first, typical under the law, commanded to the priests and people when they drew near to God, Exod. xl. 31, 32, and xix. 10, Titus iii. 5, which was a type of sanctification and holiness, Ps. xxvi. 6; secondly, superstitious, as that of the Jews, taken up of themselves, and condemned by Christ, Mat. xv. 2, Mark vii. 3, 4; thirdly, civil cleanliness, the washing of the body from all bodily uncleanness; and this is here meant and here commended unto us. This outward civil cleanliness is praiseworthy. And this washing was used among the Jews, 2 Sam. xi. 2 and xii. 20, and among the heathen, Exod. ii. 19. Eusebius* speaketh of John's bathing himself. To be cleanly is healthful to us, delightsome to others, and commendable. God required of his people cleanliness, Deut. xxiii. 13. Our Christian profession is pure and holy, which outward cleanness well befitteth; and seeing it is of good report, we are to observe it, Philip. iv. 8. This reproveth two sorts: the first are such as be sluttish, nasty, and beastlike persons, who hereby shew themselves careless of their credit, slothful, or covetous, they be offensive, uncivil, and unwholesome.† The other sort are they which will be cleanly, but yet spend too much time in trimming, washing, and starching, and are so curiously neat, and so careful to be fine and fair outwardly, as they spend their days almost in doing nothing else, and so live a proud and idle life, like the haughty dames of Israel in their bravery, walking with stretched forth necks, with wanton eyes, with tinkling feet, walking and mincing as they go, wanting humility and often modesty

in gesture, countenance, and gait. But let them read and remember what the prophet Isaiah threateneth against such lascivious wantons and luxurious minions, in the end of his third chapter.

And anoint thee. Anointing had a religious use, as we may see in Exod. xl., Lev. vii., Num. vii. 1, 1 Sam. ix. 16, which did type out the graces of God's Spirit, Ezek. xvi. 9, 1 John ii. 27. This is the best anointing, and to be laboured for. It had also a common use, as here, so in 2 Sam. xii. 20, it was usual, Mat. vi. 17, for God's blessings may be used not only for mere necessity, but also for outward comeliness and moderate delight. The creatures of God may be used not only for preservation of bodily life, but for beautifying of the body and the better setting forth thereof, as it is in truth and not counterfeited. Thus wine is given to glad the heart, and oil to make the face to shine, Ps. civ. 15. And therefore may Christians lawfully use God's creatures for outward comeliness, and to preserve that outward seemliness which is God's own work in us, by washing and by anointing. But here beware of excess, that it be also seasonable, that it be to a good end; beware of pride, of wantonness, and learn to know the time of humiliation.

Quest. Here it may be questioned, Whether it be lawful to paint the face, for it is but an oil?

Ans. Surely no. First, because this is not to preserve thy natural beauty, by oil to make it shine, but to make a counterfeit face, which is deceit and hypocrisy, which God hateth. We must lay aside all manner of hypocrisy, 1 Peter ii. 1, and this is one of them. Secondly, this is vanity of vanities; for if beauty be vanity, Prov. xxxi. 30, then much more the filthy counterfeit of it. It is great folly, for such spoil their natural comeliness at length, as experience telleth, and the prophet Jeremiah speaketh of rending the face with painting, Jer. iv. 30. Thirdly, this is great pride, for they dislike the Lord's workmanship, and adulterate it, and would be held fairer than God ever made them, and do proudly glory before men of a counterfeit visage. Fourthly, it is not held a matter of good report and honesty, which godly persons should follow after, Philip. iv. 8, but of dishonesty, such being judged to be light and lewd. In the Scripture it is the mark of a whore, and a whorish woman is described, Jer. iv. 30, Ezek. xxiii. 40, and an ungodly woman so practised it, even that harlot and murderess Jezebel painted herself, 2 Kings ix. 30; and we find by experience such to be wantons and lewdly given. Fifthly, the godly and learned fathers have utterly condemned it. Saint Cyprian saith,* it is the work of the devil, and they offer wrong to God in despising his work and framing another of their own. Tertullian† calleth it the devil's business, unworthy a Christian.

---

* Euseb. Histo. Eccles.
† Read Calvin on Deut. xxiii. 13.

* Est opus diaboli, et manus inferunt Deo, &c.—*De habitu virgin.*
† Negotium diaboli, indignum Christiano.—*De cultu fœm.*

Saint Jerome saith* that it is the fire of youth, the fuel of lust, and the sign of an unchaste mind. Saint Ambrose saith,† they which muse or set their minds upon the adultery of the countenance, do so also upon the adulterating of chastity. So as these godly men think of them but as of whores, the devil's servants, betrayers of chastity, and unworthy to be accounted Christians. Let such, therefore, as never used it beware of it; and such as have, repent; and such as do, abandon and forsake it. For as verbal lying is forbidden, so actual also; such cannot look upon God as his creatures, but as counterfeits, and such as be of the devil's making; they see not their own natural face in a glass, but the counterfeit of another, one perhaps damned in hell for whoredom already. Such as have used this sinful practice, and have turned to God, have repented of this as of an accursed work of the flesh, and as proceeding from Satan's instigation. Lastly, no modest matron ever used it, but chaste hearts have always detested it, and therefore is it carefully to be avoided.

And put thy raiment upon thee. That is, thy best apparel, or such as thou hast put upon thee handsomely. Concerning apparel I will speak somewhat at large. In innocency there was no need of raiment. Adam and Eve in that estate lived naked, and were not ashamed, neither was there cause, for that they had not sinned; but after the fall it was of necessity to put on apparel to cover our nakedness, for preservation of our bodies, and to defend them from extreme cold, heat, and from hurts which they are subject unto in going naked. So then, now we should have care for raiment, for ourselves, for such as depend upon us, Prov. xxxi. 21, and for the poor, as Job had, Job xxxi. 19. Touching this necessity of wearing apparel, it is agreed upon all hands; nature teacheth it and need enforceth it, and herein to have not only one suit, but change also for shift, if we be able; for it is lawful to have change of raiment, yea, to wear costly apparel so it be comely. Of which I will speak in order. We may have change of raiment; there is a necessity in it, a cleanliness also, and Joseph in love gave to Benjamin five changes of raiment for him to wear, Gen. xlv. 22. If any object our Saviour his forbidding two coats, Mat. x. 10, we must know it was no absolute forbidding, for there he also forbids providing of money for their journey and other things else; but this was to shew that they were to make speed, and also to teach them to depend upon his providence, for he undertook to provide for them in this journey. And by this experience of Christ's mercy towards them, he would teach them how to trust in God when he was to send them abroad into all the world after his ascension. And therefore the

begging friars have hence no ground for their idle life, and for their having but one coat. True it is that to have changes of raiment and to see our brother naked, having no clothes to put on, and yet we not supply his want, were an unmercifulness, if so by our neglect of him he should perish; otherwise we may wear change of raiment, yea, and put on costly also, with changeable colours and ornaments upon. Solomon wore costly attire, so his wife, Ps. xlv.; Joseph, Gen. xli. 42; Mordecai, Esther viii. 15; and Esau in Isaac's house, Gen. xxvii. 29; they wore also garments of divers colours, Gen. xxxvii. 7, so did Joseph in Jacob's house; and Tamar, David's daughter, 2 Sam. xiii. 18; and Mordecai was clad in white, blue, and purple, Esther viii. And as for ornaments, as ear-rings, bracelets, chains, rings, jewels of gold and silver, the Lord allowed them to his people, and to wear them upon them, Exod. xxxii. 2; and so did Rebekah wear such, sent by Abraham for Isaac's wife, Gen. xxiv. 22, 23. They be made for man's use, and therefore the godly using them and God allowing them, we may use now our Christian liberty therein. But here we must observe decency, which is a comeliness befitting the person of every one. And here must be considered, first, age, young or old, for the same colour and fashion befit not both alike. Secondly, the sex, man and woman; for these must be distinguished, as God ordained in Moses's law. Nature itself, reason, and laws of well-governed commonweals, do so ordain also.* Thirdly, the profession and calling of persons, and the difference in place; for some be public, some be private, which must be looked unto. It is therefore reproveable for public persons, out of baseness, not to go as their place requireth; and for private persons to go beyond their calling and their condition of life, although it be not above their hability, for this breedeth confusion and discord, when such also as by profession should be grave, as scholars and ministers, yet do go ruffian-like, it is worthy of reproof and punishment also. Fourthly, the manner of wearing must be observed, it must be comely, with shamefacedness and modesty, 1 Tim. ii. 9, both in men and women; we must so wear our apparel as grace and virtue, and not corruption of heart and vice, should appear to be in us. The virtues which must appear in us by our attire are these:—First, is modesty, for raiment was to cover our shame, and therefore that whorish fashion of going with naked breasts and so low uncovered as some do, is to be abhorred of modest women and chaste virgins. Sulpitius Gallus, a heathen Roman, fell out with his wife because she went about with her face uncovered, and said to her, The law limits my sight unto thee, to which thou art to approve thy beauty, and to become fair and lovely; but to be willing to be seen beautiful to others, must needs bring suspicion of an ill mind and a stain withal. I

* Ignis juventutis, fomentum libidinis, et impudicæ mentis indicium.—*Epist. ad Marcel.*
† Vultus meditantur adulterium castitatis, &c.—*De adulterio.*

* *Vide* Kick. de politeia, lib. i. cap. 10.

wish husbands to be Sulpitius-like to such wives as go thus wantonly bare-breasted, shewing how naked their hearts be unto lustful practices. But some foolish and harlotry husbands do delight to see their wives and daughters to go so; they be like Ahasuerus, who will have Vashti to come forth to shew herself; but I wish the wives in this thing like Vashti, and not to yield to their drunken-humoured husbands to go so immodestly. But they are, perhaps, rewarded as they justly deserve sometime; for can the shop windows alway stand open, and no customers come at any time to buy? Secondly, is gravity according to years, and therefore all fantastic, light, vain, and daily strange fashions, now in one, then in another, is folly and vanity, apish toying, and argueth great levity of mind, condemned by the word, Zeph. i. 8, and by all sober and grave persons. Thirdly, is frugality, for excessive cost is unthriftiness, and herein a great consumption to a man's estate, and an argument of idleness, if men go costly. The rich glutton is taxed for going costly and faring daintily every day, Luke xv., which brought him to hell at last. Fourthly, is humility, for indeed our raiment from the first cause is a sign of our rebellion against God, and that we have lost our innocency; and therefore we have no more cause to be proud thereof than a malefactor of his halter, though it be golden. It is reproved as a fault in the daughters of Judah, Isa. iii., to be so proud of their attire; and we have more reason to weep than to wax high-minded by this covering of our shame and nakedness. I wish we were like one Pambo, a godly man; being at Alexandria and there seeing a woman proud of her attire fell a-weeping,* and being asked why he so wept, said thus, Two causes move me: the one, to consider the perdition of this woman; and the other, for that I, being a Christian, cannot study so much to please Christ by innocency of life, as she doth hereby desire to please filthy and dishonest men. Fifthly, is piety, when, in time of humiliation and days of abstinence, we go as such should who feel the hand of God and apprehend his displeasure against sin, and when we so array ourselves daily as that modesty, gravity, frugality, and humility may appear therein; for why should we not even in our clothing set forth our profession, and thereby grace our religion? And this piety shall appear, if when we garnish the body we neglect not to beautify the soul with learning and religion; for a man in rich clothes, without other better qualities and endowments of mind, is, as Diogenes said, a sheep in a golden fleece. And yet such sheep have we in our English pasture, for want of grace and better education, having nothing to set them out withal but the bravery of their clothing, which Augustus Cæsar called, the ensign of pride and the nest of luxury, *vexillum superbiæ, et nidus luxuriæ;* which we find in these days to be young men's over-

* Pet. de Natalib. Eccles. Hist., lib. viii. cap. 1

throw, a let to good housekeeping, an enforcing to enhancing of rents in landlords, and in others to fall to ill shifts, when their own means of lands and revenues fail them. And thus much for this point.

And get thee down to the floor. Take the opportunity offered to procure thy welfare. So she is made by Naomi her advice to go to Boaz and to demand marriage of him; which might seem not fitting, but by Moses's law it was allowed to the woman widow without children, Deut. xxiii., to claim marriage of the next kinsman, if he neglected to take her; and it was no more immodesty for women to claim that right then, than now for one betrothed to challenge the man for her husband; for where God alloweth the thing, it taketh away the scandal and offence which otherwise might justly be given, and so others justly be offended therewith; which is not a small comfort against the uncharitable censure of unadvised persons.

But make not thyself known to the man, until he shall have done eating and drinking. Go she must, but so warily is she to behave herself, as she should not discover herself, nor make her mind known, until he had supped, and was laid down to rest, so as her mind must be shewed in private, and to him alone. The night, and in private, make modest persons utter more freely their thoughts than otherwise they would in the light, and before company. The phrase of eating and drinking implieth feasting, as appeareth hence from verse 7, and from other scriptures, Mat. xxiv., Isa. xxii. 13, Exod. xxxii. 6, 1 Kings iv. 20. So then, at such a time as this, it may seem the Israelites feasted and made merry, as a sign of gladness and rejoicing in the Lord's blessings. Of feasting I will speak afterwards in verse 7. Here note that Naomi held it the best time to speak of marriage, when Boaz had well eaten and drunken, for then are men more apt to speak freely, and to promise their good will, than at other times. This Naomi knew well, and therefore advised Ruth to make use of it. Which being so, it should make men at such times more silent and more observant of their speeches.

Ver. 4. *And it shall be, when he lieth down, thou shalt mark the place where he shall lie, and thou shalt go in, and uncover his feet, and lay thee down; and he will tell thee what thou shalt do.*

The rest of Naomi her advice to Ruth, what she was to do when she came to the threshing-floor, observe where Boaz lay, then she herself to lie down; and the end, to know his mind, and what she should do.

And it shall be, when he lieth down. After labour follows rest, and the night is appointed for the same, to refresh the wearied limbs. So the psalmist teacheth, Ps. civ. 23, and Jacob practised, Gen. xxviii. 11, and this is the right use of time. Let us spend the day in labour, and take the benefit of the night for rest, with thanks to God, and prayer for a blessing, and not be as wild beasts, as some men be, who make the day their time of rest, and the night their walking time, as fit to go abroad to raven for their prey, or to spend it in unlawful and lewd courses as ill as theft.

That thou shalt mark the place where he shall lie. This is advised lest she should in the night mistake; for wary observation preventeth error. This sheweth also that Boaz had not any certain set place to lie down in, but to lie, as best liked himself, in the floor. In those times they had no care of stately lodging; they were not effeminate and slothful, which make us now to seek for soft bedding, which breedeth lust, increaseth sloth, and maketh the body more tender, and so less able to endure pains.

And thou shalt go in, and uncover his feet. Though Naomi aimed to make Ruth Boaz his yokefellow, yet she teacheth her to proceed in humility, to go to his feet, and to lie down there; for humility is not any let, but the way to advancement, and the reward thereof is riches, and glory, and life, Prov. xv. 35, and xviii. 20, and xxii. 4. Let all them which hope for preferment labour for humility, for God giveth such grace and favour; the humble in spirit shall enjoy glory, Prov. iii. 34, and xxix. 23. Upon Mary her lowliness did the Lord look, Luke i. 48. David was humble in his own eyes, and obtained great glory; and Abigail, by so wise and humble behaviour, purchased favour in David's eyes. On the contrary, by pride cometh confusion, as may appear in Absalom and Adonijah's attempt to the kingdom; for shame accompanieth it; and pride goeth before destruction, and a high mind before the fall, Prov. xi. 2, and xvi. 18.

And lay thee down, and he shall tell thee what thou shalt do. Naomi was well persuaded of Boaz his honesty, and that he would well advise Ruth; for good counsel may be looked for of those that be truly religious and wise withal, as Boaz was; and there is no doubt of their readiness, whom experience hath made known to be loving and kind. This is it which made Naomi to speak thus confidently, that Boaz would tell Ruth what she should do. But here it may be demanded, whether Naomi did well to advise Ruth to use this means to try Boaz his mind? The manner seemeth not to be good nor approveable, and my reasons be these: First, Naomi her counsel and advice to have Ruth to go to Boaz to claim the marriage was erroneous, for he was not the next kinsman, and therefore she should not have come thus first to him. Secondly, Boaz his speech implieth that it was not a matter of good report for them two to be thus alone together, if they had been seen so. Thirdly, there was some show and appearance of evil, which should be avoided, 1 Thes. v. Fourthly, because here was an occasion of sinning offered, though not taken, nor intended; because fleshliness is that sin to which most are apt, and the most excellent have fallen into it, as appeareth in righteous Lot, strong Samson, wise Solomon, and zealous David. Yet for all this ill advice

395

and manner of doing, the Lord turned the same to good. For this is his goodness and mercy, that matters ill begun the Lord both can and will turn unto good. Thus he did with Rebekah and Jacob's dissembling to get the blessing, and with the selling of Joseph by Jacob's sons, his unnatural brethren. This example, therefore, of Ruth is not imitable. It giveth no warrant for mothers to teach their daughters to play the harlots, and to be bawds to them, nor to allow young women to go to young men, and to give their bodies to be abused, in hope of marriage; nor to make night-matches and meetings to procure husbands, whilst they hereby often make themselves whores, to their own shame and grief of friends. If it be not imitable, will some say, why is it recorded? To answer this, we must know that the actions of the godly are of divers sorts; either extraordinary, as Abraham offering Isaac, Moses his killing of the Egyptian, Israelites borrowing and carrying away the goods of the Egyptians, Phinehas killing Zimri and Cozbi, Ehud Eglon, king of Moab, and such like; these are not for imitation, but to shew that God can dispense with his law, and is not tied to ordinary courses. Or ordinary; and this is manifold, first, good and allowed of God, as Abraham's teaching his household, Job's patience, praying for his children, and works of mercy and justice, Cornelius's devotion, Paul's labour in the ministry, and a thousand such like, left written for instruction, to acknowledge the strength of grace, and are for our godly imitation. Secondly, bad and unlawful, as Aaron's consenting to the Israelites' idolatry, Lot's incest, David's adultery and murder, Peter's perjury, and such like; these are not to be imitated, but to be avoided as evil, and are written to make us to behold man's corruption, and so his desert, that thereby we may set ourselves to bewail the same, to watch over ourselves, Heb. iii. 12, 13, and that none may boast of their own righteousness, but acknowledge it God's mercy that we are not confounded, and that it is his mere goodness that saveth us. Thirdly, mixed, partly good, and partly bad; so was Rebekah her seeking the blessing for Jacob, which God had promised, and here Naomi a marriage for Ruth; but the manner in both faulty. These are written to let us see our imperfections in doing a good thing, and to teach us to examine the ways of the best, to know how far they be imitable. Fourthly, merely indifferent in themselves, neither commanded nor forbidden, as Samson his feasting of the young men at his marriage, David's delight and playing upon the harp, and such like; which are written to shew our liberty in things indifferent, and that we may use the same, so we be moderate therein. Thus we see the difference of actions, and why recorded. And these are we to mark and examine, that we be not mistaken, whether extraordinary or ordinary, whether good or bad, or mixed or indifferent, and even in these how lawful to us, how expedient also, that we may not give offence.

Ver. 5. *And she said unto her, All that thou sayest unto me I will do.*

Ruth's readiness to obey her mother-in-law, and that in all things without exception.

And she said unto her. In this conference between them two here is no interrupting of one another; Ruth heareth Naomi her counsel, and answereth when she hath heard it, which commendeth her modesty and wisdom, for it is folly to answer a matter before it be heard.

All that thou sayest unto me I will do. Ruth is as ready to obey as the other to command, and that in respect, first, of her reverence towards Naomi, and persuasion of her good mind towards her; for whom we think well of and reverence, their counsel we easily embrace and willingly obey; and yet herein may we do amiss, if we examine not well the matter; for counsel may be sometime from error of the judgment, and sometime from corrupt affection. Secondly, of her own inclination to the thing, being young, and poor, to get a rich husband; for we readily obey in that whereto we incline our mind of our own accord, there needeth little incitation.

Ver. 6. *And she went down unto the floor, and did according to all that her mother-in-law bade her.*

Ruth's performance of her promise, both in going down to the floor, and in doing there what her mother advised her.

And she went down unto the floor. The city was then higher from whence she went, though we may read of a floor up on high, 2 Sam. xxiv. 18. It may seem strange how Ruth durst attempt this, being a stranger, and fearful by nature, as women be; yet see, where desire is, there nothing can hinder, or amate the spirit, or daunt the heart.

And did according to all that her mother-in-law bade her. As it is in verses 3 and 4, so she very exactly followed her mother's advice, and in nothing followed her own mind, lest perhaps, if things had not fallen out well, she might have had the fault put upon herself. Here is an example of strict obedience unto parents, which is required at the hands of children. Ruth doth according to all that which she was bidden to do; and thus in all lawful things should children do to parents, for so God would have it, it pleaseth him, Col. iii. 20, Eph. vi. 2. It is the duty of children, and in so doing they shall be blessed. Let children learn obedience to parents, as Isaac obeyed Abraham, Gen. xxii. 6, Jephthah's daughter her father, Judges xi. 36, 37, and as our blessed Saviour did his parents, Luke i. 51, which they will do if they fear God, Lev. xix. 3, and hold their parents worthy of honour, as God commandeth, Exod. xx.

Ver. 7. *And when Boaz had eaten and drunken, and his heart was merry, he went to lie down at the end of the heap of corn: and she came softly, and uncovered his feet, and laid her down.*

This verse sheweth how she did as her mother bade her, both for the time when, and the manner how.

And when Boaz had eaten and drunk. Meaning largely and freely, as the words following intimate, which it may seem they used at such times as this. We may note, that it is lawful to eat and drink more largely at one time time than at another; as in times of feasting, which the Israelites kept in old time, in reaping the fruits of the earth, as here; so at sheep-shearing they feasted, at the weaning of children, as we at christenings, at solemn times of rejoicing, at marriages, at such times as God bestowed blessings and special favours, or did graciously deliver his people; at the entertainment of friends, and loving meetings of brethren and kindred; at such times and upon such occasions may we eat and drink, and rejoice our hearts. But yet with these caveats: First, to take heed of excess, by falling either into gluttony or drunkenness, or wanton songs, or wanton behaviour, or by foolish jesting and mocking of the godly, as the Philistines did Samson, Judges xvi. 25. Secondly, to keep such feasting seasonably, not in time of God's judgments, nor in the time of the affliction of the church, Isa. xxii. 13–15; for then it befitteth us rather to fast than to feast, Amos vi. 6. Thirdly, that we behave ourselves Christian-like; first, to praise and bless the Lord and glorify him, 1 Cor. x. 31. And here is worth the remembrance, the behaviour of the ancient Christians in their feastings together;[*] they sat not down before thanksgiving, they ate and drank moderately, so as they would not hinder their devotion to God afterwards; their communication such, as they that knew they spake in the Lord's hearing. When they had sufficed themselves, they provoked one another to speak somewhat out of the Scripture, or otherwise good things to the praise of God, by which was trial made how much every one had drunk, and finally they ended their meeting with prayer. This was a religious and Christian feasting. Secondly, in all our mirth to remember, and not forget, as David saith, Jerusalem, the church of God, Ps. cxxxvii. 5, 6; thirdly, to remember the poor which want, Neh. viii. 11. We must not be Nabal-like, to feast like a king, and be without mercy to David and his company needing our relief; nor as the rich Dives, faring deliciously, and suffering the poor to perish at our gates. These caveats observed, we may eat and be merry.

And his heart was merry. Eating and drinking make the heart merry, Ps. civ. 14, 15. Thus were Joseph's brethren made merry, Gen xliii. 34; for the spirits of men hereby are refreshed, and let loose, as it were, from cares; and this benefit we may have by the Lord's creatures, and praise God for the same, Prov. xxxi. 6, 7, so we keep a moderation, and use sobriety, as Boaz here, and not become as drunken sots, like Nabal.

* Tertul. Apol. chap. xxxvi.

He went to lie down at the end of the heap of corn. After his labour and repast, he went to take his rest, not in any dainty bedding, but even in the floor at the end of the heap; and this did he for the safety of God's blessings, and the better keeping of the corn winnowed from pilfering. Note hence, I. That painful labour maketh man not curious of his lodging. Boaz here can lie hard; Jacob, a prince's son, brought up daintily at his mother's lap, can take a stone, and lay it under his head for a pillow, and sleep soundly, being wearied with travel, which maketh rest and hard lodging very pleasant to him; and howsoever Jacob might lie better before, yet did he never rest more blessedly than in this hard bed: for now the Lord spake to him, and he saw God's angels ascending and descending upon him; for it falleth out, the more the body is pampered, the less spiritual comfort; and the less the body is cherished, the more is the soul made glad, and the nigher we be to God. Would we, therefore, not be nice, nor curious of our lying? Let us labour our bodies till we be weary, and we shall take hard lodging without dislike; hunger maketh poor fare sweet, so doth labour make hard lying pleasant. II. That it is good husbandry to seek to save, as well as to get, Prov. xxvii. 23. Boaz was noble, wise, rich, and also thriving, yet merciful, and therefore not base, but yet would, as need required, see to his own estate, and God's blessings bestowed upon him, that they might not be diminished by purloining hands. This honest care of this great man, and good man too, checketh such spendthrifts as do waste God's blessings; they be thieves to themselves, and such as depend upon them; they work their own overthrow and destruction, and in adversity they shall be without comfort; for their consciences will tell them, that they have justly brought upon themselves that evil.

And she came softly, and uncovered his feet, and laid her down. A great show of evil; for she went to a wrong man. It was also in the night, and alone, to him alone, and after his feasting too; a too bold adventure, upon her mother's weak advice in this manner of doing. True it is, the success was good; but this more of God's mercy than the fact deserved. Boaz also commended her, ver. 10; but it was not for this coming, not for the manner, but for the thing intended, to wit, to match with him, she following the rule of the word, and not lust, to seek to young men, whether poor or rich. Here we see what Naomi contrived; she did with as much cunning, as care, act it; for it is said, she came softly, secretly, and without any stir or noise to awake him, and so laid her down at his feet, waiting when he should of his own accord awake. We warily act a thing where we be loath to offend; and there are we contented to wait patiently, where we fear to do amiss, as Ruth doth here. This wisdom can we shew in attaining our desires in things of the world. Oh that we thus could behave ourselves towards God! and that we might say with the pro-

397

phet, 'My soul doth wait for the Lord, and in his word do I hope,' Ps. cxxxi. 5, 6.

Ver. 8. *And it came to pass at midnight, that the man was afraid, and turned himself; and behold, a woman lay at his feet.*

The event of Ruth's thus secretly coming in, and lying at Boaz's feet unawares to him. Where, note the time when, the event itself, the effect of it, and the occasion of both in the last words.

And it came to pass at midnight. Thus long Boaz slept after his labour and painstaking, before he did awake. Note, that the wearied body and quiet mind sleeps soundly (so Solomon telleth us, Eccles. v. 12); eat he little or much. If, therefore, we would soundly sleep, being in bodily health, let us labour our bodies; weariness is the best physic to cast any one asleep: the idle cannot sleep, they be troubled with dreams and foolish phantasies. We must also get a quiet spirit, so shall we sleep without fear; and this is to be gotten, first, by seeking reconciliation with God in Christ, so may we lie down in peace with David, and not be afraid, Ps. iv. 8, and iii. 5; Job xi. 14, 19. This made Peter sleep soundly in great bodily danger, Acts xii., and the martyrs, some of them the night before they went to execution. Secondly, by shaking off the cares of the world, Eccles. v. 12, which maketh the worldling that he cannot rest. Thirdly, by suffering no evil to reign in our hearts, as envy, malice, lust, covetousness; for these things will not suffer us to take rest, Prov. iv. 16. Fourthly, to keep ever a good conscience towards God and man; this is a continual feast, and giveth us rest.

That the man was afraid. The best are subject to fear, upon conceit of peril, and that suddenly. So was Gideon afraid, and the apostles on a sudden; and likewise Boaz here, and that upon these reasons: First, his natural frailty and weakness of faith, which also is in every one. Secondly, his ignorance, not knowing what it was, because she came in unknown to him, when he was asleep; and in such cases we be more apt to conceit evil towards us than good, because our hearts tell us, that we be wicked by nature, and deserve evil. Thirdly, the dark and dead time of the night, which is to man fearful: the psalmist speaketh of the 'terror of the night,' Ps. xci. 5. We all by experience know, how easily man's heart is made fearful in the dark; except in the sons of Belial, and the children of the kingdom of darkness, hardened in evil, and which make the night the time of their lewd practices; yet even these also will soon be stricken into sudden fear. Fourthly, this fear may more suddenly possess one in the night, as here it did Boaz, being alone: for that spirits have taken at such times bodily shapes upon them, and shewed themselves; for the night is their time chiefly, as may be seen in their coming then most commonly to witches, known by their own confession. Let us, therefore, hence take notice of this weakness, which so sheweth itself from the love we bear to our body's safety, and natural life. Now, if we fear so much for this cause bodily dangers, oh how much more should we fear to commit sin, and the wrath of God for sin, which bring destruction to body and soul, without timely repentance!

And turned himself. He gathered himself together, shrinking, as the manner is of such as in bed being in sleep, fall into a sudden fear, and turn to and fro; such a forcible operation hath this fear upon the whole body, for to decline from, and avoid the danger conceived, nature seeking to save itself, in apprehension of peril, and that of a sudden. This natural fear is more quick and sudden to seize upon the heart than the spiritual fear to avoid sin, or the displeasure of God, and so the danger of the ruin of our souls; for this danger is not so soon apprehended: here is required the grace of illumination, and of faith, before this can be wrought in us.

And behold, a woman lay at his feet. The fear possessed him without cause; and thus it falleth out often, man often feareth without just cause: the godly, through the weakness of their faith, reproved by Christ, Mat. viii. 26; the wicked, by their accusing conscience, which maketh them to fly when none pursue them, Prov. xxviii. 1; they think that evil doth haunt them, and peril soundeth in their ears, Job xv. 21. Therefore let the godly labour for strength of faith, and the wicked repent, and seek for the peace of a good conscience, that they need not to fear.

Ver. 9. *And he said, Who art thou? And she answered, I am Ruth thine handmaid: spread therefore thy skirt over thine handmaid; for thou art a near kinsman.*

This is Boaz his questioning with Ruth, her answer, with a request to him, and the reason thereof.

And he said, Who art thou? Boaz coming to himself, moderateth his fear, and containeth himself from unchaste touching, and demandeth what she was. We may note, first, though fear possess wise and godly men upon a sudden, yet they moderate it, and are not wholly overcome therewith, for Boaz here crieth not out to servants for help, neither speaketh to her as one amazed, neither falleth he into a rage with her, that she should be occasion of such fear, for howsoever the fear suddenly seized upon him, being fast in sleep before, yet was it not childish nor womanish; he soon shook it off as a man of courage, having confidence in God. He mastered his natural fear, and so should we, and not be overswayed therewith, as women and children be. Secondly, that raging lust should not seize suddenly upon honest hearts, and such as fear God. Boaz was with her alone, yet doth he not in a filthy affection seek to dishonest her, as Judah did Tamar, being inflamed with lust at the sight of her; he did it on the day time, he asked not what she

was, as Boaz doth here; lust would not afford him that leisure. This continency is praiseworthy in old Boaz, as it was before in young Joseph, Gen. xxxix.; a virtue as in these commended, so commanded by God, and much praised in some heathen, who may rise up in judgment against our wanton youth and some lecherous old men, whom God doth hate.

And she answered, I am Ruth thine handmaid. Thus Ruth calleth herself, shewing her humility, as before in chap. ii. 13, and here by professing what a one she would be unto him, humble and serviceable as an handmaiden, if she might obtain her suit. So said Abigail when David sent to her to take her to wife, 2 Sam. xxv. 41; and so humble and serviceable was Sarah, Gen. xviii. 6, for she called Abraham lord, and in what he commanded she readily obeyed. And so should good and virtuous wives do still, when husbands command but what is honest and just; not that wives should be counted in condition as servants, for as that is more than they will grant, so is it more than husbands of right ought to expect from them that be their yokefellows. But what maid-servants and handmaidens do of fear and servile duty, wives should do of love with cheerfulness, such offices as they ought to perform unto their husbands, who have authority to command. Therefore, let wives learn to obey, as God commandeth them to do in all things, Eph. v. 22, 33, and that with reverence, as unto the Lord, and as it is fit in the Lord, as the apostle teacheth, Col. iii. 18. And doubtless there would be more such than we find in these days, if they might have Abrahams to their husbands, loving, wise in instructing them, and giving them honour as the weaker vessels. Note farther, how this worthy woman doth humble and debase herself, for the godly think lowly and meanly of themselves, as did Abigail, also David, 1 Sam. xxiv. 14; that worthy centurion, who said that he was not worthy that Christ should come under his roof. Abraham likewise did call himself dust and ashes, Gen. xviii.; St Paul did greatly humble and vilify himself, 1 Tim. i. 13, 1 Cor. xv. 9; for the godly are not self-loving, they see and know what they be by nature; they are not like the angel of the church of Laodicea, which thought highly of himself, and that he wanted nothing, when yet he was poor, and blind, and naked, and miserable, Rev. iii. They know, if they have anything, that the same is from God; that the more they have, whether gifts of body, or mind, or of the world, or the graces of the soul, spiritual and heavenly, the more they be indebted, and the more they are to answer for. These things considered make them lowly in their own eyes, and to behave themselves so unto others, as all that fear God ought to do, and should go one before another in giving of honour, and not in taking it, as the world now doth.

Spread therefore thy skirt over thine handmaid. In this phrase of speech she modestly claimeth marriage of him, for some do write that it was a custom when they were contracted, that the man did throw over the woman the lap or wing of his garment, in token that he took her into his protection. The word is taken from fowls, which cover under their wings their young from danger. By which husbands are to learn that they either are or should be a protection to their wives, for the woman bestoweth herself upon the man, forsaking for his love father and mother, to be under his covert as his wife, Gen. xx. 16. She is then as himself, and he is to love her as being become one flesh; and as the head he is to care for her, as well as to rule and govern her. And therefore let husbands shew themselves to be such; and this shall they do, if they do give their wives countenance, and do grace them with all their credit; if they upon all just occasions stand for them, defend their persons, honesty, and credit against others; if they love, cherish, and nourish them as their own bodies, affording them all honest contentment, then are they good protectors. And if husbands be the wives' protection, and that they look to have them so, let them depend upon their husbands, let them keep close to them, and by a loving obedience procure protection thus from them; from which some husbands are so far as some wish them dead, and so in heart are murderers; some expose them to all misery by their unthriftiness; some run from them and leave them to the wide world; some offer them, or, at least bawd-like, are willing to have them give their bodies unto the lusts of others, that they may live thereby; others there be which murder them to be rid of them. All these are false and faithless husbands, breaking promise to their wives, made to them before God and his church; cursed caitiffs, running headlong to destruction, without honesty, love, or natural kindness to their own posterity.

For thou art a near kinsman. Here is the reason of her request grounded upon God's law, Deut. xxv., as she had learned by her mother-in-law. This is her only reason which she useth to Boaz, for that he was a good and a godly man, with whom the strongest argument to prevail is the word of God, for the word hath authority in godly men's hearts. It bindeth their consciences, and forceth them to yield; it commandeth them more than all other reasons besides. And therefore, in having to do with such, gather arguments soundly from the word of God, for these will work upon good men's hearts; and in using such reasons aright, the Lord, and not man, may be said to speak unto them; which course, though worldlings mock at, yet such as fear the Lord will weigh and consider of, for that they do desire to square and frame their whole life after the word and law of God.

Ver. 10. *And he said, Blessed be thou of the Lord, my daughter: for thou hast shewed more kindness in the latter end than in the beginning, inasmuch as thou followedst not young men, whether poor or rich.*

Boaz his reply unto Ruth, when he knew who she
399

was, wherein he blesseth her, commendeth her, and giveth the reason of such his commendation of her.

And he said. His answer is full of kindness and love, neither doth he reprove her anything at all, though he justly might, for her thus coming in this manner; but Boaz, being a good man, considered rather the lawfulness of the matter which she came for, than of the manner of seeking it; then also her ground, and the reason moving her to come to him, which was the law of God. Thirdly, the estimation of her person, being held a virtuous woman generally of all. And lastly, his fulness of charity, which taketh things in the best part, and is not easily offended, made him not to reprove her; for a good man, full of mercy and love, doth not lightly condemn the virtuous for some shows of evil, for missing in the manner where the matter intended is good. For here the matter was lawful, the ground and inducement just, the person honest and generally well spoken of, and her intendment not ill. When these things concur, we are not to take exceptions against the manner, or failing in some light circumstance. Herein let us imitate good and godly Boaz, and let us not be like such rigid censurers as those be which condemn the best things, if they be not every way as they ought. Those also which make a small fault a great offence, rejecting the whole matter for the manner, the person for a little mistake. Oh, how would a proud and churlish Nabal have taken up this poor woman, a widow and a stranger, if she had come to him for marriage, especially if she had mistaken him, as Ruth here did Boaz in sort! What shame, what impudency would he have laid upon her, and so have rejected her! And those likewise which take things indifferent in ill part, as Hanun the king of the Ammonites did David's ambassadors, 2 Sam. x., which is greatly against charity, 1 Cor. xiii., and an argument of an envious, malicious, and proud nature, as may be seen in David's brethren against him, 1 Sam. xvii. 17, 18, 28, misinterpreting his coming, being sent by his father to them.

Blessed be thou of the Lord. These words shew how well he took her coming and request made touching marriage. He scorneth her not, he putteth her not off, but accepts her, as appeareth afterwards, and even in these words, when he saith to so poor a woman relieved by his alms, 'Blessed be thou of the Lord;' which words may be taken either as a petition or as an affirmation. If as a petition, that the Lord would bless her, then are the lessons the same with those in chap. ii. 20, where the same words are used by Naomi for him, as he doth here for Ruth, excepting this circumstance, that there Naomi, a poor woman, prayeth for the rich, and here the rich prayeth for the poor, of which also before in chap. ii. 12. If as an affirmation of that which he judgeth her to be, as if he had said, Blessed art thou of the Lord: thou art an happy and blessed woman, as in Luke i. 28, for in Hebrew the word *be* or *art* is not expressed, but only thus, *Blessed thou of the Lord,* and so may be understood either *be,* to make it a petition, or *art,* to make it an affirmation, Luke i. 28, with xi. 28. And then we learn that the godly, though poor, are yet blessed; and so accounted of Boaz, that is, of a godly man, who can judge of true blessedness; for the godly have those things wherein true blessedness consisteth. As, first, God's favour in Christ, and through him are the children of his Father, therefore called blessed, Mat. xxv.; secondly, they have the fruits of the Spirit and the practice of virtue, and for this they be pronounced blessed, Ps. cxix. 1, 2, and cxxviii. 1: thirdly, they have the pardon of sin, and their sins put away in Christ, and shall not be imputed to them, and therefore are blessed, Ps. xxxii. 1, 2; fourthly, they have the assurance of eternal life, which is promised only to such, and cannot be taken from them, John x. 27, 28, and therefore most blessed, though they want these outward things, as their master Jesus Christ himself did whilst he lived here on earth. Let this comfort the godly poor, and make them to rejoice more in their godliness than the worldlings in their earthly treasure, the carnal man in his pleasure, or the vain-glorious in his honour. This should make men esteem of the godly, as David did, Ps. ci., and as Abimelech did of Isaac, Gen. xxvi. 28; also to endeavour to be like them if we account them blessed, and to esteem their reproach for righteousness' sake, to be more honour than the glory of Pharaoh's court, as Moses did, Heb. xi.; to have them to dwell with us, to have our delight in them, as David had in the saints, Ps. ci., for they are blessed. And if so, then this confuteth the carnal conceit of worldlings, who think not so of them, especially if poor; yet let such consider our master Christ, how poor he was, also the afflicted state of the saints mentioned in Heb. xi. 37, yet pronounced to be such as the world was not worthy of. And lastly, how Joseph, a prince in Egypt, did rather choose to put his sons into Jacob's family, and to be called his children, than into Pharaoh's court, to be accounted mighty among the Egyptians.

My daughter, see chap. ii. 8. Thus he might call her, as being old; for the ancient are to be as fathers, and old women as mothers unto the younger sort, in teaching them good things by word and by example, Tit. ii. 1–3; so as a magistrate he might so speak to her, as Joshua spake to Achan, Joshua vii., for magistrates are to be as fathers to the people, and to tender them as their children. But of this before. Note how she called herself his handmaid; but he is pleased to term her by the name of daughter, though she so had debased and humbled herself; for the humbling of ourselves maketh our esteem to be nothing less, but rather greater, with such as be godly and wise, see chap. ii. 10–12, where the more Ruth did humble herself the more account did Boaz make of her; for such as humble themselves shall be exalted. Let

none then think by humbling themselves that they shall lose credit and honour, as foolishly the baseborn and new start-up doth imagine; for they cannot but be suspicious of contempt who know themselves unworthy of honour and esteem.

For thou hast shewed more kindness in the latter end than at the beginning. This is the reason of his blessing of her, or accounting of her blessed, because she increased and did not decay in goodness. The truly virtuous and heartily religious are better at last than at the first, as the angel of the church of Thyatira, and as it is said of Ruth here in her kindness and love; for goodness, grace, and virtue, where it is truly planted, will increase rather than decay, for the Lord husbands such trees, John xv. 2. by his word, his Spirit, and afflictions. We must, therefore, labour for this commendation, 1 Thess. iv. 1, if we will be held truly virtuous, truly honest, kind, just, merciful, and gracious. But some are far from this praise, growing worse and worse, till they be stark naught, whether it be in respect of religion, as we see in Jehu, Demas, Alexander the coppersmith, and Judas, who were worst at last, because they were never truly good at the first; or in respect of love and kindness, as here spoken of Ruth, which love some turn into hatred, and kindness into cankered malice, and shew more ill-will at the last than love at the first, like Amnon to his sister Tamar, and Saul to David, for that love was neither good nor sound in them, as Jonathan's was to David, and Ruth's to Naomi, and hers to Ruth again.

Inasmuch as thou followest not young men, whether poor or rich. Boaz in the other words gave a reason of his blessing of her; here he giveth a reason of his so commending her kindness, which appeareth to be more at the last now than at the first, to wit, to her husband deceased, and now to her mother-in-law Naomi, because she married him in her own country, and him rather than any of her own nation, which was kindness. Then for Naomi her sake to leave her own country, and to come and dwell with her in Judah in a poor estate, this was great kindness; but now to be ruled by Naomi, being so young a woman, to seek to match with an old man, and not to follow nature in desiring young men, but the law of God, for to raise up a name again unto her dead husband, whom by this means she maketh to live again in Israel, this is it which maketh her kindness to be more at last than at the first, in loving an old man rather than any young, and him also for the dead's sake, to revive his name among the people of God. See here in Ruth how true love, obedience to counsel, and grace, do overcome nature and the law of lust; for she loved her husband, she was obedient to Naomi, and in herself virtuous, and therefore reason and religion did take place, and neither nature nor lust prevailed with her. A good example for youth to follow. Note out of these words farther these lessons: first, that as now, so then, and ever before, there have been two sorts, rich and poor, in the world; first, to shew in one what all might have been, and in the other, the poor, what all deserve to be; secondly, that the rich may have occasion to shew works of mercy, and the poor, labouring painfully and honestly, may have to whom to go unto for relief; for the rich are God's stewards for the poor. Let both seek to live together lovingly, and to help one another; the poor to lend their labour to the rich, and the rich to supply their wants; for the one cannot live without the other; all cannot be rich, neither must all be poor. Let us rest contented with our estates; let not the poor murmur with envy at the rich, neither let these despise the poor; for God hath made them both, and one to stand in need of the other. Secondly, that young persons in nature affect to marry with young persons like themselves, which is implied by Boaz's speech. So did Isaac marry, and Jacob, and so in ancient time were matches made. If ever old and young married together, it was the old man with a young woman, but never an old woman with a young man, as the wanton and lecherous often do with wanton young fellows in these days, to the stain of their sex and reproach to themselves, and often their utter undoing; for youth cannot affect old age, and therefore it is fittest that marriage be made between such as may most likely agree together; other matches prove for the most part untoward. Thirdly, the truly religious will be ruled by the law of God, and will not be led after their natural disposition. For here Ruth leaveth the young men and taketh an old man, because the law so bound her, as she conceived, taking Boaz for the nearest kinsman; because such as be truly religious have denied themselves, and do resign themselves wholly to God's good pleasure and will, saying, as Christ said, Mat. xxvi. 39, 'Not my will, O Father, but thy will be done.' Hence it was that Joseph did abstain from his mistress, David from smiting Saul, when twice he might have done it, to get the kingdom; he rather would wait and endure much affliction, for 'he that believeth,' saith Isaiah, 'maketh not haste.' And hence is it that such as fear God dare not follow the course of the world, but do restrain their nature, and their desires, and do endeavour to please God in all things. If this be the grace of the religious, let men hereby try themselves, and be as God wisheth them to be, Deut. v. 29, and as religion and grace itself requireth them to be, as David promised and prayed to be, Ps. lxxxvi. 11 and cxix. 5. They are surely, then, far from being religious, which live according to their lusts, James i. 27; those that will follow the world, Tit. ii. 11, 12, with Demas and Judas and Nabal, but not forsake it, as Barnabas, Acts iv. 37, and Zaccheus, Luke xix., did; those that will follow the flesh, as the young men did their eyes in the old world, Gen. vi., and as Potiphar's wife, who was enamoured with fair Joseph: few Josephs among the vainly and idly up-bred youths of the gentry in

401

our days. And yet such will hunt after honours and vain titles, and if they cannot merit them they will pay money for them; the insolency and pride of Haman, the aspiring arrogancy of Absalom and Adonijah, are reigning in many. And have we not scribes and pharisees which love the highest places? Is there a Jonathan among thousands? Where is a Moses that will be no more a courtier for fear of sinning? Heb. xi. Will a Saul become a Paul so well trained up? or can there be found a Manaen, Acts xiii. 1, a prince's foster-brother, to join to the church, and to become a teacher, in mere love to religion? Do they not rather scorn the calling? And yet to call these worldlings, these fleshly livers, and these vain-glorious spirits profane, irreligious, lovers of pleasures more than lovers of God, oh how would they take on! how enraged would they be! So they love to be held religious, or not to be without religion, and yet in works deny God, being abominable and disobedient, and unto every good work reprobate, as the apostle speaketh, Titus i. 16.

Ver 11. *And now, my daughter, fear not: I will do to thee all thou requirest; for all the city of my people doth know that thou art a virtuous woman.*

Boaz gave her before due commendation; here is now his consolation and comforting of her; first, by a dehortation, willing her not to fear, then by a faithful promise to satisfy her request, yielding a reason of the same.

And now, my daughter. Boaz still useth this term, both for that he loved her and desired to comfort her. We may here see in Boaz, that a loving and merciful heart is not rough in terms, as an unloving and merciless Nabal is. This we may see to be so between loving parents and children, in Abraham and Isaac, Gen. xxii. 7, 8; between kind married couples, as in Isaac and Rebekah, Elkanah and Hannah, 1 Sam. i. 8; and between loving friends and godly disposed, as in Elizabeth and Mary, Luke i. 43, St Paul, and other Christians, or labourers with him in the gospel, and also in Eli and Samuel; for loving natures, whether they be high and honourable, speaking to mean persons, as Boaz to Ruth here, or old and in authority, to such as be young, as Eli to Samuel, 1 Sam. iii. 16, or such as sit in judgment speaking to malefactors, as Joshua to Achan, Joshua vii. 19, or a master unto his servants, as Job to his, Job xxxi. 13, or one giving an alms to the poor, as Boaz to Ruth, chap. iii. 8; it is all one, they are not rough nor churlish, for they be neither proud nor impatient. And therefore, if we would be held loving and merciful, let us use loving and kind speeches. Note again, that loving and kind speeches of great and rich persons are comfortable unto the poor, as Ruth before confesseth, chap. ii. 13; and therefore Boaz doth here use them to cheer up the spirit of this poor woman; for kind words witness a kind heart, if the speakers be not dissemblers. Now, the apprehension of hearty love in the mighty gladdeneth much the heart of such as be poor and in a low estate;

let, therefore, the mighty and rich learn to shew forth kindness, and to speak lovingly. By it, David, so speaking to Amasa, passing by his fault with Absalom, bowed the heart of the tribe of Judah as one man, 2 Sam. xix. 13, 14. How did Absalom win the hearts of the people? Was it not by loving speeches and courteous behaviour, which be of an attractive virtue to gain men's affections? How singularly beloved was our late queen Elizabeth of most blessed memory, for this virtue, of all her true subjects, in that she was so affable and full of loving speeches, and of a gracious carriage towards them! The contrary we may see in Rehoboam, who, by rough and contemptible* speeches, alienated the hearts of ten tribes from him for ever. The mighty, therefore, shall do wisely to speak with mildness, to use terms of love and respect, whereby they shall procure love, reputation, and due honour unto themselves.

Fear not. That is, fear not to be deceived of thy hope, though thou be poor and I rich, let no such thought trouble thee, that I should therefore make light account of thee; for I am well disposed in my affection to thee, therefore fear not. Thus Boaz speaketh unto Ruth; for he knew, and so do we, that it is a common thing to fear the issue, where earnest desire is to obtain the thing, especially where it may in some respects seem unlikely to come to pass, as Ruth might here so conceive, when she should consider what they two were, and the great difference between them. For in such a case there cannot be a full persuasion of the event; the poorer and meaner party may justly fear contempt, and usually such a one feareth the alterability of man's nature, though haply good words may pass between them for the present. And therefore in such a case it is good and fitting for the party of whom kindness is expected, to give to the other some tokens of assurance not to doubt nor fear, as Boaz doth in this place, and in the words following.

I will do thee all that thou requirest. By this Boaz taketh away her fear and doubt, in that he promiseth her marriage. For, where a godly and honest man maketh a promise, there is no fear of performance; because he maketh conscience of his words, and knoweth himself in equity bound to the performance of the same. And therefore may we rest upon an honest man's word, though in these days many would be held honest which make no conscience of breach of promise. In that Boaz here maketh her a promise of marriage, and so contracteth himself unto her, but yet *de futuro*, as it is said, and conditionally, as the two next verses shew, we may note, that it is lawful to betroth and contract ourselves one to another before marriage. It was an usual thing among God's people in former times, Exod. xxi. 9, Deut. xx. 7, Mat. i. 18; which betrothing is either lawful or unlawful: lawful, which is made by parties that may lawfully marry, which be free in their choice, of years of

That is, 'contemptuous.'—ED.

discretion to make their choice; and therefore contracts made of such as be within degrees forbidden, of contrary religions, betrothed already to others, or defective in nature, or wanting judgment what they do, or being under government of parents and not free, are not to be allowed. Now further, this lawful contracting is either conditional or absolute, and the same *de præsenti* or *de futuro*, I *take* thee, or I *will take* thee to be my wife. If conditional, then it bindeth no farther than the observing of the condition bindeth; for if that be not kept, the parties be free, unless they give their bodies in the mean space one to another. If it be absolutely made, and by such as may so contract themselves, they be man and wife before God, and may not be sundered one from another. These things are to be therefore considered of in contracts used before marriage, for the parties' better settling of their affections one upon another, for the better acquainting themselves with the conditions and qualities of each other, and to fit themselves for house-keeping and more convenient living together, having made some honest provision beforehand.

For all the city of my people doth know that thou art a virtuous woman. The reason why he yieldeth to take her to wife; her portion was her virtues, for which she was generally commended of all. This reason did the more confirm her, and easily removed away fear, when she might perceive upon what ground he was induced to marry with her. Hence may arise many lessons: first, that virtue maketh even the poor and strangers too to become famous, as may appear in this poor widow, a Moabitish woman. So it made David famous in the days of Saul, though he sought to obscure his name; and likewise Barnabas in the primitive church; for virtue will not be hid, neither can it. And therefore such as desire renown, labour for virtue. Is not Abigail famous for her wisdom? Joseph for his chastity? Moses for his meekness? Samuel for his justice? David for his zeal? Ehud, Gideon, and Jephthah for their fortitude? and so the seven and thirty worthies of David for their valiant acts? Esther for her humility? the sinful woman for her penitency? the sons of Jonadab, the son of Rechab, for their temperance? This is the way, and the best way, to get fame and true honour for ever; and yet few tread aright in this path, but rather they will make themselves so notorious by villany, that all may know them to be vicious persons, without shame, without blushing, like those which Isaiah, chap. iii. 9, and Jeremiah, chap. vi. 15, speak of, which would not hide their sins, neither be ashamed for them. Secondy, that the godly and virtuous will take notice of such as be virtuous among them. For so do here all the people of Bethlehem, the people of God; because they love virtue, having it in themselves, they desire to encourage others that be so, and rejoice therein, and therefore do they speak thereof, and spread abroad the name of it, to make the parties which be virtuous to be honoured. This is comfort to such as live well; though they do not, nor may thereby seek praises, yet shall they be taken notice of. And by this may men consider of themselves whether they be virtuous, if they will take notice of graces in others, and rejoicingly speak thereof, to the honour and praise of the virtuous. Thirdly, that a godly man will take a wife for her virtues, as Boaz doth here Ruth; so did David for her virtues choose Abigail: for a virtuous woman is lovely, and her price, as Solomon saith, ' is far above the rubies; the heart of her husband may safely trust in her, so that he shall have no need of spoil,' Prov. xxxi. 10, 11. Let men therefore in marrying, make this choice; for such a woman is a crown to her husband, Prov xii. 4, and she retaineth honour, Prov. xi. 16. And yet this is the least reckoned of in these days; but now beauty, wealth, honour, and friends, are the motives to make marriages. Fourthly, that a good report for virtue in a woman, is a good portion, and a means of preferment. Thus came poor Ruth to so honourable and rich an husband, having neither wealth nor friends. For such a woman hath the best and most durable help of true love, even virtue; she hath the Lord to speak for her, and to procure her favour, and to cause her to be beloved. This should make women to strive for virtue, and to get a good name from it, and not for beauty and brave attire; for a good name is better than riches—than precious ointment, Eccles. vii. 1, and rather to be chosen than great riches, Prov. xxii. 1. Let parents hence learn to bring up their daughters virtuously, it is a good portion and means of preferment. This may comfort poor maidens which be virtuous, and want friends and goods, by a good report yet may they match well; let them strive, therefore, though they want goods, yet to get grace and good conditions, as piety and religion in heart, and modesty in countenance, apparel, and gesture; let them preserve chastity, and not be given to youthful company; let them be skilful in good housewifery, painful also and industrious, and having power to govern the tongue. If thus they be beautified and enriched, they have a better portion than many pounds, and fair enough to the wise in heart, so as they will give a good man contentment; for beauty is fading, and favour deceitful and vain, but a woman that feareth the Lord, shall be praised, Prov. xxxi. 30.

Ver. 12. *And now it is true that I am thy near kinsman; howbeit there is a kinsman nearer than I.*

Boaz his information of Ruth, wherein she was somewhat mistaken, granting the truth that he was a near kinsman, but not the nearest; so as here he preventeth her apprehension of the promise made, for taking it absolutely, but conditionally, as in the next verse, more at large he declareth his mind. So that here is a concession of that which she had spoken of him in ver. 9, and withal an instruction touching another nearer than himself, which she knew not of.

And now it is true. Boaz will not deny a truth, for a godly man is a lover of the truth, and will yield to it when he heareth it; for it swayeth with him, which, if it so did with every one, it would prevent tedious disputes and contentions among the learned; prevent long suits of law, put lawyers to silence in corrupt pleading, and save many pounds contentiously misspent; prevent deceit in buying and selling, and many other mischiefs, which miserably fall out for want of acknowledging the truth, which men should and would do if they hated falsehood and lying, if they had a hearty love of the truth, if they would cast off pride and the desire of vain praises, and covetousness, and the greedy desire of gain; for these hinder the truth, and where these reign, hardly will truth be acknowledged as it ought, or reign among men as it should.

That I am thy near kinsman. Four things might move him thus ingeniously to confess himself so nigh a kinsman to those poor women. First, his love to the truth, so to speak as the thing was; secondly, his holy and religious respect unto the law of God, by authority whereof she made claim to him; thirdly, his humility and uprightness of heart, not disdaining his godly poor kindred; fourthly, her own virtues, and his love which he bare to her for the same. (Of rich and poor kinsfolks I have spoken before in chap. ii. 20.) Here observe, that a loving, godly, humble, and upright-hearted rich man will readily confess himself of near kindred to his poor kinsfolk if they be virtuous; for virtue maketh them honourable with the virtuous, though poverty make them contemptible to the world. And therefore, for the poor to get an acknowledgment of them from their rich kindred, let them be virtuous, that whereas they want goods, grace may procure them favour and respect; for poor and lewd are not worthy the acknowledging, being contemptible both in body and soul.

Howbeit there is a kinsman nearer than I. So that the nighest to a right are first to be preferred thereto. This is here implied, and this reason and equity will yield. Therefore Boaz honestly maketh here mention of this other kinsman, to whom Ruth should first have gone; for both Naomi and she were mistaken in this, to come first to Boaz for the right of marrying her. Yet see how courteously and lovingly he answereth her, teaching, that such as demand in simple ignorance a matter at our hands as due, and yet in some sort not so, we are meekly to inform them, and not scornfully to reject them, as great ones now will do; for a simple error is pardonable, and it is a fruit of goodness to inform them in the right; and this would prevent contention and strife, which otherwise might grow thereupon for want of better information. Let this, then, reprove those which gladly take occasion from such mistakes to laugh at and jest away the parties, making themselves very merry with the parties' simplicity, though their meaning be both good and honest.

403

Ver. 13. Tarry this night, and it shall be in the morning, that if he will perform unto thee the part of a kinsman, well; let him do the kinsman's part: but if he will not do the part of a kinsman to thee, then will I do the part of a kinsman to thee, as the Lord liveth: lie down until the morning.

Boaz his confirmation of his promise before concerning his marrying of Ruth, wherein is noted the time when he will go about it, upon what condition he will do it, the confirmation itself by solemn oath, and his advice to rest for that night till the morning.

Tarry this night. Boaz deferreth to perform the kinsman's part for a space, though very short; and seeing it was night, and now dangerous for her to go alone from thence, he adviseth her to tarry there that night in the floor. Note, first, that upon reasonable cause, that may be deferred which cannot absolutely be denied to be done, which may be of use to check the impatience of delay, when there may be good reason and just cause of delaying the matter; secondly, that a true and loving friend careth for the safety of such as he loveth. Thus Lot took care for his guests, Michal for David's escaping from the hand of Saul; so Jonathan in this respect shewed his care and love to David, and Hushai his friend likewise. So did the disciples care for Paul's safety, Acts ix.; for true love is not only to do favours, but to expel injuries, and to prevent dangers from friends, which reproveth the ill friendship of men in these days; for some will see their friends running into evil, yet will not care by good counsel to prevent it, much less, being in trouble, to seek their deliverance, if it should haply prove either troublesome or costly; for neither of these will these counterfeit friends bestow upon those they pretend to love, when they stand in need of them. Some are worse, even Judas-like, who for gain will betray their friend, or play Ahithophel's part, turn his counsel against him for hope of favour, when he thinks his friend down the wind, and another like to rise. Such false and faithless hearts may now be found more than enow, who also will expose their friend into any danger or loss, so they may get or save thereby. Let men therefore learn soundly to try, before they too hastily trust, the pretended, rather than truly intended, love in these days; for now is falsehood in friendship, for that commonly every man loveth another for himself only, as experience sheweth; for otherwise true friends will be as Jonathan, who valued nothing of a kingdom for his friend David's sake; they will be like Hushai in advising for David's welfare; as Barzillai in relieving him in distress, and in shewing him kindness when most were against him; as Abishai in exposing himself into imminent danger for his safety. What friends can be found like the heathen mariners to Jonah, who in a tempest strove with all their powers to save him, with danger of all their lives? or like the nurse of Mauritius, the emperor's child, who offered her own to be slain by that bloody Phocas, to preserve her foster child's life, the son of the emperor? Rare examples worthy imitation, but not to be paralleled in these days. But to return to Boaz, it may be asked, Why he would suffer her to be with him alone in the floor all night? I answer, his care of her safety; for he would rather admit of an inconvenience to himself than the danger of a mischief to her, knowing the wickedness of the times then. Again, it may be he felt in himself strength, by God's grace, and also a resolution to withstand the temptation, because he was a man of years (though yet some old are wanton enough); because he was a just man (as it is said of Joseph, the husband of Mary, Mat. i.), and would preserve right to his neighbour. And thirdly, for that he had an honest and true intent to marry her, if so he might, and therefore he would not offer her dishonesty; though many of unbridled affections make such opportunities ready motives to themselves of abasing themselves one with another, because (forsooth) they mind to marry. Of which evil in this book elsewhere I have spoken. See ver. 14.

And it shall be in the morning. So Boaz, though he deferred it, yet it was but a very little while; he would not long, as Naomi saith after, ver. 18, delay the matter; for a wise man will not be over hasty, yet will he not neglect, but hasten the business which he taketh in hand. For the one is the property of a fool, but the other of a man of understanding, Prov. xiv. 15, if so be the matter do require haste; for there be two extremes in businesses to be avoided: the one is too great haste, where need is not, and this is rashness, punished in good Josias, 2 Chron. xxxv. 22, and in the heady Israelites, Numb. xiv. 40; the other is too great remissness and slackness when the matter requireth haste, which was Amasa his fault, 2 Sam. xx. 5. And therefore the matter is to be considered of, and thereby we may judge when to make haste, and when to take more time and deliberation; for that is not rashly attempted which is first undertaken with good advice, though with speed executed; secondly, done seasonably, as the circumstances of the time, place, and persons require; thirdly, when it is done by our calling warrantably. When a man faileth in these, though he take time enough, he is but a rash adventurer.

That if he will perform to thee the part of a kinsman. That is, if he will marry thee, and raise up the name of the dead; for he is before me by right to take or refuse thee, so as if he will have thee, thou canst not refuse him, then take him, and so an end hereof between us. Though it appeareth many ways that Boaz had an earnest affection to Ruth, yet would he not wrong the kinsman if he would have her; for a good and a just man, even in what he desires, will not wrong another, because the law of righteousness bindeth him to just dealing, Jer. xxii. 3, of which he maketh conscience. So requireth the law of love which

404

possesseth his heart, which is, to love another as himself, Mat. xxii. 37, and to do as he would be done unto, Mat. vii. 12. And thus should every man learn to do, and not to withhold any good from the owner thereof, and to whom it is due, Prov. iii. 27. In this kind, owe nothing to any man, neither wrong any ; for ' God is an avenger of all such things,' 1 Thes. iv. 6. Here then come justly to be reproved such as make no conscience of wronging others. Of which sort are all these : first, thieves and robbers, against which the prophet, Zech. v., and apostle, 1 Cor. vi. 10, speaketh. Secondly, partakers with such, by counsel, command, consent, provoking, flattery, concealing, receiving, defending, or (if it be in our power) by not punishing such ; for such be wicked persons, and such do hate their own souls, Ps. l. 18. Thirdly, fraudulent persons, 1 Thes. iv. 6, of which there be these : first, such as pretend law to do wrong, Lev. xix. 13, and xxv. 27, as the judge in giving wrong sentence for by-respects, who by the prophet are called thieves, Isa. i. 23. So lawyers, in crafty pleading to overthrow justice and innocency, the sheriffs in panelling. partial juries to pleasure men, and all such as be false witnesses, or procure their unjust cause to pass by giving bribes. To these may be added deceitful buyers and sellers, in praising or dispraising overmuch for advantage, Prov. xx. 14, in counterfeit wares, in false weights and measures, Deut. xxv. 13, 16. So likewise those villains, counterfeit bankrupts, damnable thieves, coin-catchers, cheating gamesters, and gnathonical knaves, who soothe and flatter to gain by others' simplicity and folly. Fourthly and lastly, such as withhold goods from the owners, and will not make restitution, as in conscience they are bound, Lev. vi. 1 ; for so God commandeth and promiseth mercy to them that restore, Ezek. xviii. 7, and threateneth the punishment for not restoring, ver. 12. It is a rule of equity and justice that requireth it, which is, to give every one his own, and the law of nature, to do as we would be done unto. Yea, we have the practice of the godly to move us. The sons of Jacob, Gen. xliii. 21, Zaccheus, Luke xix. 8, and Samuel offer it, 1 Sam. xii. 3, if they had done wrong to any. Lastly, this is the judgment of the godly learned,* that restitution should be made, affirming the sin not to be remitted except the thing taken away be restored, and also that repentance is not found without it, if there be ability to restore. Neither may this be deferred when it is in our hand, Prov. iii. 28, and when we come to worship before God, Mat. v. 23. But we must restore the thing found, borrowed, or otherwise gotten, and not justly being our own, unto the true owner himself, if we know him, or to his children, executors, or next kinsman, Lev. vi. 5, and if these be not to be found, then to God, for some pub-

lic use to the church or relief of the poor.* And this restitution must be made by me for every wrong done to my brother in body, either by myself or by my beast ; in his goods in like manner, by stealing, by eating their ground with my beasts, by burning, by borrowing and not repaying, by withholding what was delivered to be kept of fidelity, by hiding cattle going astray, or keeping things found. Herein also may justly be reckoned sacrilege, robbing of churches or churchmen of their maintenance, allowed by God and the good laws of our land, by not tithing, or tithing deceitfully.† The labourer is worthy of his hire ; let him enjoy such maintenance as by law is given him, and godly ancestors truly intended him. And be not guilty of this spiritual theft, which the very heathen would not do to their priests ; for in the great famine of Egypt, all the Egyptians' lands and goods were bought and sold, but the lands of the priests were not, but they did eat the portion which Pharaoh gave them, Gen. xlvii. 22 ; but with us, men are of so greedy, and more than heathenish appetite, that they can devour up both land, and living, and tithing, the whole portion of Christ's ministers ; so as these heathen shall rise up in judgment against these devourers, which eat up from the Lord's messengers what hath been dedicated for the maintenance of his service and worship.

Well, let him do the kinsman's part. That is, I yield him his right in thee, because he is before me, as I have said, neither will I take thee except he renounce his right in thee. Boaz, we see, seeketh not to gain her to himself without consent, neither will abuse her, but honestly behaveth himself in the night with her alone, as in the eyes of men, and open view of the world. For a godly man is not good because of men, but for that he feareth God which looketh upon him, and upon whom he looketh ; and therefore everywhere behaveth himself as he ought. Boaz here loveth her, but lusts not after her to defile her, as some would, making it a sport to commit fornication, with those whom they think do belong unto others, either betrothed maids or married wives ; but ' whoremongers and adulterers God will judge,' Heb. xiii. 4.

But if he will not do the part of a kinsman to thee. These words Boaz uttereth as the ground of his promise to marry with Ruth, to wit, if he the kinsman refuse her ; for when one renounceth his right, it is then for another ; for the release made is a setting free of that which before was tied, which is for direction to such as take houses or grounds. It is a common complaint to say, He hath taken my house and my grounds from me ; but often unjustly, as when the lord letteth not lands or houses, but to a limited time, which being expired, the same is free to let to

* St Aug. *in Epi. ad Mac.* Danæus *in Eth.* lib. ii. cap. xv. Perkins in the *Pract. of Rep.*

* Joseph. *Antiq.* lib. iv. cap. viii.
† Numb. v. 7, 8 ; read Exod. xxi. 19, 29, 30 : Lev. xxiv. 19 ; Exod. xxi. 33, 34, 36, and xxii. 1 ; 2 Sam. xii. 6 ; Deut. xxii. 2 ; Exod. xxii. 5, 6, 14 ; Ps. xxxvii. 21 ; 2 Kings vi. 5 ; Lev. vi. 4 ; Deut. xxii. 2, 3 ; Lev. v. 16 ; Deut. xiv. 22 ; Prov. xx. 25 ; Lev. xxvii. 33 ; Mal. i. 8, 13, 14.

another, except either custom bind to let the present possessor to have the refusal, or that some promise be made, which bindeth an honest man to keep it. Besides this, there is indeed a friendly courtesy in the landlord to offer to the present enjoyer that which he hath, before any other; but he is not simply bound so to do, but only of good will. Yet must I needs acknowledge that it is not a neighbourly part for any one, out of a greedy covetousness, to undermine the possessor, or by any indirect means to procure from him, at the landlord's hands, his house or lands. For this is against the law of love, to do as we would be done unto, and not to do to others what we would not that they should do unto us, as the law and prophets teach, and our master Christ commandeth; and yet this is a common practice now for want of love. Note again how wary Boaz is in making her a promise to marry with her; it is done cautelously, with condition of upright dealing between him and another. For as every promise is to be made of an honest man with due consideration (because once made, it bindeth, except there be a release) so especially the promise of marrying one another, both for the weightiness of the matter (nothing being so much concerning the welfare, or downfall of man in this life), as also for the indissolubleness of the knot; for here is no releasing one of another, but they must live together till death. And therefore let us learn to be wary in making this match; and to do this, first, consider these two things before mentioned, and weigh them well, to prevent haste and rashness herein; secondly, how fit or unfit the marriage is, and what good reasons there be to persuade to it, or dissuade it; thirdly, what is required before the marriage to further it, or else which might hinder the same. We may not rashly and unadvisedly run into this holy ordinance, as many do, first, upon foolish, light, and unadvised love; secondly, upon strong and unbridled lust, violently pressing them to sudden contracts, and often to filthy uncleanness, like brute beasts which have no understanding; thirdly, upon a fear to lose the opportunity of enjoying one another, if friends should know it, they will contract themselves and give themselves one to another, and that dishonestly, to force friends to consent; fourthly, covetousness, when men are carried away, not with the love of the party, but the greatness of a portion. These, and such like, make hasty matches, at leisure to be repented of. Here it may be demanded, Why Boaz made an *if* of the other kinsman's mind and good will, seeing first he was the nighest kinsman, and had secondly, the law of God to move him thereto? Was it not uncharitableness? I answer, No; for he knew not his kinsman's mind, as it appeareth by his trial of him the next day. Again, he knew well, that albeit nature and religion tie men to do a thing, yet worldlings will not do their duty. Cain had nature, reason, and religion, to love his brother Abel; so had Saul to respect David; but these pre-

vailed with neither of them, no more than the law here was of force to move this worldling; for such a one he was, as shall be shewed in the next chapter.

Then will I do the part of a kinsman to thee. Boaz having laid down the condition, he reneweth his promise made in ver. 11; yea, though the other refuse her, he will take her; for one man's dislike maketh not true love to decay in another man's heart; for true love is fixed upon the thing beloved, without respect to other men's affections to the same; their liking may the more increase love, but dislike cannot utterly remove it, where it is firmly settled. This experience telleth us to be true, in the love of young persons affecting marriage. And it were to be wished that our love were so strong, that our souls were so glued to religion, that though others dislike, we may not therefore cease to love it, but be as Ruth to Naomi, chap. i. 16; and so say, as she to her, though she saw Orpah depart from her. Note again that albeit Boaz made this promise to her alone, and without other witnesses, but God only; yet having promised, and sworn to keep it, he after honestly and faithfully performs the same; as in the next chapter is plain. For an honest man will keep his oath and his word, as may be seen in the Reubenites, Gadites, and half tribe of Manasseh, Numb. xxxii. 27, Josh. iv. 12, and xxii. 9; in Jonathan and David, in Judah with Simeon, Judges i. 3, 7, xii. 13; in Joseph to his brethren after Jacob's death, Gen. l. 21; Caleb to Othniel, Josh. vi. 23; the spies to Rahab, Judges i. 25; and to the man of Bethel. For an honest man hath a binding conscience when the word is passed out of his mouth, he careth for his honest name and credit, which to him is more than riches, and better than ointment. If therefore we be of upright and honest dealing, and so would be accounted, let us keep our words and our oaths; for this is common honesty, justice, and a thing of good report, which we are commanded to have care of, Philip. iv. 8. It is a mark of a good Christian, though it be to our own hindrance, Ps. xv. 4; we shall be like the children of our heavenly Father, who faileth not of anything which he speaketh, Josh. xxi. 45, 1 Kings viii. 56. Without keeping promise, men cannot be trusted; it cutteth off all commerce and traffic with men. Godly men have ever made conscience of their word; and very heathen men have been worthy of admiration in this point. And yet these things move nothing a number of baseminded, falsehearted, and dishonest Christians, unworthy the name of such, when they lose their common honesty.

As the Lord liveth. This is an oath, Jer. iv. 2. This oath he taketh, because it was a matter of great importance, and for that he would put the poor woman out of all doubt, and that she should not fear the accomplishment, though he was rich and she poor, he noble, she mean; he an Israelite, and she a stranger of Moab. From this note: First, that it is lawful to take an oath, against the anabaptists' assertion, of which see chap. i. 17; secondly, that the godly use to swear by God when they swear, and by none other. Of this more at large also in chap. i. 17. Thirdly, that the form of an oath is diversely expressed, and not one manner of way; as thus, 'I speak it before God;' 'God is my witness;' 'The Lord knoweth;' 'As the Lord liveth;' 'I protest before the Lord;' 'I call God to record,' and divers such like, besides the common form, 'by God,' and so forth; which I note to tax the usual swearing of many, who seem to hate swearing in the common form, and yet they themselves swear too often in another form : so subtle is Satan to beguile them in that, and therein to make them guilty of that, from which they take themselves to be most free. But they be deceived; for when God or his name and attributes are at any time mentioned, for this end to confirm the truth of that which a man speaketh, it is an oath. Let men take notice hereof, and cease to be common swearers. Fourthly, that it is lawful to swear in private cases, as Jonathan did to David, and he to Jonathan, the spies to Rahab, and Boaz here to Ruth, in case of necessity and in weighty matters. In such cases we may use our lawful liberty, but yet with great wariness, with great reverence of the high majesty of God; not suddenly, not in passion, not without due advisement. Fifthly, that an oath is the confirming of the mind of another in the truth of that which is spoken, Heb. vi. 16; whether of things past, spoken, or done, or of things present, or of things to come, and promised to be done. This is the end of Boaz's swearing here. If this be so, then let men rest satisfied with an oath, as Ruth doth here, and as in some cases God would have men so to do, Exod. xxii. 11; for it is the greatest confirmation of a truth that may be, except the party swearing either hath been convinced, or is at that present convincible, by good probabilities, of falsehood. If this be the end of an oath, then also let men care to swear truly, that the mind of others may trust them, and rely·up-on their faithful oath taken. But we have cause to bewail these times, in which there be such, as pro-fessing Christianity, yet will use oaths, yea, and fear-ful execrations to cozen with, to make their lies and secret villanies intended to be the less suspected, as by miserable experience some simple and plain mean-ing men may speak, being deluded by fair shows of god-liness, zeal of goodness, words confirmed by oaths, fearful execrations and counterfeit letters, that wicked hypocrites and Satanical deceivers might attain to their unlawful desires. Let men therefore take heed of men, and beware whom they trust, seeing men dare with pretence of godliness go so far in detestable villanies; but I wish him or them that practise it, to leave it betimes, else let them look for deserved doom, without serious repentance

Lie down until the morning. With these words he endeth his conference, not spending the night in vain or unnecessary prattling, as idle lovers and wanton suitors will do, but having answered her request, and shewed to her his love and honest resolution, he willeth her to lie down until the morning. By which words it seemeth she was risen up, as ready to de-part, but that he would not permit her so to do, for the reasons before mentioned, and because the night is ordained for rest, as the psalmist saith, 'At night man goeth to his rest.' Neither is it safe for young women to be·abroad in the night; it savoureth not well, it befitteth not their sex, and may endanger their chastity. We must beware of being night-walkers, for Satan, the prince of darkness, will then be the most busy. Such also as hate the light love to be in darkness, as the thief and the adulterer, Job xxiv. 15. Again, the night emboldeneth to all villany and wicked-ness, which in the day time they will not dare to do, as may be seen in the Sodomites, Gen. xix., and Gibeonites, Judges xix. 22, 25. Lastly, night-walkers have ever been suspected for ill-disposed persons.

Ver. 14. *And she lay at his feet until the morning; and she rose up before one could know another; for he said, Let it not be known that a woman came into the floor.*

This verse sheweth how Ruth rested till the morning; then, her rising ready to depart, with the moving cause from Boaz's speech, being a wary caveat unto her.

And she lay at his feet until the morning. This is added to shew their chaste and continent behaviour; for if they had offended, the Holy Ghost, who spared not Noah's drunkennes, Lot's incest, David's adultery, would not have concealed this fact, if so they had thereof been guilty. They were both honest and feared God, and therefore they would not commit such wickedness, albeit they had occasion offered. Whereby we may learn that where the fear of God and honesty beareth sway, there chastity may be pre-served, though occasion be offered to the contrary. Behold this here in old Boaz, and elsewhere in young Joseph; there was neither lechery in the one, nor strength of lust, nor youthful wantonness in the other; for their lust is bridled where the fear of God possesseth the heart, and honesty lodgeth. To be kept therefore from this evil, let these virtuous examples guide us, that lust overbear us not, as it doth in such as seek occasion to sin in this kind; 'neighing,' as Jeremiah speaketh, 'after their neigh-bours' wives.' And such also, though they seek not occasion, like the former, yet they easily take occa-sion to offend this way, with virgins, with married wives, and with those whom they think to marry with; and this last is held no offence at all by them, because they think that marriage amendeth all. But, first, it is an argument of a strong and unbridled lust, which should not bear rule in Christians. Secondly, if the man hap to die before marriage (as who is certain of life ?), the woman being with child becometh infamous, and she that should have been a wife is left as an harlot. Thirdly, it is an offence to the church, being known, and punishable by the same; which offence the godly must avoid: ' Give no offence,' saith the apostle, ' to Jew, nor Gentile, nor to the church of God,' 1 Cor. x. 32. Fourthly, and lastly, it beseemeth not the holiness of the public solemnization of marriage, to which the parties should come undefiled, as the assembly and congregation of God doth in charity judge of them. Note besides, that these two godly persons kept themselves chaste, and how others accounted also godly, and that so were, yet were very foully overtaken in this sin of the flesh, as we have example in Lot in a cave with his daughters, Judah with Tamar, and David with Bathsheba. From whence observe, that God's own dear children have not all the like measure of grace, nor power to resist temptations, and to subdue their own corruptions. In the holy word of God, we shall find three sorts of the godly; some hardly found fault with, their infirmities passed over with silence; such a one was Isaac, Boaz here; so Joshua, Samuel, Daniel, Mephibosheth, Jonathan, Zacharias and Elizabeth, Simeon, Anna, the Virgin Mary, and others. Some are noted with their frailties and light infirmities, being most excellent saints of God, as Moses, Job, Jeremiah, Hezekiah, and Josiah, and some others. A third sort are stained with foul offences, as David with adultery and murder, Judah with incest, and so Lot; Aaron with idolatry, and Peter with perjury; for the Lord affordeth not the like grace in equal measure unto all. All are sanctified, yet corruptions more sway in one than in another, as these instances shew, and as experience daily teacheth. Therefore let us not think to find the like grace in all, and the like mortification of corruption; for God distributeth his gifts, and the measure, as it pleaseth him. None are then to be condemned simply for bad persons, as if they were not in the number of God's saints, because they be not in all things like their brethren; for they, even both sorts of them, may be the Lord's, and yet in something be very much unlike. Joseph, enticed by his mistress, preserves his chastity; but David enticed another man's wife, and lay with her. Boaz alone with Ruth would not sin in fornication; but Lot alone with his daughters committed incest. Nathanael was a true Israelite without guile; but Jacob, first called Israel, of whom came all the Israelites, dissembled, and lied to his own father; Moses, a meek man, but Jonah of a very froward spirit; and yet all of them good men, and the blessed saints of God. This therefore justly reproveth those who, seeing men professing religion, and yet to differ in their courses, some to live unreproveably, and others to give great offence in their falls, though of infirmity, do utterly condemn them all as hypocrites, and as dissemblers. Yea, this checketh themselves for deadly censuring one another, when ' if any man be

overtaken in any fault, they which be spiritual should restore such an one in the spirit of meekness; considering themselves, lest they also be tempted,' Gal. vi. 1. If any man here ask, Why doth not God make all his children to be alike religiously minded, one as well as another ? I answer, The Lord may do it for these reasons : First, for the good many times of the godly themselves; for they are suffered to fall for their greater humiliation, the more to let them see their own weakness, to shew that they stand not of themselves; to make them the more to deny themselves, not to be lifted up with any conceit of their own goodness or merit, but to magnify God's mercy for their daily preservation, and for his goodness towards them; and after their fall returning to God, and feeling peace in their renewed repentance, they will the more closely stick to God, more earnestly pray, and more fervently love him; for so great good the Lord works in his children after their falls, yea, such humiliation will be wrought thereby in them, and such comfort, joy, and love in God after their recovery, as no outward crosses, nor outward deliverances, can ever do the like. Secondly, for the further damnation of the wicked, who at the falls of the godly do harden their hearts the more against all religion, thinking it to be a vain thing, and that such as follow and embrace it are no better than others, and that the best be but hypocrites, because they see some grievously overtaken, when these miserable souls should hereby be moved the more to fear their own damnation, except they repent and take a better course; for ' if the righteous scarcely be saved;' if they so hardly get out of their corruptions; if they be so fearfully overtaken, who read, meditate, hear the word, confer thereof, pray much, and humble themselves with tears; ' where shall the wicked and sinner appear ?' 1 Peter iv. 18. How can the common and careless Christian be saved ? Thus should they reason, to rouse up their spirits, to make them to seek God, and fear damnation, and not take occasion by the falls of some to condemn the profession of religion itself in others, and so to make no account thereof in themselves to the hardening of their own hearts, and so heaping upon themselves the just deserved vengeance.

And she rose up before one could know another. That she might be gone away out of the floor before the light, or at the dawning of the day, very early, ere others should be stirring. This she did perhaps out of a joy of heart, and desire to be with Naomi, to tell her the success of her counsel, which she carefully followed, as it may seem by her hasty relation of the matter unto her mother-in-law, when she came unto her; as shall be shewed in the 16th verse. Note here, that they be not drowsy-headed, whose hearts are taken up with their business; they can rise betimes, and prevent the day, whether it be the desire of getting goods, or enjoying pleasure, or to do mischief, which makes some not to rest; or that it be such joy as was here in Ruth; or a good will to do a thing, as in Abraham to obey God, he arose up early, Gen. xxii. 3, and xxviii. 18; so Jacob to get to his uncle's; Joshua to find out the transgressor in the excommunicate thing, Josh. vii. 16, to put the evil away from Israel; David to go with that which his father sent unto the host, 1 Sam. xvii. 20. So that let the heart be taken up with love, care, joy, desire, it will do anything; the spirit of drowsiness will be shaken off; for it is the careless mind which maketh slothful. To be therefore stirring, and to raise up ourselves out of the bed of idleness, we must set our hearts upon our affairs. I might also note, how darkness keeps us from the knowledge of one another; therefore in darkness man feareth not the face of man, and so is bold to do evil, because he is hid from the sight of others; and as it is in bodily darkness, so in spiritual; the ignorant and blind in soul dare do anything, they blush not, neither be they ashamed, which others enlightened are afraid to commit; neither can they discern one another; for the light of truth they have not. But yet, though men can be hid in darkness from men, they cannot be so from God.

For he said (or as others read), *and he said, Let it not be known that a woman came into the floor.* If you read *for*, it is a reason from Boaz his speech of her so soon rising; if *and*, then it is his admonition to her, that being risen, she should so get her into the city, that others might not know that they were alone together in the floor that night. Howsoever it be read, Boaz herein sheweth his care of his and her honest name and credit, which might hereby be brought into suspicion, albeit their consciences had told them, that they had done nothing worthy blame, for any act of dishonesty. From hence let us note, first, that it never was, neither yet is a matter of good report, but a suspicion rather of evil, for a man and a woman to be taken together alone in places unfit, unusual, and at times unseasonable. This the words of Boaz do plainly here give us to understand; for man is so apt to this sin of the flesh, yea, the best, without especial grace, as light occasions breed suspicions; because also men are not so charitable as they should be, if any least show of evil may seem to be given this way. Therefore let such as would not be suspected beware how they be in company alone together, when and where suspicions may arise. Secondly, that it is not enough to have our consciences clear before God, but ourselves clear of giving just suspicion of evil before men. This was Boaz his care, and St Paul's, Acts xxiv. 16; for it is not enough to have a good conscience within, but we must have care of our good name, to be well reported of abroad, 2 Cor. viii. 21, which is an excellent thing, better than riches, than ointment, Prov. xxii. 1, Eccles. vii. 1. And this the godly will endeavour to obtain, to stop the mouths of adversaries, Heb. xi. 2, 39, that they may be put to rebuke, 3 John 12, and to

procure glory to the gospel which they do profess, 1 Peter ii. 12. This being our duty, then are they reproveable which make no conscience of offence before men, because, say they, our hearts condemn not us, we know we do not what men suspect, when yet the apostle forbids offences, and to look to expediency, and not simply to the lawfulness of a thing, and to avoid all appearances of evil, 1 Cor. x. 32, and xii. 13. There are another sort worse than these, who are so far from avoiding suspicion of evil, as they are not ashamed of the evil itself, being past shame, and dare openly boast of their lewdness, without blushing, of which both Isaiah and Jeremiah do complain, Isa. iii. 9, Jer. vi. 15, and viii. 12.

Ver. 15. *Also he said, Bring the veil that thou hast upon thee, and hold it. And when she held it, he measured six measures of barley, and laid it on her: and she went into the city.*

Here is Boaz his liberality and testimony of love, noting wherein it was received, what and how much he gave, his helping her up with it to convey and carry it away. And, lastly, his and her departure into the city.

Also he said. Boaz his former speech was for her credit, but this is for her comfort; the former stood in words, but this in a good work of mercy. A good man's love appeareth in word and in deed, in good counsel, and in good works of comfort also. This sheweth love to be perfect, not feigned; this is to follow the apostle John his exhortation, 1 John iii. 18, not to love ' in word and tongue only, but in deed and in truth;' so loved Boaz, and so do all blessed men love. If therefore the love of work be wanting, and only the love of word, it is counterfeit love, and St James rejecteth it as no love, James ii.

Bring the veil that thou hast upon thee, and hold it. He took occasion from this loose veil to bestow corn upon her; for a good man, in his willingness to do good, will take the smallest occasion to shew it. This word *veil* in another place is translated *mantle*, Isa. iii. 22. It was a loose garment cast upon her, to keep her warm, and to cover her in the night. There was used also among them another veil for the day, to throw over their heads and faces for modesty's sake; such an one had fair Rebekah, Gen. xxiv. 65, whose modesty may condemn the wanton going of our women, who yet come short of Rebekah for beauty. I wish also they were not more short of her for honesty. The Arabian women, yea, and so the heathen Roman women, went covered, as do now the women in Spain, not half-naked, as many harlotries do now in England, to the shame of religion and disgrace of the gospel, having both heathen and papists to condemn them. But what care such for the gospel, which want grace? or for religion, which are of none at all, and never yet had their consciences bound to the obedience thereof, but live as libertines, doing what they list, walking after the lust of their own hearts?

And when she held it. This implieth some stay till she had folded it to receive his kindness, for he that mindeth truly to do the poor good can be content to stay till they can be ready to receive it. Boaz was not like such as seem to be willing to give the poor a penny, and yet will be gone before he can open his purse to change the niggard's silver; so they blame his not readiness to receive what they only pretended, but never from heart intended, so lewdly deluding the poor. Boaz had shewed her great kindness before, which she received, and now he offers her this mercy again, which she refuseth not. For it is no unmannerliness nor disgrace to take kindness offered of friends, though the parties before have been chargeable, and have often received of their bounty, so long as the one sort be able and voluntarily do give, and the other be poor, and not importunate, yet standing in need to receive; for poverty is a heavy burden, and may justly make excuse for them. And, therefore, such are not to be blamed which do not refuse the often offered bounties of friends; but indeed, such as need not, and will be chargeable to frank-hearted friends, such are basely covetous, and deserve reproof, rather than to have their desire.

He measured six measures of barley. Boaz had given much before by his servants; now by his own hand, yet not at random, taking out of the heap he knew not what; but he measured that to her which he gave her. Whence note from his person still giving unto Ruth, and in her to Naomi, that a liberal and merciful heart is not weary of well-doing. Cornelius, a good and devout man, gave daily much alms unto the poor, for his soul delighteth in mercy and works of charity, and desiring to be rich in good works, as the apostle exhorteth, 1 Tim. vi. These examples let us imitate and follow, we must not be weary of well-doing, 2 Thes. iii. 13, Gal. vi. 9, 10; and if we have faith, we will shew forth good works, if it be lively and not dead faith, James ii. They are therefore reproveable who be weary of well-doing; they would give once, but not often, neither at any time much; and yet we beg bread at God's hands daily, and repine if we have it not, and not only for the present, but for the time to come. It is noted of Titus Vespasian,* that he thought he had lost that day in which he had not performed some office of beneficence. Few Christians think as this heathen thought; for then would our great men give more and spend less vainly, that the poor might fare the better. Another sort are here faulty, who continue to give now and then, but are loath to increase their liberality, as God increaseth his bounty in mercy towards them; for if they grow rich, it is he that giveth them power to get riches, Deut. viii. 18, Hosea ii. 8. The third sort are such as turn their love wholly to themselves, and think all little enough for themselves, and that through base covetousness, being never satisfied, so as they live of

* Sueton. in vitâ.

usury and oppression, getting from others what they can; or, through an aspiring spirit, getting goods to grow great in the world; or else, of a vain unthrifty humour of spending, can spare nothing to give to the poor, because his consuming guests (which ever lodge with him), whoredom, drunkenness, pride, and love of play, do keep him still so bare of money. Another lesson may we learn hence from Boaz his manner of giving by measure, and not hand over head, as we say, without discretion, that liberality is not lavish of God's blessings, giving in judgment, and not without consideration, for every virtue either is or should be guided with prudence. This discretion in Boaz is commendable, and they that will consider what they give before they give, in so doing are not to be reproved.

And laid it on her. See how a willing giver doth not only bestow a benefit, but helpeth the party, if need be, to receive the same; and so doth Boaz here, and so doth also our gracious God in giving his blessings to us. If we, then, be willing to do a good turn, and to bestow a favour upon any, let us not be wanting in any needful thing to further our own liberality towards them, for this will shew that what we give we give with all our hearts unto them.

And she went into the city. Our last translation is *she went,* but it should be *he,* as the Hebrew word will make good, and the testimony of the learned in that tongue.* Both went into the city, she to her mother, as the next words in the story do shew, which, by reason of the continuation and series of the narration, maketh it seem most likely that *she* went into the city, as it is commonly translated; and *he* likewise went into the city to despatch the business, and to do what he had promised to Ruth, as it is clear in the next chapter. By thus reading it, and by considering how Boaz before could lie down by the corn, but now out of his affection to marry with Ruth, can leave all to finish that business, we may learn that love is impatient of delay, and maketh a man to lay aside other cares to enjoy his beloved. Concerning the force of this affection, see it in Samson to the maiden of Timnath, Judges xiv. 2, 3; in Jacob to Rachel, Gen. xxix. 20, 30; and in Shechem to Dinah, Gen. xxxiv. 3, 8, 12, 19; for love winneth the whole man, and captivateth his thoughts to the party beloved, as may also be seen in Samson's inordinate love to Delilah, Judges xvi. 4, 16; and in Amnon to Tamar, 2 Sam. xiii. 2, 4. Seeing this affection is so strong, let us labour to bridle it, that it rule not over us for the world or the flesh; and for this end let us set it upon better things worthy our love to the utmost, even on spiritual and heavenly things, Col. iii. 1; upon Christ, as the spouse in the Canticles did, Cant. i. 2, 3, 7, and ii. 14, and St Paul; on his word, as David, Ps. cxix.; on his church, as Moses did, Heb. xi.; and on the appearing of Jesus Christ for our

* Junius, Drusius, Lavater.

final deliverance, as all should, 2 Tim. iv. 8 ; thus to fix our love will make it holy and ourselves happy.

Ver. 16. *And when she came to her mother-in-law, she said, Who art thou, my daughter ? And she told her all that the man had done unto her.*

Ruth's return from the floor to Naomi, where a question is asked and answered, with a full relation of all that which had happened.

And when she came to her mother-in-law. Ruth having sped, as you hear, and received such kindness for the present, and such hope for the time to come, home she goeth with a glad heart, and that without delay ; she hath not her bye-walks, but having done what she went about, according to the advice of Naomi, she, as I said, returneth home again. Three things might move Ruth to hasten home ; the danger of the way, being so early, before day ; the burden which she bare upon her back, to be eased thereof ; and her joy to impart to her mother her happy success. As these made her hie home, and to desire to be with her mother, so should the like make us desirous to be at our home in heaven : first, the danger we be in while here we live in this dark world ; then, the burden of sin which we do bear, of which we should be weary, and groan till we be delivered ; and, thirdly, our inward joy conceived of our future happiness for ever and for ever.

Who art thou, my daughter ? So Naomi speaketh, because it was not yet day, that she might know her, and therefore asketh who she was. It may seem by this that Naomi her house was neither bolted nor barred, Ruth coming in so easily, and Naomi not knowing who it was at the first, for poor folks need fear no robbing.

And she told her all that the man had done unto her. That is, she related all his kind speeches, and his promise of marrying of her if the other kinsman did refuse her, as appeareth by Naomi her speech in the 18th verse ; so that *done* is here put for his word and promise which should be done, which argueth her persuasion that he would do it. And it is an excellent promise of a man to be held so faithful that his promise may be said to be done, for the certainty thereof before it be done. A rare virtue in these days, even among those that would be held no common Protestants. Where almost is he of whom it might be said, when he hath promised, that it is done ? where is man's faithfulness become ? Mint, anise, and cummin is stood upon ; but judgment, mercy, and faith, the weightier matters of the law, are omitted. Naomi asketh Ruth who she was ? who answereth not to that, but forthwith relateth Boaz his kindness, with which her mind was taken up ; for we speedily relate such things as our hearts be delighted in and much taken up with : for of the abundance of the heart the mouth speaketh, whether it be cause of joy or sorrow. If then we would speak of a matter, let our

411

hearts be affected therewith, that will make us speak readily, and neglect other conference ; many cannot speak of God nor religion, and some that can will not, desire not ; the reason is, their hearts are not affected therewith, for if they were they would be very ready to speak thereof.

Ver. 17. *And she said, These six measures of barley gave he me ; for he said to me, Go not empty unto thy mother-in-law.*

The last words of Ruth in this book are here to Naomi also, shewing who it was that gave the corn, and for whose sake.

And she said, These six measures of barley gave he me. Before Ruth telleth of his good words, and here she sheweth his good works ; for good words and good works ever concur where true love is, else it is feigned, of which I have spoken before. In that Ruth doth bring home all that which was given to her mother, and kept nothing back to buy herself any necessaries by making sale thereof, it teacheth children honesty ; for honest children will not rob their parents of anything, as Micah did, Judges xvii. 1, 2, who stole eleven hundred shekels of silver from his mother, which caused her bitterly to curse him till it was restored to her again. Good children will not do so wickedly, though other think it no transgression, as Solomon speaketh, Prov. xxviii. 24.

For he said to me, Go not empty unto thy mother-in-law. Ruth telleth why Boaz was so liberal, not for her sake only, but for Naomi her sake also, and that chiefly in his kindness to her. Ruth taketh not this to herself, concealing Boaz his loving respect to Naomi, as if all had been done in favour of her own self, bringing it to Naomi as a token of her love to her, thereby thinking to bind her the more unto her by that office ; but presenting it as a favour from Boaz unto her also, relateth the truth of the thing as it passed. By which we may observe, that true and honest minds are just in all their relations, in that which they do know, without colour, without deceit ; for they love truth, and do speak it from simplicity of heart, which is the property of the godly, and which we must labour for, Ps. xv. 2. Again, the true and honest minded seek not to procure favour and thanks by that which is the bounty of another, as many do in distributing the alms and benevolence of others, as if it were from themselves, seeking to reap that which they sowed not, and to receive which they deserve not. Thirdly note, that Boaz forgets not Naomi absent ; for a faithful friend is mindful of such as he loveth, though absent. Ebed-melech the Morian loved Jeremiah, he therefore forgot him not, though out of sight, out of the court, and now in a miserable prison, but went boldly to the king for him, and reproved the lords and princes openly for doing that wrong to Jeremiah, Jer. xxxviii. 9. Darius affected Daniel, and therefore could not be unmindful of him, Dan. vi.

This is true friendship, and not like the love of such, of whom it may be said, out of sight, out of mind, like the unkind and forgetful butler of Pharaoh, who for a long space forgot innocent Joseph, who interpreted to him his dream in prison, and that to his great comfort, of whom he also prayed to be remembered, when he came to his place again; but the butler was so glad of his own prosperity, that he had no mind to think of Joseph's adversity. Such is the love of men, too common in these days; much kindness in show to men's faces, but if the back be once turned, love is likewise turned, and quite vanished away.

Ver. 18. *Then said she, Sit still, my daughter, until thou know how the matter will fall; for the man will not be in rest, until he have finished the thing this day.*

Naomi, her last words to Ruth, noted in this story, being an exhortation, in which is to be observed, to what, how long, and the reason why.

Then said she, Sit still, my daughter. Naomi having heard and seen such testimony of Boaz his love, and knowing his honest nature and true affection, she exhorteth Ruth to sit still, that is, to be of a quiet mind, waiting with patience the issue. The words are figurative, and translated from the action of the body to the action of the mind. By this that Naomi willeth her to be quiet in mind, and without fear, and restlessness of spirit, we may learn, that there is an unquietness of mind in every one naturally to have that effected, which the heart longeth after, as may be seen in Boaz, as before is noted; so in Jacob to see Joseph, when he heard that he was alive, Gen. xlv. 4, 28; in Abraham's servant, in procuring and bringing home a wife to Isaac, Gen. xxiv. 12, 56; in the Israelites, seeking to punish the Gibeonites, for the villany committed upon the Levite's wife, Judges xx. 1, 18, 19, 24, 28; and as in good, so also is the heart restless in seeking to bring evil to pass; for the wicked cannot rest, till they have done evil. See this in Delilah, in hope of money, to betray Samson into the hands of the Philistines, Judges xvi.; and in Judas, to deliver Christ to his enemies; and in Absalom, to get the kingdom from his father. Which earnestness ariseth sometime of fear, as Ruth's here fearing to fail of her desire; sometime of covetousness and desire of gain, as in Judas and Delilah; of malice and desire of revenge, as in the scribes and Pharisees, enemies of Christ; of joy and gladness, as in Abraham's servant; of an aspiring and vain glorious humour, as in Absalom; of love and affection to one, as in Shechem to Dinah. By this then may we see, whence it is that men pursue their pleasures, profits,

honours, and their desires in that which they go about so eagerly, even because they have their hearts fixed thereupon; and on the contrary, why people so little follow after godliness, so much neglect it, even for that their hearts are far from it. Thus may we learn to judge of ourselves, and thus we lay open ourselves to be judged of others.

Until thou know how the matter will fall. As if she had said, thou hast done thy part, the issue is in God's hands, which thou must wait for with patience; for when we have done what on our behalf is to be done, then are we to rest in the expectation of the issue, as Naomi adviseth Ruth here. So must we wait on God, trust in him, and commit our ways unto him, as we be exhorted, Isa. xxviii. 16, Ps. xxxvii. 5; but yet in well-doing, Ps. xxxvii. 3, and in the exercise of prayer, as Isaac did for good success to his father's servant, when he went to get a wife for him, Gen. xxiv.; and as Moses did for the victory, when the Israelites fought against the Amalekites, Exod. xvii. 11, 12.

For the man will not be in rest, till he have finished the thing. Naomi, her reason to persuade Ruth to rest, and not to let her thoughts trouble her, nor to fear by delay to be deceived of her expectation, because Boaz would not rest, till he himself had done what she desireth. An approved truth of a man in one thing, may make certain the truth of his word in another. It is equity and charity to hope well, where we have good proof of a man's faithfulness; and this is true credit, when a man's word is become of that force and validity as it maketh another to believe him without doubting. Such was Boaz his credit with Naomi; and this is it which likewise she would, and doth persuade Ruth unto. This is the credit which we must labour for, and which we may attain unto, if we fear God, and be faithful to him (for false to God, will prove faithless to man); if we be discreet and wise in our words, to know what we promise, before we make it; if we care to keep ever our word in the least thing; if we hate lying, and such as do make lies, we shall procure credit to our word. And here let such as find men careful of their word, be like Naomi, in trusting and not wronging them, by calling their word into question without cause at any time, when they are known to have ever approved themselves for honest men; for what greater injury can be offered to an honest man, ever meaning well, and careful to keep his word, than to be suspected of the breach of his word unjustly? A true-hearted man taketh that injury very tenderly; and therefore let men beware of giving offence in this kind, by entertaining unjust and uncharitable thoughts towards such as deserve it not.

CHAPTER IV.

THIS chapter is the last of the book, and the last part of the history; for the first sheweth how

Ruth came to Bethlehem; the second, how she behaved herself when she came there; the third, her contract with Boaz. And this, the solemnisation of the marriage; where is declared what went before, and how it was effected; then the marriage itself, and the great applause of the people and elders thereto. Thirdly, the happy issue thereof in the conception and birth of Obed. And lastly, a genealogy from Pharez unto David, the king and prophet of Israel, and the type of Jesus Christ, who, according to the flesh, sprung from his loins.

Ver. 1. *Then Boaz went up to the gate, and sat him down there: and behold the kinsman of whom Boaz spake came by, unto whom he said, Ho, such a one; turn aside, sit down here. And he turned aside and sat down.*

Boaz prosecuteth the matter intended; and here is shewed when, where, how, and with whom he had to do about it. Before I come to the words, note generally, that though both Naomi and Ruth had tasted of a poor and low estate, yet were they now exalted and greatly comforted, so as now no more *Mara*, but, as before, *Naomi;* for after humiliation, in time follows exaltation, after sour sweet, and after mourning joy. Many are the troubles of the righteous, but the Lord delivereth them out of all, Ps. cxxvi. 5, 6. Israel may go into bondage in Egypt, but they shall return triumphing. Joseph shall be tried, before he stand before Pharaoh; and David, before he be settled in his throne; and Moses, before he be the princely leader of the Israelites; and when thus they have tasted of the sour, assure themselves they shall feel the sweet with joy, as both Naomi and Ruth do here: for the Lord will at length set up on high those that be low, Job v. 11, that those which mourn may be exalted in safety. The Lord will humble his, to make them see themselves, to try their love, their patience and faith, and to fit them for his blessings, that they may know how well to use them, before they enjoy them; and then will he afford them their heart's desire, and make them merry and glad with the joy of his countenance. Therefore after humiliation look for exaltation: this will work comfort under the cross, and make us patiently await the time of our deliverance.

Then went Boaz. That is, that morning, not deferring what he had promised, chap. iii. 11, 13, where I spoke of the keeping of his word, which here he accomplished. See there this truth, that an honest man will be careful to keep his word, which here I will no farther insist upon. Note farther, that what is done with the heart, is done cheerfully and speedily. Boaz goeth about this without delay; yea, so did Abraham in a matter of rare obedience, Gen. xxii., yea, he rose up betimes early in the morning to sacrifice his son: for what the heart is won unto, there the whole man is set on work; if Shechem's heart cleave to Dinah, he will not defer the matter, to be circumcised, that he may enjoy the desire of the heart, Gen. xxxiv. 8, 19. By this may we discover whether the heart go with a

business. If it be done cheerfully and speedily, the heart is with it; if but slowly, and without alacrity, the heart is absent, as in many which come so to the church, and being come, sit as dead, without any liveliness, because their hearts are elsewhere.

Unto the gate. The gate was the place of judgment, as many places in Scripture shew.* Now why it was there, these may be the reasons; first, for easy access of all sorts, as well strangers as inhabitants, to the place of justice, from which none are to be kept back. In open places is the more room; secondly, for the better manifestation of justice in the sight and hearing of all, which taketh away suspicion of injustice; thirdly, for the preventing of thronging by the concourse of people, not wholesome, and sometime dangerous, in those hot countries; fourthly, that such as passed to and fro, might be called into the business, either as witnesses or parties sometime, as it fell out in this session here, with the kinsman coming at unawares; fifthly, because the gates be the strength and munition of the city; now, there for magistrates to sit, doth more grace their authority, who sit here as commanders in the place, able to command the whole town; sixthly and lastly, to put all that enter into the city in mind of well-doing, and to take heed of evil. These be my conjectures; but whatsoever the reason was, this may we learn, that public causes are for public places, and there to be determined of: for in such cases the Lord commandeth to go up to the gate of the city; as also it was the manner of the heathen thereabouts so to do. It befitteth the cause; it preventeth suspicion of sinister dealing in private; and public places do grace more authority than private meetings. And therefore this course is to be approved, and the private hearing of public business, as in criminal causes, is against the apostle's canon; and hereby great evils fall out; justice is perverted, and sin often unpunished, the offenders let go for gain, who should be made examples, that other might hear and fear, Deut. xxi. 21.

And sat him down there. Seats were prepared before for him and the rest, as the common place of justice; which sitting down of him in the public place of justice, sheweth that he was a judge and a man of authority, and the best also in the assembly, because he took the first place. Note briefly, first, that sitting is the gravest gesture for judges and magistrates in places of judgment; so ever set out, Prov. xxxi. 23, Mat. xix. 28, Rev. xx. 4; and so ever used in those parts, and likewise with us; which therefore is to be observed for the better setting forth of their authority, which they should mind to grace by all means in the people's eyes, for more reverence sake. Secondly, that God so guideth by his providence these worldly estates, that ever some are better men in place and dignity than other some: such a one was Job, chap.

* Gen. xxxiv. 20, Deut. xvii. 5, and xxi. 19, and xxii. 15, 24, and xxv. 7, Prov. xxxi. 23, Joshua xx. 4, Job xxix. 7.

i. 1, and xxix. 7-9; and so Boaz here, for the preservation of peace in church and commonwealth;
which hand of God we are to praise him for, and to
pray unto him to uphold this inequality of persons;
for else what would follow but disorder and confusion,
and every man would do what he list, Judges xvii. 6,
and xviii. 1. See this with ourselves when men of
equality meet, and have light occasions offered : oh
how do they scornfully behave themselves one to another ! Thirdly, that men of place, according to their
dignity, may take their place without stain of pride;
for Boaz doth it : it is also their right, and it pre-
serveth order, and that dignity which God hath given
them. Therefore may they take their place; yet so
as they be humble, and not haughtily-minded, neither
proudly contend for it, and so disturb public peace,
which should ever be most dear to every one, especially to men in authority. If men may take their
place, then such are blame-worthy, which, with an envious eye, find fault with any for so doing; and they
also do amiss, which out of too great humility (to
speak but so of it) do lose their due place, and there-
withal so much of due respect unto their person and
degree, yielding their place to the less worthy, and so
lift up the other in pride, and make themselves of less
esteem. But as there be some such so lowly-minded,
so are there others too highly-conceited of themselves,
who will take place of their betters, assuming to themselves more than they deserve. This is pride and hateful arrogancy.

*And behold the kinsman of whom Boaz spake came
by.* Chap. iii. 12, 13. This word of attention, *Behold*,
calleth the reader to a remarkable thing, and to an especial providence of God, in bringing this kinsman thus
hither; not as yet called or sent for. If he had been
sent for, or called, and so come of purpose, it seemeth
the Holy Ghost would not have said, *Behold.* This,
then, was the guiding hand of God to further this match.
Whence we do learn, that when God will prosper a
business, his providence will apparently be seen in
that business, and in the success thereof, as you may
see before in Boaz his coming into the field, and
Ruth's lighting upon his reapers, chap. ii.; so in
Abraham's servant guided to Laban's house, and in
Rebekah, her coming out whilst he prayed standing by
the well, and she performing everything according as
he had prayed immediately before, Gen. xxiv. Such
a providence was seen in the Midianites' coming by
to go into Egypt, while Joseph lay in the pit, that he
might be sold to them, that they might carry him into
Egypt, as God had determined, Gen. xxxvii. The like
providence in Moses's preservation by Pharaoh's
daughter, Exod. ii., is very apparent; for God's providence is his guiding hand to effect what he hath
decreed; he willeth, and then his providence worketh
the same. Which, if we will observe, we may easily
see in our courses, and say, Behold, the providence
of God, and by well marking the same, we would be
moved greatly to praise God; we would not murmur
against crosses; we would commit our ways unto him,
and wait on his good pleasure with patience in all our
affairs, knowing this certainly, that if he hath determined a thing, it shall come to pass, though in man's
reason most unlikely.

Unto whom he said, Ho, such a one, &c. This kinsman was of worth. It appeareth by this, that he sat
next Boaz, before the ten elders; that he was able to
redeem land so soon after ten years' dearth; that he
regarded so much the marring of his own inheritance;
and lastly, because he was of the same family of
Elimelech, and in birth before Boaz, yet by place it
may seem that Boaz was his better, though Boaz
would not stand upon his greatness and power with
him, but he would proceed in this business according
to equity and right, respecting so himself, as yet he
would not wrong another, but do what was most meet
to be done; teaching this, that a godly man, a just
man, will not do what he may by his power, but what
he ought by right. Such a one was Nehemiah
(Nehem. vii. 15), and Abraham (Gen. xiv. 22, 23),
who would not do according to that which was in their
hand, but what was agreeable to justice, and fit for
them to do. Nehemiah giveth the reason, because he
feared God. This was it also that made Joseph so to
deal with his brethren, and not according to his power
and their deserts. This is it which made Job not to
contemn his servant, for he knew his servant, as well
as himself, to be the Lord's. Oh then, let men of
power imitate these men of might ! it will argue that
they also fear God, Prov. xiv. 2; and upright and just
dealing is more acceptable to God than sacrifices,
Prov. xxi. 3. Men must not be like Nimrods nor
Sauls, to make their lusts a law, and their power the
bounds of their practice. Remember Jezebel, 1 Kings
xxi. 7, who took by force and fraud Naboth's vineyard, but she at length dearly paid for the same.
Note hence again, that one not before another by
birth, may be his better by authority, as Boaz was
here; so Moses before Aaron, Joseph before his
brethren, and David before his; for God advanceth
not men as they be in birth, but as his good pleasure
is. And therefore let the elder submit to the younger,
if God please to have it so; and men descended of
nobles submit to mean men advanced by God, and
that without envy or disdain; for God fetcheth beggars from the dunghill, to set them among princes,
1 Sam. ii. Promotion is not from east or west, but
from his hand, therefore must we rest contented.
Thirdly note, that a man according to his authority
may speak to another with authority, though in some
respect the same be his better, as the kinsman is here
by birth, to whom Boaz yet thus speaketh. But why
did he not name him ? Boaz did name, as these
words ' *Such a one,*' do shew; but the penman of the
Spirit passeth him by, either as not material, or rather
for that he was a worldling, loving land better than

God's law, vers. 4, 6 ; desiring the one, but not caring to obey the other. Hereby giving us to know, that he which loveth more the world and his own outward estate, than the law and word of God, is worthy to have no name in God's book, in the book of life. Therefore 'Take heed and beware of covetousness:' old father Latimer's text.

Turn aside, sit down here. Boaz willeth him to set aside his private business for this public work, and to sit down to hear the matter; the matter concerned them both, and Boaz doth call him into the court and place of judgment about it. Whence note, that it is lawful, upon just cause, for one man to call another into public places of justice to clear men's rights. For this cause, God himself appointed amongst his people public courts of justice, Exod. xxii. 8; gave them laws to judge by, and allowed men to take the benefit thereof; and godly men have sat as judges, as Moses, Exod. xviii. 15; David, 1 Chron. xviii. 14, and others; for without this, some controversies cannot be ended, so perverse and partial are many in their own cause. Which confuteth the anabaptists, who allow not of magistrates, and this course of justice in ending controversies. Yet, on the other side, albeit men may sue one another, it must not be for every trifle; it must not be in revenge, malice, and with desire to hurt my neighbour; it must be the last remedy, and when men go to law, they must do it in love, use the law as a judge and moderator, and therefore must they choose the most honest lawyers, which will not sell their tongues, and abuse their wits for gain; they are to beware of bribing any; they must not use circumventions, but be content, peaceably and lovingly, to let the equity of the law decide the matter, and therein quietly rest.

And he turned aside, and sat down. Though this man was one of some worth among them, and a worldly man too, yet he for this public business, and for to shew his obedience to authority, turneth aside from his private affairs, and doth sit down, as Boaz did will him. Whence, note first, That when any are called to public business, private are to be laid aside for the time, to further the public, as this man doth here, and as all good members of a commonwealth should do, for that public actions and public causes should be more near and dear to us than private; for in public things there is a respect unto the private, which is more safe in the safety of that which is public. Therefore, such as do neglect wholly public welfare, and attend only to the private good of their own estate, they do amiss, and even so, as if a member of the body should see to itself, and neglect the body, which is the way at length to bring ruin upon itself, which it seeks to prevent. This reproveth such as being able and fit men for public businesses, do labour yet by all means to avoid them. As also, much more such as being called by public authority, yea, and bound by oath to the same, do nevertheless live as if

415

no such duty were imposed upon them, and are wholly taken up with the thoughts of their own private and household affairs. This so great neglect of that which is public, is no small detriment to the commonweal; this great care of every man for himself and for his own private, and little, or rather none, for the public, is the cause of so great and so many evils everywhere among men. Secondly, that men are to yield readily to lawful authority commanding, whatsoever worth they be of, which are so commanded. Men must be like the Israelites, and do as they said they would do to Joshua, even to obey readily in all things, and so to uphold his authority, as also they would oppose themselves against such as would not obey, Joshua i. 16–18. David was very obedient unto Saul, albeit he was anointed himself, he stood not upon his right, but waited the Lord's time, and was willingly obedient. Thus should we be to lawful authority, as the apostle exhorteth, Rom. xiii. 1–4, Titus iii. 1, and that by many reasons, in the epistle to the Romans, though in those times the kings and governors were heathen and bloody persecutors. This condemneth those which are like Korah and his company; and like Absalom and his associates in conspiracy, which are so far from obedience, as they rise up in open rebellion against lawful authority. Such were the counterfeit catholics; and such be they ever in heart, though not alway in action, in this our sovereign's dominions. This also checketh those which, though they hate treason and rebellion, and will not disobey supreme authority, yet will despise inferior officers; but they are commanded the contrary, as the apostle Peter teacheth, 1 Peter ii. 13; for not only the king as supreme, but also such as be sent of him, are to be obeyed of conscience for the Lord's sake.

Ver. 2. *And he took ten men of the elders of the city, and said, Sit ye down here. And they sat down.*

Here is set down the assistants in this business: how many, what they were, whence taken, and their sitting down in the place of judgment with Boaz and the kinsman, after that Boaz had willed them so to do.

And he took ten men. The elders and people were gathered together, it may seem, before unto the gate; whether it was that they were especially sent for, or that they hearing that Boaz was gone up to the gate of the city, and so came voluntarily, as it was perhaps their manner so to do when they heard of any to go up to the place of judgment, it is not certain; but the elders were there and the people also, ver. 11, and of the elders, he chose only ten to sit in the place of judgment. Why only ten, is no reason given; it may be, the number was chosen according to the ten years of Naomi her absence in Moab, chap. i. 4, or according to the number of the ten commandments, to put them in mind of their duty, or for what else, I will not further conjecture; it was a number thought fit in this case for the hearing and determining of the matter.

This we note in Boaz taking of these men, men of authority, that public causes are to be handled before public persons, and of them a competent number for the determining thereof, Deut. xxv. 7, Joshua xx. 4; for therefore are such appointed, public persons for public causes; and by such as have authority to end matters, the thing in hand is more firmly established, and if there have been before, or might after, contention arise, the same hereby is cut off and prevented. And therefore, in such cases, let such fit persons and so many be judges, as may by their authority end businesses between one another.

Of the elders. Here I will note, first, what elders were; secondly, of whom chosen; thirdly, of what sort of persons; fourthly, why set over the people; and lastly, why called elders. For the first, elders were men of authority, 1 Kings xx. 7, 8, distinguished from the people, and joined with others, so as it is said, the *princes and elders*, Ezra x. 8, Judges viii. 6, 14–16; *judges and elders*, Deut. xxi. 2; *elders and officers*, Num. xi. 16. Under this name were the chief in the commonwealth comprehended, both out of Israel, Joshua ix. 11, Num. xxii. 7, and in Israel, as in many places it fully appeareth; and therefore princes are included in elders, Judges viii. 6, 14–16, and rulers and elders made one, Ezra v. 9, 10, and vi. 7, 8. The chief of the king's house were called elders, 2 Sam. xii. 17, and such as in every city bare rule, Deut. xxi. 3, 19, 20; for those which were appointed in every city to be judges and officers in Deut. xvi. 18, are everywhere after called by the name of the elders of the city, Deut. 20, and xxii. 15-18. Thus the Lord ordained governors to rule his people. For the second, they were chosen by the people, and admitted by Moses, as himself in a place witnesseth, Deut. i. 13, which was to them a great liberty and freedom. For the third, they were of the best, able, and fittest men, Exod. xviii. 21,* thus to be qualified; first, to be men of wisdom and understanding, Deut. i. 13, and not childish and simple persons; for that is a punishment upon the people, to have such over them, Isa. iii. 4; secondly, to be good men, religious, and fearing God, 2 Chron. xix. 11; for such should rule over men, 2 Sam. xxiii. 3, as have conscience towards God, under whom, and for whose glory they are to rule; and with those the Lord will be, 2 Chron. xix. 11; thirdly, to be men of truth, as Jethro adviseth, Exod. xviii. 21, that is, true men, Gen. xlii. 11, as Joseph's brethren call themselves; such as are that which they seem to be, not pretending one thing and intending another, but in the course of justice do follow the truth of the cause, as the truth thereof shall appear unto them; fourthly, to be men hating covetousness, Deut. xvi. 19, else they will take bribes, Prov. i. 19, and love dishonest gain, and pervert justice, Ezek. xxii. 27, 1 Sam. viii. 3; fifthly, to be known men in these things, Deut. i. 13. When such are set over a people,

* See Zipper. de Lege Mos. lib. iii. cap. 9.

let us praise God and rejoice; and where such be wanting, pray to God to send them; and where the contrary be, lament and bewail the estate of such a people. Touching the fourth, why they be set over a people? For the praise of the good, and the punishment of the bad, 1 Peter ii. 13, 14; and to rule in justice and in judgment, and to govern the people, 2 Chron. ix. 8, for that we be all of a rebellious nature since the fall of Adam. Now, to govern well, magistrates and men in authority must do two things: first, they must find out offences, they must inquire, and search out the same diligently, Deut. xiii. 12, Job xxix. 16, Deut. xvii. 4; for one rebellious Jonah may hazard many men's lives, and the sinking of the ship, Jonah i. ; so one Achan may weaken a whole army, Joshua vii., and therefore it is necessary to seek them out, that sin may be punished, and God's wrath appeased. Secondly, they must justly proceed against offences, and that thus: first, they must set God's fear before them, as Jehoshaphat exhorts, 2 Chron. xix. 7. Secondly, they must do it in the spirit of courage, Deut. i. 17, 2 Chron. xix. 11, Job xxix. 17, and xxxi. 34, not fearing the face of any, though many, though mighty. Thirdly, they must deal equally, without respect of person, hearing the small as well as the great, not wresting judgment, but judge the people with just judgment, Deut. i. 17, and xvi. 18, 19. For the last, why called elders? It may be they were chosen of the ancient of the people, or for the most part of such: for the Hebrew word here (מזקני) cometh of the verb which signifieth to be waxen old; and the assembly of the elders is called the *Synedrion* of the old men, συνέδριον γερόντων, by the Grecians; and of these is it most meet that judges and magistrates be chosen; first, for their wisdom and experience, though wisdom doth not always abide with the aged, Job xxxii. 9. Secondly, for that such give counsel with more mature deliberation, and have not the force of affection to over-sway them, as youth hath, which therefore is rash, and giveth often ill counsel, of which Rehoboam tasted and repented. Thirdly, for the gravity of their countenance, which giveth grace and credit to their authority, and so are not so subject to contempt, as the young in years be; for the hoary head is to be honoured, Lev. xix. 32, and age is a crown of glory if it be found in the way of righteousness, Prov. xvi. 31. Fourthly, because they have a strong motive to persuade them to upright dealing, even their old age and the nighness of death. This made some heathen to be upright and stout against the mighty,* as Solon against Pisistratus, and Cecilius against Cæsar; the former said, his old age made him so to withstand the attempts of the tyrant, and the latter told his friends that his old age, and being also childless, made him dare to speak so roundly and freely against Cæsar. We see, then, what reason there is that the governors should be an-

* Plut. lib. *An senibus sit gerenda Resp.* Laert. Tul. *de senect.* Val. Max.

cient men, such as well might be called elders, not only for authority, but for their years and gravity.

Of the city. To wit, of Bethlehem; for in every city, by God's appointment, there were officers and judges, the elders of the people, Deut. xvi. 18, Ezra x. 14, 2 Chron. xix. 5. How many were in every city is not certain; in this, besides Boaz and the kinsman, were ten. And it is said, *ten of them*, implying more. In Succoth were princes and elders threescore and seventeen, Judges viii. It may seem, that the number of them was either greater or lesser, according to the populousness of the inhabitants, and largeness of the cities; only in Jerusalem was the great *Synedrion*, consisting of the seventy-two elders constantly. In every city were courts of justice, and every matter came before those elders; as matters concerning idolatry, rebellion, and obstinacy of children given to riotousness; also murder, adultery, theft, and injuries offered, and slander; so matters of marriage, and sale of land, as here in this place.* The punishments† which they inflicted were pecuniary sometime, sometime beating and whipping, and sometime death itself; likewise to this death were put enticers to idolatry, and such as committed it; also a young woman that should play the whore in her father's house, and those that committed adultery; likewise the sacrilegious person, the blasphemer, the wizard, and the obstinate, gluttonous, and drunken son, all were stoned, Lev. xxiv. 14, and xxi. 9, and xx. 14. Some were to be burnt, as the priest's daughter playing the whore, and the incestuous person; and this death may seem to be before the law for whoredom, Deut. xxi. 22. Some were hanged for some offences; but before the punishment was inflicted, and before sentence was pronounced, there was diligent inquiry of the fact, and also competent witnesses to justify the same, Deut. xvii. 4, and xix. 15, 19; for not one, but two or three witnesses were to establish a matter; and if any false witnesses were found, that was done to them which they had thought to have done to another. Thus we see, how these elders proceeded in justice, from whom there was no appeal in any matter, but in that which was too hard; and then were the parties to go to Jerusalem, unto the priests, the Levites and judges there, and abide that sentence without gainsaying, and that upon peril of their life. From the consideration of these things afore delivered, touching superiority, and courts of justice everywhere, and such a court from which could be no appeal, we may observe, first, that superiority of some above the rest is the ordinance of God, for the well governing of a commonwealth. The chief and best is that which is monarchical, when a king ruleth over the people, so be he as Moses describeth, Deut. xvii. 19, 20, and not as Samuel, 1 Sam. viii. 11, 18;

for God set first one, even king Moses, as he is called, Deut. xxxiii. 5, over the people, and Moses prayeth that one might be set over the people, lest that the Israelites should be as sheep without a shepherd, yea, though then there were captains over thousands, hundreds, and tens, and the seventy elders upon whom the Lord had put his Spirit. Again, we read that the Lord saved his people by judges or princes, raised up to lead them and to be judges over them, Judges iii., and iv., and vi. Furthermore, when the Israelites were seated in Canaan, and that there were the seventy-two elders, also in every city elders, yet is it said, that every one did what seemed him good, because there was no king in Israel, Judges xvii., and xviii., and xxii. Moreover, Israel never came to be renowned, freeing themselves from all their enemies, and subduing them which were round about them, till they had a king over them. Lastly, it is the wisdom of nations, both civil and barbarous heathen, 1 Sam. viii. 5, besides the church of God, to allow of this kind of government, such as the Lord hath now placed over us, that so every man may not do what he listeth; and therefore are we to rest thankful therewith, and praise the name of our God. Secondly, that in well governed commonwealths (like that of Israel, ordered by the wisdom of God himself), there should be many courts of justice, and so many, and so near the towns and villages, that the people might have speedy recourse thither, to end any cause which might fall out among them. In every city in Israel, in every tribe and city thereof, were courts of justice, Deut. xvi. 16. In Judah were an hundred and twelve cities, which was but a little circuit, even so many courts for justice and judgment, to which the towns and villages resorted which belonged to them; and in them, as is before noted, were all matters handled, without going any farther. This would prevent long journeys, and so great expenses of subjects; this would sooner bring causes to the hearing, and matters to an end; this were the way to have sin more easily and sooner punished. The Israelites did not stay till quarter-sessions, till assizes every half year; till which time causes must rest, prisoners lie and die in prison, or else learn such villanies there, as they will be ever the worse for when they be delivered. The Israelites were not constrained to take long journeys every term to the chief city of their kingdom to try matters, as we do, and as we were wont to do, even to go much farther, to Rome from England, heretofore; but all had courts for every matter, for all offences, for controversies of every nature, hard at hand, and daily kept for any to have access unto. Which I thus speak of only, not to condemn utterly our courses, but to set out the political estate of the Jews, a platform of government devised by God himself, and therefore worthy imitation of all nations, and that before any other whatsoever; for the wisdom of no lawgiver can be compared to the wisdom of this heavenly lawgiver. Thirdly, that it is meet

---

* Deut. xvii. 3, 5, and xxi. 18, and xix. 11, and xxii. 21, 24; Exod. xxii.; Deut. xxii. 14, 18.

† Deut. xxii. 19, and xxv 2; Lev. xix. 30; Deut. xiii. 10, and xvii. 5, and xxii. 21, 24; Joshua vii.

that such a court of justice be in every well ordered state, whose sentence should be definitive, and with which men should rest. So was it in Israel, from which none might decline upon pain of death, Deut. xvii. 11, 12. This would curb contentions and unquiet spirits, which be full of molestations, when by their purse they can maintain their will, bringing causes from court to court, and about again, only to make the weaker party weary, and so to wring from him his right, or else to be utterly undone in following the suit: a grievous sin, and that which crieth aloud in the ears of the Lord, though lawyers fill their purses by such devilish devices. Their money perish with them, which make themselves rich by such iniquities!

And he said, Sit ye down here. Thus spake he to the ten elders, when the kinsman was set down. Which sheweth, that as Boaz was a great man, so also the kinsman was of greater place than they, seeing he was placed before them, yet they did not of themselves do anything, neither did enter upon the business before these were set: so did he esteem of them and their authority. Whence may be noted, that wise men in government do so behave themselves, as they will take heed to do nothing that might weaken the authority of such as be fellows in office, judges, justices, and officers with them; for they know, that what they derogate from them, they take from themselves, as they be magistrates. And therefore must magistrates uphold such as be in authority with them; though some perhaps for their person be unworthy, yet must they be regarded for the place they bear; and this shall they do, if, as Boaz here, they give them place with them, then not presume to handle matters apart without them, equally belonging to all; and thirdly, to be content to have their own causes heard and judged by them. The contrary hereto doth argue light esteem of fellows in commission, if not contempt.

And they sat down. Here was no exception taken against Boaz in anything; he commanded in a sort, and they obeyed, for the spirit of envy and pride were banished, else the matter had not thus been done in such peace and quietness; for where one taketh no more upon him than he may, and other yield what they ought, being humble and not haughty, there everything is done peaceably, as we see here; but where a Moses meeteth with a rebellious-spirited, proud Korah and his company, there all things fall out contrarily. The word *to sit* is used sometime to consider of, to advise, to take care of; and the gesture of sitting, which was the gesture of kings and judges, 1 Kings i. 48, Prov. xx. 8, Mat. xix. 28, 2 Sam. vii. 1, is a gesture of rest, quietness and peace; to teach this, that men in the seat of judgment should be advised, considerate, careful what they do, and of a quiet spirit, without perturbation. Such a one was Joshua, in his proceeding against Achan, Joshua vii. 19, 25; he

spake mildly, lovingly, without passion, without words of bitterness, or contempt, yet did he not neglect to execute justice upon him, as he well deserved, and the cause required; he derided not the prisoner, he railed not upon him; but with a fatherly gravity and words of like authority he spake unto him. His example is for imitation, and a check to some deriding and scoffing spirits, sitting as judges upon life and death.

Ver. 3. *And he said unto the kinsman, Naomi, that is come again out of the country of Moab, selleth a parcel of land which was our brother Elimelech's.*

Thus Boaz beginneth his speech of the sale of land, who it was that would sell it, how much, a parcel, and to whom it did belong before, as thereby shewing her right unto it, not as an inheritrix, but as a dowry to her, as his wife.

And he said unto the kinsman. Before Boaz uttered the cause of his coming into that session, he saw all settled, and audience given; for though he earnestly affected the business, as may appear by that which hath been delivered of him in the former chapter, yet would he carry the matter wisely and discreetly; hereby teaching this, that the wisdom of a wise man keepeth him so, as he is not carried beyond discretion; for wisdom maketh him to understand his way, to be also well advised, to work by understanding, and to order his ways with discretion, Prov. xiv. 8, and xiii. 10, 16. Such therefore as be overswayed with any passion, either of love, or anger, or what else exceeding discretion, want wisdom at that time to bridle their disordered affection, and unruly passion, which is often brutish, without religion, and therefore unbefitting a godly man. Note farther, that Boaz having a cause, he in this great session of ten elders, besides the rest, declareth the matter himself, it being a happy liberty in that commonwealth. It was not like those places, where men cannot be allowed to speak in their own cause, though they be never so able, but they must hire others to speak for them; by which it cometh to pass, that causes are spun out to an exceeding length, and not often faithfully handled; for men hired to set their wits and tongues on sale, what will they not do? Doth not our age produce enow evil, lamentable and cursed fruits hereof? And have we not cause to bewail the manifold mischiefs and ensuing miseries, which this generation of evil men bringeth forth daily among us?

Naomi, that is come again out of the country of Moab. Of her person, and return from that place, see before, chap. i. 6. Here she is propounded as the saleswoman; the land she had by Elimelech her husband, as the last words of this verse shew, as her jointure or dowry, for wives had land among the Jews and Israelites, 2 Kings viii. 6. And good reason there is that wives should be provided for by them which have lands to leave them, because they are one with the husband, they have laboured together, and love binds the husband to have care for her after death ; for her comfort, her better esteem even with her own children ; for if they have anything, then children will love and honour them, and glad will they seem to be which of them may have her company, and may please her best ; but if she have nothing, they will be as glad which may be rid of her. Therefore let husbands have a care to provide for them, and not be like some husbands, which give all or most to children, and little or nothing to wives, but what law will give them ; and that he may so do, let the wife labour to deserve well of the husband ; and yet though she deserve well, let him not give all to her, and little to children, as some do, and so undo both herself and children with an after-choice of a bad husband.

Selleth a parcel of land. That is, determineth to sell a portion or piece of land left her by Elimelech. She was grown poor, and therefore might sell her land ; for so we do read, that the poor might sell land or houses ; and this selling and buying is lawful, Lev. xxv. 25, 29, as we may see by God's approbation, and the practice of the godly in buying and selling, Gen. xxiii. The manner of purchase, and sale, and conveyance is shewed in the prophecy of Jeremiah, chap. xxxii. 6, 44. It must be without oppression; and this will be avoided if men fear God. But the Lord allowed not the sale but upon necessity : he must become poor first. The Jewish interpreters upon that place of Leviticus say that no man but the poor might sell his inheritance ; others might not sell, to put money in their purses, to make merchandise, or other things, save only for food and necessary livelihood. How justly, then, are here condemned among us such as sell their lands for to spend at play, to run a-whoring, to go gaily, and in costly raiment, to keep hawks and hounds, to travel into idolatrous countries to see fashions, and to learn not good manners, but bad conditions with apish compliments ! Others also which sell their possessions because they would live idly, to put the money out to usury, and so live lazily, but yet cursedly, upon the sweat of other men's brows, these and the other should say with Naboth, God forbid that I should sell my fathers' inheritance, especially selling as these do, to bestow and lay out the money so accursedly. But let such unthrifts know, which sell their land to waste upon their lust, that they do wickedly rob their posterity, they weaken their present estate, they bring upon themselves beggary, and so contempt and misery, and that very justly, and do, as much as lieth in them, root out their names from the places where their ancestors, by God's blessing, had planted them ; and when all is spent, they expose themselves to many temptations, to take lewd courses to help themselves, which bring many to a shameful end. Let them remember that if they cannot live with their estates, how can they live without them. Pains they cannot take ; they have idly been brought up, which often is the cause of this prodigality. To beg they be

ashamed, because of reproach justly to light upon them, therefore must they fall to stealing, and so come that way into the magistrate's hands, that they may be punished for their former villanies, which the magistrate took no notice of, or made no conscience to punish.

Which was our brother Elimelech's. Thus Boaz calleth him, who was but his kinsman, though near. This was usual among the Jews and Israelites so to call one another ; yea, it is observable that God's people, in all ages, have called one another brethren, before the law, under the law, and in the time of the gospel ;* and good reason so to do, for they have all one father, and all one mother ; which should teach us brotherly love one towards another ; to love as brethren, that is, with respect to our Father, and we his adopted children ; for whoso after this manner loveth is translated from death to life. Also such as love like brethren are familiar, they have a feeling of each other's estate both in prosperity and adversity, rejoicing or sorrowing, as it falleth out, and that because they be brethren ; they do also shew readiness to help one another, as brethren should do, and they hold it a shame to do them wrong. Therefore let us love, and love as brethren, and try it by these true brother-like marks of love, which, if a man do, he shall find little brotherly love among men ; for few love a man in this respect, as he is the child of God ; few are familiar with the virtuous for their virtue's sake. And who mourneth with them in the true cause of their mourning, or rejoiceth with them in their joy ? If men so do, where is their helping hand to further their joy, or to help them when they be troubled for righteousness' sake ?

Ver. 4. *And I thought to advertise thee, saying, Buy it before the inhabitants, and before the elders of my people. If thou wilt redeem it, redeem it ; but if thou wilt not redeem it, then tell me, that I may know : for there is none to redeem it besides thee ; and I am after thee. And he said, I will redeem it.*

Boaz here sheweth why he telleth the kinsman of Naomi her selling of land to offer him the sale first. In which offer note, first, what the offer is, to buy it ; then, before whom ; thirdly, the manner of propounding it, as left free to his choice, to redeem or not to redeem ; fourthly, the reason why offered to him in the first place, and that by Boaz ; lastly, the kinsman's answer, taking the offer.

And I thought to advertise thee. To wit, of the sale of the land. And this Boaz doth, for that he had to deal with a worldling, with whom he would deal plainly, in telling him first of that which most affected him, and of the earthly commodity, before he spake of marrying Ruth. Whence we may learn, first, that world-

* Gen. xiv. 14, Exod. ii. 11, Lev. xix. 17, Deut. xiii. 19, Rom. i. 13, Mat. vi., Gal. iv. 26, 1 Pet. ii. 17, Rom. xii. 10, Heb. xiii. 1, 1 Thes. iv. 9. 1 Jchn iii. 14.

lings are carried away most with wordly respects, therefore Boaz doth thus begin with the kinsman; for worldlings savour only of the earth, like moles which live in it; and though they now and then come up out of the earth, they by and by run again into it. They are like the serpent, whose seed they be, living upon the dust of the earth, gold, silver, and transitory goods, the sight and enjoying whereof is to them as food and life. Their wisdom also is from below, which is ' earthly,' making men covetous; and ' sensual,' making men delight in beastly pleasures; and ' devilish,' full of craft, fraud, wicked policy, and subtle devices, James iii. 15. This wisdom below followeth the things of this world, even the lusts of the eyes, which are earthly; the lusts of the flesh, which are sensual; and pride of life, which is devilish. Therefore let us hereby try our worldliness, and whether we be such as worldlings be; the signs whereof be these: first, when we are more moved to do anything for profit and gain than for the commandment of God, or charity, or any other motive by which the godly are drawn on to do that which they should do. Secondly, when our hearts are wholly set upon the world, minding altogether earthly things, which sheweth that there is our treasure, because our hearts be there. Thirdly, when we grow more covetous as riches increase, setting our hearts upon them, Isa. xxxii. 6. Fourthly, when we speak like worldlings, who can utter their thoughts freely in these earthly matters, but are in spiritual matters very blockish, if not senseless. Fifthly, when we be not liberal-minded, for a liberal person is set against the niggard and churl, Isa. xxxii. 5, who is called in Hebrew *nabal*, a fool, for, so is the covetous worldling; also *kelai*, of a word (כלה) which signifieth to consume, for that he wasteth himself in the world and for the world. By circumlocution he is said to be one ' greedy of gain,' Prov. i. 19, one that loveth silver, and abundance, and is not satisfied, Eccles. v. 10. The Grecians calleth him φιλάργυρος, *philarguros*, one that loveth money, Luke xvi. 14, and πλεονίκτης, *pleonectes*, one that would have more, never contented; and therefore to be covetous and contented are put as contraries, Heb. xiii., the one being forbidden, and the other commanded. This is the worldling. Secondly, note that an honest man dealeth plainly and not covertly with others in these worldly businesses. Boaz concealeth not the commodity which the kinsman might reap in marrying of Ruth; he propoundeth not her, and concealeth this; for an honest man hateth fraud and deceit; he doth to others as he would that they should do to him. If, therefore, we would be held honest, let us deal uprightly and plainly with others with whom we have to do; for it is sincerity, it maketh a man's word of credit, and bringeth him into the reputation of an honest man; and let this be remembered, that fraud and deceit God will certainly avenge, 1 Thes. iv. Thirdly, note that albeit man may not deceive his brother, yet is he to proceed

wisely, to use prudence and discretion in his affairs; as knowing what to speak first, what next; for there is time for all things, as Solomon saith, so in this also. And it is no fraud to utter one thing before another, and so to speak truly, to further the matter in hand; to conceal also a thing for a time, so it be with no ill intent, not to deceive, or hurt my brother any way, it is not to be condemned, but rather to be allowed, as a point of wisdom and prudence in a man, and therefore may it be observed honestly and justly, without stain or crack of credit.

Saying, Buy it before the inhabitants, and before the elders of my people. Both the elders and people were gathered together, as we may here see, and in verses 9, 11. Here the inhabitants are named before the elders; in the 9th verse the elders before them, and in verse 11 these before the elders again, as shewing how one dependeth upon the other, the elders upon the people, and the people on them by mutual relation, one assisting another, the officers the people, by their power and authority, and the people these by aid and help, as they should be commanded, which is peaceable happiness in a commonwealth. In that they be called Boaz his people, it sheweth the greatness of this man's power in Bethlehem, as lord and chief governor there, of whose greatness I have spoken before. He doth here bring this matter thus into the public assembly, for that it was public, for more peaceable proceeding, for better assurance, ratification, and confirmation of the business, when it should be concluded there before such elders and so great assembly of people. Lastly, because it was to be finished in the gate of the city, by the law of Moses, Deut. xxv. 7, 8; so it was not done in vain glory, or from an high spirit, but for that reason and necessity so required. Matters of importance are so to be handled for place and person, as may best serve to end the same peaceably, without farther ado, if it may be.

If thou wilt redeem it, redeem it. Boaz doth not urge him, but leaveth him to his choice; he telleth him of the land, but urgeth him not with the law, because he did not much care whether the kinsman would redeem it or no, having a desire to match with Ruth himself. Whence we may observe, that there a thing is rather propounded than heartily urged where the mind is not bent to have it effected; that we usually leave to men's choice which we are very indifferent in, not much caring whether it be or be not. So do many preach, propounding the doctrine of godliness rather than earnestly urging the same, because they be indifferent towards their hearers, not much caring whether they serve God or no. By this may the hearty affection or coldness in a cause be judged of. Here note by the way how the kinsman the redeemer was a type of Christ, Isa. lix. 20, who became, by taking our nature upon him, our brother and Redeemer, who redeemeth us, first, from sin, Titus ii. 14, from a vain conversation, 1 Pet. i. 18, that we might be a peculiar people to God, zealous of good works; secondly, from our enemies, Luke i. 74, 75, that we might serve him in holiness and righteousness all the days of our life; thirdly, from under the law, Gal. iv. 5, that we might receive the adoption of sons; fourthly, from the curse of the law, Gal. iii. 13, 14, that the blessing of Abraham might come upon us, and that we might receive the promise of the Spirit; fifthly, from the wrath to come, 1 Thes. i. 10, and so to give us the inheritance of life and glory.

But if thou wilt not redeem it, then tell me, that I may know. Note, first, that a man is either to perform his duty, or to render up his right to another that will, for else he is as the tree which keepeth the ground barren, Luke xiii., and good for nothing but to be cut down and cast into the fire. A good lesson to idle and negligent ministers, who should either take pains to teach, or yield up their places to such as would; else let them look for the end of the unfruitful tree, and the reward of the unprofitable, wicked, and slothful servant, which was cast into utter darkness, where is weeping and gnashing of teeth, Mat. xxv. 30; secondly, that one man knoweth not the mind of another till it be revealed and made known unto him, as Boaz acknowledgeth here, and as the apostle teacheth, 1 Cor. ii. 11, and Solomon also, Prov. xx. 27, and therefore are we to be charitable in censuring men's hearts, when we know not the intent thereof till it be revealed, as by words, for of the abundance of the heart the mouth speaketh; or by works, for, as our Saviour saith, 'By their works you shall know them;' or by signs and tokens, by looks and gesture, for where the eyes be lofty, the heart is haughty, Ps. xiii. i. 1, and ci. 5, and the gesture stately, the mind is great. Thus may we judge of the mind and heart; for by words, works, and gesture may they be known, and 'their countenance,' saith Isaiah, chap. iii. 9, 16, 'doth witness against them.' And therefore should we look to these, and strive to have an outward carriage comely and decent as befitteth Christians, if we would not have the inward man censured and thought evil of.

For there is none to redeem it besides thee. The reason why he advertiseth the kinsman; for that he was the next, if the other refused, and the other had the right before him. An honest and just-dealing man will not enter upon another man's right without his leave, and first acquainting him therewith; for otherwise wrong should be offered to him, which an honest man is loath to do, love bringing him to do better unto his neighbour, as we see by Boaz here; whose example let us be willing to follow, as we would be accounted just and honest. Again note, that in the sale of land, he is to have the first offer, who hath a right thereto after the present possessor, before another, if such a one be able and willing to buy the same, if either the law would make him heir, or the bond of natural love should persuade thereto. In so doing, an even course is kept, love is observed, houses and

421

families are upheld, when that which belonged to a family or kindred is kept among themselves, and not alienated unto another house or stock; which, therefore, for men's outward name, and better strengthening of their family, is fit to be observed.

And I am after thee. As if he had said, I rather than any other propound this unto thee, because, if thou wilt not do thy duty, I will, being the next kinsman. They are most fit to put others in mind of their duty, which have a more special reason and calling thereto than others, and a mind and ability to perform what others do neglect; for where these concur, as they did in Boaz, the party admonishing cannot justly be excepted against. And therefore let us look whether we, in going to urge others to their duties, have a calling by special reason so to do, else may we be condemned for too busybodies; likewise, whether we have a conscience in ourselves, that we be not guilty of unwillingness to do our duty in that which we press others unto, lest it be said to us, 'Physician, heal thyself.'

And he said, I will redeem it. This sheweth that he was a worldling, for his kinsman, after so long a famine, had ready money to purchase, but not a penny to give to poor Naomi and Ruth, as Boaz did. Boaz was rich, and had wherewith to redeem the inheritance, but he was merciful. So he was a rich man *in* the world, but not *of* it, as a worldling is; for a worldling is one of the world, loving it, seeking it with greediness, hoarding up, and ready ever to be buying, but without mercy to the poor, as this kinsman seemed to be. By this learn to behold a worldling, and a godly rich man, both getters, both full of coin, both ready to purchase; herein they differ not; but the one hath regard to the law of God, so not the other; one hath a merciful heart to be liberal to the poor, and so hath not the other; the one in his purchase hath respect to the good of his brother, the other regards wholly and only his own commodity; for he is unsatiable, being like the dry sandy ground which drinks up rain; like the dropsy, the horse-leech, the grave, and barren womb, which be never satisfied. No more is the covetous worldling; his increasing and getting satisfieth him not, but rather maketh him the more greedy of gain. Which miserable corruption is much to be bewailed, and happy contentment is to be sought after, as the apostle exhorteth, Heb. xiii. 5.

Ver. 5. *Then said Boaz, What day thou buyest the field of the hand of Naomi, thou must buy it also of Ruth the Moabitess, the wife of the dead, to raise up the name of the dead upon his inheritance.*

Boaz propoundeth now the thing principally intended. In which may be noted, when it was spoken of, what, and the end why.

Then said Boaz. When he saw him forward to buy the land, and as one prepared thereby, in his understanding, to have the offer of Ruth made to him, then he propounded her, teaching this, that then a matter is fit to be spoken of, when the party may seem to be prepared thereunto ; and this is wisdom both concerning spiritual and corporal things. Thus may we see how Boaz did here ; so the wise woman of Tekoah did to David, 2 Sam. xiv. ; and in like sort Nathan to David, the prophet to Ahab, 1 Kings xx. 39, 40, 42 ; and thus did Joseph prepare his brethren, before he discovered himself to them. And in this manner doth God in shewing his will to us. He prepared his people in giving the law, Exod. xix. ; and John Baptist must prepare the way before Christ come with the gospel ; and so must Paul be prepared with humiliation, before the Lord tell him his good pleasure, and put him into his function to carry his name unto the Gentiles, Acts ix. And thus did Peter, before he propounded the choosing of Matthias, and the word of glad tidings to the Jews, Acts i. and ii., for in doing this, we may greatly further what we do intend. And therefore let us learn this wisdom, to put it also into practice.

What day thou buyest the field of the hand of Naomi, thou must buy it also of Ruth the Moabitess. The reason of this speech of buying first of Naomi, then of Ruth, is this : Naomi was Elimelech's widow, to whom the land did belong, and whom the kinsman should have married ; but seeing she was too old to marry, and to bear children ; and now Ruth young, and the widow of one of Naomi her sons, she was to supply Naomi her defect ; and she, when the land was to be redeemed, must also be married to the kinsman, albeit she was a Moabitess ; for God's law was not partial, but extended in Israel, in that case for which the law was given, to the woman, whether she were an Israelitess, or of another nation, and married to an Israelite. Note here, that Boaz at the first propounded not so much as he intended ; yea, what is principally intended is often last propounded, as here, or wholly concealed, usual with statists ; as we may see in Saul, who propounded the marriage of his daughter to David, as if he honoured and loved him, when the end of his policy was to destroy him, 1 Sam. xviii. 9, 17, 21, 25. Jeroboam propoundeth tranquillity and rest to Israel, and that he had care to save them from so great cost and trouble, as to go up to Jerusalem there to worship ; he would, for their ease, have them to worship at Dan and Bethel the golden calves ; but this their fleshly ease, effected by this devilish policy, was not intended, but the safety of himself, and the confirming of the kingdom to himself, of which yet in the end he was deceived, 1 Kings xii. 26, 27. Seeing that less is at first propounded sometime than intended, and the main thing now and then concealed, as these examples shew, and as we may see it in the serpent, that grand politician, unto Eve ; let men learn to be wise to sift the drift, if they have to do with men of wisdom and of a deep reach ; else avoid them, if their own apprehension be too shallow to conceive them, lest by credulity they be overthrown. But it may here be asked, seeing Boaz did propound not that which at the first he chiefly aimed at, whether it be lawful so to do ? I answer, Yes ; for to propound one thing before another is not evil, neither to conceal sometime part of our mind, as we may see in Samuel, so advised by God himself to speak, 1 Sam. xvi. 2, yea, that may be sometime spoken, and in some case, which may seem to further a thing in hand, and yet be the way to prevent, and tend to the welfare of another, as the counsel of Hushai to Absalom, 2 Sam. xvii., which counsel was not to overthrow Absalom, though by God's hand it fell out so, but to provide for the safety of David, and to cross the counsel of Ahithophel, which tended to the utter destruction of David, the Lord's anointed ; which was honest and godly policy, in which no evil but good was intended of Hushai his part, which differs much from the damnable policy of Saul and Jeroboam, which subtle men most commonly follow and put in practice. We may also observe here maintenance for Naomi, and marriage for Ruth, so as both the widows were cared for ; for of widows God hath ever had an especial care, Exod. xxii. 22, 23. To a widow must Elijah go to preserve both his own and her life, 1 Kings xvii. ; for a widow must Elisha work a miracle to discharge her debts, 2 Kings iv. 1, that she and her children also may live. For widows left childless, a law was made for their marriage, Deut. xxv., and maintenance allowed for such, if she were a priest's daughter, when she returned to her father's house, Lev. xx. 13. And therefore let men have respect to the widows, as James exhorteth, chap. i. 27, who maketh it a chief sign or character of our religion before God.

The wife of the dead. This sheweth how Ruth came to have a right in an Israelite to marry with him, because her husband was an Israelite ; and the law was, that the widow of such a one the next kinsman should marry, if he died without issue. But yet this is not all, for Orpah was the wife of the dead too ; she was married to Chilion, brother to Mahlon ; but Ruth's religion, and coming with Naomi to dwell among God's people, give her this benefit of God's law. By which we may learn that religion, and not any earthly privilege, doth interest us into the law of God and the benefit thereof ; for otherwise Orpah had as much right by the law to the kinsman and to Boaz as Ruth had. If, therefore, we claim a benefit by the word, let us be religious ; for godliness hath the promise of this life, and the life to come ; but unto the wicked no hope, so long as they so remain, but to them the threatenings and curses be due.

To raise up the name of the dead upon his inheritance. This was Moses's law, Deut. xxv. 5, and ordained for divers causes : first, to shew that by death the right of inheritance was not lost, for it is called *his* inheritance, which figured out this, that by death we lose not our right of heaven, which is called our inheritance ; secondly, to provide that the widow should not be without children, thereby typing or figuring unto us, that the church should not be left barren; thirdly, to make the dead to live again, and his name to remain among such as were in the land of the living, so teaching that the dead should rise, and enjoy life everlasting; fourthly, to preserve the name of the dead, Deut. xxv. 6, that it should not be put out, so giving us to know, that God keepeth our names in remembrance, and we shall not perish; fifthly and lastly, to preserve the honour of the first born, when he that was begotten by the kinsman, was to bear the name of the dead, and not his name which begot him; so God would teach us, that Christ, the first begotten, should be honoured, and such as were begotten by spiritual fathers, the ministers of the word, should carry Christ's name, and from him be called Christians, and not by the name of their teachers, as if they begot people to themselves, but only to Christ, to keep up his name amongst his saints for ever. Besides these ends, and this typical and figurative meaning, we may observe that, by Moses's law, kindred were to uphold the name of their house, that it perished not; for it was a great curse to have a man's name rooted out, Ps. cix. 13, Jer. xxii. 30. And though that law do not bind us, yet the law of natural love, and loving respect to our own kindred, the name and credit of those which we come of, yea, and the honour which our family may come unto by obtaining antiquity, should make us uphold it; for ancient families have a certain honour upon them for antiquity's sake, though otherwise but poor and mean. Now, to keep up a name, and that in good credit, we must observe and fulfil these things: First, plant religion, and keep that among us, for so God will uphold and strengthen us, and bless us and ours: ' The godly shall be had in an everlasting remembrance, but the name of the wicked shall rot.' Secondly, bring up our children, and so teach them to bring up theirs, in honest courses and callings, and not to let them live idly and vainly; for nothing prevents evil more, nor upholds a man's estate better, than to live with industry and diligence in a calling; and what overthroweth houses, and bringeth men to ruin, making gallants to sell away their inheritances, but that they have been idly brought up, without callings, without honest employments? Thirdly, keep our genealogies, from our ancestors, and the increase of our posterities, to behold therein the Lord's blessing, and to rejoice in our increasing the Lord's church. Fourthly, we must help them up again, which by God's hand fall into decay. Common charity and natural love do persuade hereunto, and our own credit also, in keeping our name from contempt, if that respect may move us; for the more poor, the less esteem, and the greater contempt. Fifthly, we must labour to prefer our kindred to good marriages, to good places, as they shall be fit, and occasions offered, as far forth as we shall be able to the utmost. Sixthly, we must love one another entirely; which shall appear, first,

by our inquiring after one another, when we be separated; secondly, by visiting one another near, and sending one to another further off; thirdly, by being glad to see any of them, though descended many degrees from us: for the further off, the better appeareth the antiquity of our kindred, and the greater increase of our house; fourthly, by being desirous that one should make use of another before any other whatsoever, for this combineth them very nearly in affection; fifthly and lastly, to defend them in their just causes, and to be as one man to preserve them from wrongs and injuries offered them unjustly. This do, but yet only as far as may stand with public peace, for that must be preferred before kindred, yea, and our own estate and lives, lest we run into factions and partakings, and so cause civil dissension, which must be most carefully avoided; but otherwise, being no breach of public peace, no wreck of conscience, nothing against justice and legal proceedings, we must defend them, and in their good courses uphold them in love and charity. If every house and family would do thus, should not men be happy? should not every one rest in peace under his own vine? The rich friends would supply the want of their poor kindred, and the poor would honour them, and lay down their lives for them. Charity would rule as queen; and justice would sit in peace; religion would flourish, and the land would be blessed, and people made renowned, admired and feared. Before I end this verse, here it may be asked, Whether the law of Moses, Deut. xxv. 5, mentioning a brother, be to be understood of natural brethren, or only, as the Hebrews use to understand brother, a near kinsman, and not a natural brother?

Ans. It is to be understood of a natural brother, for the law was in use before it was written, Gen. xxxviii. 17, 18, and so then understood by Judah and Tamar, God dispensing therewith; and Naomi thus understood it also, chap. i. 13, though, if there be no brother, the nighest kinsman then must marry the widow. Therefore Ruth claimed it of Boaz, and Boaz did propound it to the nearer kinsman. Besides these, learned men do take the law to be so meant.

Ver. 6. *And the kinsman said, I cannot redeem it for myself, lest I mar mine own inheritance; redeem thou my right to thyself; for I cannot redeem it.*

The kinsman's answer to Boaz concerning his propounding of Ruth to him. He refuseth her, and giveth his reason; then he resigneth his right to Boaz, and repeateth again the words of refusal as a reason of his resignation.

And the kinsman said, I cannot redeem it for myself. He could before redeem it, but now he saith he cannot. He loved the land, and in that respect he was ready to fulfil the law; but he cared not for the woman, the poor widow, and in this regard the law was not respected of him. So we see how that worldlings are partial observers of God's law: some part they take and some part they leave, even as it liketh them; they look to the bare letter, but not the spiritual meaning; they shun the act, but for words and thoughts they do take no care; the sins in the grossest kind they avoid, but the lesser, as they account them, they make little or no conscience of; that which concerneth their pleasure and their profit according to the law they are ready to do, but, on the contrary, where the law crosseth them, that they cast behind them, as this kinsman here; they hate popish fasts, but love drunken feasts; they abhor superstitious worship and cost about it, but they can be content to live off sacrilege and the maintenance due to ministers, though given by ancestors to the church, with an execration or curse upon such as shall change them to any other use. Other men's duties they can hear of, and urge the law to them, but to be told of their own, and pressed to the performance thereof, they cannot endure. The reasons of this partiality are these: First, the want of the true love of God, and reverent fear of the power and authority of the lawgiver; for where this love and fear is, there will be respect had to all the commandments, without partiality, as we may see in David, Ps. cxix. 6, and in other holy men of God. Secondly, the unbridled lust of man unsubdued, and not brought into the obedience of Christ by the power of the word, as St Paul speaketh, 2 Cor. x. 5; for if the word ruled in their hearts, they would not be thus partial in obeying God's will, but be like Zacharias and Elizabeth, ' walking in all the commandments of God unblameable,' Luke i. 6. Thirdly, their love of pleasure and worldly profit more than God himself, which appeareth by this, that they will lose neither of these for religion's sake. Herod will do many things, but his pleasure with Herodias he will not forego. Ananias and Sapphira will give much, sell all to give to the church, but not give all; they will think more of the matter than give away all at once, though still they will pretend it. Such Herod-like and such Ananiases there be, which have not denied their pleasures nor their profits for religion's sake, which therefore maketh them partial in their obedience to God. Fourthly, the love of praises of men, John xii. 42, 43, and fear of them, make them to make baulks in their service to God, now omitting this, then that, and here trespassing, and there offending against the law; to get this man's praise, and not to displease that; being bound only to man, but loose in their hearts to follow their own wills in respect of any conscience towards God. Fifthly, the deadness and benumbedness of their consciences (for want of looking into God's law, and the searching out of their ways by the same), which never troubles them for neglect of their duties, nor for the breach of any part of the law. Sixthly, a carnal persuasion of their good estate, and that in thus doing they be not so much to blame. Because they thrive in the world, they get many friends, and they see others also to be their companions with them herein of the best rank in the world, and

such as profess to be better, yet are taken tardy in foul faults; and therefore are they hardened hereby in this their halting service and partial obedience to God. Let us take knowledge of this to bewail it, then to remove these causes, and to labour for the contrary graces, that we may serve God with all our hearts. Note again how he saith, *I cannot*, when he might have said, *I will not*; but hence we see that what man will not do, that he excuseth with *I cannot do*. So did the high priests and elders answer our Saviour, saying they could not tell, Mat. xxi. 27, when indeed they would not tell him what they thought of John's baptism; for *I cannot* is a more modest speech than *I will not*, and it carrieth a reasonable excuse with it; for in reason we think that what a man cannot do he should not be urged to do, and therefore do men use to say they cannot do that which they have no will to do, either of a froward spirit, which is to be condemned, or upon respect of some inconveniences, which may in some sort be excused with *I cannot do*, to wit, with conveniency; but this must not excuse or hinder our duty of charity, to neglect the helping of our brother in this his necessity, or to omit to do what we ought or may well do; for so to say *I cannot* is untruth and an evil excuse.

Lest I mar mine own inheritance. Thus this kinsman excuseth his refusal of Ruth. He might think, perhaps, being a worldling, that he might mar it if he married a young woman, and so be overcharged with children, or that in marrying Ruth he should be burdened with poor Naomi; or he having children by another, should by this bring a new charge upon him, and occasion discord by children of divers women, which seldom agree, as may be seen in Ishmael and Isaac, and Jacob's sons; or he might have another wife (as upon this place some do note), and so by taking this the house might be filled with contention, as we may see when Abraham took Hagar to Sarah, also in the wives of Jacob, Elkanah his two wives, and as is very like between the wives of Lamech, the first bigamist; or lastly, he might think, having a good inheritance of his own, by taking Ruth, and begetting a son to the dead, and so perhaps having no more, should thereby raise up the name of the dead upon his inheritance, and want one for his own, which he would not so mar, as he saith, whatsoever his thought was, thus to move him to speak. We may learn that a worldling is careful to preserve his outward estate, that it be not marred, as he here speaketh, for such a one is wise in his generation; he loveth his riches and wealth, and he feareth want, and it is not amiss to care to get honestly and to preserve our lands and goods when we have them, for they are God's gift, and we are made his stewards over them, to keep them carefully and to employ them according to his will, and not after his lusts; yea, this we are commanded to do, and urged by Solomon thereto by many reasons, Prov. xxvii. 23—27. This care had Abraham, Isaac, Jacob, Gen. xxxiii. 13, 14, and Naboth, 1 Kings xxi.; and the apostle telleth us that every one is to provide for his family, 1 Tim. v. 8, as the good housewife doth, Prov. xxxi. ; and parents are to lay up for their children, 1 Cor. xii., which they cannot do except they be painful, frugal, and do care to uphold their estates, and therefore thus far a worldling is not to be reproved ; but as far forth as he careth for the world with neglect of religion in himself and in his family (whenas first we must seek God's kingdom, as Christ commandeth, Mat. vi. 33, and that in the first and not in the last place), and as far as he keepeth it with shipwreck of conscience, upholding it by ill means, and having no care to do good works ; which two, that is, the neglect of God's service and of keeping of a good conscience, if they be avoided, men may in the care of their outward estate be well warranted to keep and prefer God's blessings bestowed upon them, ever in faith to God and love to our brethren ; for, with all care we ought most of all to uphold our spiritual estate, that we mar not that and lose our hope of heaven, but let the care of the one put us in mind of the care of the other, as every way more excellent. Note farther from this man, that worldlings think by obeying God's law they shall mar their earthly estate, that religion will overthrow them ; and thus they imagine, first, because they see God's word to cross their worldly courses, whereby they do use to get and uphold their estate, which indeed cannot stand with religion pure and undefiled before God. Secondly, because they are persuaded that they must do as men of the world do, else they shall not thrive, howsoever religion itself binds them to the contrary. Thirdly, because they trust not God, nor rely upon his word. Fourthly, for that they see many which go for religious men to be poor, and not to thrive as they do, or desire to do in the world, which they impute to their overstrictness in religion, and therefore do conclude with themselves that to live after the rule of God's word is the next way to beggary, which they will by their worldly courses prevent if they can. But let us beware of such atheistical thoughts, and be far from these imaginations of worldlings, first, because riches are from God, Deut. viii. 18, and not by man ; man cannot make himself rich by any means if God's common blessing be not assistant thereto. Experience also teacheth us this : when we see men industrious, yea, provident and wise as others, yet can they not attain the half that others come to. Secondly, because these outward blessings, even these are promised to such as do live well and obey God, Deut. xxviii. Thirdly, for that many men in living carefully to please God and to serve him, have come to great wealth, as we may read of Abraham, Isaac, Jacob, Joseph, Job, Boaz here, David, Jehoshaphat, and many others. Fourthly and lastly, for that men by their rebellion against God have lost great estates, and deprived themselves thereof, and their posterity, by their wickedness, as is evident in the example of Saul, Jeroboam, and others. And therefore let us not think our worldly estate to become worse by careful living after God's laws, but rather better and more sure, as

425

Job's was, about whom the Lord made a hedge for his safety. And remember for a conclusion, that such as fear the Lord shall want nothing that is good. 'O taste and see,' saith David, Ps. xxxiv. 8–10, 'that the Lord is good ! Blessed is the man that trusteth in him. O fear the Lord, ye his saints, for there is no want to them that fear him ! The young lions lack and suffer hunger, but they that seek the Lord shall not want any good thing.' Note thirdly hence from these words of the kinsman, that the fear of worldly loss in a man's outward estate maketh him neglect the law of God, as this man doth here ; for God's word prevaileth not ; it hath not a commanding power over the conscience of a covetous man, because his heart is glued to his riches, Luke xviii. 22, 23 ; a base fear through unbelief possesseth him that he himself may come to want, and the love of riches so betwitcheth him as he valueth them above the Lord's precepts, contrary to David's account of God's word, Ps. cxix. 72, 103, 111, and xix. 9. That we may become, therefore, obedient to God's law, let us cast off this atheistical and heathenish fear.

Redeem thou my right to thyself. The kinsman is here willing that Boaz should take his right ; that which before he said he would redeem himself, now he is contented that another should redeem it. So worldlings are content to yield sometimes their right unto others, as, namely, that which they cannot come by, that which they cannot keep, that which they cannot have but with more cost than the thing is worth ; or when by getting a little there is hazard to lose much, and likewise that which for present fear they yield unto, as Benhadad did restore cities unto Ahab, 1 Kings xx. 34, because he was in his hand, and in peril of his life, which he would by that means redeem. Otherwise, worldlings willingly forego nothing. Therefore their yielding of their right at any time upon the foresaid by-respect is not thanksworthy.

For I cannot redeem it. None but can pretend some excuse or other why they do not what they ought. In this man may we observe two things, inconstancy and want of charity, for before he would redeem it, now he will not ; before, yea ; now, nay. Three things make men inconstant. First, levity of mind ; this is a natural infirmity, and to be pardoned. Secondly, ignorance and want of foresight of the inconveniences, which maketh him rash at first and to repent afterwards, and so to change his mind, as this kinsman doth. This is somewhat excusable, though not altogether without blame, for a man is to do that which is gone out of his mouth, though it be to his own hindrance, Ps. xv., if nothing else hinder the performance. Thirdly, dishonesty, which is when a man maketh no conscience of anything he saith or doth, but as he seeth advantage therein to himself ; saying and gainsaying, doing and undoing as he seeth it to tend to his own profit. This is flat knavery, and justly to be condemned. Of this we must take serious knowledge, and bewail the first in us, prevent the second by good consideration and deliberation, and hate the last as detestable falsehood and dishonesty, not to be practised among Christians. Uncharitableness in this kinsman herein appeareth, that he hath no care of the name of the dead, nor respect unto the two poor widows, Naomi and Ruth. The land he loved and liked well, but the women he would have nothing to do with; he had a mind to enrich himself in worldly substance, but he had no will to shew mercy to the poor, for a worldling thinks himself born for himself, seeking his own good, but not the good of another, contrary to the true property of charity, 1 Cor. xiii. This uncharitableness must we take heed of, and abandon self-love, the true cause thereof, and labour for charity, the evidence of our faith in God and true union with our brethren in Christ.

Ver. 7. *Now this was the manner in former time in Israel, concerning redeeming, and concerning changing, for to confirm all things; a man plucked off his shoe, and gave it to his neighbour: and this was a testimony in Israel.*

These words are a declaration of a custom in Israel, and brought in here to shew the reason of the kinsman his drawing off his shoe in the verse following. In this note the antiquity of this custom; also, where, about what, to what end, what it was, and the ratification.

Now this was the manner in former time. It was no new device, but an old custom, though nowhere in Scripture mentioned before. In commending this custom from antiquity, we see that antiquity hath ever been of credit to commend a thing unto us. By this the prophet commendeth religion and worship of God to the people, Jer. vi. 16; and by this prevailed the scribes and pharisees with their traditions, by saying it was said of old, and done by the forefathers, Mat. vi., xv. Thus the papists seek to grace their superstition and will-worship, for that which is of old hath many approvers of all sorts, which maketh it to be of such estimation. Seeing this is so, let us learn to know true antiquity from counterfeit, the antiquity of truth, which is of God, and that of error, which is of the devil; and that which we find to be antiquity of truth, that to uphold, and to reject the other; so shall we approve of the truth of our religion as most ancient, and renounce popery as a new novelty, and a religion sprung up but of late. This should also make us to be wary, and to take good heed that we ascribe not the name of antiquity to anything but that which may be proved to be sound and orthodox, yea, albeit being a thing but indifferent, lest, if it be evil, we, by attributing antiquity thereunto, do credit and add confirmation unto it by speaking thereof as being ancient; and when we so inform others, when we approve of it, and practise it, and instruct, teach, and allow our children so to think and do, if the thing be good and

of approved antiquity, it is well done so to speak and practise; but if evil, we do amiss in misleading others, by gracing any way such a thing with the credit of antiquity, whenas we rather should use all means to disannul and cancel the same.

In Israel. Old customs have prevailed amongst God's people, both civil and religious customs, John xviii. 39, and that both good and bad. Good the godly have observed, as did Joseph and Mary, Luke ii. 27, 42. Bad the people have followed, such as were and be addicted to the will of men, and to the examples of their forefathers, Jer. xliv., to great and learned men's practices, 2 Kings xvii. 34, 40, being led by their own bringing up to follow the opinion of the most, and not to be guided by the law and precepts of God. Thus were the high places kept up in Judea, the golden calves worshipped in Dan and Bethel; so popish customs having taken place, we find hard to be removed; and heathenish customs sometimes among the ignorant and vulgar people are kept and observed in divers things at some seasons of the year, of which in this clear light of the gospel Christians should be ashamed. Some customs are not to be condemned simply, but only in regard of the abuse; as for friends to meet and feast, to make a feast at weddings, Judges xiv. 10; to rejoice, to sing, to play on instruments, yea, sometime to dance, Jer. xxxi. 4, so it be that the Lord's-day be not profaned, nor made the appointed day for these things, as most commonly it hath been, Isa. lviii. 13, for that day is set apart for better ends and holy purposes; also, so that moderation be used herein, as in feasting, to avoid drunkenness and gluttony; in mirth, wanton songs, lascivious speeches, abuse of God's name and his word; and in dancing, the mixed companying of men and women, for in Israel the women danced together, Judges xi. 34 and xxi. 31, 1 Sam. xviii. 6, Jer. xxxi. 13, and the men alone. As for the other, it is an allurement to vanity and folly, as daily experience may teach them that impudently will gainsay the same. So, then, let us distinguish customs, and as they be good so use them; if otherwise, cut them off, and suffer not an ungodly custom to have any authority, or to be a law in thine heart, for ofttimes evil customs do overmaster good customs. Wherefore let Hagar be expelled, that the promised seed may have his right and place.

Concerning redeeming, and concerning changing. Of redeeming land, buying and selling, before hath been spoken. Here is mention of the exchange of one for another, as Ahab offered unto Naboth, in which, as in the other, equity is to be observed. These words brought in here shew about what matters this ancient custom was observed, namely, in and about matters of the world. In which they had their liberty, as we have now in these things, and not to be found fault with or disallowed; neither need men to have any scruple in using them, nor to call them into question, when they see not therein any apparent impiety or gross superstition.

For to confirm all things. To wit, which was done or spoken touching the redemption or change. So here is the end of the ceremony for civil use, not for superstition. It was for confirmation and establishing of the right of one upon another, for custom is as a law binding one to another in that which is done according to that custom. It is good, therefore, to take heed how we settle a custom.

A man plucked off his shoe, and gave it to his neighbour. This was the custom or the ceremony used according to the custom then in Israel about such things. Several countries have several customs. We deliver up our right by taking up a piece of earth, and do lay it upon the deed or writing when we give up our right in freehold; in some places by a straw in copyhold land; some pull off a glove. Here is plucking off a shoe, to signify by the shoe his right to the land, by plucking off his will to forego it, by giving it to his neighbour the resigning of his right, so as the ceremony lively setteth out the thing. But it will be asked, Why was a shoe used in this? It may be to note that the man acknowledgeth hereby that now he had no right to set his foot upon it without the leave of the other; according to that with us, no man having a right, without the owner's good will, so much as to walk over another man's ground; but if he will he may commence a suit against him *de pedibus ambulandis:* but such extremity is utterly void of charity, and to be hated among Christians.

And this was a testimony in Israel. This act made good the bargain of sale or exchange in Israel, for a common custom maketh sure a thing delivered according to that custom where it is of force and use. The practice of that custom shall testify against them, and confirm their deed, where that custom is in use, for many customs are in many places and do differ. Let therefore such a custom be carefully observed, and beware of the breach thereof.

Ver. 8. *Therefore the kinsman said unto Boaz, Buy it for thee; so he drew off his shoe.*

This is a conclusion of the bargain between them. Shewing what the kinsman both spake and did, granting Boaz liberty to buy it, and observing the custom amongst them, to ratify the same in the resigning of his right.

Therefore the kinsman said unto Boaz. That is, because he said he could not redeem it, he saith to Boaz, Buy thou it; and because the custom was so he drew off his shoe, for this word *therefore* hath reference to both clauses. Here is a worldly man, yet he dealeth in the resigning of his right very honestly, and so as by law and custom the same might be confirmed and made good to Boaz. Hereby we see that some men out of common honesty, being worldlings, will so pass away their right to another as it shall stand good by

427

law to them, for they will observe in such things moral honesty. They love their credit before men, they care to preserve such just dealing for their more free commerce with others, and to prevent future troubles, which they might occasion otherwise by any trick of dishonesty when it should appear. This we find true by experience among ourselves, which is very praiseworthy, and a comdemning of such as pretend a greater show of piety, but have not half the honesty which some civil worldly men have; for if we pass an estate to any, why should we not make the purchase good to the utmost according to law? Honesty and equity require it at our hands, if we be not deceivers, as some be, who make sale of that which secretly they have conveyed to others before; which practice, yea, and every such like deceitful dealing, is very theft and damned villany.

Buy it for thee. Before the kinsman in verse 6 willeth Boaz to redeem it to himself, here he saith, Buy it; so that to redeem was to buy the inheritance, of which somewhat in the next verse.

So he drew off his shoe. Thus he observed the custom, to confirm the right unto Boaz. Two things are here done to put over his right: first, his word, and then his deed. One was not enough to convey it over unto Boaz, therefore both are conjoined. So doth the Lord deal with us in giving us a right in the eternal inheritance. He giveth first his word, then his deed, setting to his hand and seal to confirm his word, which internally is the Spirit and heavenly graces thereof, externally the sacraments; so that which is bought by Christ is conveyed unto us. God giveth us good assurance, as here the kinsman to Boaz. Good assurance is to be given and taken in passing of right from one to another, Gen. xxiii. 18, Jer. xxxii. 6–8. It is honesty on the one side, and wisdom on the other. And therefore herein let us be both honest and wise. But now for plucking off the shoe, we must know that we find it two ways used, religiously and civilly. Religiously, in reverence to God, as did Moses, Exod. iii. 5, and Joshua, chap. v. 15, in drawing near unto him, which signifieth the putting off of foul and carnal affections, and to draw near with a pure heart unto God; and in witness of great humility, as David did, 2 Sam. xv. 30, acknowledging a sensible feeling of the heavy hand of God, and his afflicted estate then, which by sin he had justly brought upon himself, Isa. xx. 2. Civilly, this plucking or putting off the shoe was, first, for conveniency to wash the feet; next, for confirmation of sale of land, as here; and, thirdly, for disgrace, when the kinsman would not perform the part of a kinsman according to the law of Moses, Deut. xxv. 9. This is not here meant; for by the law the woman, after she had claimed marriage of the kinsman privately, then also she complained to the magistrate. If the kinsman should refuse to do the office of a kinsman, then is she to pluck off his shoe, and spit in his face, which some expound to spit before his face.

But here is a voluntary plucking off of his own shoe, and also the former verse sheweth it to be a custom touching redeeming and changing; and thereupon the kinsman useth it to resign his right, and to confirm it unto Boaz, and not as an act of disgrace to himself, for not yielding to do the kinsman's part, which was not claimed at his hands by Ruth either privately or before authority; and therefore I take that this putting off the shoe, and that spoken of in the law of Moses, Deut. xxv., are not one and the same.

Ver. 9. *And Boaz said unto the elders, and unto all the people, Ye are witnesses this day, that I have bought all that was Elimelech's, and all that was Chilion's and Mahlon's, of the hand of Naomi.*

Boaz here taketh witness of that which is done. The witnesses are the elders and the people; the matter which they are to be witnesses of is the sale of all the land of Elimelech, Chilion, and Mahlon, and the purchase thereof at Naomi her hand; the kinsman resigning his right to him, that he might buy it to himself.

And Boaz said unto the elders, and unto all the people. Boaz esteemeth of the elders as men in authority; but yet he neglecteth not the people, whom also he calleth upon to be witnesses also. This was his wisdom, to procure love of all, as appeareth by their prayer made for him afterwards, ver. 11. Here in this verse, and the rest following, we may see the happy success of that which Boaz took in hand; for it was a good matter, for a good end, and done in a right manner. Now, when a thing which is lawful is taken in hand, and done well, to a right end, there may be expected a good issue; as may be seen in David's setting upon Goliath. It was an honourable attempt, the manner of his proceeding was lawful, he waited for it, and had public authority to set him forward, and the end was God's glory and safety of Israel; for God is with such, and his power shall assist them, and his favour shall give them good success, as he promiseth unto such. And therefore, if we would prosper, let us observe these things in our attempts; for if the end be good in thy intendment, and the thing unlawful, the act is sinful; if the matter be good, and the end sinister, this marreth the matter; but if the matter and end be as they should be, yet if the manner be amiss, we may for this miscarry, as we see in David's removing of the ark, 2 Sam. vi. 6, 1 Chron. xv. 13. This let us observe in coming to the word and sacrament, 1 Cor. xi.

Ye are witnesses this day. Boaz saith that they are witnesses, for that they saw and heard what was done at that time, in that assembly, between him and the kinsman; so as we see that what men come for, and are called to see and hear, that are they witnesses of; so saith he, and they also confess it in verse 11. By this may we know who to produce for fit witnesses in a matter, such as personally are seers and hearers of

that which they testify; and as they be fit witnesses, so then are they sound and faithful, if they will truly and without respect of person affirm that for truth which they know to be so; for it is one thing to be a fit witness in respect of a man's knowledge, and another thing to be a faithful witness, to speak truly what he knoweth. Seeing what we see and hear maketh us fit to be produced for witnesses, when occasion shall serve, let us, in matters of moment, for upholding of truth, justice, and peace, observe well what we do see and hear, that we may be true and faithful witnesses, to maintain truth, justice, and peace, without all partiality.

That I have bought all that was Elimelech's, and all that was Chilion's and Mahlon's. Here is shewed whereof they were witnesses; one thing is here specified, the other in the next verse. This here is of the purchase of land, whereunto he calleth them to be witnesses, for better confirmation of the land, and the right thereof to himself; for witnesses are for to establish a matter, Deut. xix. 15. So we see in Boaz a care to make sure the estate. A wise man will seek to make sure that which he purchaseth; as Abraham also did, Gen. xxiii., and Jeremiah, Jer. xxxii. 10, 11, 25, who had for confirmation of the land, first, the evidence drawn; then the same sealed; thirdly, the same done according to law and custom; and, lastly, before witnesses. Thus the Scripture commendeth unto us a care herein from these examples; it is wisdom and prudence to secure our estates in the best manner, so it be just and honest, for so shall we prevent future contentions which after might rise about it. And if ever men had cause to look about them in any age, now they have; for it may be said, as Jeremiah said in his time, chap. ix. 4, ‘Take ye heed every one of his neighbour, and trust ye not in any brother; for every brother will utterly supplant.’ Here may be noted Boaz his uprightness also, who desireth to have others to take notice of his doings, and to have that public which should be public; for an honest mind is desirous to be public where the matter requireth it, as in buying and selling of land, in the course of justice, in the ministry of the word, in solemnising of marriage, and such like. It argueth an honest intention, not caring who seeth it; it will clear him of the slander or suspicion of fraud and circumvention. And therefore in such cases labour to be public, for only they which do evil, or intend it, hate the light; honest minds care not who seeth them. It is no good sign of a good intent when buyers will mark* in secret to buy lands of others, of such as be young prodigals or old spendthrifts, or such as must sell for need; for those hope to make a prey, and to get that for a little which is worth much. But such gain is unjust; and where fraud and oppression is, there will God be an avenger, 1 Thes. iv. Lastly, note hence, that it is lawful for a rich man to buy

* That is, ‘traffic,’ hence ‘market.’—ED.

land of others when it is offered, as here, whenas also need is of some parcel for a special use; as Abraham did buy a burying-place, Gen. xxiii.; and Omri, the hill of Samaria, 1 Kings xvi. 24; and when it is for good uses, Lev. xxvii. 22, as for the maintenance of God's public worship, to build an altar, as Jacob, Gen. xxxiii. 19, and David, 2 Sam. xxiv., did; so now to buy land for maintenance of the word, for schools of learning, for hospitals, and to set poor on work. Again, he may buy to help a poor man that for need must make sale to supply his want with money; but such a purchase must be made in mercy, in great equity, and without oppression, in the fear of God, Lev. xxv. 14–17, 25. And, thirdly, when the salesman is his kinsman, then to buy as a friend and kinsman, to preserve the land in their name, but especially to do the kinsman good; and that in two things, in giving to the utmost what it is worth, and in being ready at all times to let him redeem it again, if ever he shall be able. Thus may a rich-landed man buy land; but here he must take heed, first, that he entice not others to make sale of their estates which be not willing thereto, as Ahab did, 1 Kings xxi. 2, 4, which wrought that mischief which afterwards ensued. Secondly, that he make not a prey of a poor man, not of any other which standeth in need to sell, Lev. xxv. 14. Thirdly, that he buy not upon a greedy desire, and an insatiable covetousness, to have all about him; for the prophet denounceth a woe and judgments against such, Isa. v. 8–10. Fourthly, that he buy not in the days of a general calamity, but rather employ his money in works of mercy. This was a virtue in Nehemiah, chap. v. 16. They therefore err who think they may buy as much as they can if they have money, conceiving no other use thereof but to buy and purchase therewith only for themselves, to make themselves great. And this reproveth those which are so greedy of buying land, as they run into the usurers' books and borrow what they may to purchase, till the use of the money eat up a good part of the land, and themselves at the last become beggars, and so leave their children poor, their friends in bonds, and not a few lenders perhaps in the lurch. Such is the fruit of a greedy covetousness. But, we may say, as it is lawful to buy, so is it lawful to sell. True, of which before somewhat is spoken already, yet here a little more of the same matter. A man may sell to sustain his poverty happening by God's hand, as did the Egyptians, Gen. xlvii. 18, 20; to recover their livelihood and health, as did the diseased woman, Mark v. 25; to pay debts, as did the poor widow, 2 Kings iv. 7, to be free from bondage, and to save her life. For goods and lands are for our use; and liberty, life, health, and credit are more to be esteemed than any lands or possessions. A man may also sell to others for their need, as Ephron sold to Abraham a field, Gen. xxiii.; Hamor to Jacob, Gen. xxxiii.; and Araunah to David, 2 Sam. xxiv. And, thirdly,

for to relieve the want of their brethren, as they did in the primitive church, Acts ii. 45, and iv. 36, 37, and v. 1. In such cases may men sell, but not to uphold prodigality, whoredom, idleness, pride and vanity.

Of the hand of Naomi. The right, it may seem, of all the lands of these three was in Naomi her hands, when they died childless. Thus the law left her well, as our law doth many widows now, and the love of kind husbands. But that too many widows wax wanton, and do, in following their lust and fantasy, overthrow themselves and their estates too. They follow not this holy and modest matron, who sought no marriage for herself in her old age (as some with us do, to their shame), but she had care for her beloved daughter-in-law, Ruth. If she had such lands to sell, may some say, why lived she so poorly, and suffered Ruth to go and glean, and live upon the alms of Boaz? Naomi had not the possession of these lands, being sold away before, but the right first to redeem, if she had been able, which she put over to Boaz, when the kinsman refused to redeem them, and so to help Ruth in her marriage.

Ver. 10. *Moreover, Ruth the Moabitess, the wife of Mahlon, have I purchased to be my wife, to raise up the name of the dead upon his inheritance, that the name of the dead be not cut off from among his brethren, and from the gate of his place: ye are witnesses this day.*

Boaz relateth the second thing of which they were to be witnesses, which was concerning his marriage; where note, first, with whom; secondly, how obtained; thirdly, to what end, is double; and fourthly, the calling of them again to witness it.

Moreover, Ruth the Moabitess. This was she whom he had promised to marry, and whom he now went about to make sure to him, though she were a Moabitess. Here it may be demanded, whether persons of diverse religions may marry together? *Ans.* If they be converted, they may. So Moses married Jethro's daughter, Salmon Rahab, and Boaz Ruth here, and Sheshan married his daughter to his servant, an Egyptian, 1 Chron. ii. 34;[*] but otherwise they may not. God forbade it his people, Deut. vii. 3; such matches were condemned, Ezra x., Neh. xiii.; the yoke is unequal, as St Paul speaketh, 2 Cor. vi. 14; it was reproved in Esau, and herein was he a grief unto his parents, Gen. xxvii. This is not to marry in the Lord; it is dangerous to the soul, if the heart should be drawn from God, as was Solomon's, 1 Kings xi. 1; and such matches hath God cursed, Neh. xiii. 26, Deut. iv. 7, as we may see in Jehoshaphat matching his son with Ahab's daughter, 2 Chron. xix. 2; it had almost rooted out his whole house, chap. xxi. 6, 13. Fathers and councils do condemn it, and therefore beware of making such matches.

The wife of Mahlon. See for this before, chap. i. 4,

* See Zipper. de Lege Mos. lib. 4, cap. xviii.

and in this chapter, verse the 5th, where Ruth is called the wife of the dead, and here shewed to be Mahlon, the elder brother to Chilion, the husband of Orpah, who by her apostasy lost her blessing in Israel, which Ruth obtained by her constancy.

Have I purchased to be my wife. We see hence a good man will be at cost to obtain a good wife. Abraham will send far a messenger to this purpose, Gen. xxiv., with camels loaden, and with jewels of silver and gold. Jacob will serve seven years, and seven too, but he will have Rachel, Hos. xii. 12, Gen. xxviii. and xxix. Boaz here will purchase a poor Ruth for her virtues; for indeed a virtuous woman's price is above rubies, she will do her husband good all his days, Prov. xxxi., she is worthy therefore the getting, and worthy to be honestly maintained; and yet we see most care least for such an one, but they will labour and spare no cost to get one that is fair, though beauty be deceitful vanity, Prov. xxxi. 30, and sometimes such a one is not over honest; or one rich, loving the portion better than the party, marrying basely and after living discontentedly; or for birth or friends, when the one lifteth up the heart with pride, and the other becometh chargeable. Beauty maketh not blessed, but virtue; not goods, but grace; not natural generation, but spiritual regeneration; no friends here, but the sweet favour of God, which he only affordeth unto the virtuous. See further from hence the love of Naomi to Ruth, who giveth her right to Boaz to redeem the land for advancement of Ruth; for loving parents will do much for the preferment of their children. Naomi here liveth unmarried, she doth all she may to get Ruth a good match for her own sake, and in love to the dead, that of her may be gotten one to bear the name of the dead, as Boaz speaketh in the words following. Which honest and loving care of Naomi checketh such widows as, being well left by the dead, do, either of covetousness and carelessness, neglect to marry their children, living only for themselves, or else of a wanton lust do cast themselves away upon such as will both undo them and their children.

To raise up the name of the dead upon his inheritance. Of these words somewhat is spoken before on verse the fifth, which I will not repeat. Here Boaz allegeth these words as a reason of his marrying this young woman; they are the words of the law in Deuteronomy, chap. xxv. 6, 7, and so are the next following; to which law Boaz had respect in thus matching with Ruth, from whom we learn these things: First, that a wise man will prevent an offence, which by others might be taken at him, when he considers the occasion thereof; for Boaz telleth them the true ends of his marrying thus, lest the beholders and hearers should have censured ill of him, as of lechery, he being old and she young; or of folly, she being poor and he rich; she base, and he honourable; or of an inclining in her to idolatry, he being an Israelite, and she

a daughter of Moab, of that race which enticed Israel to sin, and brought a great judgment upon the people, Num. xxv. And this he did for the care and credit of his name, which is highly to be esteemed, Eccles. vii. 1, Prov. xxxii. 1, and in love unto those there gathered before him, in whom he would prevent the offence, which on their behalf might be taken, though not on his part given. And thus must we learn to do, both to beware of offences to all sorts, 1 Cor. x. 32, Mat. xviii.; and also where we perceive that any might take an offence, there wisely to prevent it in them if we can, and not be like such as give themselves to all licentious liberty to live as they list, as almost every one doth in these days, not caring for a good name of a grave and sober Christian, or of adorning their holy profession, or of displeasing the godly minds of others; but to live only like libertines, after their own lusts, opening the mouths of the adversaries to speak ill of the gospel of God. Secondly, from Boaz we may learn, that a godly man in his marrying is guided by God's law, and hath respect unto God's good pleasure therein. So had Abraham in matching his son Isaac, and Isaac in marrying of his son Jacob; for such as be godly, make the Lord's will and word their rule in all things, much more in a matter of this weight and consequence. They know it to be God's ordinance, and therefore will advise with God about it; yea, they know that God hath not left men herein to their liberty and lust, to marry as they like best, but hath limited them, and in his word hath taught them with whom, how, and to what end to marry. And therefore in marrying we must be ruled by the Lord, which will appear by these things: If we see what calling we have to marry before we enter into this troublesome estate, as reason and religion should persuade us; if we see that we have a just cause to marry, then to consider with whom God alloweth us to marry; if we seek out such a one as not only with whom we may marry lawfully but also fitly; and therefore to pray earnestly to God for such a one, for God maketh fit matches, Gen. ii. and a virtuous woman is his gift. It is a happy thing to match fitly, and more hard than to match lawfully. If, lastly, we use marriage, as God hath appointed, for increase of posterity, Gen. ii., and to avoid fornication, 1 Cor. vii. (the first end was before the fall, the latter after), and withal for mutual society, help, and comfort, which one ought to have with another; which cannot be except there be fitness, grace, true love, humility, and patience. But who are thus led by the Lord in their marrying? Men seek wives now without any respect to God's will and pleasure; they follow the lust of the eyes, the lusts of the flesh, and pride of life. Thirdly, we may observe how the virtuous are to match, so as they may raise up a seed of the righteous among God's people, for the preservation of the church and religion, as Boaz here had a care to raise up the name of the dead upon his inheritance. But this cannot the married do, except they themselves be true lovers of goodness, and have a special care to train up their children religiously, first, in knowledge of God, else are they atheists ; of the true God, else heathenish idolaters ; and of the true worship of this God, else but will-worshippers ; then to inform them in the doctrine of faith, without which grace they can never profit by the word, nor ever please God, Heb. iv. 2, and xi. 6 ; the sum of which belief is set down in the articles of our creed. Next, to teach them how to pray aright, which is the means to confer with God, to speak to him, to obtain blessings from him, and without the practice whereof men are but as beasts, and a mark of such as think there is no God, Ps. xiv. The sum of our prayer, and the perfect rule of direction for matter, and manner, and end, is set down by our Saviour Christ. Lastly, to teach them obedience, and to walk in God's commandments, without which, all knowledge and faith is vain, 1 John ii. 4, James ii. ; the sum of what we are to obey, is in the ten commandments, which children must be taught and instructed in. Here may be noted this also from the words, that the dead do live again, as it were in their posterity, which keep their inheritance ; for children, and the preservation of their father's inheritance, do keep alive the name of the dead. Therefore let children have a care hereof, lest they destroy the name of the dead, as many prodigal children do.

That the name of the dead be not cut off from among his brethren. This is another end, the other being the means to prevent this, for the raising up of the name of the dead, preventeth the cutting of it off from among the brethren. Concerning the word *brethren,* hereby is meant others than very natural brethren ; for the people of God before and under the law, as in the primitive church under the gospel, were wont to call one another brethren, of which I have spoken before out of the third verse. For *cutting off.* This may be when one will not marry to have children, or marrying are not blessed of God with children, or having children, are cut off by God's just judgment, and so the name perisheth, as it befell Jeroboam, 1 Kings xiv. 10 ; Ahab, 2 Kings ix. 8 ; Jehoiakim, Jer. xxii. 30, and xxxvi. 30 ; and as God doth threaten the obstinate sinner in Deuteronomy, chap. xxix. 18, 19. Howsoever this cutting off be of posterity, we may learn hence, that the decay of posterity is a cutting off of a man's name from among his brethren, as the words here and in the law imply, Deut. xxv. 6. And therefore let people pray for this blessing of marriage, and thank God for their posterity and fruit of the womb. Abraham most highly esteemed hereof, Gen. xv. 2 ; and the psalmist maketh a reward to such as fear God, Ps. cxxvii. 3, and cxxviii. 3 ; yea, children are a crown to the old men, and it was a heavy curse upon Jehoiakim to be made childless, Jer. xxxvi. 30, and xxii. 30 ; and it was threatened in the law as a punishment for sin, Lev. xx. 20. They be much to

431

blame, then, which do marry of purpose with such as they think are past bearing of children, or with others apt for children, but yet in heart desire to have none, or perhaps but one or two, rather to dally with, than to be troubled with ; but such children often prove a scourge to these parents, through their foolish affection and too great indulgency, because they have no more.

And from the gate of his place. These words shew that Elimelech was a man of authority among them, an elder and judge in the gate, which honour Boaz would uphold in marrying with Ruth, that his name might not be cut off from the place of authority, here understood by the gate. Good men seek to uphold the honour, and to preserve the dignity of one another, as the fifth commandment teacheth ; which being our duty, we must care to observe, both to the dead and to the living. To the dead, as Boaz doth here. Now their honour we preserve when we speak of them with honour, as David did of Abner, 2 Sam. iii. ; when we maintain their good name against calumnies and slanderous reports ; and when we imitate their virtues, and seek to uphold their posterity, especially when they shall deserve well, and follow the steps of the dead in well-doing. Thus shall we truly and with praise preserve their honour, though we do not as the papists, dedicate days in honour of them, and make them intercessors to God for us, to the great dishonour of Christ. And as we should maintain the honour of the dead, so should we the honour of the living, by acknowledging their dignity, in age, place, and gifts, by speaking thereof, as is meet, without envy or disdain, and by doing reverence in our outward behaviour according to their dignity. Here may also be noted, that men of place and authority may soon leave their family in a low estate ; for Elimelech's wife was poor Naomi, and glad of the help of her daughter-in-law's gleanings. How poor was the widow left, for whose relief the prophet Elisha wrought a miracle, 2 Kings iv., being, as is supposed by some, the wife of an honourable man, Obadiah, Ahab's steward, 1 Kings xviii. 3, who did feed an hundred prophets of God in caves, in the time of famine ! This may fall out sometime by God's hand in punishing the fathers, that they can leave nothing to children ; sometime for trial, as in Job's case, who was brought to great misery, and sometime a man's own doings may bring him under the power of authority, which may justly deprive him of his honour and estate, as it befell Abiathar in the days of Solomon, 1 Kings ii. 26, 27. Let not men be therefore proud of their parents' present glory ; an alteration may soon come, as we see in Jeroboam and Baasha, in Ahab, Jehoram, and Jezebel ; in Haman also, Athaliah, and others ; for God's power, princes' authority, and a man's own way, may soon bring down his greatness, and also a ruin upon his whole house, Ps. lxxv. 6, 7.

Ye are witnesses. That is, as if Boaz had said, not only of the sale and purchase of the land, but also of this my marriage with this young woman Ruth, which here we see to be public, and in the gate of the city, in a civil court and place of justice. Whence note, first, that marriages are to be made publicly, before sufficient witnesses, as was Jacob's, this here, and that to which our Saviour was bidden, John ii. This is fit for the honour of marriage, for the better ratification thereof, and to prevent pretences of marriages; for if marriages were not public, but privately huddled up, some might pretend marriage, and live together as man and wife in show, and yet be but lewd livers; so others, weary of one another, might say they were not married, and so unlawfully separate themselves. Therefore let marriages be public, and in a public place, as here it was, and as now by our laws we be bound thereto; and avoid private making of marriages, and in corners, for they are often made in haste and end unhappily. Secondly, that marriage in old time was only a civil action; there was no need of a minister to make it, it was lawfully and sufficiently done, when it was made openly, by such as might marry, among the people, as we may see in the marriage of Isaac, of Jacob, Esau, Samson. Which confuteth the papists, that make marriage a sacrament, as if marriage were only lawful in the church, and not among the very heathen; when yet from the beginning it is common to all mankind, and allowed to all sorts. True it is, that we do make such marriages lawful only when ministers make them, but this is not with a papistical opinion of a sacrament, nor for that our church condemneth marriages otherwise made in other nations as unlawful, but the church and state have so ordained, for the greater reverence to God's ordinance, when his ministers shall bless the same, in the public congregation, with the prayers of the church; and when they shall teach them their duties, which do marry. Thus gracing God's holy ordinance by their praying and teaching, the one for benediction, the other for instruction, and therefore worthily ordained, and so of us to be religiously observed.

Ver. 11. *And all the people that were in the gate, and the elders, said, We are witnesses. The Lord make the woman that is come into thine house like Rachel and like Leah, which two did build the house of Israel; and do thou worthily in Ephratah, and be famous in Bethlehem.*

The assembly make answer unto Boaz: first, acknowledging themselves to be witnesses, and then praying for a blessing upon the woman, and then upon him; that she may be lovely and fruitful, and he to do so worthily, that he may come to be renowned.

And all the people that were in the gate, and the elders, said. In so great a company (no doubt), differing in nature and conditions, yet we see here how they do all agree before Boaz to applaud him. May it be

imagined that none had a by-thought, to see an old man to marry a young woman, one rich and noble to take a poor and mean maiden? Yet before him all say well unto it; for great men have to their faces great countenance and applause of the people in that they take in hand. The people will like all that David doth, 2 Sam. iii. 36; so will four hundred prophets allow of Ahab's purpose to go to battle against the Syrians, to recover Ramoth-Gilead; for people fear to offend, they desire to please their betters. And therefore this should teach those of place and wealth, upon whom many do depend, to take heed what they do, for they may set others on to godliness, and they may move others unto wickedness; they cannot fall themselves alone, but be like the great dragon, Rev. xii., with their tail pulling many down with them. Let David set up religion, multitudes will follow him to the house of God; let Jeroboam set up idols and devils, the Israelites will worship them; let Ahab worship Baal, all will do so; and let Jehu destroy him, and they will help him to do it. People are like a shadow, following authority; like wax also, which will take any print. In themselves are nothing, but allow and disallow, as they see great ones do before them. And therefore let no men of place regard their applause, thinking that well done which the vulgar approve, or flattering dependents; for they will not speak as the truth is, but to humour persons; not what they think to be right, but what they know another liketh of, and would have them say.

We are witnesses. That is, we acknowledge ourselves to be so as thou sayest; we are witnesses, and will upon any just occasion be ready to shew ourselves so. Whence note, that what men are called to witness, being either eye or ear witnesses thereof, or both, that should they be ready to testify, as these here profess themselves to be, and as did the Israelites, in the behalf of Samuel, before the Lord's anointed, 1 Sam. xii. 45. 'A faithful witness,' saith Solomon, 'will not lie.' And therefore let us in such a case be ready and faithful witnesses, for the truth sake, for justice and peace sake among our brethren. Many times ready and faithful witnesses prevent suits and keep peace, where otherwise there would be strife and contention. This reproveth those which, being able sufficiently to bear witness, yet for fear of displeasing will not; these want fervent love of the truth, and offend against the commandments, which bind men to preserve the dignity, life, chastity, goods, and good name of our neighbours. Now, if any of these be endangered, and we by our witness might set them free, and will not, we are guilty thereof. Again, this checketh, or rather condemneth, those that for favour will either add or detract in their witness-bearing, so seeking to please man, and to displease God, giving a deadly wound to their own consciences. Thirdly, such as do speak only what is done and said, but yet to another end and meaning than was intended, as

Doeg dealt with Ahimelech, and the false witnesses against Christ. These wicked persons sin against the commandments, Exod. xx., they trespass in one of the seven sins which God hateth, Prov. vi. 19, and are an abomination to the Lord, Prov. xii. 22, who ordained in the law a punishment anwerable to that which by their false witness should have been inflicted upon another, Deut. xix. 16, 19. Such God threateneth to punish, Prov. xix. 9, for they offend greatly; they hinder the true course of justice, they deceive the judge, they hurt their neighbour, and they abuse the holy name of God, which they call to witness falsely. Let men therefore take heed hereof.

The Lord make the woman. Here they begin to pray for them, and all jointly together. Of praying to God I have before spoken. Here farther may be observed, first, that marriage is to be solemnized with prayer, and others are to pray for the married parties, as these do here; and Bethuel, Laban, and her mother, did for Rebekah, Gen. xxiv. 60, and as our church ordaineth now at marriages; and that for these three causes : first, for the holiness of the action, being God's holy ordinance, and an honourable estate instituted in paradise, and in the time of innocency, and to be therefore undertaken holily and reverently, with supplication and prayer unto God; next, for the unholiness of our persons in ourselves, who by our corruption pollute the ordinance of God; and as we be of Adam's race, so have we our children conceived in sin, and brought forth in iniquity, and beget such as be after our own likeness, Gen. v. We have cause then to pray, and that fervently, to God to bless and shew mercy unto us. And thirdly, for the troublesomeness of the estate of marriage, which may cause us to pray heartily, for it is full of temptations and trials. And therefore let it move us to pray for them, after the example of the people here and these elders; and not be like such as at the time of marriage only stand staring and looking on, or through vain thoughts do laugh and make a sport thereof, or else spend their thoughts upon the delight of future vanities, dancing, drinking, lewd songs and ribaldry, more heathenish than Christian-like. And if others are to pray for the married parties, then much more should they pray for themselves; but alas, how far are most from it, having their thoughts spent upon vanities! Secondly, note that in public prayer the assembly should be of one accord, as all these were here, both the elders and people, as also elsewhere, 2 Chron. v. 13, Neh. viii., Acts i. 14, and ii. 26, and iv. 24. This is unity, and the other confusion, when people are otherwise exercised than in giving their assent to that which is publicly performed.

That is come into thine house. That is either already come, or that certainly shall come, as if she were already in the house. This sheweth the cohabitation of man and wife, and that they are to dwell together, as Peter speaketh, 1 Peter iii. 7, 1 Cor.

vii. 5; and God placed the first man and wife together in paradise, and Abraham and Sarah lived together; so did Isaac and Rebekah, Jacob and his wives, and so did David with his, 2 Sam. vi. 20. And this is fit and necessary for mutual comfort and society; therefore the apostles took their wives with them, 1 Cor. ix. 5; and it is for this cause altogether a fault, when any wilfully live separated from their wives, or any unnecessarily without a calling, out of an idle levity, will become travellers into other countries after they be married; when the apostle warneth them not to defraud one another, except with consent, and that but for a time, and for this end to give themselves to fasting and prayer, and then come together again, lest Satan tempt them to incontinency.

Like Rachel and Leah. Rachel is first named, because she was Jacob's wife first by covenant, and his best beloved. Two wives he had; and it was and is lawful to have one wife after another, as Abraham had Keturah after Sarah; for they that cannot abstain, it is better to marry than to burn, 1 Cor. vii. 9, 36; and when the one is departed, the other is free to marry again in the Lord. And therefore it is an heretical opinion to forbid second marriages, which the godly practised, and the apostle alloweth upon good reasons. But to have two wives at once is not lawful, for it is contrary to the Lord's first institution of marriage, who joined together but one man and one woman, Gen. ii.; it is against the apostle's doctrine, who teacheth every man to have his own wife, and every woman her own husband, 1 Cor. vii. And we may read of the first offenders, how one was out of the church, a blasphemous Lamech, Gen. iv., and the other in the church, a profane Esau, chap. xxvi. 34. And albeit holy men had many wives, it was their fault, God only being pleased to pass it over in his mercy; but allow thereof he did not, as appeareth by the prophet Malachi's words, chap. ii. 15; and therefore are they not herein to be followed. It is a blessed law which of late time hath been enacted in this nation, against marrying two wives at once. In praying that Ruth might be first like Rachel, who was amiable and lovely to Jacob, and then like Leah, who was fruitful, they may seem to pray for two things of the Lord : the first was, that there might be true love and good liking between Boaz and Ruth, for true love and good liking ought to be between husband and wife; specially so commanded, Eph. v. 25, Col. vi. 19, so practised by Isaac, Gen. xxiv. 67, and by Elkanah, 1 Sam. i. 5, and other godly men; and it is that which maketh marriage comfortable, and the parties to live quietly together with mutual contentment. Oh, therefore, let us pray for this love, and not only pray, but endeavour to use the best means to procure and hold it. And to effect this, the married persons are to take heed of strange affections, which might alienate their minds one from another; then to behold rather the good qualities and virtues of one another than the infirmities and things to be found fault with, for love covereth a multitude of offences. Young persons before marriage cannot see one another's faults, and if they do see them, yet their love is such as they can pass them by. Why, is not love in marriage as strong, nay, stronger, seeing now two are made one? Isaac took Rebekah, and she was his wife, and he then loved her; but now men love their Rebekahs afore marriage, and then, taking them for wives, they hate them, or not love them as before. Moreover, the married parties are to be ready to perform mutual duties cheerfully; yea, they are to strive which should be most loving in their duties of love, and should also provoke one another thereto. Lastly, they should often think of the solemn covenant made betwixt them, and by that and other godly reasons press themselves, the husband himself, and the wife herself, to their duties; yea, they should bewail their own and one another's corruptions before God, and pray against them, and for God's good graces to make them dutifully loving one to another. Thus doing shall they, by God's blessing, both procure and keep love. The second thing they prayed for was, the increase of children, which was the first blessing to man and woman, when God had made them, Gen. i. 28, and the first and principal end of marriage, and which God promised unto his people, Zech. viii. 5, Gen. ix. 1. In old time it was held a reproach for women to be barren, Luke i. 25, 1 Sam. i. 26, and the Lord did threaten it as a punishment, Lev. xx. 20, Jer. xxii. 30; yea, and inflicted it upon some, Gen. xx. 18, 2 Sam. vi. 23. Surely it is the want of a blessing, as the psalmist teacheth, Ps. cxxvii. and cxxviii. And, therefore, let us pray for this blessing, as Abraham did, Isaac, Manoah, and Hannah, from which these are far who so marry, as they might be without hope of children; such also as murmur at God's blessing through unbelief, fearing not to have to maintain them, unlike Leah, who comforted herself and praised God for children, Gen. xxix. 32, 35. Some would have some one or two, as it were to play withal, or to inherit that they have, but many they cannot away with; but these are most to be condemned who use means and medicines to prevent children, or sin in the sin of Onan, whom the Lord slew, Gen. xxxviii. 9, for it is murder before the Lord. Lastly, from the prayer made to the Lord for love between them and the increase of children, we may observe two other things: first, that love between man and wife cometh of God, and is his gift; for, as the psalmist saith, It is God that maketh them that are in one house to be of one mind; and therefore we ought to pray to him for it, and where it is, to praise him heartily for the same; then, that children are the gift of God, as may appear by many scriptures, and by the prayers made to God for them, Ps. cvii. 38, and cxxvii., and cxxviii, Gen. xx. 18, and xxix. 31, and iv. 1, and xxix. 35. And therefore must we acknowledge them from God, as Eve did, and Leah; if we want them, pray to him

for them, as Hannah and others did, and then care to bring them up well, and dedicate them to God's service in some lawful calling, in thankfulness for his so great a mercy.

Which two did build the house of Israel. That is, God made them fruitful to bring forth to Jacob a family, of whom came the Israelites, the peculiar people of God. They two are only mentioned, their maids are left out, but understood in them, for that they were the wives' gift unto Jacob, to bear children for them when they bare not. They are said to build the house when they brought forth children, which metaphor is used, because in Hebrew the name of a son (בן) cometh from a word (בנה) which signifieth to build; so as the bringing forth of children is as the building up of an house, by which a family is named for the cohabitation of man and wife together; so we call our kindred and stock our house. Note here, howsoever men have the name of the house, and by them cometh the posterity to be honourable, yet are women the builders up of the house, and are the especial instruments of the increase of posterity; for when men had no children, it is said, the women were barren, and their wombs shut up; and when men had any, it is said, the Lord gave the women to conceive. In them, therefore, is either the increase or decay of posterity, yet both from God, as he either pleaseth to bless or to deny the blessing. By *Israel* is meant *Jacob*, touching which name of Israel note these three things: the change of the name by God himself, Gen. xxxii. 28, and xxxv. 10, to comfort Jacob in great fear for his brother's coming against him, and to shew his more excellent estate than before; for the change of a name was to express a more happy condition, as may appear in a new name promised to the church, Isa. lxii. 2, and given also to Abraham, Gen. xvii. 5, 15; and here before Jacob's name was called Israel, it is said, the Lord blessed him, Gen. xxxii. 26–28, and gave him the name, so as with the change of the name was the change of his estate foretold. The signification of this name, which is the next thing, is prevailing with God, Gen. xxxii. 28, whence we in Christ are called, ' The Israel of God,' Gal. vi., for that we prevail with him through Christ. The third thing is the event, according to the name, for he prevailed against Esau by God's mercy; for though he came against him with four hundred men, yet was his heart so mollified at the sight of his brother, as he with tears embraced him for joy of their meeting, Gen. xxxiii. 4, and xxxvi. 6; and afterwards, when Jacob was in Canaan, Esau gave way unto him, and went into Edom, and left him the land. Thus God made good his promise to Jacob, and made him *Israel*, a true prevailer; for God giveth no signs to his children, but he maketh the same good in the effects and the event answerable thereunto. So much for the words; but in this that these elders and people do pray for a blessing of children from the consideration of God's former mercies to others, and also do take their example from such as did build up Israel, God's church, and not Babel; Bethel, and not Bethaven; we may learn, first, that God's blessings to others before us are a motive to us that come after, to beg the like blessings in the like case from God, reserving to himself his good pleasure and will, which, in asking the common blessings of the world, is ever the condition either to be expressed or understood; for God's mercies shewed to others are not only for their present good which receive them, but to shew how ready the Lord is to shew the like mercies to others, if they themselves by their sins hinder not the same. Therefore let us consider of God's mercies to others, to be thereby encouraged to ask the like of God for ourselves in the like case, with submission to God's good will and pleasure. Secondly, that such children are to be desired as may be to build up Israel, that is, God's church; such these pray for here. This is the most happy blessing of the womb; thus shall the wife be as the pleasant vine, and the children like olive branches, which a man may behold with comfort; for by them God is glorified in his mercy, the church increased, parents comforted, and children made happy, sons being as plants growing up, and the daughters as corner-stones polished, Ps. cxliv. 12; these be the arrows which make the man blessed that hath his quiver full of them, Ps. cxxvii. 5. But, alas, how few desire such children! Most desire them for their name, for to possess their inheritance after them, but not for the enlargement of God's church; for if so, we would not marry for mere pleasure, as many do, or for the world, as not a few do; but in the Lord, with such as fear God, and so for religion's sake, and have a care to bring up our children in the knowledge of God, and not in the corrupt manners of the world, and fashions of the times, as most do unto vanity; or but unto mere civility, as many do, which are well accounted of, yet never bent their thoughts to true piety in the education of their children.

And do thou worthily in Ephratah. This Ephratah is said to be Bethlehem, Gen. xxxv. 19, and xlviii. 7; yet some distinguish them thus, as Ephratah to be the country, and Bethlehem the city, the one signifying *increase,* the other *the house of bread;* which being so, it noteth that where the country is fruitful, and *Ephratah,* increasing, there the towns and cities are *Bethlehem,* store-houses, and houses of bread. So was it in Egypt, in the days of Joseph; for the increase of the field by God's blessing on man's husbandry maketh plenty of food in the places of our dwellings. Our meditation upon this should make us thankful to God, who hath for a long time made our country and fields *Ephratah,* and our cities and towns *Bethlehem.* And let us take heed of sin, which will cause the Lord to turn our plenty into scarcity, and make a barren wilderness of our fruitful land, for the wickednsss of us the inhabitants which dwell in it, Ps. cvii. 33, 34;

435

for we do greatly provoke him to wrath, in abusing his blessings to pride, idleness, gluttony, drunkenness, whoredom, and want of mercy to the poor, as did wicked Sodom in her fulness. But let us take heed; for the Lord will not ever strive with us thus in mercy; his justice cannot ever suffer it.

The words, 'do thou worthily,' are read also thus, 'get thee riches;' which may well stand, and may be a fit request for Boaz and Ruth after they be married and have increase of children, teaching this, that marriage needeth maintenance, as we all know; for it is chargeable, and that in these respects, in housekeeping, in bringing up of children, and in being liable to rates and seizements, according to the ability of the parties married. And, therefore, let such as intend to marry, provide honestly aforehand for the maintenance of marriage, as Abraham did for Isaac his son, Gen. xiv., and not rush, through unbridled lust, as many young lads and lasses, poor and beggarly, do in these days, to their own hurt, and the putting of a burden upon their neighbours, when they cannot maintain their charge. If any have improvidently married, and now do feel the smart thereof, let them lay their hands to labour, and be the more painful to get, to uphold their family, as Jacob did, Gen. xxx.; and if they be godly and faithful in their labour and service, God will bless them, as he did him, in their measure, and as he in his divine wisdom shall think meet for them. If we take the words as they be in the translation, 'do thou worthily,' let us note that a man may be said to do worthily in a double respect, either in respect of his person, when he doth that which well befits him, according to his birth, his education, his age, his place, and his holy profession of a Christian, as men do expect from such a one; or in respect of the deed done, when it is so done, as the virtues which should concur to the doing thereof do lively appear, and shew themselves in it. To apply this to riches, in the getting, keeping, and employment of them, a man doth worthily, first, in the getting, when these virtues appear: *industry,* painfully labouring, as Jacob did; *equity,* in using only lawful means lawfully, avoiding all fraud, deceit, and unjust courses to get riches; then *piety,* which is a holy depending upon God for a blessing upon the lawful means which he daily begs at his hands, not resting upon his own wit or painstaking; and, lastly, *contentation,* Heb. xiii. 5, not eagerly pursuing after riches, as most do, who fall into temptation, and a snare, and into many foolish and noisome lusts, which drown men in destruction and perdition, 1 Tim. vi. 9. Secondly, in keeping, a man doth worthily, wherein is shewed *frugality,* a virtuous sparing, and not a niggardly keeping in, unbefitting his ability, his place and person; so also *equity,* even in this, when he will not withhold from another that which is not his own to keep; for injustice may be as well in keeping as in getting. And, thirdly, *piety,* which is, when he sets not his heart on riches, trusts not in them, nor is lifted up above his brethren, but knoweth himself under God, in the midst of his wealth, walking therefore religiously and humbly. This man so doing, doth worthily. Thirdly, in employing or laying out, he doth worthily, when he is *liberal* to good uses, for the use of God's church, as was David and his princes ; and Solomon for the temple ; the Israelites before for the tabernacle ; and Hezekiah and the people for the priests and Levites, 2 Chron. xxxi. 4, 5, 6, 8 ; so for the commonwealth, and place of his dwelling, and withal to lay out for his own family, to maintain himself, wife, and children, as befitteth his place, and after his ability ; so to take care, and freely to give to nourish his whole family with food sufficient, not neglecting the poor, but to be ready to lend to some, and to give to other some, as their needful estates shall require. Thus shall he by liberality and charity do worthily in laying out.

And be famous. This well followeth after the other. They pray that he may do worthily, and then become famous. It is a duty to pray one for another, especially for men of authority, that they may do worthily, and become renowned thereby, Ps. xx., 1 Kings i. 37 ; for their greater authority, and because their example of well-doing and fame therein will be a great means to persuade others to well-doing, or else a bridle to curb them for fear of offending. Let us then pray for men in place to do worthily, and to become thereby renowned, to provoke others to follow them, and that virtue may be countenanced by them, as it will be by those which be famous for virtue. Note again, that to do worthily, procureth fame, and renown, and good report. So David became famous, 2 Sam. viii. 13 ; and Solomon by his wisdom and acts, 1 Kings x. 1, 2 Chron. ix. 5 ; and likewise others obtained good report, Heb. xi. 2 ; and the fame of our Saviour was spread abroad by his life, doctrine, and miracles ; and even Ruth, a poor woman and stranger, by her virtues was made known in Bethlehem, chap. iii. 11. And this cometh to pass by the excellency of well-doing in the minds of such as love it themselves, who cannot but in heart approve, and in tongue extol it, and set forth the due praises of such as do worthily. The Lord also putteth this blessing upon well-doing, that the doers shall receive honour and praise of men. So got David praises even above Saul, 1 Sam. xviii. 7, and was honoured by the commendations of his fact before the king. Therefore, when we see men to do worthily, let us set out their praises, for their encouragement, and to prick forward others to well-doing, and not be like the envious scribes and pharisees, seeking to diminish the honour of Christ ; nor like Saul, who sought the life of David ; and the Ephraimites, the destruction of Jephthah, for their worthy deeds, Judges xi. and xii. ; such a black poison is envy, as it bedarkeneth the name of well-doers as much as it can, rather than to make it famous.

In Bethlehem : Here is the place where they desire to have him famous, where he was brought up, where he had his means to live, and place of authority ; teaching hereby, that it is there chiefly required for a man to do worthily, where he oweth that duty ; as where he hath been brought up, where he hath his estate to live by, and where God hath seated him. So did our Saviour worthily in Nazareth, Luke iv. 16–18 ; Jephthah among the Gileadites, for their good, and the welfare of all Israel, if Ephraim had so taken it. This is a memorandum to ministers, there to do worthily where God placeth them, and where they have their living, and not be like some that can do worthily abroad sometimes, but at home will take little or no pains to teach their people. This also should put gentlemen and men of place in mind to do worthily in the country, in good house-keeping among their tenants, from whence they have their revenues ; and not get up to cities, there to keep a private table, to increase their estate, or else to uphold their pride. Neither yet is it enough for men to dwell in the country, as divers do, but do not worthily, their neighbours being never a whit the better for them, but are either so niggardly, as they benefit none, living only to themselves, or else so prodigal, as they rob their tenants with borrowing, and divers other ways, both sorts overcharging them.

Ver. 12. *And let thy house be like the house of Pharez (whom Tamar bare unto Judah), of the seed which the Lord shall give thee of this young woman.*

These words be the third part of their prayer. They did first pray for the woman, as the builder of the house, as before it is said of Rachel and Leah ; next for the man, because he is the glory of the house ; now for the posterity, because they do continue it. Here note what is prayed for, an honourable posterity, set out by the house of Pharez, whose father and mother are mentioned ; then, of whom it must come, and by whose gift and goodness.

And let thy house. That is, thy children and posterity : so as they praying before for the parents, and now for the children, do teach this, that they which truly wish well in love to the parents, cannot but be well-minded to their children and posterity, 1 John v. 1 ; so did David to Mephibosheth, the son of Jonathan, 2 Sam. ix. and xix. ; to Chimham, the son of Barzillai ; and to Hanun, the son of the king of Ammon ; for how can we love the fountain, and not the stream ? the root, and not that which springeth from it ? Let us try hereby true love to parents, by the love we bear to their children.

Be like the house of Pharez. Pharez signifieth a *breach*, because in the womb he strove for the birthright, and brake out before his brother Zarah, who had put out his hand to come first forth, to be the first-born, but plucked back his hand again. Zarah may set out the Jews, who were the first of God's people, but by apostasy lost their birthright ; Pharez may set out the Gentiles, who made a breach upon them, and got the birthright and the honour to be called now the people of God. There be two sorts of Pharezes, one heavenly, which strive for to be of the first-born of God. This is a blessed striving, which few contend for. There is another earthly, when brethren contend for to get the elder brother's inheritance from him, and do labour to get him disinherited. The neglect of the former is unholiness, and the pursuing of the latter is too great worldliness. These words, to ' be like the house of Pharez,' give us to know, that he was greatly blessed and honourable in his posterity, seeing they desire that Boaz's house might be like his. Now men wish not such a thing to great persons, but where there is an estate answerable to their greatness, and may well befit them, and be held a blessing unto them; and yet this Pharez was base gotten, and that in incest also. Whence we may see, that basely begotten may become very honourable, so as it may be happy with others to be blessed like them for worldly respects. Thus also was Jephthah honourable, Judges xi., a man of valour, made the head over all the inhabitants of Gilead, and yet the son of an harlot. Thus it pleaseth God to shew mercy on whom he will shew mercy; which may comfort such as be base born, that if they bewail their birth, and repent and believe, the Lord will have mercy likewise on them, and register them in the bead-roll of the saints, as Jephthah is, Heb. xi. Again, this may teach, from these elders and people, that they are to be esteemed honourable whom God doth make honourable; for these speak highly of Pharez for all his birth; and the Gileadites thought worthily of Jephthah, and did him honour; yea, the Holy Ghost hath vouchsafed to honour him, and to put him among the faithful, though he was by birth a bastard. They, therefore, do amiss, who despise men for their birth, when otherwise they be worthily qualified, and better conditioned than those, perhaps, which be more lawfully begotten. True it is, that a bastard was not to come into the congregation for ten generations; but God can dispense with his law, and where he so doth, let us do them honour, and not debase whom the Lord exalteth.

Whom Tamar bare unto Judah. Judah was one of Jacob's sons, and one of the twelve patriarchs, and begot this Pharez on this woman Tamar, who was his daughter-in-law. The history is in Gen. xxxviii. Whence we may note briefly, that great were the falls of many of the holy patriarchs; as nine of them, in the conspiracy against innocent Joseph, Gen. xxxvii. 2, 3, 11, whose death they intended, because he told his father their ill report; for that also Jacob loved him more than all of them, and because he told them his dream, for which they the more envied him, and were the more bent against him. But more particularly Reuben fell into that foul sin, to lie with his father's concubine; Simeon and Levi, brethren in

evil, who, under colour of religion, sought to revenge themselves, and abused the seal of God's covenant to shed much blood; and Judah here committeth incest with Tamar. Thus may we see, that men of note, children of godly parents, and pillars of the church, may fall very fearfully; as may also appear, besides these, in Aaron, in Samson, Abiathar, David, Solomon, and many others. Such is the strength of corruption, when we are left of God, and therefore are we to fear and to look to our standing; watch and pray continually, lest we fall into temptation and be overcome. And also we may observe how Jesus Christ was contented to come of such as were tainted with foul vices, as of men stained and polluted with incest, as Judah; with adultery and murder, as David; with idolatry, as Ahaz; with witchcraft and sorcery, as Manasseh; so of women defiled, as of this Tamar; of Rahab the harlot; and of Bathsheba, which sinned in adultery with David: to shew hereby, that he, our blessed Saviour, came into the world to save sinners, which is for the comfort of the penitent, 1 Tim. i. 15. And here also such as be godly may learn not to be discouraged, not to be daunted, neither to account worse of themselves, because they have had of their kindred foully tainted with vices. We see here the innocent Lamb of God to have been of such, and yet he the Holy One of Israel. Let such, then, put themselves to silence, who seek to disgrace the well-deserving by the stain of ancestors, or some of their kindred. By thus doing, men should offer wrong to Jesus Christ, which every saint of God is very far from; and who is he that should not be disgraced, if this might serve to disgrace a man? Note farther, how these words come in by a parenthesis: whether uttered by the elders and people, or else put in by the penman of the Holy Ghost, it is not material; but here we see how God would have a remembrance of the birth of Pharez, with his honour and outward blessings from God; for that it is good in our great glory and outward prosperity to be put in mind whence we be. Thus God put David in remembrance, 2 Sam. vii. 8, and Jeroboam; for so such persons shall have cause to praise God for his mercies, and be kept humble, and not forget themselves, as men commonly do in their peace and prosperity. Let such, then, as be raised up from a low estate, remember whence they are, and be willing to hear thereof from others; for God's mercies shall be the more known, admired, and glorified, whose praise we must seek with the very utter contempt of ourselves, if so the case shall require. How great a sign of pride is it then, and of a will to obscure God's mercies, when men shall chafe in themselves against such as shall mention their mean or base birth! But if men may not forget whence they be in their worldly advancement, then may we not forget our natural birth in our spiritual exaltation, when we be made the children of God, kings and priests to him, of children of wrath, and bond-slaves to Satan. If the remembrance of the other put us in mind of God's mercy, much more this, for between them is no comparison. Lastly, note that it is said, that Tamar bore Pharez unto Judah. Mothers bring forth children to the fathers of the children; so it is said that Leah bare sons to Jacob, Gen. xxix. 34; for the father is to bear the name, and take the child into his care and tuition, whether born in wedlock or otherwise. Let fathers, therefore, take care of such as they beget, for to them hath the mothers brought them out.

Of the seed which the Lord shall give thee of this young woman. Hence may be observed, that an old man may marry a young woman; as here Boaz did Ruth, and Joseph did the Virgin Mary; but not for wantonness, but for issue and posterity, as Boaz doth. Allow, therefore, of such marriages in such a case, but beware of an old man lecherous, who is one that God hateth; so an old woman wantonly affected to marry with a young man. Secondly, that children are God's gift, Gen. xlii. 9, of which at large before, which must move us to thank God for them, and to train them up to his service, and to acknowledge them his gracious gift, as Jacob did, Gen. xxxiii. 5. Thirdly, that true prayer is not without faith, for it proceedeth from it, as the apostle teacheth, Rom. x. 14; and here the words plainly imply that these elders and people were persuaded that God would give to Boaz children of Ruth, for they said, 'Which the Lord shall give thee.' As taking it for granted that he would give him children, which they were persuaded unto from the young years of Ruth, then from the obedience of Boaz, who married Ruth only to raise up children to the dead, that his name might not perish, according to the law of God, Deut. xxv., which he herein chiefly respected; and, thirdly, because this was the line and stock out of which the Messiah should come, according to Jacob's prophecy; and therefore they knew that of these should come issue to fulfil the prophecy. In praying, let us also with these believe, so are we commanded, James i. 6; and if we do believe, we shall obtain what we ask, if the Lord think it needful for us, Mat. xxi. 22, for the prayer of faith availeth much if it be fervent, James v. 15-17. Fourthly and lastly, hence observe, that prayer is a means to make an honourable house, and to continue it in the following posterity. Therefore David used prayer in this case, 2 Sam. vii. 25, as these do here for Boaz's house in his posterity; and so did Abraham pray for Ishmael to continue in the Lord's sight, Gen. xvii. 20, who promised him mercy, and an honourable issue to many generations from him. Let us use this means to uphold and continue our house. I have spoken of many good means before (out of ver. 5), let this be added to them. But men in their worldly wisdom seek by other means, without prayer, to continue their posterity in honour; as by these, first, by great purchases for their children. But doth not Solomon tell them, Prov. xxvii. 24, that riches are not for ever? And we find it true by experience. Secondly, by building stately houses, and calling them by their own names, thinking that their houses shall continue for ever, and their dwelling-places to all generations. But doth not the psalmist tell them that 'this their way is their folly'? Ps. xlix. 13. Is not the tower of Babel thrown down? Gen. xi. 4, 8; and, became not that their confusion, by which they sought a name, and to continue together? Thirdly, by entailing of lands upon the heirs male from one to another for many generations; but could there be a surer entail than the kingdom of Israel to David, which yet was almost quite cut off by Solomon's idolatry, so as Rehoboam lost ten tribes in his days? Entail it as sure as they can, yet the iniquity of the children will make it to be cut off. God liketh not that men should by their devices tie his blessings to whom they list, for vain-glory's sake, and to keep up a name. And do not we see lawyers, which teach parents to entail, how they can teach their children to untail it again. Fourthly, by matching with great houses, and by this they think their house shall stand; but did not Ahab, by marrying with Jezebel, the king of Sidon's daughter, root out his whole posterity? and did not Jehoshaphat, by marrying his son to Ahab's daughter, do almost the like? Fifthly and lastly, by procuring great places of honour in the commonwealth, oh then they think they are surely founded; but doth not Solomon tell them, Prov. xxvii. 24, that the crown endureth not to every generation? But let these consider of Haman and of his high place, and yet how suddenly he came to a fearful end; and with this let them not forget the treasurer Shebna, Isa. xxii. 16, 17, 21, who graved, as it were, his habitation in a rock by policy, and by making strong sides for himself. But doth not Isaiah say, that the Lord would lead him into captivity, and violently turn him, and toss him as a ball, and drive him from his station, and bestow his place upon another? And therefore, without the Lord, all these means are weak to uphold a house; yea, such a house sin will undermine and cause to fall. Let none, therefore, rest on these weak props, but pray unto the Lord for his blessing, which maketh strong the habitation of the righteous.

Ver. 13. *So Boaz took Ruth, and she was his wife: and when he went in unto her, the Lord gave her conception, and she bare a son.*

Here is the full accomplishment of the marriage, the holy liberty thereof, and the blessing of God upon the same, both for conception and bringing forth a son.

So Boaz took Ruth. Where he took her it is not mentioned; whether after this assembly was dismissed, or before, is not certain; some think she stayed with Naomi, expecting the success, as Naomi advised in chap. iii. ver. 18, and so from thence did take her. It may be she was, while this assembly was together (after Boaz had publicly declared his mind, and bought the land and her at the hands of the kinsman), brought in thither, and so he there did solemnly take here; for in the end of the former verse it is said, 'Of the seed which the Lord shall give thee of *this* young woman,' as implying her then there present. And *he took her* implieth the marriage, as appeareth elsewhere in other places, Gen. xxiv. 67, 1 Sam. xxv. 43, Judges xiv. 8. And the next words in the text shew, that it was not like Shechem's taking of Dinah to deflower her, Gen. xxxiv. 2, but to make her his wife by lawful wedlock, which was ever public, and not done privately in corners. So then the meaning of the words is, that Boaz did marry Ruth, and so was his wife; and with us, such as do marry, do take either other by the hand, and do by word of mouth say, that the one doth take the other to live together as man and wife. And it may be that the word *taking* is put for *marrying*, to note the free consent of mind and heart; then the right and interest which the one hath in the other; and, thirdly, the care and protection of the husband which he taketh of his wife, and the woman's acknowledgment to have betaken herself unto the man as her head and husband. This Boaz's taking and marrying of Ruth sheweth how a nobleman (for his father was the prince of Judah, 1 Chron. ii. 10) may marry with a mean poor woman, so she be virtuous, as his father did Rahab before, and Ahasuerus did Esther, and no disparagement; though Boaz had further reason to lead him thereto, as his own words before declare, ver. 10. Again, we see how an Israelite might marry with a woman a stranger, so she were a convert. And lastly, that a good man will keep his honest word; for what he had privately promised, chap. iii. 11, 13, he here now maketh good to the utmost; of which two last points I have spoken before.

And she was his wife; that is, by his taking and marrying of her. So we see that lawful marriage is that which maketh man and woman husband and wife, So is it said of Rebekah, Gen. xxiv. 67, that 'Isaac took her,' and she was his wife; and in like case of the woman of Timnath which Samson did marry, Judges xiv. 8, 15. It is not living or lying together, as lewd persons may do, nor yet mutual affection, but the entering in God's holy ordinance, which maketh the woman the wife. Therefore, to live honestly, and to make a woman thy wife, marry her lawfully. Now in this that the marriage is so shortly described, without mentioning of any such feasting and merriments, as is often with us, with too much riot and excess, it may here be demanded, Whether it be lawful to make feasts at marriages, and then to be merry? *Ans.* It is lawful to be merry in sobriety, to rejoice and sing, so it be with grace in our hearts, as the apostle speaketh, Eph. v. 19. And we may make feasts, as Laban did at Jacob's marriage, Gen. xxix. 22, and

439

as Samson did at his, Judges xiv. 10, as the custom was among the Philistines, which he observed; yea, our Saviour was at a feast when some were married, and did by divine power supply their want of wine, John ii.; and by the parable, Mat. xxii. 2, and xxv, it seemeth to be an usual thing to feast, and to have solemnities observed besides at marriages. Here only beware of wantonness, riot, and excess, and then may they eat, and drink, and rejoice their hearts.

And when he went in unto her. This is expounded in another place, to go to her into the chamber, Judges xv. 1; for brides had a private chamber, into which the bridegroom entered on the marriage day, Joel ii. 16; but here is modestly implied the act of marriage, set out also in Scripture by other terms, as of knowing, lying with one, giving due benevolence; never speaking hereof but by a periphrasis and circumlocution; and therefore are we hereby taught, that when necessity enforceth to speak of that, which in proper speech is not comely to utter, it is to be expressed so as chaste ears may not be offended. This the Holy Ghost, in thus setting down this thing in these modest terms, teacheth; and it serveth to reprove such as abuse their tongues to wantonness, and lascivious and immodest terms, to make others merry, and to be held pleasant companions; but such fools, as Solomon calleth them, make a sport of sin; for these offend against the commandment and charge given by the apostle, Eph. iv. 29, Col. iii., Eph. v. 3; they corrupt good manners by their ill words, 1 Cor. xv. 33; they trespass against the seventh commandment, and do contrary to that which the apostle teacheth and exhorteth unto for the government of the tongue both in speaking and singing; yea, these do grieve, not, as they think, only men, such as they judge over-precise, because they will not run with them into the like excess of riot, but the blessed Spirit of God, Eph. iv. 30. And let these know, that if men must give an account unto God for every idle word, then surely for such filthy communication and bawdy songs, which fleshly spirits made themselves merry withal, which godly men have condemned, calling such a speech the chariot of adultery, because it bringeth many to such a lewd practice. Heathen by laws have forbidden it,* for that it polluteth the mind, filleth it with wickedness, and maketh such impudent; and also did punish the same, as is reported of the Romans,† that so the dignity of the laws and discipline among them might remain, as one saith, inviolable. What a shame and impudence is it then in such as would be called Christians, and yet cannot by reason nor religion of Christ be restrained from such petulancy and wantonness. Note again here, how this is spoken after marriage, and not before, to teach that such as be married may lawfully company together, Gen. xxix. 21, and that by warrant from God, who said, after he had made man, and joined Adam and

* Athenian law, *apud Stobæum.* † Au. Gell.

Eve in marriage, Increase and multiply; and the apostle teacheth, 1 Cor. vii. 3, 5, that then neither of them hath power over their own body, and hereof maketh a double use, to render due benevolence, and not to defraud one another. Then they are to be reproved which before marriage company one with another, as incontinent and violently lustful persons do, and such as being married do defraud one another. And here this condemneth the church of Rome, which alloweth man and wife, upon the vow of chastity (forsooth), to live asunder one from another, contrary to the apostle's doctrine and exhortation, 1 Cor. vii. 5.

The Lord gave her conception. Hence it is evident that the gift of conception is from the Lord; and this is true not only in such as be altogether barren, as was Sarah, Rebekah, Hannah, the Shunamite, and Elizabeth, but in such as be at the first fruitful; this also is from his gift, Job x. 8, 10, 11. And therefore is it to be ascribed to him, he is to be thanked for it; we are not to think, as Rachel did, that a husband can give children; it is no strength of body, nor good complexion, that can make fruitful, but the blessing of God. And we may further learn here, that the Lord alloweth of the honest act of marriage, for he commandeth due benevolence, 1 Cor. vii; he calleth the marriage bed undefiled, Heb. xiii. 4; he blesseth it, and giveth the gift of conception; he allowed thereof before the fall, Gen. i., and hath in mercy ordained it as a remedy against sin, 1 Cor. vii. 2. This, therefore, confuteth such as have judged the companying together of man and wife to be a sinful act, absurdly and profanely abusing this place for it, 'those that live in the flesh cannot please God;' as if that which God himself hath allowed, and most holy men of God have done, should be now that which should debar them of God's favour, when yet these popish harlotries can dispense with God's law, and keep their whores, and yet not live in the flesh, but be holy men! But let them know, that whoremongers and adulterers God will judge, Heb. xiii.; when marriage is honourable, and the bed undefiled, and the liberty to be used and allowed for procreation of children, to avoid fornication, with hearty thanks unto God for his ordinance. Here note farther the difference which the Scripture maketh between conception of a woman a wife and of another. In copulation out of marriage, it is said of a woman, that she conceived, as Tamar by Judah, Gen. xxxviii. 18, Hagar by Abraham, Gen. xvi. 4, and Bathsheba by David, 2 Sam. xi. 5, but never as here, that 'the Lord gave her to conceive;' for the other is by his common blessing, as among brute beasts, but this by his favourable approbation and gracious blessing, as Jacob said of his children unto Esau, Gen. xxxiii. 5.

And she bare a son. After the gift of conception followeth childbirth, not forthwith, but in due time of life, Gen. xviii. 10, which is sometime at the ninth month, but commonly at the tenth. It was not enough that she should conceive, and after have an abortive birth, but that God in mercy should preserve the child alive in the mother's womb to be timely born; for as not to conceive, but to be barren, was a punishment, so conceiving, and to bring forth an untimely birth, is in the same nature. The Lord therefore here sheweth his goodness, not only in giving conception, but a happy deliverance unto Ruth, and a timely birth; so the Lord followeth his with his mercies. Now, in that it is said to be a son, and not a daughter, it is to note the greater blessing. For it is a greater blessing to have a son than a daughter. And therefore we do find, when God would make the barren to bear, and such as had begged that blessing at his hands, he gave them sons, as we may see in Sarah, Rebekah, Rachel, Hannah, Elizabeth, and in others. Because the son is the upholder of the name of the family, he is in nature the more worthy; for the woman was made for man, and not man for the woman, as the apostle teacheth; and the man is a more fitter instrument for the good of the church or commonweal, albeit sometime the Lord hath done wondrously by women. Besides these reasons, the males among the Israelites were a greater blessing; for that the man-child, and the continuance of the line in Judah, gave them hope of the Messiah, which they looked for; and the male child bare upon him the seal of the covenant of God, which was circumcision, that God would be their God, and of their seed after them. Therefore praise God for this blessing and birth, for both, but more specially for this, as beholding therein the Lord's mercy to keep thy name upon the earth, among thy brethren, and saints of God. Lastly, note the effectual power of the prayer which they made, ver. 11. The Lord heard them; for here we see Ruth, before barren, is now become fruitful. So as we hereby do learn, that the hearty and faithful prayer of the godly is never in vain; for the people and elders desired that Ruth should be fruitful, and she was so; and also that Boaz's posterity might be honourable and renowned, and so it was, as we may see in the 21st and 22d verses of this chapter. For an effectual prayer of righteous men availeth much, as James saith, James v. 16, 17, and proveth by an instance of the prayer of Elijah, and as may be seen in the prayer of Moses, of Asa, 2 Chron. xiv. 11, 12; Jehoshaphat, 2 Chron. xx. 6, 14, 15; Isaiah and Hezekiah, 2 Chron. xxxii. 20; and of many more, which is to encourage us to the exercise of prayer in faith and fervency of spirit. If any think that those afore named were extraordinary men, and that therefore we poor and miserable persons, in comparison of them, cannot look to have our prayers so effectual with God; I answer, first, that James takes away this objection and fear of acceptance with God; for he saith, that 'Elias was a man subject to the like passions as we are,' yet he prayed and was heard; secondly, that we have assistance of God his Spirit, teaching us to pray with groans which cannot be expressed, because we know not how to pray as we ought; and, thirdly, that Christ prayeth for us, and in him we offer up our supplications, and so shall be heard. This lesson also teacheth us to esteem greatly of the prayers of the godly, seeing they be so effectual, and desire them to pray for us, as the Israelites did Samuel, and St Paul the faithful and saints of God, as may appear in almost every of his epistles, so highly did he account of their prayers for him.

Ver. 14. *And the women said unto Naomi, Blessed be the Lord, which hath not left thee this day without a kinsman, that his name may be famous in Israel.*

Praise and thanksgiving unto God at the birth of the child. The parties rejoicing were the women; their joy was uttered to Naomi, the manner was holy and religious, praising God; the matter thereof, or the moving cause, was, that God had not left her without a kinsman; and the hopeful end thereof, that his name may be famous in Israel.

And the women said. That is, such godly women as were at the child-birth, these rejoiced in Naomi's behalf. For it is the duty of one to rejoice in the welfare of another, when God bestoweth his blessings upon them. As these do here, the neighbours of Elizabeth, Luke i. 58; Jethro, at the prosperity of Israel, Exod. xviii. 9; and the friends of Job at his recovery, Job xlii. 11. This we are commanded to do, to rejoice with those that do rejoice, Rom. xii. 15; the godly are members one of another, 1 Cor. xii. 26; and therefore must needs have a fellow feeling; it is a fruit of love and charity, and that we love our neighbour as ourselves, Mat. xxii. 19, which if we do, we will rejoice in their welfare, as we do in our own. But let this be with them in lawful things; for charity rejoiceth not in iniquity, 1 Cor. xiii.; let us rejoice with them in their happy and blessed welfare, whether temporal, as former examples shew, or spiritual, as St Paul rejoiced in the behalf of the Philippians and Colossians, Philip. i. 3, 4, Col. i. 3, 12; and St John in the graces of the elect lady and her children, 2 John ver. 4. This reproveth three sorts: first, such as envy the prosperity of others, as Sanballats and Tobiases, Neh. ii. 10; like Egyptians, Exod. i., which cannot endure to see others prosper by them. These are void of charity, which is without envy, 1 Cor. xiii. 4; and they are like the devil, that being cast from heaven, could not endure to see man in paradise; or like devilish men, Cain, Saul, and the scribes and pharisees, the enemies of Christ. Secondly, such as rejoice with their friends in their prosperity, though they get up by unjust means, and by unlawful practices uphold themselves. This is not true love, 1 Cor. xiii. 6; for here is more cause of mourning than of rejoicing; for what joy can it be to a godly heart to see his friend rich and in glory by usury, bribery, oppression, deceit, and fraud, which came for plagues

441

upon him from heaven, and are the highway to hell and damnation? But outward prosperity so dazzleth the eyes, and deludeth the heart, as the plagues of the soul, and vengeance due for the same, they either see not, or believe not; therefore they rejoice like worldlings with such as themselves. The third sort are they, which cannot rejoice with others in their spiritual welfare, that men are become godly, as St Paul and John did, but rather despise them for it, because they themselves savour not of the things of God, they love darkness rather than the light. If they do rejoice herein, it is rather for the good which conversion brings in worldly respects, than of religion itself, as that hereby they leave to be unthrifty, and do care to live in the world, and such like, which is no rejoicing at their heavenly graces, but for worldly profit, and for such things as religion maketh good in regard of the outward things of this life; as profit, good report in a common acception, civil carriage, and so forth. This is a worldly, and not a spiritual rejoicing with those that truly rejoice in the Spirit.

Unto Naomi. And why to her more than to Ruth? Because she was the principal instrument for the effecting of the marriage, and she stood in most need of comfort, having endured a long time affliction. For those chiefly are to be cheered with the consideration of God's mercies and blessings, who have been most humbled; as these do here Naomi; for they speak so to her, as if this blessing had been only for her comfort, saying, He hath not left *thee* without a kinsman, he shall be to *thee* a restorer of life, and so forth. And therefore when we see any to have been much cast down, and that the Lord beginneth to shew them mercy, let us speak thereof cheerfully unto them, and comfort their hearts; for they know how to use well God's mercies, their former humiliation hath prepared them, hath schooled them, so as they will not wax proud with the Lord's blessings, as others do.

Blessed be the Lord. Words of praise and thanksgiving to the author of this blessing. Thus begin they their joy and mirth; for the joy of the godly is holy and religious; for the matter of their joy is good and lawful, the manner with grace in the heart, as the apostle exhorteth, Eph. v. 19, and the end, to set forth the Lord's glory, of whom with praises they make mention. This was the joy of Moses and the Israelites, Exod. xv.; of Deborah and Barak, Judges v.; of Jehoshaphat and Judah, 2 Chron. xx.; of Zacharias and Elizabeth, Luke i.; for the godly take occasion from all the good which befalleth them to be mindful of the Lord, from whom they know they receive all blessings, whatsoever they be, and whosoever be the instruments thereof to them; with David therefore, Ps. ciii., they say, 'O my soul, praise thou the Lord, and forget not all his benefits!' If this be the joy of the godly, what wickedness then is it in those, who in their mirth, and in the midst of God's blessings, do put away the remembrance of God, and the thought of his precepts; spiritual songs, and gracious speeches mar utterly their mirth; the presence of the godly is hateful to them, and hindereth their merriments; for they cannot rejoice but in vanity; their talk is ribaldry, their songs wantonness, their laughter madness, and the delight of their hearts mere sensuality; the mirth of these must turn into mourning before they die, else shall their music be elsewhere weeping, wailing, and gnashing of teeth. And here, before I end this, women may learn how to behave themselves at the birth of children, as first in prayer, then in praises; pray they should for pardon of sin, and bewail, in the woman's pangs, original corruption; in the birth, our spiritual pollution; and praise God they ought for safe deliverance, acknowledging it his mercy and goodness, as these do here. Many things might move them hereto, and to be far from the behaviour of some, who instead of praising God, sit down to be merry, and to spend their speeches idly, prating of others, yea, sometimes in lewd slandering of their neighbours, or in filthy scurrility, wherein the midwife, which should be a mother of modesty, is often chief; when such should be chaste, grave, and godly matrons, who by their office and godly counsel might do much good, if they were as they ought to be; but so lewd are some of them, as they cannot endure the company of better disposed persons. Their praises should be like the midwives in Egypt, Exod. i., women fearing God, able to instruct, to comfort, to pray unto God, and to praise him for his goodness.

Which hath not left thee this day without a kinsman. This is it they bless God for, that God had given to Naomi a young kinsman, a kinsman indeed, which will so shew himself. Naomi had a kinsman very nigh unto her before, chap. iii. 12, but he shewed himself not like a kinsman, and therefore was here passed over as no kinsman. For as men indeed shew themselves, such they be, and so are to be esteemed, otherwise they have but a name of a brother, father, kinsman, friend, Christian, yea, minister, magistrate, and have not the truth, and substance of such. They be but merely titular, and glory in shadows, as most do, who are nothing answerable to that title and name of nature, of love, of fellowship, or of office and place, which they are called by or settled in. Note further, that it is of God that the godly poor are not left comfortless of some friend, one or other, both able and willing to help them. Thus the women here tell Naomi, and do bless God therefore in her behalf; for if God should not raise them up succour, who would respect unto them? Because poverty causeth contempt, or neglect at the least, and the religion of the poor is but held counterfeit, and themselves hypocrites, so the world judgeth of them. And therefore when God raiseth up friends to take knowledge of them, and to do them good, great cause have they to bless God, as they here do, both for hope of supply of wants, and also preventing of injuries, which honest

poor, by such able and good friends, are less subject unto than others which want them.

That his name may be famous in Israel. This is the hope they have of this young Obed; and one mercy of God in giving this son unto this honourable family is, that he might be renowned among God's people. Whence note these two lessons: first, that much is expected and looked for from the children of great and godly parents, both in respect of the parents and also of the children. For it is supposed that parents being godly, will have care to instruct, and if need be to correct their children, to pray for them, and be good examples to them; and being great, that they will use the best means and procure the best helps for their good education, and leave them sufficient to shew forth the fruits of godliness. And if thus parents do, who may imagine otherwise, till the contrary appear, but that the children of such will demean themselves as they should? And who can expect but good from the children of godly parents? Should not the father's graces provoke children to goodness? and their greatness to abhor base practices? Good children will not degenerate from good parents, whose goodness will more persuade to well-doing than greatness to make them proud and wicked, as some Absaloms and Esaus have been, and yet are, to the grief of religious parents, and at length to the shame and confusion of themselves. Secondly, here may be observed, that God giveth children to the better sort, great and honourable, that they may become famous amongst God's people. So conceived these godly women of this son of Boaz; for, indeed, all the blessings of riches and honour given unto parents, are not only given for their own good, but amongst other ends, for the better enabling of them to bring up their family in good order, and especially their children in the ways of God, for his service and honour, as they have more means to provoke them thereto. Let therefore such parents here take such a course with their children, as they may make them, by God's blessing, famous in Israel, in God's church, and among his people, which they may effect by these good means: first, by being every way and at all times a good example of piety to them, as David was, Ps. ci., and Zacharias, Luke i. Secondly, by instructing them carefully in godliness and religion, as parents are commanded, Eph. iv. 4, and as David did instruct Solomon, Prov. iv. Thirdly, by seeing them set to the practice of that which they are taught, and to have an especial eye thereto. Men teach their children good manners among men, for civil carriage of their outward man, and will see therein if they offend, and reprove them; so should they thus see to them in their Christian good manners and behaviour towards God and good men, and in every Christian duty towards all. Fourthly, by settling them in some particular calling, as Adam the monarch of the world did his sons, to keep them from idleness, from being busybodies, and from a world of wickedness, which such as live but of* a calling run into. Fifthly, by restraining them from ill company, idle, wanton, prodigal and profane persons, and exhorting them to have fellowship with such as fear God, also with civil and honest men well reported of, well brought up, and well disposed unto goodness. Sixthly, by commending, countenancing, and encouraging their well-doing, both by present rewards and promises of future good ; but if they do ill, then fatherly to admonish at the first, to withhold them from evil by love rather than by slavish fear ; but if this will not prevail, then to rebuke sharply, and to punish as the cause shall require. Thus if parents would do, there is no doubt but, by God's mercy, many men's children of place may become famous in Israel, and not be so infamous as some be, to parents' shame and their own overthrow.

Ver. 15. *And he shall be unto thee a restorer of thy life, and a nourisher of thine old age ; for thy daughter-in-law, which loveth thee, which is better to thee than seven sons, hath borne him.*

This is still the continued speech of the women to Naomi ; the scope whereof is still to comfort her, in foreshewing what this babe should be unto her, and the reason why they so speak of him.

And he shall be unto thee a restorer of thy life. Naomi had many crosses, she had lost her husband and children, yea, and her outward state in the world, which made her, as it were, dead with sorrow, which these women and godly neighbours well considered of, and here therefore do enlarge their speech for Naomi's greater comfort ; to teach us, that true friends, affected with others' miseries, cannot but meditate many arguments of comfort in the days of their felicity. For the joy of their hearts is unfeigned for their friends' prosperity, as truly as before they were moved with their calamity. Thus let us learn to try the sympathy of men's hearts towards other in prosperity and adversity.

A restorer of thy life. So they speak, as if by her former misery she had, as it were, been lifeless. Whence note, that heavy crosses, as poverty, old age, widowhood, and loss of children, do bedead the spirit even of godly persons. So these words imply, and experience teacheth. For no affliction is joyous for the present, but grievous, Heb. xii. 12. How much more when many come together ! Therefore let us have compassion of the afflicted, and labour to raise up their spirits, especially of poor afflicted widows, for it is a part of pure and undefiled religion before God, James i. 27. This condemneth such of cruelty as will vex the afflicted, or be miserable comforters, as Job's friends were to him. Secondly, we may learn, that godly children are as restorers of life to their parents, Prov. x. 1, they make them glad. Let children labour to be such that they may cheer up their parents' hearts, and not be, as too many be, causers

of heart's grief to them, making them to go down with mourning to the grave, for such are foolish children, Prov. xv. 20, and x. 1, and xvii. 25.

And a nourisher of thine old age. Note, first, that old age needs nourishing, for it maketh man feeble and to want heat, 1 Kings i. 1, Eccles. xii. 3 ; also to be subject to diseases, as to be blind, as was Isaac, Gen. xxvii., and Jacob, Gen. xlviii. 10, and to be lame, as Asa, 1 Kings xv. Therefore in the youth of summer provide somewhat for the winter of old age, and when thou hast provision for age thank God therefore. Secondly, that children are to be nourishers of their parents in their old age ; as Joseph was to Jacob, Gen. xlv. 11, and Ruth, but a daughter-in-law, here to Naomi, chap. iii. 18; and such a one the women hoped Obed would be. Let children learn this duty. For, first, nature teacheth it, in the stork ; and branches of trees, receiving the sap from the root, do return it again to it towards winter. Secondly, Reason teacheth to be thankful, and to do good to them that have done us good. From parents children have being, bringing up, and their preservation, whose love, care, pains, and cost, children can never recompense. Thirdly, it is one end why they be born ; for if a friend be born to help his friend in adversity, Prov. xvii. 17, then much more children to help their parents, who are bone of their bone and flesh of their flesh. Fourthly, parents are children's glory, Prov. xvii. 6, therefore should they make much of them. Fifthly, here to add the commandment, Exod. xx., to honour our parents. Now how are they honoured, when in want they are not relieved ? Sixthly, such as succour their parents may expect a blessing from their children. Those children, therefore, which are without natural affection, sin against God, against nature, reason, and religion. But children will perhaps say, Our parents are froward and hard to please, and therefore they make us weary and unwilling to keep and nourish them. *Ans.* First, consider how froward you were in childhood, and yet poor parents carefully kept you and cast you not off. Secondly, when old age cometh, you may be such. Do then as you would be done unto ; learn to bear with your parents, to teach your children how to bear with you. Thirdly, note how children can bear with rich parents well enough, while they hope for profit, and fear to lose what they look for. If hope of gain can make children put on such patience, then let true love do it much more.

For thy daughter-in-law, which loveth thee, which is better than seven sons, hath borne him. This is a reason of the women's hope of this child's kindness towards Naomi. From these words we may learn these things : First, that there is a good hope of children's love, which come of loving parents, that they will love such as their parents have loved. Thus the women conclude ; and this was a lesson which David taught his son Solomon, 1 Kings ii. 7 ; and Christ

* That is, 'without '—ED.

443

loving those whom his Father loveth, teacheth so much. Let, therefore, children be thus affected, especially if their parents have set their love aright, upon such as were worthy of love. Secondly, that there may be great love between a mother-in-law and a daughter-in-law. Ruth's love towards Naomi was very great, she left her country and kindred for her, chap. i. 16, 17; laboured painfully for her, chap. ii. 18, 23; and Naomi was not wanting to seek the good of Ruth, chap. iii. Let these two be examples to such; and to make them loving, strive to be religious, and to fear God, as these did; for religion will work what corrupt nature cannot effect. Let them perform mutual duties, and let stepmothers know that they step in to be instead of natural mothers, and so let children take them, so will they love one another. Thirdly, that true love cannot be hid, for it so will express itself as others shall take notice of it. These women knew Ruth's love; so did Saul, Jonathan's to David; the people, Christ's love to Lazarus, John xi. 36, for true love will break out as fire. Try true love by the manifestation thereof. Joseph may hide his a while from his brethren, Gen. xlv. 1, and David from Absalom, 2 Sam. xiii. 39 and xiv. 1, but it will break out at length. They, therefore, but boast vainly of love which never express it. Fourthly, that true love in adversity is not lost in prosperity. Ruth is still said to love Naomi though thus exalted; so did Hushai David, so did Job's friends, chap. ii, howsoever they erred in judgment. Let not love be altered with our estates, nor honour change good conditions, as it doth in too many. Fifthly, that the loves of a stranger may sometime exceed the love of many children by nature. The women prefer Ruth's love above seven sons, that is, above many sons. Such God by favour can supply what is wanting in them by nature, and make a stranger's love surpass. Let this be comfort to the distressed.

Ver. 16. *And Naomi took the child, and laid it in her bosom, and became nurse unto it.*

This verse sheweth the education of the child, by whom, and how.

And Naomi took the child. This the old woman did voluntarily, out of her true love both to the mother and the child. She was in the house of Boaz, that great rich man, we here see, and so well provided for in her old age, yet would she take pains, and not be idle. So we see, that the godly, though old, and well provided for, yet will set themselves to labour, and do something; for they make conscience of their time, not to spend their days in idleness, which they know to be a foul sin and the nurse of many. They will labour to be an example unto others, and to spur the younger on to take pains. Though they live of themselves, yet they owe a duty to God to be doing what they may; and if they live upon others, herein they shew their good will, to be as little chargeable as they may, and to be thankful after their strength and

power. Now, this holy woman is herein to be imitated; and let none think that they may be excused to live idly, either for age, so long as they can take pains, or for that they have enough to live upon, because God giveth none riches to live a lazy life; but such, even old persons, should live either in labour, as St Paul willeth the widow of threescore years old, 1 Tim. v. 4, or in teaching and instructing others, Titus ii. 3, 4; a blessed exercise for old folk, which will give them comfort in the end of their days.

And laid it in her bosom. This sheweth her love, and with what tender affection she took him into her hands. Four things might move Naomi thus affectionately to love the babe: First, her love to the mother, who so exceedingly loved her. Secondly, her love to Boaz the father, who had so mercifully dealt with her. Thirdly, her love to her husband Elimelech, departed, whose name was raised up again by this child, upon his inheritance. Fourthly, her great hope of joy and comfort from the child itself, as the women foretell in the former verse. Howsoever it was, here we may see, that parents carry a hearty affection towards their children; they be in their hearts and bosom; for if this love was in Naomi, a mother-in-law, we may well conclude it in natural mothers, which may appear many ways, in their great pains and care in nursing them, and in bringing them up; in their grief and sorrow, when their children are any way diseased, as we may see by the tears of the father, and cry of the mother, which Mark and Matthew make mention of, Mark ix. 24, and vii. 25, Mat. xv. 22; in their kind embracing of them as here, and as did the father of the prodigal son; in their great joy to hear of their welfare, as Jacob did rejoice to hear of Joseph, Gen. xlv. 27, 28; in their easy natures, soon reconciled to their children, when they humble themselves before them, as we see in David to Absalom, and the father of the prodigal son; lastly, in their great lamentation at the death of their children, as David did for Absalom, though a most unnatural son, and the widow which followed her son to the grave, which Christ raised up to life again. No other reason can be given, but that natural and inbred love to children in parents, else some children are so hard-favoured and ill-conditioned, as parents could not so love them, but only for that they be their children. Let children hence learn to be thankful to God and their parents, and shew love to them again in all obedience.

And became his nurse. That is, a help in the mother's nursing of it, as by holding it, lulling of it asleep, giving of it meat, warming of it, and such like helps for the nourishing of the life of the babe, and not giving it suck, for she was too old to do this. We may find in Scripture two sort of nurses: dry nurses; such a one was Rebekah's, Gen. xxiv. 59, to help to attend on the child, and to ease the mother somewhat, as Naomi doth here; and in helping to nourish and bring up a child; in this sense a father is called a nurse, Num. xi. 12. The other sort are milk-nurses, such as give suck unto children, as in Scripture we find only those to be their mothers, even them that bare them, to bring them up also, that as they afforded them the womb to bear them, so the breasts likewise to give their children suck. And this is the mother's duty, if possibly she be able ; not birth, wealth, nicety, nor idleness can exempt them from this duty, as it doth a number of wanton dames, that they may be fitter to follow their lusts. That mothers are to give their own children suck, it is apparent by these reasons ; the natural instinct in beasts teacheth every other creature having paps to give suck ; yea, the sea monsters draw out their breasts and give suck to their young ones, saith Jeremiah, Lam. iv. 3 ; and therefore, such as neglect this duty, are worse than these beasts, which we hold unkind if they let not their young ones suck. It is the principal use and end of breasts in women, when God sendeth them children, though too many now make them only stales and bawds of lust. The workmanship of God should make them do this : First, in placing them so high, as in no other creature, even neighbouring upon the heart, the shop of heat, to convey the blood sooner into the breasts ; so as the heart works for the infant, to teach mothers to have affection to this work. Secondly, so placing them, as the mother is taught in nature to embrace the infant, to lay it to her breast, the more to work love between the mother and the babe. Thirdly, in making them to have this faculty to turn blood into milk. And lastly, God's providing, as soon as the infant is perfect for birth, milk in the breast for the infant ; so as God and nature call them to this duty, except any will say that God hath done all this in vain, and might have spared his workmanship. The very name of a breast, *mamma*, should put them in mind hereof, the first syllable whereof is that which an infant doth soonest speak, calling the mother *mam ;* as if nature had given this first to the babe, so easily to frame, to utter this word, to put the mother in mind of her duty, and to give it her breast. Again, God in the work of nature hath not only given breasts, but heads or nipples for the infant to suck the milk out of her breasts ; and to help it, hath made the skin about the nipples more rugous and rough for the child's tongue to hold by. The heathen philosophers, endued but with the light of nature, teach this,* and affirm, that the mother's milk implants in children the love of mothers ; yea, mothers love commonly those children better, which they nurse, than the rest ; and reason may be given, because the mother giveth, and the child receiveth, by sucking her breasts, more of her substance, than they which do not. Children love their nurses, we see by experience, and better than their mothers that bare them, so long as they be without judgment to discern, and only follow nature for the nourishment of life. It is not so natural, say

* Arist. and Plutarch.

445

also these heathen, to be nursed of another, as of the mother, in whom it is conceived ; for differing bodies have differing temperature, and therefore the taking away of the infant so soon from the accustomed nourishment in the mother, must needs breed an alteration. A learned man * thinks this to be the cause of the degenerating so much of great men's sons, and of their so little love to their mothers. It is a token of no great love to children, when their mothers put them over to strangers ; it is just with God, if mothers after find their children over strange to them, being but rather half than whole mothers,† mothers of necessity, and not of good will; for perforce they bring forth, but it is true love which maketh a mother to give suck ; safety to themselves desireth the former, or else to die with it in the womb ; but love only to the infant procureth this latter at their hands. Besides all these reasons, the examples of all the godly women in Scripture teach mothers now this duty. That right honourable Sarah, the wife of a most honourable man, and mighty in substance and power, nursed her son Isaac, Gen. xxi. 7. Princely Job was nourished by the breasts of her whose womb did bear him, Job iii. 12 ; queen Bathsheba nursed Solomon, Cant. viii. 1. What shall I speak of holy Hannah, 1 Sam. ii. 23, the mother also of Moses, Exod. i., of Samson's mother, Judges xiii. 42, and others ? The mother of Jesus our Lord and Saviour, whom all do honour, she did give her blessed babe suck ; all women call her blessed because she bare Christ. And was she not as blessed in giving him her breasts to suck ? Luke xi. 27. Yes, verily. Some good ladies at this day disdain not this duty. And what should hinder them? Such persons may give suck, and then deliver the child over to a dry nurse to attend it in all other things, which help the poor cannot have. Lastly, as there is a blessing of the womb to bring forth, so of the breasts to give suck, Gen. xlix. 25 ; and the dry breasts and barren womb have been taken for a curse, Hosea ix. 14. Let mothers, therefore, take knowledge of these things, to press them to this duty of nursing their own bowels, that, in giving still of their own substance, they might the more work love in their children towards them. Their excuses are idle, and are of no force against these reasons, for true motherly love is seen in nursing ; for lust brings to conceive, necessity forceth to bring forth, but only true and natural love causeth a mother to nurse her child.

Ver. 17. *And the women her neighbours gave it a name, saying, There is a son born to Naomi ; and they called his name Obed: he is the father of Jesse, the father of David.*

Here is the naming of the child which was born of Ruth, where note who named it, the reason, the name thereof, and what he came to be, shewed in his honourable and royal posterity in his son and grandchild.

* Kick. in his Oecono. † Note this, you unnatural mothers !

And the women her neighbours. The women here are those before in ver. 14, very godly and religious, as appeareth by many things before spoken of. These godly women were Naomi and Ruth's neighbours, such as dwelt together with them, as the word (שכן) signifieth. Here may be noted who be fittest to be called to such businesses, the honest neighbours and kinsfolk, as was at the birth and circumcision of John Baptist; for kinsfolk they expect it, and have therein an interest and cause of rejoicing in the increase of their lineage, and therefore may not be carelessly neglected. And neighbours are to be called, as those which be nigh at hand and helpful at need, who, being near, are better, as Solomon saith, than a brother far off. But here, observe farther, what manner of neighbours they were which these godly women had, even such as themselves, for godly women delight to have about them such as themselves, for the wicked and they cannot accord; they have differing heads and hearts. Over the one God ruleth, over the other Satan; the one is regenerate in heart, the other unregenerate, and therefore cannot but jar in word and deed, the one being an abomination to the other, as Solomon speaketh, Prov. xxix. But the godly having one head, Jesus Christ, and one heart, Acts iv., they will reap benefit one of another, by instructing, admonishing, comforting, and praying one for another. Therefore, to shew yourselves godly, be ye delighted to have them about you.

And gave it a name. It is said the women gave it. We find that sometimes the fathers gave the name, as Abraham to his son, whom he called Isaac; mothers often, as we may see in Leah and Rachel, Gen. xxix. and xxx.; so kinsfolk now and then, as we may note out of Luke i. 58, 59. And here in Ruth the neighbours gave it, yea, sometime a stranger named the child upon just occasion, as Pharaoh's daughter did give the name of Moses to him, which the parents did not alter; so as it seemeth this was not strictly stood upon, though most commonly the parents give the name. If any here ask concerning the time when children were named, I find that it was sometime at the birth of the infant; so Rachel, Gen. xxxv. 18, and the wife of Phinehas, 1 Sam. iv. 21, gave their children names upon their departure; but being in such cases, it seemeth not to be ordinary. It may be thought to be usually at the time when the child was circumcised, as we may perceive at the naming of Isaac, Gen. xxi. 4, and John the Baptist, Luke i. 59. And thus do we give names at the baptizing of infants, that as they did, so we may put children in mind of the covenant made in baptism, of their badge of Christianity, and of their ingrafting into Christ, and how they were admitted as God's children into the household of faith, and as heirs of the kingdom of heaven.

There is a son born to Naomi. That is, for the good and comfort of Naomi, as is before shewed out of the

15th verse, and as may be gathered by the like phrase elsewhere, Isa. ix. 6, Luke ii. 11; so as in these words is a reason of the name which they gave unto the child. Whence note that the godly in ancient time gave names, not by hap-hazard, but as good reason did lead them thereunto; for they gave names in obedience to God's commandment, who appointed sometimes names unto children; to know also whence they were and whence taken, Gen. xvii. 19 and xxi. 3, Luke i. 13. Thus Adam was so called of the matter whereof his body was made; so Moses of the place whence he was taken. Some had a name from their miserable estate and condition, as *Enosh;* some to call to remembrance some favours of God. Thus *Simeon* was so called of his mother Leah, and Joseph for the like reason called his sons *Manasseh* and *Ephraim.* Sometime names were given from some thing which fell out at the birth; hence *Pharez* had his name, Gen. xxxviii. 29, and *Ichabod* his, 1 Sam. iv. Some were named so from that which should come to pass afterwards, as Solomon was, for that in his days should be rest and peace, 1 Chron. xxii. 9. Some had their names from some things to be effected and done by them; so was our 'Lord called Jesus, because he should save his people from their sins,' Mat. i. 21. Besides these inducements to impose a name, they did sometime call them after their ancestors, to keep them in remembrance, Luke i. 59, 61. We must learn to imitate the holy men of God in these things, to express our own graces, or to teach our children some duties, or to call to mind the works of God, or to remember holy men and women, to imitate their virtues. And we may not think this to be too precise a practice, seeing God's wisdom interposed itself sometime, both in giving names and in changing of names; and the reverence due to the holy sacrament administered, adviseth us to a due consideration hereof in honour of the sacrament. And a good name may call sometimes a man to the remembrance of his duty. I know that a name maketh not a man good, for some have good names, but their condition stark naught: yet a good name may sometime occasion a man to think of goodness; and howsoever the party so named doth make no use of it, yet it is commendable in the imposers thereof, who imitate the example of godly men in the old time, the saints also in the primitive church, and the godly disposed at this day, which reproveth such as give names idly without sense or reason, ridiculous names, heathenish rather than Christian, and some such names as be very profane. But of this thus much.

And they called his name Obed. That is, as they gave him his name, so thus was he called; which words may imply that the name once given was with authority confirmed, so as the infant was commonly so called without alteration, neither were ever any names altered but upon some extraordinary occasion; for to suffer a change thereof is either folly or worse, if good and honest causes move not thereunto.

Obed. This signifieth *serving*, because he should serve as a comforter to old Naomi, as the women said, ver. 15, which is the reason of this name ; to teach him and also all children their duty, which is this, to labour to be a comfort unto their parents, of which before in ver. 15. Now this they shall do if they live in obedience to their parents, with fear to offend, yielding ever to be ruled by them ; if they seek to imitate their parents' virtues, and to follow them in all good things ; if they frame their courses to godliness, striving to have an heavenly Father also for their guide and direction ; if they settle themselves to a good course of life, to live within some honest calling, either in the church or commonwealth ; if, lastly, they live in mutual love one with another, like Job's children. These things will comfort parents, which, therefore, let children labour for ; let them be *Obeds*, serving thus to their comforts ; let them be *Isaacs*, to make their parents to laugh for joy, and not *Benonis*, sons of sorrow, like *Cains, Esaus,* and *Absaloms*, wicked, profane, and unnatural.

Note here one thing more before I come to the next words, how that this child is not called either Elimelech or Mahlon ; and yet was he given to raise up the name of the dead upon his inheritance, that might not be cut off from among his brethren, and from the gate of his place, ver. 10, and for this end did Boaz marry Ruth ; whence, therefore, we may perceive that the preservation of the name of the dead stood not in another's bearing of his name, so to be called as he was, but rather in the issue having a right to the inheritance and enjoying of it, that it might not be alienated from the kindred and stock of the dead. Which being so, sheweth the gross folly and wrong which some shew to their near blood, in disinheriting daughters and passing their inheritance unto mere strangers for a very bare name, as if that were to hold up their name, when oftentimes it cometh to pass that such sell away the inheritance, and so root out their name, which is better kept by continuing an inheritance in their blood and bowels than by the sound of a word upon the person of a stranger. This folly we see by examples to be condemned and cursed before our eyes in not a few.

He is the father of Jesse, the father of David. These words are added to shew, first, who this Obed was, or rather what a one he came to be in his posterity, even very honourable and of high renown. Here we see that as ancestors may grace posterity, so honourable offspring may grace ancestors and forefathers. Again, by these words we understand when this story was written, even in the days of David, and that also when he was chosen of God from his brethren ; for else Jesse his eldest son should have been named, and not David, who was the seventh and youngest son of his father. Thirdly, these words shew whereto this history tendeth, to bring us unto David, that sweet singer of Israel, the chief type of Jesus Christ, the Saviour,

not only of the Jews, but likewise of the Gentiles, of whom he was pleased to come, to be their Saviour also, as it appeareth to us at this day, blessed be God for ever. Amen.

Ver. 18. *Now these are the generations of Pharez : Pharez begat Ram.*

Here is the last part of this book, and the conclusion of this chapter, containing a genealogy from Pharez to David, ten generations, as they be reckoned in order, in this and the rest of the verses, from the father to the son, and from the son to the end of the tenth generation. The occasion of this genealogy was from the last words of the former verse, speaking of Obed's being father to Jesse and grandfather to David ; and to shew this the Holy Ghost beginneth a genealogy from before Obed's time, in seven of his ancestors, and descended to David his grandchild.

Now these are the generations. Usually the genealogies of the godly are recorded, but sometime the generation of the wicked, as of Ishmael and Esau, are set down, Gen. xxv. 13, xxxvi 9, xxi. 13, and iv. 17–19 ; not so much for their sakes, as to shew the truth of God's promises made to the faithful concerning some of them, or to shew some wicked instruments in their posterity, as in the genealogy of Cain. The genealogy of the godly is set down for these ends : first, to shew how God registereth up his people in a book of remembrance, as being precious in his eyes ; secondly, to shew how he hath had from time to time, throughout all ages, a race of righteous people, a peculiar generation to himself, in despite of Satan's malice and all his bloody instruments ; thirdly, for help to chronology, as may be seen in Gen. v., from the lives of the patriarchs ; fourthly, to shew the descent from the first Adam to the second, as appeareth in the evangelists, where Matthew entitleth his first chapter ' the book of the generation of Jesus Christ,' Mat. i., from Abraham to Joseph, and then Luke from Joseph to Adam, Luke iii. This genealogy here in Ruth is to teach the truth of Jacob's prophecy concerning Christ's coming of the tribe of Judah, for here it beginneth at Pharez, Judah's son, and descendeth to David, the royal prophet and type of Christ ; also to shew why the house of Pharez was so extolled, in ver. 12, by the elders and people ; and thirdly, to let us know for what end this story was written, not to praise and set out the virtues of a couple of poor women, but to shew from whom David came, the figure of Christ, even of Ruth, a Gentile, a Moabitess. Lastly, this may be to shew the efficacy of the prayer of the people at Boaz's marriage, wishing by this seed Obed his house to be as famous as Judah's house was by Pharez, as it was indeed. For, as Nahshon and Salmon, princes, came of him, so of this Obed came Jesse and David, and so a royal posterity.

Of Pharez. The catalogue beginneth here, and from this man, though misbegotten incestuously, the honour of the families is fetched. For so in truth it was, the Lord making Pharez renewned in his posterity; whence note, first, that the holy writers are without partiality. They write as things be; they omit not, for fear of disgrace, that which is true and ought to be set down; they will not spare any, friend, foe, far off nor near, no, not themselves. Moses will write his own faults, his wife's, his brother Aaron's and Miriam's; Samuel will not slip over his son's miscarriage, nor Jonah his own rebellion against God, and his peevish brabbling with him; Jeremiah will record his own impatiency, and St Paul his bloody rage against the saints, for indeed they are led by a better spirit than that of the world; they also cast off self-love, and they prefer the truth and god's glory above all, which may persuade us to the reading of these holy histories full of varieties, and yet truths not to be found in any writings of men. And this should teach such as undertake to write stories, to deal truly, without fabling, and to avoid partial relations,* that we may read true histories, and not fictions and falsehoods, to the deceiving of the posterity, which should be thereby instructed. Secondly, that men hold themselves honoured to come of such as have gained honour in the world, though otherwise stained in their birth; for so here it is accounted honourable to come of Pharez, as many with us do, to come but into this island, which William the Conqueror obtained, how base soever he was by his birth; for outward honour and glory procureth estimation and becloudeth birth, so as that no notice is taken thereof. Now, if outward honour effect this, with what honour may we think ourselves honoured, when God, the emperor of heaven and earth, is willing to acknowledge us to be born of him, and to be called his sons? But of this few glory, because it is only spiritually discerned, and for that such as be so honoured with God find here many crosses, and so are in contempt with the worldly-minded.

Now, in handling the rest of the names, I will shew you out of them that as one naturally begets another, so the elect of God are to be qualified, one grace, as it were, producing another. The first in this natural generation is Pharez, which signifieth *separate;* so in the supernatural work of regeneration the elect must be first *Pharez,* separate by their effectual calling by the word and by the Holy Spirit in their conversation from the vain world, 2 Cor. vi. 17; for such are the children of God, and such ought they to be, as the apostle exhorteth, Eph. v. 11, or else we be not of this spiritual regeneration. Such then as are companions with wicked, and so live, they are no *Pharezes,* and so none of Christ's line.

* Nam quis nescit, primam esse historiæ legem, ne quid falsi dicere audeat, deinde, ne quid veri non audeat, ne qua suspicio gratiæ sit in scribendo, ne qua simultatis?—*Cic. de Orat.,* lib. ii. *Vide* Josephum, Antiq. lib. xvi. cap. 11, ubi merito culpat Nichol. Damasceni historiam, Herodis res falsis laudibus ornantem.

Ver. 19. *Pharez begat Hezron.* So is it plain, Gen. xlvi. 12, Mat. i. 3, 1 Chron. ii. 5, who went down with Jacob into Egypt, Gen. xlvi. 26, contrary to the opinion of some popish writers. The name signifieth, *in the midst of happiness;* and such be the elect, after they become *Pharezes.* They must needs be *Hezrons,* full of joy; when they feel the benefit of their separation, they are glad people, even as the Israelites, separated from the Egyptians and their heavy bondage.

Hezron begat Ram. 1 Chron. ii. 9, Mat. i. This Ram or Aram was not Hezron's first-born, but Jerahmeel, to give us to know that the Lord tied not himself to the first-born, but he chose sometime the second, as here, and sometime the youngest, as David; and so he doth at this day, which is the cause of the difference of children, from one father and one mother, having the same education, some doing well, other some ill. The name signifieth *high;* for so are the elect with God, Deut. xxxii. 10, Zech. ii. 8; and being once *Hezrons,* joyful in the ways of God, they seek and set their minds on things above, as the apostle exhorts all risen with Christ to do, Col. iii. 1. They be not base-minded, to pore upon the world as earthworms, but are high-minded towards God and things above; they are of a generous spirit, not suffering the things below to tread down their affections, and to draw them from God.

Ram begat Amminadab. 1 Chron. ii. 10, Mat. i. He was father-in-law to Aaron, who married his daughter Elishebah, Exod. vi. 23. This name signifieth, *my people is noble* or *free,* and so are the elect; for having attained to this height, that they become *Rams* or *Arams,* they free themselves from the world, as far as it hindereth them from setting their minds on things above.

Ver. 20. *And Amminadab begat Nahshon.* 1 Chron. ii., Mat. i. Who was brother-in-law to Aaron, the head and prince of the tribe of Judah; which host consisted of 74,600 valiant men, the first standard, Num. i. 7, and ii. 3, and vii. 12. This first offered to the dedication of the altar, for the greatest should be the forwardest to God's service and to advance religion. This also first set forward with his charge towards Canaan, Num. x. 14; so should the greatest with their families set forward to heaven. This signifieth *experiment* or *trial,* for the elect of God having gotten to be *Amminadabs,* and become free, they taste of the Lord's goodness, and can say with David, Come and see what the Lord hath done for my soul. They keep in remembrance the kindness of the Lord, and can speak of his noble acts.

And Nahshon begat Salmon. 1 Chron. ii. 11, where he is called Salma; he married Rahab, Mat. i. 5. Thus in the line of Christ are brought in Gentiles for our comfort, of whom he came, as well as of the Jews, and is our kinsman, as well as theirs. This signifieth *peaceable,* and so are the elect; for after they become *Nahshons*, experienced in God's goodness, they have a peaceable conscience, they have a quiet mind, without murmuring, without doubting, without gainsaying the will of God in anything which may happen, though it cross them in this world never so much ; they be peaceable also towards others, because the wisdom from above, with which they are endued, is peaceable, James iii. 17.

Ver. 21. *And Salmon begat Boaz.* 1 Chron. ii. 11, of whom I have spoken before. It signifieth *in strength ;* for when the elect are *Salmons*, that they find inward peace with God, and that they know God to be with them, then they say to their souls, as the angel to Gideon, ‘ Go in this thy strength ;’ for in the Lord they are valiant, and by his help may do worthily, being confident in God.

And Boaz begat Obed. 1 Chron. ii., Mat. i. Of this also before. It signifieth *serving.* Such are the Lord's elect, they are his servants ; for when God hath made them *Boazes*, and put strength of grace into their hearts to withstand their spiritual adversaries, they will become obedient *Obeds.*

Ver. 22. *And Obed begat Jesse,* 1 Chron. ii. 13, Mat. i., who dwelt at Bethlehem, and was an ancient man in the days of Saul, 1 Sam. xvi. 1. This signifieth *a gift* or *offering ;* and such be all true Obeds. When the elect become serviceable and obedient, the joy they feel in the Lord's service maketh them *Jesses*, even to offer themselves to God as holy and acceptable sacrifices, Rom. xii. 1.

And Jesse begat David. 1 Chron. ii. 13, 15, Mat. i. Of this kingly prophet and prophetical king I might speak more at large than might seem suitable to this brief exposition. I therefore refer you to the Books of Samuel, and the first of the Kings, and the first of the Chronicles, and to the Book of Psalms, which lively set out this holy man, a man after the Lord's own heart. His name signifieth *beloved ;* and such are the Lord's elect, and they may know themselves to be so, God witnessing his love to them ; for when they be once *Pharezes*, separated from the vain world ; *Hezrons*, joyful and glad in this their separation ; *Rams*, lifted up in mind to heavenly things ; *Amminadabs*, a free people from spiritual thraldom, having gotten the spirit of adoption ; *Nahshons*, experienced in God's love ; *Salmons*, peaceable ; and *Boazes*, going on in this their strength ; and *Obeds*, obedient, and that freely, as *Jesses;* what doubt is there but they be *Davids*, even beloved of God ?

To conclude this chapter, and so this whole history, we may here see how, from a mean estate, some can arise to great honour, as Ruth from gleaning to be the wife of Boaz, and the grandmother of a king and prophet. Thus poor Mordecai was exalted, and that on a sudden, from sackcloth into silken robes fit for a king, from fear and danger of death to great honour, and to be feared. And thus came Joseph from a prison, to be a prince in Egypt ; and David from keeping sheep, to be the king of Israel ; all which is the work of God, as Hannah singeth, 1 Sam. ii. 8, David publisheth, Ps. lxxv. 6, 7, and cxiii. 7, and Daniel teacheth, Dan. iv. 17. It is easy with the Lord suddenly to make a poor man rich, and to exalt him to honour. And therefore let such as be low not envy the advancement of others lifted up, it is of God ; and let them not repine nor murmur to see themselves neglected, for if God held it good for such, and for his glory, to be lifted up, as he can do it, so, verily, he would do it as well as he doth others ; for God respecteth no person, but doth what he pleaseth in heaven and in earth, and what is most for his glory, though we judge perhaps otherwise. Another thing may we note for the comfort of the godly, that great is the reward of religion. Ruth was of the Lord mercifully rewarded, as we have heard ; so was Rahab by faith preserved, and all with her brought from among cursed Canaanites to be among the Israelites ; yea, to become the wife of Salmon, a prince in Israel ; and lastly, to be vouchsafed this mercy, to be recorded with the faithful in the catalogue of the most renowned, Heb. xi. ; yea, and to be mentioned with Abraham for her good works, the fruit of true faith, James ii. What got David for his upright heart, though he seemed to be neglected of his parents, and sent to keep sheep, and not called to the feast till Samuel caused him to be sent for ? Was not he for all that esteemed of God, and chosen before all his brethren ? The Lord will not let goodness be unrewarded, for godliness hath the promise of this life, and of the life to come. And in this let all that truly fear God comfort themselves, and look up to the recompence of the reward, which in due time they shall receive to the full, if they faint not. Blessed be God, and his name be praised for ever more. Amen !

END OF BERNARD ON RUTH.

www.ingramcontent.com/pod-product-compliance
Lightning Source LLC
Chambersburg PA
CBHW080557090426
42735CB00016B/3262